Defending the Land of the Jaguar

Defending the Land of the Jaguar

A HISTORY OF CONSERVATION IN MEXICO

Lane
Simonian

UNIVERSITY OF TEXAS PRESS
AUSTIN

Requests for permission to reproduce material from this work
should be sent to Permissions, University of Texas Press, Box 7819,
Austin, TX 78713-7819.

∞ The paper used in this publication meets the minimum requirements
of American National Standard for Information Sciences—Permanence of
Paper for Printed Library Materials, ANSI Z39.48-1984.

Library of Congress Cataloging-in-Publication Data

Simonian, Lane, date
   Defending the land of the jaguar : a history of conservation in Mexico /
Lane Simonian. — 1st ed.
      p.   cm.
   Includes bibliographical references and index.
   ISBN 0-292-77690-X
   ISBN 0-292-77691-8 pbk.
   1. Conservation of natural resources—Mexico—History.   2. Environ-
mental protection—Mexico—History.   I. Title.
S934.M6S55   1995
333.72'0972—dc20   95-1487

To my Mother and Father for their love of nature and people

Be careful with the things of the land. Make something, cut wood, till the land, plant nopales, plant magueys. You will have to drink, eat, and dress.

—The Huehue Tlatolli (collection of advice from Aztec elders to their children— fifteenth or early sixteenth century)

My father says it [crop failure] is because of a lack of water and rain, because before making the *milpa* [the field created through slash and burn agriculture] they left some trees that could rapidly grow into forests and store water, but now they do not do it. All of the forest is being cut now. There is no shade and the land is dry. Now there is so much cutting that there is neither water nor forests only hunger.

—Maya descendant Edilberto Ucan Ek

That jammed city of toxic air and leafless trees may be the first to know asphyxiation by progress. One of the world's oldest civilizations suffers mankind's newest affliction. Mexico City warns the rest of the species of all that has gone wrong with modernity's promised millennium of happiness.

—Novelist Carlos Fuentes

It is not that we have been expelled from paradise. Rather we have expelled paradise itself.

—Essayist Fernando Benítez

Contents

MAPS

TABLES

PHOTOGRAPHS

Preface

Part of the purpose of this book is to recount why Mexicans devoted themselves to the protection of the environment. Natalia Grieger of the Mexican Green Party told a particularly compelling story in this regard. In Germany, she used to take long walks with her children through the snowdrifts, yet they rarely became ill. But in Mexico City, where the climate is almost always pleasant, they were plagued with respiratory problems. Grieger became an environmentalist out of a love for her children, city, and country.

Grieger still regards Mexico City as a great city, but one marred by traffic, noise, and smog. Under such conditions, it is no wonder that so many of its residents seek solitude and beauty wherever they can find it. Thousands flock each weekend to Chapultepec Park or to the National Park Desierto de los Leones in the coniferous forests above the Valley of Mexico. Others venture further each winter to marvel at the millions of butterflies that carpet the fir trees in the highlands of Michoacán and the state of Mexico. For some, at least, the enjoyment of the peace, beauty, and fresh air of their natural surroundings will mark the beginning of their struggle on behalf of the environment.

I have told the history of conservation of Mexico filtered through my own experiences, particularly the summers that I spent as a child stirred by the magnificent seashores, rain forests, alpine meadows, and mountains of Olympic National Park. I grew up seeing nature not as a conglomeration of resources but as a source of beauty and life. Certainly, some of the natural world must be used for the economic benefit of people, but I firmly believe that development is possible without the abuse of the environment that we witness today in Mexico and in many other parts of the world.

I hope that the study of environmental history will become more international in its scope. In many places, people have fought to protect nature. Their stories should be told, even though for so long they have been a distinct minority.

Acknowledgments

Without the support of Lawrence Badash, David Brokensha, Sarah Cline, Wilbur Jacobs, Carroll Pursell, and my adviser Roderick Nash, I would not have been able to study the history of conservation in Mexico. I thank each of them for encouraging me to pursue my unconventional interests.

Along with Nash, Badash and Cline offered many helpful suggestions on earlier drafts of this book. Their fairness, integrity, and friendship were deeply appreciated. I was fortunate as an undergraduate student at the University of Oregon and the University of Nevada-Reno and as a graduate student at the University of California at Davis and Santa Barbara to have had so many fine teachers.

I am grateful to the Graduate Division at the University of California-Santa Barbara and to the University of California Consortium on Mexico and the United States (U.C.-Mexus) for providing funds for this study.

I thank all the librarians and staffs who assisted me in this research. I relied most extensively upon the services of the archivists, reference librarians, and pagers at the Bancroft Library, the National Archives, the National Agricultural Library, the Archivo General de la Nación, the SEDUE Document Center, the Biblioteca Nacional, the Instituto Nacional de Antropología e Historia Library, and the Instituto Mexicano de Recursos Naturales Renovables Library. I am especially grateful to Walter

Brem, Assistant Curator to the Bancroft Library, for directing me to so many valuable sources and for all the enjoyable conversations.

I thank Enrique Beltrán, Gertrude Duby Blom, Carmen Elizalde Aguilar, Martin Goebel, Arturo Gómez-Pompa, Ronald Nigh, Joe Quiroz, and Mario Ramos for speaking with me at length about conservation in Mexico. I am equally grateful to the many people who collected information for me.

María Lucía Flores Sánchez and her family gave me not only room and board in Mexico City but also made me feel at home. My quietly affable roommates, "Nacho" and Enrique Contreras, were excellent company. Enrique gave me a wonderful introduction to his community and to his country by making me a part of his family's independence day celebration in Pachuca. I immensely enjoyed, as well, my outing with Bob Haas and the Audubon Society of San Miguel de Allende.

Some of my best memories of Mexico were the times I spent with Margarita and María del Rayo Ramírez in Puebla. Their intellect and generous spirit are warmly remembered. May they be able to visit the mountains which they love for many years to come.

My friend Bill Stoughton worked painstakingly on the photographic reproductions. I have long admired his beautiful pictures and remarkable vitality.

John Perkins and Angus Wright, who acted as internal reviewers for the University of Texas Press, offered excellent advice on how to improve the manuscript. I am solely responsible for any remaining errors in fact or judgment.

The staff at the University of Texas Press took an early and active interest in this work. I am grateful for their steadfast belief in the importance of the subject.

Finally, I thank my family and friends for their humor, encouragement, and kindness.

Defending the Land of the Jaguar

Introduction

The venerable Mexican conservationist Miguel Alvarez del Toro (b. 1917) once lamented that "it is difficult to find a country less interested in the conservation of its natural resources than is Mexico."[1] Indeed, the exploitation of natural resources has been the dominant theme in Mexican environmental history. The Spanish crown, nineteenth-century Mexican politicians, and twentieth-century "revolutionary" governments all envisaged the large-scale exploitation of the region's natural wealth as the key to economic prosperity. Along with ambitious officials, Indians, colonists, miners, farmers, cattle grazers, and industrialists stripped away the resources at their disposal. Even the pre-Conquest Indians of Mexico, who, according to many environmentalists and Native American scholars, were supposed to exercise "land wisdom" by virtue of their heritage, had a detrimental impact upon the environment.[2]

Considering the many glaring examples of environmental abuse in Mexican history, it would be easy to conclude that Mexico has never had a history of conservation. Moreover, if the conventional wisdom is true that poor people cannot afford to protect natural resources, then there would seem to be no basis for conservation in Mexico. The general lack of government support for conservation and the tremendous obstacles to conservation in Mexico, however, should not be taken as proof of the absence of environmental concerns. In fact, a number of individuals dedicated their lives to the protection of nature.

Why did some Mexicans wish to save the natural world? A few conservationists delighted in the beauty of nature or had a deep respect for the rights of all living creatures. More commonly, though, Mexicans advocated conservation either because they feared that economically valuable resources were being exhausted or because they believed that people's well-being depended upon the maintenance of stable ecosystems. Not surprisingly, most Mexican conservationists directed their attention to the protection of forests because of their evident economic and biological value.

Governments, too, more readily recognized the value of forests than the value of such other renewable resources as wildlife, soil, and water. Thus, Mexico's long history of forest legislation was not matched in other areas. Spain sought to protect only economically valuable species in the New World, and independent Mexico did not enact a national wildlife law until 1894. Mexico did not launch a national program for soil and water conservation until the 1940s. Government officials did not easily appreciate the aesthetic and ethical arguments for wildlife conservation. They belatedly, and then usually only lukewarmly, appreciated the importance of soil and water conservation for agricultural production.

Some rural peoples conserved their resources independent of any government conservation programs. Among them were *hacendados* who undertook works to prevent water loss and soil erosion on their estates and *campesinos* who adhered to the wise agricultural practices of their ancestors. A small segment of the rural population, as well as a few urban professionals, recognized the importance of maintaining the health of the land.

The pre-Conquest Indians of Mexico were, with qualifications, the region's first conservationists. In some instances, they carefully managed the natural world in a conscious attempt to impede environmental deterioration. Alongside this, they admired the beauty of nature and revered many wild plants and animals. Yet, at the same time, the ancient peoples of Mexico often held religious beliefs and engaged in agricultural practices that resulted in the exploitation of the environment. Indeed, several rulers had to curtail their subjects' use of natural resources in order to reduce the pressures that they were placing upon the land with their extractive activities and large populations. For instance, the king of Texcoco, Nezahualcóyotl (ruled 1418–1472) enacted a forest conservation law to deter his people's abuse of shrinking woodlands.

During the fifteenth century, an official policy of conservation had begun to emerge in central Mexico.[3]

Mindful of the destructive results of deforestation on the Iberian peninsula and determined to maintain an adequate supply of timber for its
own needs in the New World, the Spanish crown enacted a tough forestry code for its overseas colonies. Among its provisions, the code restricted the use of fires to clear forests, required permits for wood cutting, and mandated reforestation. The crown wanted to eliminate the
wasteful use of forest resources by colonists and by Indians. Royal officials, though, never succeeded in strictly enforcing the forestry regulations, particularly against locally powerful colonists and impoverished Indians, to the latter of whom sympathetic officials occasionally
granted clemency from the law.

During the nineteenth century, some politicians and private citizens
warned against the dire economic consequences that would result if
Mexicans continued their relentless assault upon the forests. A smaller
group of Mexicans feared deforestation for another reason: the destruction of the forest cover would result in soil erosion, prolonged droughts,
severe floods, and an unhealthy environment (less oxygen, fewer trees
to absorb "bad vapors," chimney smoke, etc.). The negative consequences of deforestation were more pronounced in Mexico than in
many other countries because of its rugged topography and highly vari-
able rainfall. Thus, Mexican conservationists had solid evidence for
many of their claims that the removal of forests was detrimental to
people's well-being.

During the first half of the twentieth century, Miguel Angel de Quevedo was the principal advocate for the conservation of forests on biological grounds. He was the architect of almost every forestry initiative
between 1900 and 1946, the year of his death. The apex of Quevedo's
public career came when President Lázaro Cárdenas (1934–1940) appointed him head of Mexico's first autonomous conservation agency. As
Cárdenas's conservation commissioner, Quevedo established Mexico's
national park system and undertook a vigorous campaign to restore and
protect Mexico's forests. The three pillars of Quevedo's forestry program
were reforestation, the small-scale development of forest products, and
the strict protection of forests near cities and along watersheds. Quevedo's strict enforcement of forestry laws produced a backlash. Peasants,
agriculture officials, and even conservationists accused Quevedo of pur-
suing draconian measures.

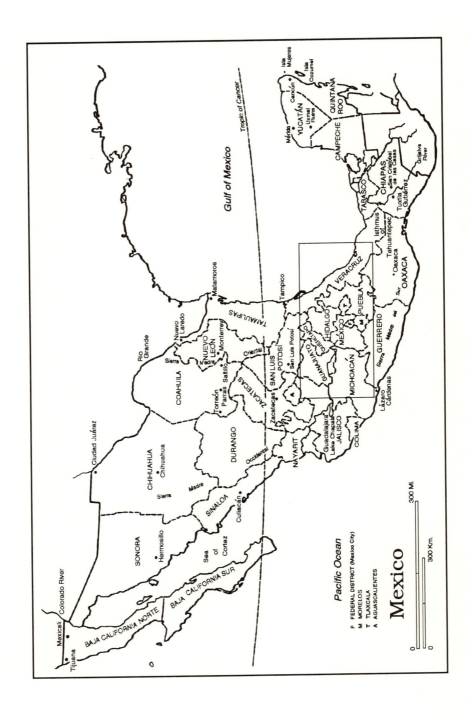

Mexico

F FEDERAL DISTRICT (Mexico City)
M MORELOS
T TLAXCALA
A AGUASCALIENTES

Pacific Ocean

Gulf of Mexico

Tropic of Cancer

BAJA CALIFORNIA NORTE
BAJA CALIFORNIA SUR

Tijuana
Mexicali • Colorado River

SONORA
Hermosillo •

Sea of Cortez

CHIHUAHUA
Ciudad Juárez •
Chihuahua •
Sierra   Madre   Occidental

SINALOA
Culiacán •

DURANGO

COAHUILA
Torreón • • Parras
Saltillo •

Rio Grande
Nuevo Laredo •
NUEVO LEÓN
Monterrey •
Sierra   Madre

TAMAULIPAS
Matamoros •

Tampico •

ZACATECAS
Zacatecas •

SAN LUIS POTOSÍ
• San Luis Potosí
Oriental

NAYARIT

JALISCO
Guadalajara •
Lake Chapala

COLIMA
Lázaro Cárdenas •

AGUASCALIENTES

GUANAJUATO
QUERÉTARO
HIDALGO
MÉXICO
F
M
T

VERACRUZ
PUEBLA

MICHOACÁN
Sierra   Madre   del   Sur

GUERRERO

OAXACA
• Oaxaca
Isthmus of Tehuantepec

TABASCO
CHIAPAS
• San Cristóbal de las Casas
Tuxtla Gutiérrez •
Grijalva River

CAMPECHE

YUCATÁN
Mérida •
Cancún •
Uxmal • Ruins

QUINTANA ROO
Isla Mujeres
Isla Cozumel

300 Mi.
300 Km.

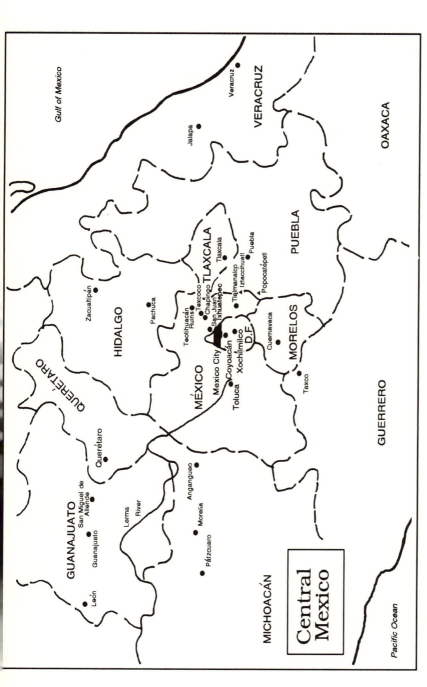

Map 1. Mexico. Adapted from Cathryn L. Lombardi and John V. Lombardi, with K. Lynn Stoner, *Latin American History: A Teaching Atlas* (Madison: University of Wisconsin Press for the Conference on Latin American History, 1983). Reprinted with permission from the University of Wisconsin Press. Base map from Robert Jones, *A History of Latin America* (Lexington, Mass.: D. C. Heath and Company, 1978). Reprinted with permission from Robert Jones Shafer.

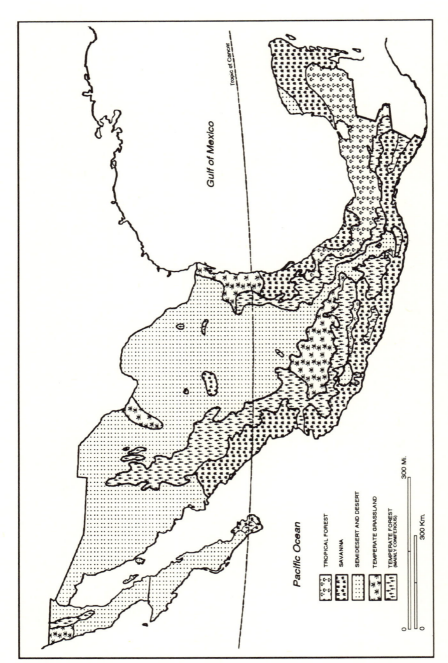

Map 2. The Vegetational Zones of Mexico. From Gilbert J. Butland, *Latin America: A Regional Geography* (London: Longmans, Green and Company, 1960). Reprinted with permission from Longman Group Limited.

After Quevedo's tenure, conservation officials adopted a different tack: they promoted the use of resources. According to these officials, the use of resources encouraged conservation because people would care for that which was economically valuable. This philosophy neatly dovetailed with the desire of high-level government officials to ensure a steady supply of resources for industrialization and agricultural "modernization." Notwithstanding some good words, Cárdenas's successors viewed restrictive conservation policies as anathema to their larger economic ambitions.

In the wake of government disinterest and public apathy concerning the protection of nature in the post-Cárdenas era, three conservationists, Enrique Beltrán, Miguel Alvarez del Toro, and Gertrude Duby Blom, worked tirelessly to convince public officials and private citizens of the folly and tragedy of their destructive actions. The common strand in their varying philosophies is that human survival depends upon the survival of the natural world. Their overall influence was limited, but Beltrán, Alvarez del Toro, and Blom did inspire a new generation of conservationists.

By the 1970s, a small conservation movement had arisen in Mexico. Mexican conservationists embraced the idea being promoted by international organizations during the early 1970s that development had to be sustainable. In other words, without the maintenance of a resource base (forests, soil, water, etc.), poverty would become a permanent state of affairs in the world. Mexican conservationists demanded the replacement of environmentally destructive development programs and land use patterns with environmentally sound alternatives.

The administration of Luis Echeverría (1970–1976) responded rather coolly to these demands, but it did move on a related front by enacting the nation's first pollution control law in 1971. During the 1970s, the government's goal was to control pollution through technology while allowing industrialization to continue apace. By the 1980s, Mexican politicians acknowledged that the nation's horrendous pollution problems could only be abated by clamping down on heavily polluting industries and by changing people's life-styles. Political rhetoric, however, usually exceeded political action.

Dissatisfied with the government's response to environmental problems and worried about the consequences of environmental degradation for human health and the health of the natural world, a few individuals organized a small but vocal environmental movement during the 1980s. The movement entreated for a return to the ancient Indians' respect for nature. From the pre-Columbian Indians to the current Mexican environmental movement, Mexico has had a long, if weak, tradition of conservation.

In addition to its intrinsic value, the history of conservation in Mexico provides a useful comparison with the history of conservation in the United States. The two histories have been dissimilar because of the large geographical, cultural, social, demographic, political, and economic differences that exist between the two countries. These differences explain why the Indians of Mesoamerica more severely altered their environments than did the Indians of North America, why Mexico enacted a national forestry law three decades before the United States, and why the Mexican environmental movement arose later and with less public support than the U.S. environmental movement.[4] Important parallels exist between the conservation histories of Mexico and the United States as well. Both the Spanish and British crowns enacted forest conservation ordinances for their colonies. Franklin D. Roosevelt and Lázaro Cárdenas used conservation to improve the conditions of people as well as the health of the land. During the early 1970s, President Richard Nixon and President Luis Echeverría sought to control pollution through technological innovations. A broader and more important parallel is that historically both Mexican and U.S. citizens have tried to conserve resources for economic and ecological reasons.

The following account is the first general history of conservation in Mexico. Throughout its pages resonate many philosophies regarding the necessity of bringing economic pursuits into balance with environmental realities, but not one is more important than humankind's responsibility for the survival of the biosphere. Especially now, with the development of a small, but vibrant conservation and environmental movement in Mexico, it is an appropriate time to explore the motivations and efforts of those who tried to protect Mexico's natural heritage.

Chapter One

THE MAGICAL AND THE INSTRUMENTAL

Nature in the Pre-Hispanic World

As part of their observance of the first international earth day (22 April 1990), Mexican environmentalists gathered around the ancient monolith representing Coatlicuetonantzin, mother earth.[1] Here, they paid homage not only to an ancient Mexican god but also to the ancient Mexicans themselves. Members of today's environmental movement wish to restore the reverence that the pre-Conquest Indians held for the natural world. They also want to reestablish the sound resource management techniques of the ancient Indians into a nation that is on the verge of ecological collapse. The environmental community believes that if Mexicans adopted traditional land use practices and were able to embrace the environmental thinking of their ancestors that the country might yet be able to surmount the current ecological crisis.[2] For them, Mexico's future hinges upon recovering traditions and practices from the ancient past. As the writer Carmen Aguilera has expressed this sentiment: "The knowledge of plants and animals which yesterday gave fear, imagination, and enjoyment to our ancestors is a mode of contributing to what continues to be needed today and which we will need in the future [to check environmental degradation]: teachings from the past with deep roots, lessons, and hope."[3]

By portraying the ancient Indians as the consummate environmentalists, environmental leaders are contributing to the revolutionary dogma that glorifies past Indian civilizations. Although their condemnation of the Spanish Conquest is rarely as direct as that of the *indigenistas*, the implication of their pronouncements is nevertheless clear: the roots of the country's environmental crisis lay in the Spanish suppression of native religions and their introduction of detrimental land use practices.

But are the Indians of pre-Conquest Mexico the proper role models for those who wish to create an ecologically sustainable society? Did they themselves exhibit the environmental wisdom that the public and scholars have traditionally assigned to them? Some historians and anthropologists have begun to question whether Indians did in fact live in harmony with the natural world. Anthropologist George A. Collier, for example, maintains that the Indians of highland Chiapas (in southwestern Mexico) were altering the land even before the Spanish came. Most notably, they had used fire to clear large tracts of forests for agriculture. Certainly the introduction of livestock into the region after the Conquest worsened environmental conditions, as Collier admits, but he argues that this does not negate the fact that the Indians were also agents of environmental degradation. Based on his studies, Collier rejects the notion that the Indians were environmentalists by nature. In fact, he suggests that native peoples often lived in "obvious disequilibrium" with the natural world.[4]

By labeling all the earliest immigrants to the hemisphere Indians, the Europeans created the false impression that they were a homogeneous group. Even today, many scholars lump native peoples together when discussing their relationship with nature. Important differences in land use patterns existed among Indians, however. For instance, in the arid regions of what is today northern Mexico and the U.S. Southwest, the Indians "conserved" the land in some cases and altered it in others. Hunters and gatherers utilized the desert extensively and in a diversified manner. In doing so, they reduced their impact upon particular ecosystems and on particular plant and animal species. Some of the indigenous farmers planted crops that were drought resistant, built small dams to trap eroded particles, relied upon flooding to water their crops, and planted trees along stream banks to stabilize soils.[5] Other agriculturalists diverted water by means of small irrigation canals and catchment basins, modifying microenvironments in the process. In response to the new distribution of water, new plants grew in areas that were once too dry to support them; the natural flow of rivers was disrupted; soil composition was altered; evaporation rates changed, affecting humidity and precipitation; and the migratory patterns of birds and animals shifted.[6]

Other groups altered the environment more extensively. For instance, the Hohokam built sophisticated irrigation systems, which affected macroenvironments, not just microenvironments.[7] The Indians utilized the environment in a dissimilar manner partly because of differences in their implements and population sizes.

In Mesoamerica (the region from central Mexico to Panama), a relatively primitive technological base supported a very dense population. At the time of the Spanish Conquest, perhaps as many as twenty-five million people lived in central Mexico alone, principally sustaining themselves on crops grown on fields cleared by fire and planted with a digging stick.[8] Given their numbers, it is not surprising that Mesoamerican peoples had a profound impact upon the environment.

Did religion temper the utilization of resources in Mesoamerica and elsewhere in Mexico or was the impact of Indians upon the land solely determined by population levels? Were there any differences in native religions that might explain variations in the exploitation of wild plants and animals? An examination of Indian thought regarding nature indicates that at times religion did have an effect upon their treatment of the land.

Many pre-Conquest Indians felt an ambivalence toward the natural world. On the one hand, they were terrified by the tumultuous environment in which they lived: droughts, floods, hurricanes, eruptions, earthquakes, and such ferocious animals as jaguars, mountain lions, and crocodiles, all threatened their existence. On the other hand, they took immense pleasure from the generosity, rhythms, and resplendence of nature: the colorful flowers, graceful trees, gentle animals, life-giving rains, and impressive landscapes. Nature brought both pleasure and pain. Though some aspects of it were to be feared and other aspects of it praised, nature itself was neither good nor evil.[9]

The ancient peoples voiced their deep admiration for the beauty of nature through poetry. A Maya poem expresses delight in the moon-lit sky:

> The beautiful moon has arisen over the forests;
> lighting the middle of the sky,
> where it remains suspended,
> illuminating above the land all the forests.
> It has arrived in the middle of the sky,
> radiating its light upon all good things. . . .
> There is joy in all good men.[10]

An Aztec poem reveals the attachment of people to the natural world:

> Do men have roots which are true?
> No one is oblivious
> to your richness, which are your flowers.
> Inventors of yourself!
>
> Our common home is the land.
> In the place afar,
> Is it also so?
> In truth it is not the same.
>
> On the land: flower and song.
> We exist here![11]

The Indians of pre-Hispanic Mexico immensely enjoyed the beautiful aspects of their surroundings. This, however, did not prevent them from utilizing natural resources. As Friar Toribio de Benavente Motolinía observed, animals from which the Indians took pleasure could also be killed: "The Indians [the Aztec] enjoy the song of birds as well as shooting them with darts."[12] The native peoples were not preservationists at heart.

The Indians revered and feared different animals and plants. Their attitude toward forests offers one of the most striking examples of the ambivalence that the ancient peoples of Mexico felt toward the natural world. The forests were dark places, cold places, places that harbored dangerous animals and evil spirits. The forests, though, also contained sacred trees. The Nahua (a group of Indians that included the Aztec) and the Tarahumara believed that trees contained the souls of their ancient ancestors. The Tzotzil, Zapotec, and Mixtec thought that some of their ancestors emerged from the roots of trees.[13] For many groups, the roots of trees were envisioned as both an entrance to and an exit from the underworld. The Indians associated trees with both life and death, with chaos and paradise.[14]

In recording the oral traditions of Chamula (a Tzotzil community in the highlands of Chiapas), Gary H. Gossen compiled the following images of the forests:

> Ever present in nature, particularly in the forest, are the forces that
> would overcome . . . order and return the world to the chaos of dis-

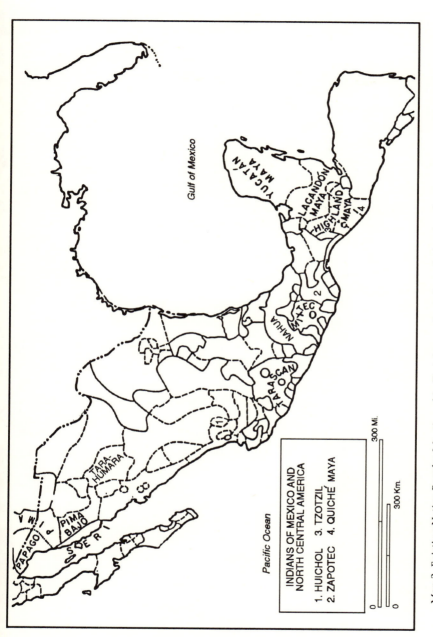

Map 3. Existing Native Peoples Mentioned in Text (approximate boundaries after the Conquest). Adapted from Harold E. Driver, *Indians of North America*, 2d ed. rev. (Chicago: University of Chicago Press, 1969). Reprinted with permission from the University of Chicago Press.

tant space and past time. These include demons living in remoter, wild parts of Chamula that cause eclipses by attacking the moon and the sun, threatening the very source of order-giving heat and light; snakes and other transfigurations of the earth lord, whose domain is the wooded mountain that humans should avoid lest he harm their souls; and other dangerous deities. Negative events are associated with the setting of the woods, which symbolize lowness, coldness, darkness, threat, and behavior that is not rule-governed.[15]

The forests and mountains contained caves, which were the intermediate zones between the earth and the underworld. Consequently, those who were lured into the caves disappeared forever from the land. Dwelling within many of the underground lairs were earth lords who were responsible for lightning, thunder, and all forms of precipitation. When angered, these deities could create droughts.[16] It is possible that the Tzotzil associated the large-scale disturbance of forests with a lack of precipitation. Perhaps they even altered some of their forestry activities in order not to provoke the woodland spirits.

The association of forests with danger was widespread in Mesoamerica. The Franciscan friar Bernardino de Sahagún, who sought to reconstruct the Nahua world through the use of Indian informants, recorded the following apprehensive description of the forests:

It is . . . a place of cold: it becomes cold; there is much frost, it is a place which freezes. It is a place whence misery comes, where it exists; a place where there is affliction—a place of affliction, of lamentation, . . . of weeping; a place where there is sadness . . . ; a place which arouses sorrow, which spreads misery. . . . It is a disturbing place, fearful, frightful; home of the savage beast, dwelling place of the serpent, the rabbit, the deer; a place whence nothing departs, nothing leaves, nothing emerges.[17]

Sahagún's native informants further describe their trepidation of the forests:

There is no one; there are no people. It is desolate; it lies desolate. There is nothing edible. Misery abounds, misery emerges, misery spreads. There is no joy, no pleasure. . . . All die of thirst. . . . There is hunger, all hunger. It is the home of hunger; there is death from hunger. All die of cold; there is freezing; there is trembling; there is clattering, the clattering of teeth. There are cramps, the stiffening of the body, the constant stiffening, the stretching out prone. There is fright, there is constant fright. One is devoured; one is slain by stealth; one is abused; one is brutally put to death; one is tormented. Misery abounds.[18]

The forests contain deities, animals, and attributes (coldness, darkness, etc.) linked to death and chaos. The physical dangers presented by the forests—lack of water, lack of food, frostbite, hypothermia, attacks by wild animals—may have contributed to the spiritual fear of the woods.

The Maya were frightened by the forests, too. A Maya legend relates that there once existed luxurious trees for making the milpa in the forest of Belhalal, near the old walls of Uxmal (on the Yucatán peninsula), but that the people never wanted to plant there because within the forest lived a creature who swallowed all those who came near. The story suggests that despite possible misgivings, the Maya eventually did cut the forest near Uxmal, perhaps because of population pressures.[19]

The Maya were wary of specific trees as well. They identified the *chechem* as a sad and bad tree, for it poisoned human beings. Until discovering that they were immune from the *chechem*'s venom, the birds did not make nests or sing in its canopy. The deer, too, stayed at a distance, unless, driven by thirst, they drank the water beneath its boughs. But woe befell any person who was enticed by the refreshing shelter afforded by this treacherous tree: "The *chechem* tricks those who do not know it, attracting them by its shade, during the hours in which the sun cuts like a knife and breath burns the mouth upon respiring. Poor one who is trusting and reposes under the tree for that person shall never be the same." Indeed, according to Maya lore, those who slept beneath the shade of the *chechem* almost invariably died. Even people who managed to arise and run with all their might would be lame and crazy for the rest of their lives.[20] The *chechem*'s bark or wood may indeed have been toxic, and therefore the Maya may have avoided it when making their milpas.[21]

The Indians of ancient Mexico attributed positive as well as negative qualities to trees. Trees were part of the Nahua's and Maya's conception of paradise. According to Sahagún's informants, the forests were "a place of verdure, of fresh green. . . . A place of compassion, of sighing."[22] The Nahua believed in an earthly paradise, distinguished by an eternal spring and a cornucopia of fruits and vegetables, and in a celestial abode populated by gentle animals, beautiful birds, and a variety of trees.[23] The

The ceiba—sacred tree of the Maya. Departamento Autónomo de Publicidad y Propaganda.

Maya said that the souls of their dead went under the ceiba tree, into a good land of rain, mist, and lush vegetation.[24]

The ceiba was a prominent part of the Maya cosmology. According to their lore, the great mother ceiba arose from the middle of the world as a reminder of the victory of the gods of the sky over the gods of the underworld.[25] The Maya planted the tree in the middle of their plazas and villages as an affirmation of its place at the center of life and at the center of the earth. They also grew the ceiba in the middle of their homes for protection and tranquillity. The Maya lovingly described it as a beautiful and joyful tree whose wide and smooth trunk and branches were as large and as straight as a roof. Radiant butterflies with green and blue wings flew around its limbs and the birds and the "good wind" made their homes in its canopy.[26] The Maya regarded the tree to be a compassionate and sacred being. Even today, descendants of the Maya do not chop down some species of ceiba when clearing land for their milpas.[27]

The Indians of Mexico held other religious beliefs that elicited respect and restraint in the use of the forest. The Maya believed that if trees were cut without permission of the gods, the sky would fall and the end would come to the earth again.[28] The Nahua invoked the name of their god Quetzalcóatl before chopping down a tree.[29] According to the Spanish priest Jacinto de la Serna, the Nahua asked permission from the tree itself for its use: "The Indians attributed a rational soul to trees believing that long ago trees were people. That is why before cutting them, they greet them and ask them for permission to cut them, which they reluctantly do."[30] The Tarahumara shared with the Nahua the belief that trees had rational souls. Like all living creatures, trees felt pain and joy. When a tree was angered or insulted, it would take revenge upon its offender.[31]

The Indians deified plants that they felt had medicinal value.[32] During the late nineteenth century, the Norwegian explorer Karl Lumholtz surprisingly observed how the Tarahumara treated worshiped vegetation: "Those [plants] that are supposed to possess curative powers are venerated. This fact, however, does not save them from being cut into pieces and steeped in water, which the people afterward drink or use in washing themselves."[33] The Indians utilized plants that they esteemed for a variety of purposes, including medicines, fuel, and construction. In some cases, religion and utility may have merged in a manner that led to the protection of some species (such as leaving the ceiba on the milpa in order to gather its fruit or avoiding the poisonous *chechem*). Indians may have also been careful in their use of the forest in order not to provoke a god or a wild deity. Woodcutters and farmers, though, could undertake their activities as long as they secured the permission of the trees or of divine beings. Though perhaps reluctantly, the Indians accelerated their exploitation of woodlands as their populations grew.

Unlike Europeans, the pre-Conquest Indians feared the forests, but they did not hate them. The dangerous spirits and animals of the woodlands had to be respected. Human beings had neither the power nor the right to remove them. Thus, the Indians accepted the spiritual and physical dangers of the forests. Contrastingly, Christians sought to remove these dangers by eliminating the forests.[34] Moreover, the biblical injunction to subdue the earth had no counterpart in native religions. By turning forests into fields, Indians were not attempting to please any god by advancing civilization. They were simply attempting to increase food production to meet mounting demands.

Some groups did exploit forests for religious reasons. The Tarascan of Michoacán, for instance, burned many piles of wood to their gods before going to war (royal officials made certain that people planted, cut, and collected wood for these religious ceremonies).[35] The Tarascan thought that by performing this rite their gods would cause afflictions among their enemies.[36] They attributed the Aztec's troubles with the Spaniards to their neighbors' abandonment of wood sacrifices to the gods:

> Let the strangers [the Spanish] kill the Mexicans because for many days they have not lived right for they do not bring wood to the temples but instead, . . . they honor their gods only with songs. What good are songs alone? How are the gods to favor them if they only sing songs? We work much more than is customarily required for the needs of the gods. Now let us do a little better, nay more, bring in wood for the temples, perhaps they will forgive us, for the gods of the heavens have become angry with us.[37]

In order to save his state and his people, the Tarascan king felt compelled to burn greater amounts of wood to satisfy the gods. Religious beliefs sometimes contributed to the exploitation of forests.

In native religions, animals, like plants, were part of the spiritual world, but their specific status and treatment varied markedly between different groups. Those peoples who relied primarily upon hunting for their subsistence (or who remained connected to their hunting roots) had strong taboos that guarded their use of wildlife. For instance, a Papago hunter always knelt over a dead deer and apologized, explaining that the deer was needed for food and should not be angry. Like a number of other North American Indians, the Papago felt that the animal spirits would harbor game or cause diseases if the people treated wildlife with disrespect or unnecessary cruelty.[38] Religion set the parameters for the Papago's utilization of wildlife.

The religious views of the Indians of Baja California may have protected one species against exploitation altogether. The native peoples of the peninsula apparently abstained from hunting mountain lions, fearing that a killed cat would return to take revenge upon its attackers.[39] In the minds of hunters and gatherers, wild animals were powerful magical beings whose prerogatives could not be transgressed by human beings without grave consequences.

Most of the agricultural peoples of Mexico followed a different code of conduct toward animals.[40] Since survival now depended principally upon the success of agricultural harvests rather than upon the abundance of game, cultivators were much more concerned about appeasing the rain, sun, and fertility gods who controlled the success of the harvest than in pleasing the animal spirits (they also tended to believe that it was the gods rather than the animal spirits who caused famines and diseases). Ironically, one of the chief means of satisfying the agricultural deities was through the sacrifice of game. The Dominican friar Diego de Landa described a Maya ceremony that in its basic outlines was replicated in many other parts of Mexico: "In a day of this month . . . chosen by the priests, the hunters hold another festival . . . which serves to placate the angry gods who work against them and their sown fields, and give to them the blood spilled from the game because without the sacrifice horrendous things would happen."[41] In this case, the religious significance of animals ensured their deaths rather than their survival.

The subordination of animals to the sky gods is recounted in a number of Mesoamerican legends. In the creation myth of the Quiché Maya, the *Popul Vuh*, the sun turned the original "voracious" animals, such as the puma, jaguar, and rattlesnake, into stone.[42] In one of their legends, the Toltec related how the animal gods fiercely resisted their overthrow by the celestial deities.[43] The hare god defiantly attacked the sun with arrows, but the sun caught the projectiles and shot them back, killing the hare. The sun god pursued all the other animal gods until only one, Xólotl, remained. After unsuccessfully begging the sun deity for his survival, Xólotl desperately transformed himself into several animals and plants before his magic was exhausted. At this point, the sky gods killed the last animal god with an obsidian point. From then on, the sun and the moon had no rivals.[44]

Despite their demotion, however, animals were more than mere living beings. They were closely connected to human beings and the gods. The Huichol thought that their ancestors were mostly animals, especially serpents, jaguars, and mountain lions.[45] The Zapotec underscored their bravery by claiming to be the offspring of lions and other wild beasts.[46] The Olmec identified themselves even more closely with the powerful wildcats, making sculptures that had human bodies and jaguar faces.[47] The gods took upon the guise of animals, too. Usually, they did so in a form commiserate with their status, so that the mighty sun god became a jaguar and the earth god a snake.[48] The Indians of Mesoamerica associated many animals with gods that reflected the animals' personalities. Thus, the Nahua identified the coyote with the god of war and the god of song because they regarded it to be both an aggressive and social animal.[49] The Maya associated the sprightly monkey with the god of the arts, music, and games.[50] Native peoples further linked wild animals to the gods as consorts. This was the case with the Tzotzil and the Quiché Maya, who thought that wild animals acted on behalf of the earth gods in defending the forests against human intrusion.[51]

Animals also served as the companions and guardians of human beings. The Tzotzil, Zapotec, and Tarahumara felt that animal soul companions protected them from danger.[52] The Tarahumara, for instance, regarded the mountain lion to be a good animal that looked after people: "When he sees an animal such as the bear or the coyote approach a man, he roars to warn the man; and if the man pays no attention, the lion attacks the animal to save the man; therefore strips of his skin are worn around the necks and ankles as a protection."[53] Other animals could perform valuable tasks only when alive. Thus, the Tarahumara avoided stepping on toads: "The horned toad holds the world. It says: 'Don't tread on me! I am the colour of the earth and I hold the world; therefore walk carefully, that you do not tread on me.'"[54] Likewise, the Tarahumara were careful not to disturb rattlesnakes, whom they considered to be the companions of sorcerers. Lumholtz reports that "a Mexican once killed a rattlesnake, and the Indian grew very angry and said that the snake had protected his house; now he had no one to guard it."[55] Finally, the Tarahumara were grateful to animals that intervened on their behalf before the gods:

> . . . animals are by no means inferior creatures; they understand
> magic and are possessed of much knowledge, and may assist the Tar-
> ahumares [var.] in making rain. In spring, the singing of the birds,
> the cooing of the dove, the croaking of the frog, the chirping of the
> cricket, all the sounds uttered by the denizens of the greensward, are
> to the Indians appeals to the deities for rain.[56]

The Tzotzil and the Zapotec perceived that their personal fate was tied to their animal guardian. Thus, a provoked earth god could harm a Tzotzil by expropriating his or her animal companion. The Zapotec believed that they and their wild friend followed the same course in life, such that if the animal was wounded or died in some manner so also would the Indian. If, on the contrary, some accident happened to the Indian, it would also happen to the animal. In this symbiotic relationship, the Zapotec seemingly had a strong incentive to protect his or her animal guardian (and vice versa).[57] So, although people no longer believed in animal spirits or animal gods that exacted retribution for their mistreatment, wildlife continued to command respect as the companion of gods and of human beings.

Dense populations rather than a less animistic religion was the principal cause of the depletion of natural resources in Mesoamerica. Indeed, some native peoples became concerned about the extent of the environmental degradation that they had generated. A few rulers even enacted regulations to restrict the use of natural resources. The peoples of Mesoamerica may have attempted to be careful with the land through the adoption of different agricultural techniques as well as through their laws, but this goal was not always achieved. The intensive utilization of resources spurred by population pressures resulted in environmental deterioration, the extent of which is still being debated among scholars of pre-Hispanic Mexico.

An old theory for the disappearance of Classic Maya civilization (by the early tenth century) was that the Maya had exhausted the fertility of the soil through slash and burn agriculture. The milpa could only support crops for two or three years before the land had to be left fallow again to regain its fertility. In the two main areas of Maya settlement, the Petén and Yucatán, the land must be left fallow from four to seven years and from fifteen to twenty years, respectively (the soils of the Petén are more fertile than those of the Yucatán and therefore require a shorter fallow period).[58] The old theory postulated that the Maya population grew to such a level that they had to shorten fallow periods to continue to increase food production. By shortening fallow periods, they depleted the fertility of the soil. The result was crop failure, starvation, and the depopulation of Maya centers.

Proponents of this theory assumed that modern-day Indians in the region practiced the same form of slash and burn agriculture as their Maya ancestors. But the ancient Maya (as well as some of their descendants) created their milpas with greater care.[59] They left trees on the land, perhaps in order to reduce soil erosion, to produce organic debris, and to speed the process of reforestation.

During the late 1920s, some scholars began to challenge the notion that the Maya exclusively practiced slash and burn agriculture. Based upon archaeological evidence such as the remnants of terraces and land demarcations, they deduced that the Maya utilized permanent agriculture.[60] Subsequently, Mayanists found anthropological and ethnohistorical data that indicated that the Maya developed a diverse system of agricultural production. This system included kitchen gardens for the production of a variety of vegetables and fruit trees and raised fields, which consisted of the soil and organic debris upcast from adjacent drainage canals.[61] The Maya may also have planted trees in the fertile crevices between stones and within the confines of artificial rock enclosures for the production of food, medicine, and fuel.[62]

Some scholars concluded that the Maya adopted these techniques to make their agriculture sustainable in the tropics. Specifically, the kitchen gardens reduced pressures to clear forests for agriculture and allowed for longer fallow periods for the milpas; the raised fields provided well-aerated, moist, and fertile soils for agriculture; and terraces impeded soil erosion and collected water that increased the moisture and fertility of the soil. The Maya may have successfully adapted to the tropical environment by achieving a balance between shifting and permanent agriculture.[63]

If, however, the Maya responded to population pressures by converting vast expanses of forests into farmlands, then they would have faced a new set of problems. In modern times, sedentary farming has failed in the tropics because of the rapid loss of soil nutrients, inorganic matter, and soil moisture and friability (the land becomes infertile; once tropical vegetation is removed, heavy rains leach minerals out of the exposed soil, and the sun bakes the ground into a hard crust). Perhaps, as some scholars suggest, the Maya circumvented these problems through mulching, manuring, and terracing and thus were able to practice permanent agriculture in the tropics on a large scale.[64]

Other Mayanists have reached a far different conclusion: they argue that the collapse of the Classic Maya civilization was due to a population that had outstripped the productive capacity of the land itself. As a result, the Maya suffered either massive starvation or widespread food shortages that in turn may have triggered ruinous rebellions or wars.

At present, no proof exists that the Maya population had reached or exceeded the carrying capacity of the land. The apparent speed of the Maya collapse, as well as the apparent absence of large-scale emigration, suggests a more cataclysmic event than the gradual onset of an agricultural crisis as the amount of land necessary to support a growing population dwindled. Other factors, such as climatic changes, prolonged droughts, plant diseases, or internecine warfare may have led to catastrophic declines in agricultural production and hence the depopulation of the Maya lowlands (so far, anthropologists have only ascertained that the Maya collapse occurred during a period of warfare). How close the Maya came to reaching the limits of the land may never be known.[65]

Undoubtedly, the Maya did cause some degree of environmental degradation. Studies of Maya settlements in lacustrine regions indicate that agriculture and urbanization resulted in deforestation and soil erosion.[66] In these regions, the Maya either did not use sound resource management techniques, such as terracing, or these methods were insufficient to check environmental deterioration.

In lacustrine zones and elsewhere, the Maya not only cleared forests for farming and for settlements but also used their stone axes to chop down trees for firewood, for buildings, and to fire kilns for the production of ceramics and lime (the latter was used to build ceremonial centers).[67] In coastal areas, Maya communities may have burned considerable amounts of wood to evaporate salt from brine water.[68] These activities contributed to deforestation in Maya Mesoamerica.

The Maya's agricultural undertakings may have had a particularly detrimental effect upon wild plants and animals. If the Maya did clear large tracts of forest for permanent agriculture, then some tropical species must surely have become extinct.[69] Even with shifting agriculture, the structure of the forests (the size and distribution of tree species) would probably have been changed, and the ranges and numbers of some animal species would have been reduced. As a passage from an ancient Maya book indicates, animals did perish as the result of slash and burn agriculture: "The forests burn for the planting of corn, and all burns, and the animals of the land die, the same the deer, that entangles its antlers in the branches; as the rabbit that hides in its burrow."[70] At the very least, then, Maya land use practices caused a decrease in plant and animal populations.

The Maya also diminished wildlife populations (and flora) through direct exploitation. Though primarily an agricultural people, the Maya also collected wild plants, hunted, and fished. Maya murals depict marketplaces replete with animals (some alive and some dead) and animal products, including coatis, macaws, turkeys, deer, armadillos, rabbits, suckling pigs, iguanas, wax and honey bees; the skins of ocelots, jaguars, and deer; and a variety of bird feathers (the Maya mainly used skins and feathers for ceremonial purposes).[71] In the sixteenth century, Diego de Landa observed descendants of the Maya bringing in large catches of fish from the sea. In addition, he commented upon how the Indians hunted all the big birds in the trees. With the diffusion of the bow and arrow through southern Mexico (brought into the region by the warring Aztec), the Maya could hunt more animals than had been previously possible with their traps and nets. Technological developments, as well as population growth, contributed to the diminution of wildlife in southern Mexico.[72]

In central Mexico, soil erosion and deforestation were serious problems even before the arrival of the Spanish. From his studies of alluvial deposits in the region, geographer Sherburne Cook concluded that in many locations the loss of topsoil began long before the Conquest. Furthermore, he found a close correlation between the severity of soil erosion and population densities. In particular, regions occupied by the Mixtec in Oaxaca (556 persons per square mile in 1520), by the Nahua in Puebla (1,245 persons per square mile), and by the Tarascan in Michoacán (1,754 persons per square mile) exhibited "severe to locally complete" erosion at the time of the Conquest.[73] The Indians of central Mexico moved up the steep hillsides as agriculture in the valleys could no longer support growing populations and as soil erosion made farming on lower slopes impossible.[74] The loss of topsoil from the upper elevations was yet more rapid than it had been lower down. To make matters worse, the short downpours that routinely occur in the region from late spring to early fall stripped away exposed soils. Eventually, the deterioration of the land would have threatened the survival of those peoples.[75]

The Indians of central Mexico burned away woodlands to plant corn. At the time of the Conquest, the Nahua cultivated approximately 15 percent of the land on the central plateau, much of which had been previously forested.[76] The collection of firewood placed an additional strain upon the region's forests, as it provided the primary source of fuel for the highlands' nearly eleven million people. The use of wood in construction, including the calcination of lime for the building of temples and pyramids, was yet another cause of deforestation.[77] The Spanish remarked upon the Aztec's extensive use of wood for canoes, boxes, tables, doors, pillars, roofing, lintels, columns, planks, and boards.[78] Sahagún's Nahua informants described the forests as a place "where trees are cut, where there is logging, a place of beams."[79] Merchants sold bronze and copper axes in the marketplaces of Tenochtitlán, the capital of the Aztec empire,[80] and Aztec rulers collected wood as part of their tribute from other Indians.[81] Timber was an important part of the Aztec economy.

Some Indians in central Mexico were concerned about soil erosion and deforestation. To impede erosion, native peoples made terraces out of rock, land, and maguey.[82] The Nahua spared some of the plateau's forests by planting crops on beds of mud and decayed organic materials (the *chinampas*) in the shallows of lakes. Because of the valley's temperate climate, several harvests could be produced each year from this highly productive form of agriculture. Following King Nezahualcóyotl's construction of a dike across Lake Texcoco in 1449 to prevent flooding, salinity levels of the southern lakes in the Valley of Mexico were reduced to such a low concentration (due to their separation from the brackish waters to the north) that they could support large-scale *chinampa* production. After the Famine of One Rabbit (an Aztec time cycle) in 1454,

Indians in the Valley of Mexico expanded the raised fields to provide a buffer against the heavy frosts and prolonged droughts that had culminated in massive starvation. By the second half of the fifteenth century, *chinampas* covered approximately nine thousand hectares on Lakes Xochimilco and Chalco, with each hectare feeding between fifteen and twenty people.[83] These fields, then, could support most of Tenochtitlán's 235,000 or so inhabitants.[84] The Indians apparently did not cultivate the ridges or slopes of the mountains surrounding the Valley of Mexico but instead planted on the flat lands and near their houses.[85] Whether intended or not, the *chinampas* aided soil and forest conservation by reducing pressures to burn steep wooded hillsides for farming.

A few pre-Conquest rulers enacted forestry regulations. Perhaps, the first to do so was the thirteenth-century Chichimec prince, Nopaltzin, who prohibited the setting of fires in the mountains and countryside without a license and then only when necessary.[86] Though Nopaltzin's motives for this edict are unknown, he was likely concerned about the effects of uncontrolled use of fires upon wildlife and forests, both of which were important resources. The Tarascan kings, who valued forests as a habitat for wildlife, as a source of many products, and as a supply of wood for ceremonial purposes, appointed forest guards to oversee the activities of lumberers.[87] Concerned by the growing scarcity of trees, the king of Texcoco, Nezahualcóyotl, restricted the areas where people could cut wood for buildings and for ordinary uses. Nezahualcóyotl declared that those who cut trees within protected areas would be put to death (he later modified this decree by allowing his subjects to collect dead wood and branches within the reserves).[88] The scarcity resulting from the unrestricted use of timber resources had led to the first forestry regulations in Mexico.

The Indian elite attempted to maintain nature within their midst. Between the late 1420s and the early 1430s, the Nahua kings created forested parks (including Chapultepec, the oldest existing park in the New World), botanical gardens, zoos, aviaries, and fishing ponds to indulge themselves in their enjoyment of wild plants and animals. According to the Spanish chroniclers, these nature reserves were places of wonder. They contained "forests full of deer, rabbits, hares, and other animals surrounded by rivers and fountains and admirable ponds that cannot be but extolled."[89] The forests "were planted with a variety of trees and fragrant flowers, and in them a multitude of birds . . . sung harmoniously."[90] Urbanization produced a desire to retain a contact with nature and to protect such areas as parks.

The Indians of central Mexico coveted wildlife for utilitarian and ceremonial purposes, as well as for its aesthetic value.[91] According to their legends, the Tarascan settled in the region around Lake Pátzcuaro in order to exploit its rich fisheries and the abundant game. Despite becoming a largely agricultural people, the Tarascan remained skilled hunters and fishers. They caught the lake's tasty fish with fish hooks and nets. During the winter months, they surrounded migratory waterfowl with their canoes and killed them with trident-form spears. Hunters supplied the Tarascan kings with deer, rabbits, ducks, quail, and other birds to use in sacrifices or for food.[92] The Tarascan also killed animals for the skins to make their clothing. The people who settled on the shores of Lake Pátzcuaro never ceased to make ready use of the fish and game at their disposal.[93]

The Aztec, too, were excellent hunters and fishers. The Spanish chroniclers related how they used nets and darts to kill many birds and fish, which provided a significant source of protein for the inhabitants of the Valley of Mexico.[94] In the "fresh catch section" of the Aztec markets, vendors sold black and white fish, shrimp, snails, salamanders, tadpoles, river oysters, turtles, turtle eggs, and more than a dozen aquatic birds ranging from ducks to herons. The meat stock also included rabbit, deer, weasels, moles, wild boars, snakes, iguana eggs, worms of the maguey, and grasshoppers. In addition to food items, merchants sold the pelts of jaguars, mountain lions, otters, deer, and badgers.[95] The Aztec kings regulated fishing, if not hunting. Royal officials punished fishers who caught more fish than they could eat or sell.[96] As resources became scarcer so too did the need to eliminate waste.

The Aztec and their neighbors killed animals to meet ceremonial and material "needs" as well as for food. They engaged in ritual hunts and sacrificed wolves, deer, hares, rabbits, small dogs, pheasants, lizards, and human beings to placate their gods.[97] Bird feathers and animal skins were among the most prized items of tribute.[98] Besides their ceremonial importance, these items were used by royalty for their personal pleasure. The kings of Texcoco had rugs made of jaguar skins, blankets made of eagle feathers, and tapestries made of rabbit fur.[99] In their utilization of animals, the peoples of the central plateau had far exceeded their subsistence needs.

By the time of the Spanish Conquest, the Aztec were straining the environment of the central highlands. Their use of wood for fuel and for construction and their clearing of land for agriculture had taken a toll upon the forests.[100] Many hillsides were badly eroded.[101] Their large-scale hunting of migratory birds and ducks had thinned those popula-tions.[102] The Aztec had not exhausted their food supply, however. Schol-ars have almost universally rejected the theory that the Aztec practiced human sacrifice in order to augment (through cannibalism) their mea-ger supply of animal protein.[103] When Hernando Cortés conquered the Aztec, the Valley of Mexico and the adjacent countryside were not on the verge of ecological collapse.[104]

On the other hand, the Aztec were far from living in some kind of mythical harmony with the land.

By contrast, the Spanish altered the environment of Mexico on a grand scale. In most cases, they had diverged further from the spiritual beliefs and subsistence practices of their ancestors than the native peoples of Mexico had from theirs. Although principally from an eco-nomic standpoint, a few Spaniards did recognize the threat that scarcity of resources posed to their society. This recognition provided the prin-cipal line of continuity between the different cultures.

Chapter Two

THE SPANISH RESOLVE

Conserving Resources

for the Crown

Some of the inhabitants of the Iberian peninsula held the same religious respect for the natural world as the Indians of pre-Columbian Mexico. Like many native Mexicans, for instance, a Basque woodcutter asked permission before chopping down a tree in deference to its feelings. A few dwellers in the primeval forests of the Pyrenees still profess that forests become angry when they are sold, so that people who pass within them risk being crushed by falling trees. At one time, the denizens of Asturias (a province in northern Spain) avowed that a satyrlike creature defended the forests and all life within it by frightening away woodcutters and hunters. In fact, many Iberians once felt that the earth was inhabited by spirits and divine beings.[1]

By the time of the Conquest, however, many Spaniards had demystified and disempowered nature. They did not believe that wild plants and animals were magical beings that could either assist or harm them. Nor did they consider themselves to be part of a natural world whose forces lay beyond their direct control. In addition to divesting nature of its spiritual powers, the Spanish often overlooked the importance of being careful with the things of the land. As a whole, they exhibited more confidence than the Indians of pre-Hispanic Mexico in their ability to alter nature without harming themselves.

The Spanish, however, were not completely oblivious to the consequences of resource degradation. They had witnessed the results of environmental deterioration on the Iberian peninsula, from eroded hillsides to flooded valleys. By the time of Columbus's voyages to the New World, the Spanish monarchy had begun to take steps to confront regional shortages of wood. The Spanish crown promulgated conservation laws for their colonies as well, in part because they had witnessed the process of resource depletion at home.

Spanish conservation policies were driven by economic considerations. The crown attempted to protect those renewable natural resources most important in the functioning of the colonial economy. Above all, the Spanish wanted to conserve the colonies' forest resources. Spanish kings and viceroys were concerned that without restrictions and without reforestation, the timber crucial to mining operations, shipbuilding, and construction would be depleted. Resources of lesser value, such as most wild animals, or greater availability, such as water and soil, received far less attention from the crown.

The Spanish approach to resource management was narrow. True to their country's legalistic heritage, royal officials attempted to protect resources in their colonies through decrees. For the most part, the Spanish dispensed with the techniques that the Indians had used to conserve the land. Perhaps a few Spanish missionaries restored pre-Hispanic terraces that native peoples could no longer maintain because of the decimation of their populations by epidemic diseases, the expropriation of their lands, and their entry into a wage labor system. Most of the colonists, however, allowed them to fall into disrepair, preferring instead to direct the large amount of labor necessary for the upkeep of terraces toward other tasks.[2]

By introducing the plough and livestock into the New World, the Spanish exacerbated the problem of soil erosion, thus making the adoption of soil conservation measures even more critical than during pre-Columbian times. A few colonists counseled their compatriots against the profligate use of the land. Early in the seventeenth century, the cosmographer Henrico Martínez issued one of the most dire warnings. He postulated that the flooding of Mexico City was directly related to the clearing and plowing of land on the surrounding hillsides. According to Martínez, soils eroded from mountainous plots were filling in the lakes of the region. Since the amount of rainfall remained constant, the water had nowhere to go but over the rim of the lakes, inundating the city. Martínez cautioned that with the passing of time, the residents of Mexico City would increasingly suffer from the poor agricultural practices of their rural kin.[3] Martínez was one of a handful of colonists who considered the prevention of soil erosion to be imperative. The Spanish crown's response to this problem, however, was muted. The Law of the Indies (the Spanish legal code for its colonies) included restrictions on forest use and grazing, part of whose purpose was to prevent soil erosion. This, however, was the extent of Spain's soil conservation policy for its overseas possessions.

Likewise, Spanish officials rarely placed a high priority on the careful management of water resources. Spanish water law focused on the allocation of water rather than on the elimination of its wasteful use. Thus, while the Law of the Indies addressed the issue of water rights in some detail, it was silent on the matter of water conservation. In the arid north of New Spain, local officials and irrigation users were more apt to couple the issues of water distribution and water management than were overseas administrators.[4] This was the case in 1789, when the founders of Hermosillo, Sonora, dictated that no one should use more water than was absolutely necessary. They also required irrigation users to construct their diversion outlets of stone and lime to prevent the loss of water through the breakage of the central canal. Many town plans called upon irrigation users to return all surplus water from their ditches to the originating source. Though laudable from a conservation perspective, this proviso inadvertently fostered water pollution, since the recycled water often contained salts, garbage, chemicals, and waste. To protect public health, some municipal councils established fines for water contamination. There is no indication that the Spanish were concerned about the detrimental effects of irrigation, particularly desiccation, upon fragile ecosystems, though. Along with deforestation and the consumption of water and vegetation by livestock, irrigation contributed to the increasing aridity of northern New Spain.[5]

Public officials rarely instructed private landowners to adopt water conservation measures (Hermosillo was an exception). A few far-sighted *hacendados* initiated such measures on their own without any encouragement from the government. For instance, the Sánchez-Navarro family, who owned an extensive hacienda in Coahuila, lined some of their canals with masonry to prevent seepage.[6] Most irrigation works, though, were not built to save water. Measures to reduce water loss, such as constructing strong irrigation gates, lining ditches, or storing water underground, often were not taken by the colonists because of the planning and expense involved. Consequently, thousands of gallons of water evaporated or seeped into the soil.

More so than most, if not all, of their predecessors in the arid north, the Spanish relied upon extensive irrigation systems to make the desert bloom. Other adaptations to the dry environment, such as the collection of semiwild plants, the use of floodplain agriculture (using brush dams on the arroyos to block water from the fields) and the reliance on drought-resistant crops, such as squash, entailed an existence that was too nomadic and too small scale for the Spanish. They chose instead to build irrigation canals and to appropriate water previously controlled by Indian communities.[7] From their experiences on the Iberian peninsula, the Spanish learned that irrigation made agriculture possible in semiarid lands.[8] Their assessment of the capability of this technology, though, was often too optimistic.

There were important Spanish antecedents to efforts to conserve wildlife and forests in the New World. Between the fourteenth and sixteenth centuries, Spain had developed a wildlife code, and the monarchy's concern for the protection of wildlife became stronger over time.[9]

The intent of the earliest Spanish hunting regulation was to protect human beings rather than wild animals per se. In 1348, King Alfonso XI prohibited the use of "large iron traps which can fell bears, boars, or deer because of the dangers that can befall men or horses which travel in the forests." Gradually, the focus began to shift toward the conservation of wildlife. During the fifteenth century, Spanish kings restricted the types of weapons that could be used in hunting and fishing in part to prevent the overexploitation of animals. In 1435, King Juan II prohibited the dumping of poisonous substances into rivers to kill or paralyze fish, and in 1465, King Enrique IV forbade the use of traps, nets, or shotguns to kill doves.

Rulers also took steps to ensure the reproduction of animals. King Enrique III acted in pursuance of this goal when he prohibited hunting during the breeding season (specified as the months of March, April, and May) and proscribed the collection of eggs.

The crown's efforts to protect wildlife intensified during the sixteenth century in response to the increasingly severe impact that habitat destruction (especially deforestation), overhunting, and overfishing were having on Spain's animal populations. To protect the realm's fisheries, King Carlos I (reigned 1516–1556) prohibited fishing with sheets, blankets, linens, and certain types of nets, capturing fish by drying up streams, and fishing during the spawning season. To maintain an adequate supply of game (hunting was one of the aristocracy's favorite sports), Carlos forbade hunting with hounds and firearms and during snowfall or other inclement weather when large numbers of animals sought shelter or prey. In 1617, King Felipe III rescinded the prohibition against firearms because, as he said, the regulation had "not resulted in the abundance of game that had been hoped. People hunt secretly with other instruments that are quieter and which have a more destructive impact upon game [populations]." Spanish monarchs were intent on conserving species for consumption and recreation.

Royal officials often exempted more plentiful animals, such as rabbits and birds, from hunting regulations. The crown went a step further by encouraging the killing of predators. The monarchy justified its policy as follows: "Because the wolves do such harm to cattle, we order the giving of licenses to all cities and villages within our realm so that they can order the killing of said wolves, even being with young, and can give a bounty for each head."[10] Wildlife conservation did not extend to animals deemed to be dangerous to people or to their livestock.

By the time of its overseas conquests, Spain had cut down large tracts of its forests. The collection of firewood, the use of wood for shipbuilding, and the burning of forests for pasturage had all taken a heavy toll on Spain's woodlands. The conversion of forests into pastureland had singularly transformed the Spanish landscape. The eighteenth-century Spanish naturalist A. J. Cavanilles sadly noted how sheep grazing had deformed the character of the land in the province of Galacia: "Years past there were beautiful pines, and other trees were also dense, but they [the pastoralists] burned them and destroyed them so that those existing nowadays are few. That pernicious technique which the pastoralists used to create abundant pasturage has caused great harm."[11] For many centuries, sheepherders, through their powerful trade association, the Mesta, had guaranteed themselves the "right" to burn Spain's forests.

The Spanish monarchy had played an important role in the expansion of the sheep industry. In 1273, King Alfonso X chartered the creation of a national association for the sheepherders of Castile—the Mesta—so that pastoralists could better protect their interests and thus create more wealth for the kingdom. At the same time, though, Alfonso attempted to protect the rights of other resource users. In his law code, for example, the king required anyone who set fires that engulfed forests or fields to pay for the harm that they caused. He also required livestock owners to compensate fruit growers and farmers for any damages that their herds did to the owner's trees, grape vines, or crops (similarly in the New World, Spanish monarchs pledged to stop cattle ranchers from encroaching upon Indian farmlands and all livestock grazers from converting woodlands into pasturage).[12] Ultimately, though, the great increases in the number of sheep and the crown's growing support for the Mesta would endanger farms, vineyards, and forests.

The Mesta reached the height of its power during the first half of the sixteenth century. Eager to fill their coffers with precious metals from the overseas wool trade, while making debtors out of England and Flanders, King Fernando and Queen Isabel expanded the privileges of the Mesta and granted it greater access to common lands. Partly as a result of the crown's munificence, sheepherders increased their flocks from 2.5 to 3.5 million head between 1516 and 1526.[13]

This population explosion came at a great cost to Spain's remaining woodlands. Moreover, the monarchs did little to stop sheepherders from converting forests into pasturelands. Because of the great wealth generated by wool exports, the crown had allowed pastoralists to damage the very resources that its conservation policies were designed to protect. The monarchy's dependence upon precious metals from the New World would lead to an equally regrettable exemption of the mining industry from crown forestry laws.

Gradually the power of the Mesta declined. During the mid-sixteenth century, municipalities became increasingly successful at challenging the association's privileges. Town councils passed ordinances that established stiff penalties for the burning of forests. (Although sheepherders were the worst violators, other livestock owners and farmers also set fires, either to clear the underbrush or to remove the forest itself.) Some towns even prohibited sheepherders from cutting branches to feed their flocks because this practice threatened to stunt the growth of trees. The crown became less willing to intervene on behalf of the Mesta on such matters, in part because it now had a new source of wealth in the form of silver and gold from the Americas. However, by the time the Mesta's power had begun to wane many of the country's forests and soils had already been badly damaged.[14]

King Fernando and Queen Isabel, disturbed by the extent of deforestation around Spanish towns and villages, enacted their country's first forestry law in 1496. According to their decree, woodlands around human settlements were to be

> . . . conserved for the public's well-being and not cut without a license except for those trees which are so tall that the people of said cities can use them for wood, not cutting them at their base just the branches so that they can regrow, and the other trees which are not

so large can be used for acorns and for sheltering cattle during winter.[15]

In 1518, King Carlos and Queen Juana ordered the planting of oaks and pine trees throughout Spain. Their rationale for this proclamation was as follows:

> Because we are informed by officials of the realm that they are cutting and destroying our forests and they do not plant anew . . . the result of which is that there is no cover for cattle in times of inclement weather and a great lack of wood. . . . We will remedy this situation by appointing officials to oversee the planting of oaks and pines so that there is better pasturage and shade for cattle with the least harm possible to farmers.[16]

Some rural peoples had developed a harmonious relationship with the forests. On occasion, cattle grazers used the ground cover to feed their herds and the forest canopy to protect them during the winter months. In the fall, villagers collected acorns to feed their livestock after the snows fell or themselves when harvests were poor. Many days they ventured into the woodlands to hunt and fish and to collect spring water, honey, medicinal herbs, cork, fruits, and a host of other products. The crown was trying to protect both a supply of wood and the forest-based economy.[17]

The passing of the traditional forest economy troubled not only the Spanish monarchy but also the celebrated novelist Miguel de Cervantes (1547–1616). Through his protagonist, Don Quixote, Cervantes lamented the end of humanity's symbiotic relationship with the land:

> In that holy age [the Golden Age] all things were held in common. In order to provide for his (or her) daily sustenance, no one had to do more work than raise a hand to the robust oaks, which generously invited everyone to take its sweet, ripe fruit. The clear springs and running brooks, in magnificent abundance offered to people their delightful and transparent waters. In the cracks of the rocks and in the hallow trees a republic of solicitous and considerate bees offered to whichever hand, the fertile harvest of their sweet labor. The vigorous cork-trees, without any motivation but courtesy, discarded their broad light barks. . . . All was peace then, all friendship, all concord: the heavy blade of the crooked plow had not yet dared

to open and expose the holy bowels of our first mother; that she without compulsion, offered through all the parts of her fertile and spacious bosom, whatever could nourish, sustain, and delight the children who possessed her.[18]

Through reforestation, the crown attempted to restore the natural wealth of the realm, but as Cervantes knew, the past could not be recovered. The crown, though, had the opportunity to prevent resource scarcity from occurring in its colonies.

In New Spain, the conservation of wildlife was not a major concern of Spanish officials. Nearly all of the wildlife ordinances were local in nature.[19] Most of New Spain's wildlife populations were too large and of too little economic importance to warrant crown protection. And though hunters killed many animals, their numbers seemed too small to affect what appeared to be an unlimited supply of game.[20]

One of the species that the Spanish did value in New Spain was the oyster because of its pearl. Earlier, the crown recognized that the pearl industry could become a lucrative business. During the sixteenth century, the Spanish monarchy enacted a series of regulations designed to guarantee the collection of the royal fifth (in this case, a fifth of the value of the pearls) and to maintain oyster populations. To accomplish the latter goal, the crown banned the use of *chinchorros* (large boats that could haul in many more of the mollusks than was possible with canoes), required that oysters not fully grown be returned unopened to the sea, and prohibited fishers from collecting more oysters than they could disembowel (to prevent the rotting of oysters on the shore).[21] Despite these measures, however, royal officials were unable to restrain the exploitation of oyster beds. The Jesuit missionary Miguel del Barco (1706–1792) noted that by the mid-eighteenth century the number of oysters had "diminished greatly so that they have almost been exhausted in some places."[22] One soldier had collected 275 pounds of pearls.[23] Although without much tangible effect, the crown had at least afforded legal protection to the oyster because of its economic value. Other species did not fare so well from a policy perspective.

As in Spain, predators fared the least well of all. The use of dogs to tree mountain lions and other large cats was a common practice in New Spain. Once treed, the animal was shot.[24] In Baja California, missionaries were intent on killing mountain lions because of the threat they posed to livestock and even to human life. In their campaign against the mountain lion, the missionaries enlisted the support of Indians by offering them gifts and by convincing them to place aside their fears of the cat. The missionaries demonstrated the "cowardly" nature of the cat by exhibiting how it ran up trees when set upon by dogs.[25] Miguel del Barco told of another ploy used by the Spaniards to reshape the Indian's perception of the mountain lion. To dispel the belief that a dead lion would take revenge upon its attacker, a missionary killed a mountain lion to show the Indians that he himself had not died.[26] The missionaries had demystified the natural world for the Indians and had provided them with an economic incentive to kill wildlife. As in other regions of North America, Europeans had changed both the Indian's spiritual and economic relationship to the natural world.

The Spanish curtailed the Indians' utilization of wildlife by banning animal sacrifices and by expropriating hunting grounds. But overall, they fostered an increase in the native peoples' exploitation of animals through the introduction of new weapons. In the case of the Valley of Mexico, the Indians still hunted migratory birds, but now with firearms instead of darts and nets. By the end of the eighteenth century, native and non-native hunters were killing 120,000 ducks annually in the basin.[27] The changes wrought by the Spanish in the technology and ideology of hunting in Mexico sometimes produced dramatic alterations in the native peoples' use of animals.

In contrast to its lax attitude toward wildlife conservation, the Spanish crown worked vigorously to protect its timber resources in the New World. In 1539, King Carlos directed *encomederos* (Spaniards who had been granted access to Indian labor) to plant trees to provide their vicinities with a supply of wood.[28] The viceroy of New Spain, don Antonio de Mendoza, was also troubled by the specter of timber scarcity. In 1550, he was sufficiently alarmed by the destruction of forests near the mining community of Taxco that he forbade the setting of forest fires in the region.[29] In his reports (ca. 1550) to the incoming viceroy, don Luis de Velasco, Mendoza solemnly reflected that "in a very few years, a great deal of forests have been cut [in New Spain] and having consideration of this, there will be a shortage of wood before there is a shortage of metals." Mendoza understood that the extraction of precious metals, upon which the Spanish colonial economy was primarily based, was impossible without the existence of wood for fuels, shafts, supports, and buildings. Mendoza cautioned Velasco that the destruction of the territory's forests would mean a major change in the order of things. He directed Velasco's attention to forestry laws already in existence and advised him to continue the enforcement of these laws. If he did so, then the social and economic dislocations that deforestation would produce could be averted.[30]

During the seventeenth century, the pace of forestry regulations slackened perhaps because of the Hapsburg kings' preoccupation with Continental wars and internal rebellions or simply because of their satisfaction with existing laws.[31] In any case, the Bourbon kings (whose line began in 1700) formulated policies designed to gain greater control over their colonies' valuable timber resources. In 1765, Carlos III decreed that licenses were required to cut wood on private as well as on common lands and that for each tree cut three more had to be planted.[32] In 1803, the monarchy (headed by the feeble Carlos IV) crafted the final and most comprehensive colonial forestry law.

The Ordinance of 1803 was a component of Spain's program to "safeguard" its colonies against the economic and military intrusion of foreign powers, especially the British. Through this particular edict, crown officials sought to restrict foreign access to coastal hardwoods and to maintain an adequate supply of those same hardwoods for Spain's navy. To achieve these ends, they prohibited Spanish merchants from selling wood to another country without a permit, permitted only marked trees to be cut within twenty-five leagues of the sea, and stated that only in case of an urgent necessity could trees be cut before they reached their maturity (perhaps only if Spain's navy suffered heavy losses). In addition, they mandated the planting of "useful" trees in suitable areas and proscribed the grazing of livestock in areas where they could harm the new trees. Finally, they encouraged the use of coal as an alternative to firewood. To enforce this ordinance, the Bourbons created a special corps of forestry guards serving under the director general of the Armada.[33] Spain's most ambitious forestry law would come to naught. The ordinance was in effect only seven years before the war for independence began in New Spain.

The crown's efforts to conserve forests was not merely a legal exercise; royal officials needed the compliance of colonists and Indians. It was in this triangular relationship between crown, colonist, and Indian that the fate of New Spain's forests lay.

The crown wrestled with the issue of the extent to which Indians should be allowed to use natural resources. In 1541, King Carlos declared that all forests, pasturelands, and waters in the New World were held in common.[34] In theory this decree granted Indians unrestricted access to resources in those areas. In 1559, King Felipe II reiterated the crown's position that Indians should have free access to forest resources, but added a disclaimer: "It is our will that the Indians can freely cut wood in the forests for their own use. And we order that no one puts impediments in their way except that they do not cut them in a manner which prevents them from growing and regenerating."[35] The crown particularly decried the Indians' practice of slash and burn agriculture. According to royal officials: "The native peoples' use of the milpa to cultivate land causes great harm [to the forests]."[36] Colonial authorities also reproached the Indians for cutting young trees at their base for firewood and for the making of charcoal.[37] The viceroys of New Spain forbade both activities in areas where forests were needed for mining, construction, or shipbuilding.

In part, the Indians' destructive use of forest resources ensued from crown policy itself. Taxation and the forced sale of goods had pushed Indians into a monetary economy. One means of meeting these exactions was through a more extensive exploitation of natural resources, particularly forests. The Indians would sell wood in town markets and use part of the money to meet their tribute obligations. The explorer Alonso de la Mota y Escobar described the routine as follows: "The Indians utilize the forests to cut wood for planks, beams, and other purposes. They bring the wood to the city to sell and with this proceed to eat, dress, pay tribute, and pass their lives."[38] Concurrent with the new exactions was the Spanish expropriation of Indian lands, the upshot of which was that the Indians had to exploit fewer resources more heavily, particularly as Indian populations rebounded from the decimation ensuing from the Conquest and from disease.[39] In those areas where the Spanish intrusion was less intense, such as Oaxaca, traditional land use patterns continued and resources were better conserved.[40] Spanish economic policy did not create the problem of resource misuse in the New World, but it did create new pressures that intensified resource exploitation by Indian communities.

The question of what constituted the Indians' fair use of forest resources and what constituted a just forest protection policy would be a recurrent one in Mexican history. However, unlike most post-Independence politicians, Spanish officials held some sympathy for the Indians' plight. They understood the conditions that contributed to the Indians' exploitative use of resources. As the Spanish intendant Bruno Díaz de Salcedo (ca. 1798) observed:

The unfortunate Indian cannot plant trees because Monday they walk to the forests with their wives and children where they spend two days cutting wood, and on the third and fourth days they descend to the villages often with the women and children carrying what they have cut, and they sell it for a *real* at most and that is on the lands of the poor Indians because if they went onto the rich *hacendados'* lands they would be beaten, and when the owner gives them a license to take out some wood, not only do they have to pay for it, but they must also work, and before long they lose whatever they have gained.[41]

To a certain extent, colonial officials exonerated the Indians for their misuse of natural resources, arguing that their misery caused them to proceed in such a fashion.[42]

Spanish officials listened to Indian grievances regarding the colonists' exploitation of the forests. In the Chalco region of the Valley of Mexico, the Spanish viceroy don Martín Enríquez responded to Indian complaints by announcing his determination to enforce forestry regulations:

In that the Indians of the village of Tlalmanalco have informed me that the Spanish and other people cut and destroy the forests in a manner in which if there is no remedy soon one will finish said forests, which would be of great harm and loss of all the republic being where principally one provides wood for the buildings of this city [Mexico City]; . . . I order that no person without my license cut any trees and then not at its base, observing the kingdom's laws.[43]

Viceroy Enríquez, though, also promised to punish Indians who set fires in the region with one hundred lashes and expulsion from the province for one year. By comparison, Spanish arsonists faced the same one-year exile and a one-hundred-peso fine. The Indians and Spanish officials did have one common interest: both wanted to limit the colonists' exploitation of natural resources.

In both British and Spanish America, the home country's desire to control timber stocks almost invariably conflicted with the aspirations of the colonists (the British enacted forestry laws principally to protect trees for ship masts). In the case of the British colonies, settlers intent on running their sawmills for their own profit successfully subverted their government's conservation efforts.[44] Spanish colonists were more accustomed to crown control over their use of natural resources, but they did not enthusiastically support or even obey the crown's resource policies.

Spanish officials repeatedly complained that colonists did not comply with the laws. Bruno Díaz de Salcedo conceded that government officials sometimes lacked the will to prosecute colonial lawbreakers: "They [influential colonists] do not observe crown laws regarding reforestation nor have crown officials which have governed this province [San Luis Potosí] for more than two centuries been able to make them comply, because they are powerful men whom crown officials need."[45] Díaz de Salcedo urged that, although the woods in his jurisdiction were among the best in the world, it was necessary to take care of them and not to exploit them, but his plea fell on deaf ears.[46]

Spanish (and British) colonists complained that their government's forest policies were absurd given the abundance of woodlands in the New World. Among the complaints that the Spanish crown received were some from local officials who charged that their superiors were out of touch with the physical realities of the land. In San Luis Potosí, a provincial official questioned why he had to comply with the crown's policy prohibiting the cutting of trees at their base when his jurisdiction contained lush forests. In fact, the official said the law was a hindrance to his "constituents," since trees had to be removed to keep roads open and to make fields. Spanish colonists were upset by the rigidness of forestry decrees.[47]

The appearance of abundance was one of the greatest obstacles to the conservation of resources in New Spain. The conquistadores and early explorers, in particular, were awestruck by how bountiful the resources were in this new land. Many later settlers continued to believe that the natural wealth of New Spain was unlimited in spite of increasing evidence to the contrary.

The early accounts of New Spain described a land whose natural endowment far surpassed that of Spain:

There are in this province of New Spain great rivers and springs of very good sweet [fresh] water, extensive woods on hills and plains of very high pines, cedars, oaks, and cypresses, besides live oaks and a great variety of mountain trees. . . . The fields are most agreeable, and full of a most beautiful herbage that grows to the [height of the] middle of the leg. The soil is very fertile and abundant, producing everything sown in it, and in many places gives two or three crops to the year.[48]

The friar Toribio de Benavente Motolinía also marveled at the new land: "It is abundant and so grand the richness and fertility of this land called New Spain that it cannot be believed."[49] Other chroniclers effused over the plentifulness of wildlife and the richness of the pastureland in New Spain.[50] The Jesuit José de Acosta summed up his own exuberant accounts of New Spain by claiming that it was the land most provided for and supplied in the Indies.[51] Indeed, many settlers agreed with Acosta's conclusion that New Spain was the jewel of Spain's colonies.

Initially, Spanish settlers believed that even the semiarid and arid lands of the north held great possibilities. As Father Juan Cavallero Carranco anticipated: "The coasts of Sonora are worse than those of the Californias and are less pleasant to the eye, but going inland twenty leagues, there are all forms of commodities and wealth; the same could also be true of the Californias."[52] Cavallero Carranco's expectations were not to be met, however. As the explorer Fernando de Rivera y Moncada described his journeys in Baja California: "In my ten days march from Mission Santiago to La Pasión (Dolores), I did not find a single shelter except in the mining camp of Ocio. . . . And from there on, neither ranch, nor house, nor even the least shelter along the road. . . . For want of water, pasture lands are lacking. The greater part of the country is a sandy waste sown with thorns and thistles."[53]

The great deserts of northwestern New Spain presented a formidable barrier to settlement and development. The Spanish have the same word for desert and wilderness, *desierto*, which is derived from the Latin *desertus* meaning to abandon.[54] In contrast, wilderness comes from the Old English words *wild deor,* meaning the place of wild beasts, and is related to the Old English word for forests.[55] Both Spanish and English associated wilderness with a place they considered to be hostile, lonely, and fearful, a place that had to be conquered. However, most Spanish settlers did not inhabit a wilderness. The majority of those who came to New Spain settled in the central highlands, a region with a hospitable climate and a tractable Indian population (in direct contrast to the conditions that existed in the English colonies and in northwestern New Spain). In fact, it was a land similar in many ways to Spain.[56] The Spanish colonists did not have to conquer this new land, they only had to extract its wealth, and given the seeming abundance of natural resources, most Spanish colonists felt that they could exploit the territory's riches unceasingly.

Not every person in New Spain ascribed to the belief that the colony's resources were inexhaustible. In the early seventeenth century, Alonso de la Mota y Escobar detailed how the environment around the noted mining community of Zacatecas had been altered since its founding in 1540:

> There was at its [Zacatecas'] beginning many groves of trees in the ravines which now have all been cut for the foundries so that if there are a few wild trees, nothing else has remained. And thus it is that the wood is very expensive in the city, because it is brought in eight to ten leagues on roads. During pagan times, the surrounding plains and forests contained the most famous territory of roe-deer, hares, rabbits, partridges, and doves that had no equal in the world.[57]

Near the end of the eighteenth century, the subdelegate of Charcas (in the province of San Luis Potosí), Rafael Sánchez Cassamadrid, wrote to Bruno Díaz de Salcedo that the once abundant forests of Astillero had almost all been consumed for stairs and galleries.[58] Though resource scarcity (particularly around mining communities) had become more apparent by the late eighteenth century, few colonists shared Sánchez's alarm.

Apart from the growing scarcity of wood, a small group of Indians, colonists, and foreigners attributed unwanted environmental consequences to the destruction of the forests. In the seventeenth century, some of the inhabitants of the Chalco region blamed deforestation for the disappearance of streams.[59] During the latter part of the eighteenth century, the scientist José Antonio Alzate y Ramírez noted a decline in rainfall in the Valley of Mexico, which he attributed, in part, to the removal of the region's woodlands.[60] One of Alzate's contemporaries, the Prussian explorer Alexander von Humboldt asserted that the centuries-old pillaging of the forests around the valley had produced a more arid land, since water rapidly evaporated from soils exposed to solar rays and dry winds. He further observed that flooding had become more severe because there was almost no vegetation cover to impede the runoff of soils into the lakes of the basin and to block the confluence of streams during heavy rains.[61] Despite the ill effects resulting from the destruction of forests, however, Spanish officials had only recently begun to undertake reforestation measures and then only in the immediate vicinity of Mexico City. As Humboldt noted: "They (the Spanish) destroyed, and daily destroy, without planting anything in its stead, except around the capital, where the last viceroys have perpetuated their memory by promenades (paseos, alamedas), which bear their names."[62]

One of the grand ironies of the crown's forest policies was that the crown itself was a chief agent in the destruction of the forests of the colony. In the first decade following the Spanish Conquest, the mining industry took a particularly heavy toll on the forests of New Spain as tons of charcoal were used to fuel smelters for the extraction of ores. Although the mid-sixteenth century invention of the amalgamation process (the use of mercury to separate ore from the rock) reduced the rate of deforestation in the colony, Spaniards still used great quantities of wood in mining operations for buildings, mine shafts, and the smelting of ores resistant to amalgamation.[63] Astonishingly, many mine owners carelessly lined their works with wood despite the growing scarcity of wood on the central plateau.[64] As Humboldt assessed the situation at the beginning of the Independence period: "I am far from thinking that the American procedure of amalgamation, so tedious and imperfect as can be, can be abandoned on the central plateau of Mexico, where by the negligence of its inhabitants, the country has been entirely despoiled of its forests."[65] But it was not simply the negligence of its inhabitants that led to the depletion of New Spain's forests. The crown depleted woodlands for shipbuilding and construction, as well as for mining. Estimates are that at the time of the Conquest approximately three-fourths of New Spain was covered by forests.[66] At the end of the colonial period, Humboldt estimated that only one-half of New Spain was forested.[67] In a period of less than three hundred years, Mexico had lost one-third of its woodlands.

However, the crown's efforts to conserve forests in its colony cannot simply be dismissed as a failure. At least a few colonists and Indians did comply with the laws. Some of them cut only the branches of trees. Others planted cut-over land with fruit trees or conifers. Without a forestry code, the extent of deforestation in New Spain could only have been worse.[68]

On 4 January 1813, the liberal Spanish parliament, the Cortes, declared that all lands with forests or without them (except for those communal lands needed by the people) on the peninsula and in the New World would be reduced to private property (the parliament ruled in the absence of King Fernando VII, who had been taken hostage by Napoleon). By this broad stroke, the legislators resolved to increase agriculture and industry, to help citizens without property, and to reward the defenders of the country at home and in the New World.[69] In June 1813, the Cortes transferred authority for the conservation and repopulation of the remaining common forests to local officials.[70] Thus, Spain's control over its overseas forests officially ended.

In disposing of the public forests and in abdicating responsibility for forest conservation to local governments, the Spanish parliament foreshadowed the principal course of Mexican land policy up to the Revolution (1910–1920). Most nineteenth-century Mexican politicians opposed any kind of restrictions upon the use of private forests and were reluctant to commit the national government to the protection of the region's dwindling public woodlands. A few Mexicans, though, felt that it was imperative for the country to protect its valuable resources. Slowly, the semblance of a conservation policy reemerged.

Chapter Three

CONSERVATION DURING UNFAVORABLE TIMES

Independent Mexico until

the Revolution

When Mexico gained its independence in 1821, three centuries of land use regulations fell into abeyance. Mexican politicians, committed to their agenda of stimulating an economy devastated by the wars for independence (1810–1821) and in establishing their own political control, paid little attention to the conservation of natural resources. Development and order became an even greater obsession among the Mexican elite once economic and political stability were finally achieved (the Liberals overcame the last obstacles to their rule when they executed Archduke Maximilian in 1867).[1] For most of Mexico's Liberals, conservation was simply a hindrance to their grandiose economic plans.

Yet critics of the callous treatment of the land did arise in Mexico during the nineteenth century. Predominantly, their concerns centered around the loss of critical resources rather than around the importance of wild areas for the rejuvenation of the human spirit. In fact, only a small segment of the literati was attracted to philosophies, such as romanticism and transcendentalism, that emphasized the aesthetic and spiritual qualities of the natural world.

For most Mexicans, the contrasts that Europeans and American romantics had made between the sublime beauty and the awesome forces of nature, on the one hand, and the ugliness of factory towns and the routinized nature of urban life, on the other, were not readily apparent, for Mexico remained a largely rural and nonindustrial society throughout the nineteenth century (in 1900, 88 percent of the Mexican popu-

Hunters relaxing in the outdoors. Lito. del Comercio.

lation lived in the countryside).[2] Furthermore, those who promoted industrialization in Mexico during the latter part of the nineteenth century embraced material "progress" as an unmitigated good. For them, romanticism, insofar as it entailed a celebration of the natural world and of the "noble savage," constituted not only an outdated European philosophy but one antithetical to their cause. Alien to the bulk of the population and despised by the Mexican elite, romanticism in many of its facets could not establish deep roots, and so a strong romantic impulse in favor of the protection of nature did not present itself in Mexico.

A few Mexicans, however, did hold a romantic view of nature. Pedro Blazquez, a Mexican sports hunter, noted that the air of the city—contaminated as it was by coal-burning stoves, fecal material, and factories—was a precursor to ill health and death. By contrast, the atmosphere of the countryside was a source of health and life, as plants purified the air by absorbing carbon dioxide and other gases. More and more people, he claimed, recognized the benefits of leaving the pollution and tumult of increasingly crowded cities for the clean air and placidness of the rustic environment.[3] José Santos Coy, owner of a forested property in the northern Mexican state of Coahuila, also praised the beauty of the rural landscape: the sweet valleys, the meadows carpeted by grasses and flowers, and the streams that ran through islets of green. He believed that the countryside was the only place capable of comforting the harried soul, at least in beings inclined to contemplation and isolation.[4] The engineer José M. Romero spoke in equally reflective terms about the remaining forests in his home state of Hidalgo in central Mexico:

> On the road from Pachuca to El Chico . . . the traveller has to stop frequently to behold the magnificent and powerful solitude, illuminated by the rays of the sun whose golden threads radiate through the pine groves, and whose formidable silence is only interrupted by the song of the *zenzontle*, by the whisper of the wind among the trees, or by the noise of water cascades that fall at one's feet. A storm in these forests is a scene so powerful and majestic that a person can see, and only a strong heart is capable of observing it without fear.[5]

A small group of Mexicans viewed the natural world as a place of powerful forces, pure air, solitude, and great beauty, all of which stirred the human body and spirit.

José María Velasco. Valley of Mexico from Molino del Rey, 1895. Spec. Exhib. Private Collection. Reproduction authorized by the Instituto Nacional de Bellas Artes and the Philadelphia Museum of Art.

Transcendentalism also had a few adherents in Mexico. Pedro Blazquez felt that nature presented the "rich panorama of creation."[6] He interpreted the harmonious songs of birds and the murmuring of brooks as providing a "mysterious hymn of love and recognition" to "the supreme maker of the world." Blazquez implied that it was in the wild areas that one felt closest to God.[7]

Mexico's most famous transcendentalist was the great landscape painter José María Velasco (1840–1912). A deeply religious man, Velasco portrayed nature to show "his love of God and God's love of mankind." He spent his career painting the Valley of Mexico, with its hardened boulders, lofty volcanoes, and transparent air, all of which he imbued with a sense of tranquillity and mysticism. He believed that the valley was a demonstration of the perfection of God.[8]

Velasco was not a romantic artist. He did not embellish his vistas with sublime mountains or ethereal hues. Instead, he painted the Valley of Mexico as it was.[9] In addition to depicting the works of God, he portrayed the works of human beings: the railroads, factories, and power plants. He neither glorified nor villainized these new fixtures. For Velasco, they were simply a part of a changing landscape.

Velasco held a mystical attitude toward nature, and yet he also studied it scientifically. He wrote a book on the flora of the central plateau, illustrating it with his own lithographs, and taught his students the value of scientific observation and investigation. He himself extensively explored the Valley of Mexico and one of its volcanoes, Popocatépetl. The product of Velasco's religious beliefs and his scientific bent were landscapes that were both mystical and realistic.[10]

Unlike the U.S. transcendentalist John Muir (who also had a scientific bent), Velasco did not become a propagandist for wilderness protection. He was more akin to another U.S. transcendentalist, the writer Ralph Waldo Emerson, in that he was satisfied in expressing his love of nature and his love of God through his art.

Although Mexicans, who ascribed therapeutic and spiritual values to nature, did not form a movement for wilderness preservation, several of them were part of a small minority who called for the conservation of natural resources.

During the nineteenth century, most Mexican conservationists advocated the protection of nature for two reasons. First, some individuals feared that the country was on the brink of exhausting its natural resources. Particularly disturbing to them was the continued depletion of the nation's forests. Mexico's economic prosperity depended upon politicians curbing the voracious consumption of its woodlands. Second, Mexicans advocated conservation on biological grounds. They particularly focused on the role that forests played in regulating natural cycles. For them, the connection between forest conservation and people's well-being was evident: forests maintained a stable environment that advanced human health and safety.

Mexicans became aware of the economic and biological necessity of forest conservation earlier than people in the United States did. The Mexican government enacted a law to conserve forests on national lands in 1861, three decades before the first law of its kind was passed in the United States (the Forestry Act of 1891). A government minister identified the connection between deforestation and drought a quarter century before U.S. geographer George Perkins Marsh drew the same connection in his classic book *Man and Nature; or, Physical Geography as Modified by Human Action* (1864). Marsh's discussion of the consequences of deforestation (drought, flooding, diminished stream flow, siltation, and soil erosion) came as a revelation to his compatriots. By contrast, Mexicans had long recognized the negative effects that deforestation had on natural cycles.

History and geography had led to a heightened awareness in Mexico of the dangers posed by deforestation. Mexico entered into the national period with relatively few of its forests intact (as opposed to the United States, which still had large tracts of forests in the West). The myth of inexhaustibility was more easily punctured in Mexico than it was in the United States. Furthermore, in contrast to the relatively flat landscape of the United States east of the Rockies, Mexico's mountainous topography provided its citizens with many drastic illustrations of how deforestation exacerbated soil erosion and flooding. Others read about these problems in the works of Martínez and Humboldt, whose treatise on New Spain was available in translation. Mexicans also had access to a body of literature by eighteenth-century Spanish naturalists on the connection between the lack of forests in Spain and the paltry flow of streams, the dryness of the atmosphere, and the sterility of the soil.[11] Both from firsthand experience and from the observations of others, Mexicans had more knowledge to draw upon regarding the consequences of deforestation than did people in the United States. Nor were they so wedded to the doctrine of individual freedom that they dispensed with regulations altogether as U.S. citizens did until the end of the nineteenth century.

In contrast, wildlife policies were based almost exclusively upon economic considerations. Animals did not seem to have the same biological importance as forests. A few Mexicans argued for the protection of wild animals because of their aesthetic qualities, but their influence upon public policy was minimal.[12] Most Mexican politicians made the same distinction between valuable, worthless, and harmful animals as their colonial predecessors did. Thus, for most of the nineteenth century, the Mexican approach to wildlife conservation focused on maintaining stable populations of economically important species rather than on developing a wildlife code that would protect a wide range of species.

Many of the early wildlife conservation laws were aimed at preventing the commercial exploitation of animals by foreigners. In an 1824 edict, the Mexican government forbade nonnationals from hunting and trapping fur-bearing animals.[13] Between 1825 and 1830, maritime officials issued a series of decrees, designed in part to exclude foreigners from the sea otter trade in Mexican California waters. Most notably, in 1826 they restricted coastal trade to national vessels with two-thirds of the crew composed of Mexican citizens.[14] The exploitation of California's sea otter populations by non-Mexicans continued, however, as Mexico did not have enough vessels to adequately patrol the coast. In 1831, the governor of California, Manuel Victoria, alerted federal officials that foreigners, who had bought lucrative contracts from Mexicans, were killing young sea otters near the coastal islands where the mammal bred. He warned that these interlopers were thus destroying the species.[15] Victoria's predecessor, José María Echeandía (1826–1830), had included a clause in hunting licenses that specified that sea otter pups could not be killed.[16] The unmet goal of both these governors was to restrict the harvesting of sea otters to conservation-minded Mexican hunters.

California officials also attempted to protect their valuable timber supplies against foreign exploitation and domestic misuse. Jolted into action by reports of the destructive impact that U.S. citizens were having upon the forests near San Francisco, the 1834 territorial commission of California enacted a decree that prohibited the exportation of timber and required a license for woodcutting and for the transportation of lumber from port to port.[17] In 1845, officials from Los Angeles mandated that all timber cut on public lands within their district be used for the common good, such as for firewood and construction.[18] Authorities in California utilized the powers originally invested in them by the Spanish Cortes to protect their precious woodlands.

When California became part of the United States in 1848, U.S. officials disposed of all the preexisting restrictions on the cutting of timber. An equally important part of the story, however, was that during the second half of the nineteenth century, Mexican politicians became increasingly willing to permit the exploitation of their resources by foreigners and their own citizens for the sake of development.

Some Mexican officials realized that forests had a value beyond the price of timber. In 1839, Interior Minister José Antonio Romero implored that forests be protected to alleviate droughts:

> For several years, the Republic has suffered from drought; harvests have failed and cattle have died. Reason and experience point to the devastation of the forests and the denudation of the hills and mountains as influential causes of such calamities. Consequently, it is necessary not only to restrict the cutting of trees, but for the preservation of the health and welfare of the people and the protection of

agriculture and industries depending upon it, to encourage the restoration of wasted forests and the planting of trees along public
roads and in such places as they could otherwise be useful.[19]

Romero presented his recommendations in the name of the president of
the Republic of Mexico to the governors of the states and territories.[20]
Ironically, Romero's message was ignored by national leaders, who still
considered forest conservation to be largely a local matter.

One of those who heeded Romero's warnings was the governor of
Veracruz, Antonio María Salonio. In 1845, he enacted a forestry law that
authorized the creation of tree protection boards (juntas), part of whose
purpose it was to locate sites suitable for the formation of tree nurseries
and to oversee the planting of trees along roadsides and other common
places. In a novel application of the public works levy, Salonio required
all able-bodied men between the ages of sixteen and fifty (except for
military personnel and members of the clergy) to work one day a year in
the nurseries and another day planting seedlings.[21] The governor directed that some of the trees from the nurseries be planted along ave-
nues and in plazas in order to beautify the towns and cities of Veracruz.

The juntas' primary mission was to conserve and restore the woodlands of Veracruz. Salonio instructed the boards to conduct annual sur-
veys of the state's forests, distinguishing the ancient trees from the
younger ones. In conjunction with this, he directed the juntas to enter
into agreements with woodcutters and timber users, including factory
owners, on the number of trees that they would have to replant. The
governor required all forest users on the public and common lands to
obtain permits from the local juntas. Those who violated this provision
would not only forfeit the wood that they had cut but also pay a fee
equivalent to its value, lose their woodcutting instruments, and plant
twice the number of trees that they had felled or deposit money to accomplish this task. The boards, though, had only nominal jurisdiction
over private lands. In part because of this, they were unable to halt the
loss of Veracruz's forests.[22]

During the mid-1850s, the agent general of the Ministry of Agriculture, state and municipal officials, and the Society for the Improvement
of Materials (a citizens' group with affiliates in different parts of the republic) urged authorities to stem the destruction of forests by imposing
restrictions upon woodcutters and by mandating reforestation.[23] The
newly created Ministry of Public Works (1853) began to take action on
these matters. In August 1854, it issued a decree that required a permit

for the export (on either domestic or foreign ships) of wood used in construction or cabinetmaking.[24] In October of that same year, the ministry asked mining commissions throughout the republic to determine the number of leagues covered with forests within their jurisdiction, the kind of trees that grew in these forests, and whether their products were used for firewood and charcoal or for carpentry and cabinetmaking. The commissions were instructed to verify the number of trees that were cut monthly and to reforest denuded areas.[25] A comprehensive forestry survey and major reforestation program, however, were not undertaken for another half century.

In 1854, the Society for the Improvement of Materials called upon the Ministry of Public Works to protect the forests around the Valley of Mexico. According to the society, population pressures and the demands of industry had consumed many of the region's woodlands such that each day the inhabitants of the region felt more intensely the scarcity and expense of timber, firewood, and charcoal, the unhealthiness of the atmosphere (due to the absence of trees to purify the air), and the diminution of water supplies. The society expressed its hope that the government would take immediate action to resolve this grave situation.[26]

Two years later, the national government addressed a request from the *ayuntamiento* (city government) of Mexico City that woodlands be protected to ensure the city's water supply. The government acknowledged that it had erred by allowing woodcutters in the Desierto de Carmelitas (later known as the Desierto de los Leones) to take the greatest wealth possible in the shortest time possible. In doing so, it had prejudiced the well-being of Mexico City's residents, whose survival depended upon the springs originating along the valley's western flank. Federal authorities came to the conclusion that the destruction of the forests in the region had resulted in a diminished stream flow, since there were fewer trees to pull water up to the surface and to provide shade to reduce evaporation. For the care of a water source so important to the inhabitants of the capital, the government decreed that the Desierto de Carmelitas would remain the full dominion and property of the *ayuntamiento* of Mexico City. The decree allowed the municipality of Mexico City to auction off land in the Desierto, but only if the buyer agreed to conserve its springs (by not cutting trees) and to submit to the oversight of the *ayuntamiento*.[27]

Further prodded by complaints that Mexico was losing its best woodlands, Liberal President Ignacio Comonfort issued a circular in 1857 in which he declared that as much as possible the cutting of trees should be prevented. At the same time, he assured industrialists and miners that they would not be deprived of timber for their operations. Comonfort's solution was to return to the colonial forestry ordinances, which, he asserted, were still in effect. He specifically cited the directives that firewood could only be collected from the branches of vigorous trees and that woodcutters had to plant four trees for every one they cut (three trees during the colonial period). Comonfort promised to punish severely those who broke this decree.[28]

In 1861, the Liberal government of Benito Juárez enacted the first national forestry law in Mexico. This statute, which applied only to public lands, required woodcutters to plant ten mahogany and cedar trees for every tree that they chopped down. First of all, though, prospective loggers had to submit a permit application to the Ministry of Public Works, indicating the area in which they intended to operate and the number of trees that they planned to cut. If the ministry approved the application, a subinspector and a forest guard accompanied the permit holder to the site and marked its boundaries. The government set a fine of six pesos for every tree cut without a permit, with the proceeds being used to augment the salaries of four forest guards and one subinspector. In addition, private citizens who reported the clandestine cutting of trees could claim one-third of the penalties assessed. Forestry officials and private citizens thus had a financial incentive to oversee the enforcement of the law.[29]

A number of individuals emphasized the narrow scope and ineffectiveness of the country's forest legislation. Leopoldo Río de la Loza, a chemistry professor, noted that forest guards and the general populace stood to make more money by collaborating with lawbreakers or by cutting down the trees themselves than by reporting violations of the law. Those guards who were honest faced the nearly impossible task of policing vast territories, usually encompassing remote and mountainous regions. Here, the local inhabitants often transported illegally cut timber on well-hidden paths in the woods. Moreover, the law applied only to national forests; the government allowed private forest owners to use their timber in any way they saw fit.[30]

In 1865, José M. Romero, a member of the scientific commission of Pachuca (in the central Mexican state of Hidalgo), indignantly remarked that woodcutters and the mining company Real del Monte exhibited high scorn for the nation's forestry laws. For their part, loggers cut trees at whatever height they pleased and refused to plant four trees for every one they felled. Romero wailed that "the axe of the woodcutter has become a terrible enemy of these forests."[31] He reserved his greatest scorn for the Real del Monte Company, which had cut all the nearby forests to feed its steam engines, factories, and amalgamation sites, without having planted a single tree or followed any forestry provisions. Romero asserted that the company's contempt for Mexico's forestry regulations led to "fatal results that afflict all the classes of Pachuca." He noted that people had to walk great distances to collect firewood and that the price of construction materials was so high that many residents could not afford to build a house. Even more detrimental, the once abundant springs that supplied the city of Pachuca were nearly dry because the cutting of trees had resulted in increased evaporation and the lack of infiltration of water into the soil. Romero observed that it was now common for the population of Pachuca to be without water for two or three days and without hope of abundant supplies even during the rainy season. For all these reasons, it was incumbent upon the government to regulate the destructive activities of the mining company.[32]

Others voiced their frustration with the lukewarm response of public officials and private citizens to appeals for forest conservation. Tomás Mancera, a miner from Hidalgo, sadly observed the state of the region's forests during the mid-1860s: "Woodcutting continues such that the delightful and abundant forests of the Mineral [de Pachuca] remain only in name; the numerous pines which once existed here will be very difficult to replace as they took hundreds of years to reach maturity: this with notable prejudice to the public's health as the streams dry for want of trees."[33] Mancera stated that the most direct means of protecting the area's remaining forests would be to use the abundant coal supplies from Zacualtipán, Hidalgo, to power steam engines and locomotives. He felt that other options provided little hope for success. Mancera doubted that a patriotic appeal to property owners could be used to safeguard the community's interest. Nor could the government be of much assistance. Even when authorities tried to enact and enforce useful conservation laws, local inhabitants and woodcutters did not cooperate. More typically, inertia or political upheavals resulted in the government taking no action at all. Thus, the depletion of Mexico's forests continued unabated.[34]

Some individuals attempted to correct what they regarded to be deficiencies in the existing forestry code. In an 1862 law designed to protect and expand orchards, the governor of Baja California, Teodoro Riveroll, stated that because trees and bushes mightily contributed to increasing the rains so scarce in the region and because the wise prohibitions against the cutting of the forests had been forgotten, no one could fell trees, even on one's property, without the permission of the *ayuntamiento*.[35] Riveroll felt that such a step was necessary because the public interest was being jeopardized by the property owners' misuse of the land.

Near the end of the French Intervention (1862–1867), Leopoldo Río de la Loza drafted a forestry ordinance, taking the forestry law in Veracruz as his point of departure. Río de la Loza called for the establishment of tree nurseries and reforestation programs nationwide. In regard to the latter, he proposed that all rural property owners (or their tenants) annually plant five trees for every *caballería* (a land unit equivalent to 33.3 acres), with awards being given to those who planted more.[36] In addition, each year municipalities would have to plant one tree for every one hundred inhabitants and the Department of Highways, the owners of private roads, and railroad magnates would have to plant one tree for every league (about four miles) of road. Along with reforestation, Río de la Loza sought to expand restrictions upon forest use. In his ordinance, he included limitations on the access of industry to wood: bark taken for industrial uses could come only from trees that were in poor vigor, blown over by the wind, or dead. He further stated that the extraction of turpentine and other resins should never be taken in such a manner as to cause the death of the tree. He declared that under no circumstances could forests be set on fire. Anyone who violated this provision would have to pay for the cost of the fire and also would have to work six months to four years on public works projects. And last, he proclaimed that a license from a tree protection board was needed to cut in any forest.[37]

Río de la Loza's proposed law marked a major advance over previous regulations. Archduke Maximilian, though, was unable to implement the ordinance because of his untimely death, and after his execution, the Liberals returned to their policy of the unrestricted use of private lands.

For a time following the French Intervention, the Mexican Geographical and Statistical Society (created in 1833) acted as a leading voice for forest conservation in the nation. The membership declared that one of its most important tasks was to stir in national, state, and local governments an awareness of the "calamity of deforestation."[38] In partial fulfillment of this pledge, the society appointed a commission in

1870 to assess the state of Mexico's woodlands and to offer recommendations regarding their protection and restoration.

This group, headed by Ignacio Ramírez, addressed two fundamental questions: Why was forest conservation necessary and how could Mexico best attain this end? The commission displayed its Liberal sympathies by offering a narrow vision of the government's role in promoting conservation and by focusing almost exclusively upon the economic value of forests.

As part of its business, the Ramírez commission responded to the desire of a number of communities in Mexico to gain control over forests within their jurisdictions. For all intents and purposes, Ramírez and his colleagues rejected this bid for the extension of local control over private woodlands. They told city officials to "trust in the private interest and if this does not correspond to the communal interests then you can ask for authorization."[39]

The point that local leaders were trying to make was that the threshold at which private interest conflicted with communal interests had long since passed. They argued that it was imperative that their forests be protected not only to ensure an adequate supply of wood for fuel and construction but also to ensure an adequate supply of water, to prevent floods, and to moderate the climate.[40] The Ramírez commission scornfully responded to these arguments for forest conservation:

> Little do we need to stop in these details [about the alleged biological value of the forests] except to ponder what is strangely forgotten about the forests; they do not need a bold and fabulous mission as invented by Druidism or Naturalism in order to call the attention of all social classes to their value: they are our principal source of wood for construction and fuel.[41]

Ramírez and his colleagues took a harder stance yet when they argued that many of the biological functions attributed to the forests were simply false. They emphatically stated that forests were the result, not the cause of rainfall. While conceding that forests reduced evaporation, the commissioners insisted that any type of vegetation would perform the same function. They concluded that building canals and wells was a more effective means of providing water than protecting forests and planting trees. Forest conservation was needed for a stable economy not for a stable environment.[42]

As part of its undertakings, the commission examined forest policies in Western Europe and the lack of such policies in the United States. The group admired many of the forestry measures that had been adopted by European countries: the Germans had protected their forests and had developed practical techniques for forest management; the French had developed a strong forestry code that applied both to its public and private forests (the commission's only complaint was that the French code had impinged upon the rights of property owners); and even the English had begun to take measures to protect their forests. In stark contrast to Western Europe, the United States had not taken any steps to protect its forests. The committee members analyzed this failure as follows: "The United States with its model of positivism exploits its forests wherever they are found. . . . The individual and private sovereignty is a sacred dogma of their political economy, and for their institutions. They don't possess public forests since they sell them."[43] The commissioners stated that if Mexico had an inexhaustible supply of wood and other fuels, as was the case in the United States with its huge California forests and large reserves of oil and coal, then Mexico would not need to concern itself with conservation so much. Yet, as they noted, even in the United States, legislation and science had begun to concern itself with reforestation.[44]

The Ramírez commission then announced its overriding concern: Mexico was losing a resource of inestimable value. Already wood could not be found for long distances around many villages and had become so scarce that many people could not afford it. And the situation would only become worse as railroads and industries laid claim to an increasing share of Mexico's forests:

> But despite so little need and so much wealth, the hand of man denudes the soil until whole regions are disfigured, where one puts up a factory, the forests disappear and in half the Republic the poor collect the most insufficient fuels for preparing humble foods for their families. . . . What will happen when all the nation is moved and industry imperiously claims its principal source of fuel?[45]

The committee concluded that for the sake of economic prosperity it was imperative for Mexico to conserve its forests and to plant trees.

The Ramírez commission argued that the best opportunity for the protection of Mexico's forests lay in education and research. As part of this effort, the Mexican Geographical and Statistical Society promised to sponsor silviculture studies, placing special emphasis on those areas most needing trees. According to the commissioners, such studies that impressed upon people the importance of using land rationally would be more valuable for the protection of the land than new laws, although the latter could also play a role in some circumstances.[46]

The Mexican elite considered the Indians to be the group most in need of education regarding the rational use of forests and yet also the most incorrigible. The Society for the Improvement of Materials criticized Indian communities for cutting trees at their trunk rather than just taking their branches, for chopping down trees before they had reached their maturity, and for setting fires that they did not control. The group blamed these practices for causing a rise in wood prices. It ruefully noted that "the Indians cut trees at their own whim without obeying the ancient ordinances of the forest and without adopting any method which reason dictates would be to their benefit."[47] Leopoldo Río de la Loza was equally critical of the Indians' "irrational" use of forest resources. Echoing colonial officials but in a less sympathetic tone, an exasperated Río de la Loza declared that "the Indians have and still continue to exploit in an arbitrary manner the public wealth [the forests]; they have resisted all means that have been taken to civilize them on this point."[48]

Liberal politicians shared Río de la Loza's frustration. Matías Romero, an influential diplomat and businessman during the regime of Porfirio Díaz (1876–1911), shuddered at how the Indians used priceless wood as a source of fuel: "There are still large forests in Mexico, . . . where wood is worth nothing. I have seen many poor people, living near such places, using for cooking their foods, woods of the most expensive kind such as ebony, rosewood, mahogany, cedar, etc."[49] Manuel Payno, a professor of history and a former Liberal politician, also felt compelled to comment upon the Indians' abuse of forest resources. Payno recoiled at the onslaught that Indian communities were making upon the forests of Ajusco (a mountain south of Mexico City):

The Indians cut as much wood as possible taking daily thousands of loads of charcoal without submitting to any order or rules. . . . The grand trees whose age can be calculated at 200 or 250 years and the venerable cedar can only be found on the steep canyons and escarpments on the volcanoes because there man cannot uproot them, nor wound them with their destructive hatchets. Nevertheless, nothing escapes the ferocity of the Indian *carboneros*.[50]

Payno reported that Indians had cut all the old trees on the flanks of Ajusco and that now they were in the process of felling all the new growth too. He castigated the Indians for cutting wood that, because of its immaturity, was practically worthless:

> There is another mountainous region [north of Mexico City] in which there are many well-established Indian villages that exclu-sively occupy themselves in the cutting of woods that they sell to nearby villages and cities; some of these woods are little valued by the architects and carpenters because most of them are of small di-mensions and cut before the wood has reached its full maturity. This makes it inappropriate for manufacturing and of little durability for housing.[51]

As during the colonial period, the expropriation of Indian lands had helped precipitate the Indians' rampant destruction of forests. The dif-ference between the colonial and national periods, however, was that government officials now stood firmly behind those who wished to ex-propriate Indian lands. The Liberal reform law, known as the Ley Lerdo (1856), forced corporations, including Indian communities, to divest themselves of the lands that they were not using as part of their opera-tions. Part of the goal of this law was to replace the "inefficient" Indian cultivator with the "productive" yeoman farmer. During the Porfiriato (the period of the Díaz regime), the expropriation of Indian lands reached a fever pitch. So that large-scale capitalistic agriculture could take the place of subsistence agriculture, the Díaz administration gave *hacendados* and foreign investors the right to displace Indians from their land.[52] Indians who resisted becoming laborers or tenant farmers on the haciendas were forced into intensive exploitation of natural resources, since wealthy landowners had expropriated the fertile lands the Indians had farmed. One journal writer unwittingly hit upon the crux of the matter: "The forests are being destroyed by peons who would rather gather roots in the mountains than work on the haciendas."[53]

The Porfiriato marked an accelerated exploitation of the land itself. In 1870, Manuel Payno posed a question that presaged this period. After conceding that Mexico was a fertile land and that many trees regener-ated through their own seeds, Payno asked: "What is more powerful, the fertility of nature or the barbarism and avarice of man? Which are the forces more active, the creative forces of nature or the destructive forces of man?"[54]

During the Díaz administration, "the destructive forces of man" were aided by the vast expansion of the railroad system.[55] Both directly and indirectly, the "iron horse" consumed Mexico's forests. Enormous quantities of wood were used for stations, posts, ties, and fuel. In addition, the mining activity that railroads stimulated depended upon wood for timber supports and buildings. Mexico's growing industrial sector, also spurred by the development of railroads, required timber as well. The Porfiriato marked the greatest assault on Mexico's forests since the colonial era.

Railroads also contributed to the decline of Mexican wildlife. Because of the railroads, big game hunters gained access to many new areas. Mining and lumbering, which followed the railroads, destroyed critical habitats. When a turn of the century flier for the U.S.-owned Rio Grande, Sierra Madre, and Pacific Railway waxed about the attractive openings in mining, lumbering, and stock raising in Chihuahua (a northern Mexican state) and boasted about it being the greatest game country on earth, it was in fact sealing the end of an era of abundant wildlife in northern Mexico.[56]

The expropriation of Indian lands and the construction of railroads were part of the Porfirian strategy to develop the country. According to the *científicos*, Díaz's brain trust, Mexico was a nation endowed with rich raw materials that when once systematically exploited (with the aid of a modern transportation system and wealthy investors) would transform Mexico into an industrial giant. Driving the *científicos*' ambitions were two anticonservation philosophies: antipathy toward "vacant lands" and positivism (the same philosophy that the Ramírez commission said had led to the destruction of forests in the United States).

In his contempt for "vacant lands," Díaz was building on a Western tradition whose origins lay in the biblical injunction to subdue the earth. This injunction gained practical application during the Middle Ages as northern Europeans cleared forests and drained swamps to expand agriculture (and as Spanish sheepherders converted forests into pasturelands). In the seventeenth century, the English philosopher John Locke permanently linked capitalism to the elimination of "vacant lands." Locke argued that the day laborer in England was better off than the Indian king in America because British property owners had put the land to productive use. According to Locke: "Land that is left wholly to nature, that has no improvement of pasturage, tillage, or planting, is called, as indeed it is, 'waste'; and we shall find the benefit of it amount to little more than nothing." Contrastingly, the individual who puts "waste land" to use was benefiting the entire community.[57]

The Spanish crown had not ascribed to this philosophy. On the contrary, they believed that unrestricted individual exploitation of the land harmed the community. The crown attempted to retain under its jurisdiction forests, pasturelands, and waters for the common good. The nineteenth-century Mexican Liberals rejected Spain's communal traditions by expropriating Indian lands and by opening up public lands for exploitation by the middle and upper classes. They eliminated the distinction that the Spanish had maintained between forested and agricultural lands. Hence, they allowed agriculture to expand at the expense of the forests (only the vast expanse of many haciendas prevented their owners from exploiting all of the land). The Liberals' disdain for "vacant lands" was motivated by their belief that development depended upon the utilization of such lands. By the time of the Díaz administration, the liquidation of "vacant lands" had become part of the modus operandi.

The second philosophy that the Díaz administration embraced was positivism. According to the French philosopher Auguste Comte (1797–1858), the founder of positivism, progress involved the evolution of knowledge and society from one based on religion to one based on science. The positivists emphasized the importance of a scientific education in developing a rational and ordered mind that would contribute to the well-being of society. Comte specifically appealed for a religion of humanity in which the leaders of the bourgeois state would preclude revolutionary upheavals by advancing the welfare of the population as a whole. Thus, the Comtean mantra: love, order, and progress.[58]

The *científicos* adopted the means of Comte's philosophy but changed the ends. According to the *científicos*, society could be scientifically run, but they defined progress not in terms of improving the conditions of humanity but in terms of unleashing investment to further development. And order, which in the Comtean system was to be tempered by a degree of liberty, now meant protecting the interests of a rapacious elite.[59]

Antipathy toward "vacant lands" and positivism were doctrines that could easily be wedded. Mexico's progress depended on putting "vacant lands" to use. Officially, the Díaz regime defined "vacant lands" as lands not given for public use or unowned by corporations or individuals.[60] In fact, though, lands not being used in a manner in which the Díaz regime wished them to be used were considered vacant.[61] For all practical purposes, the public domain was reduced to the areas difficult to reach or sparsely populated.[62]

The Porfiriato would seem to be one of the least propitious times for the development of conservation concerns in Mexico, but in fact the excesses of the period produced just that result. Much of the interest in the protection of natural resources was solely economic in nature, but scientific arguments in favor of such protection continued to be made.

Some Mexican officials realized that the country had an economic stake in the conservation of natural resources. To attract foreign investment, Mexico had to guarantee an adequate supply of raw materials. Already, a few foreigners had raised concerns about the availability of timber for railroad building in Mexico. In 1866, Alfred Mordecai, a U.S. railroad engineer working on the British-financed Veracruz–Mexico City Railway, noted that the pine forests above Veracruz provided the only local source of wood for the line.[63] In 1872, the directors of the Mexican National Railway (a U.S. venture) observed that "Mexico is very sparsely supplied with timber, yet its comparatively dense population and numerous mines require a large quantity. This must be transported from the forests wherever they exist." The company was relieved to have found good sources along its proposed route.[64]

Many foreign investors and members of the Mexican elite continued to believe that Mexico was a treasure house of raw materials, but some individuals challenged this notion. Matías Romero, for one, observed that after four hundred years of constant consumption, the forests in close proximity to towns had been destroyed. Now, the nation's lumber supply was being sorely taxed by the expansion of railroads and factories among other factors. Romero assured his readers in *International Review* that the government was aware of the gravity of the situation and would adopt measures to save timber.[65]

The Díaz regime did take steps to reduce the consumption of wood by railroads. Authorities encouraged the replacement of wood-burning locomotives with those using coal. They also mandated the creosoting of wooden tracks to increase their longevity and the use of iron rather than wooden ties.[66] Some government officials concluded that the scarcity of wood had become a relatively serious problem.

A few government officials recognized that forests were essential to the maintenance of a stable environment. In an 1880 circular, a government official detailed the many ways in which the public welfare depended upon the protection of woodlands. One only had to witness the legacy of deforestation—badly eroded soils, floods, and dried up streams—to appreciate the role that forests played in maintaining water supplies and stabilizing soils. Trees also assisted in the regulation of the atmosphere by maintaining the proper level of oxygen in the air and by absorbing the carbon emitted by industries. In addition, trees contributed to a more salubrious environment by preventing the development of marshes. From the quality of the air to the quantity of water, humankind profited tremendously from the existence of forests.[67]

The academic community supported claims that trees were a critical component of the environment.[68] In 1892, Jesús Alfaro, a medical student, published a small thesis in which he identified the many biological, chemical, physical, and medicinal benefits provided by vegetation. According to Alfaro, trees and other plants were "the most precious guardians of health," for not only were they a great storehouse of medicines, but they also impeded the spread of many diseases.[69] He claimed, for instance, that trees helped reduce the incidence of malaria by drying soils (particularly in swampy areas) and by blocking humid airs. They also contributed to the public health by moderating the climate through evaporation (Alfaro believed that abrupt changes in climate were one of the principal causes of disease), by creating air rich and pure in oxygen, and by preventing dust storms.

Alfaro expounded upon the critical role that trees played in regulating the environment: they increased rainfall, blocked soil erosion, reduced the heating of the soil through solar radiation, and curtailed flooding by absorbing water into the subsoil. He contended that the planting of trees had converted areas with a dry, hot, unhealthy climate into benign places to live. In contrast, the cutting of trees had changed verdant areas into deserts. He went so far as to claim that people in forested areas lived longer than people in nonforested areas. Alfaro's thinking represented a nascent ecological perspective in that he recognized the important role that forests played in regulating chemical, physical, and biological cycles.[70]

Some Mexicans concerned about deforestation questioned the validity of the biological arguments being made on behalf of forest conservation. In a tract entitled *There Are Forests Because It Rains, or Does It Rain Because There Are Forests?*, José Santos Coy argued that forests did not produce rainfall. Santos Coy (a forest owner from Coahuila) based his argument on two observations: frequently rain did not fall over forested areas, and rain continued to fall over areas in which forests were being cut.[71] He believed that the justification for forest conservation lay in the grandeur of the ancient forests rather than in their purported contribution to rainfall. Santos Coy ventured that even those unmoved by the spectacle of rustic beauty would agree that there was a certain risk of barbarism in destroying forests that were the work of centuries. He was, nevertheless, painfully aware that some parties persisted in the ruin of these irreplaceable woodlands for monetary gain. Most disturbing of all to Santos Coy were those who destroyed the beauty of their own surroundings: "And even among rural folk . . . are those who believe in the value of money or gold. . . . I speak of them, because these property owners are condemned to decadence, to ruin, . . . who want to squeeze out the juice leaving only the skin of the fruit."[72] Santos Coy concluded that laws could accomplish nothing if people wanted to destroy their woodlands. Only when people understood that the harm that they did to their land by cutting their forests outweighed the monetary gain would they change their activities.[73]

To a certain extent, high-level government officials were influenced by arguments in favor of resource protection. In 1894, the Díaz regime enacted a forestry law that, among its most significant provisions, authorized the government to establish forest reserves on national lands.[74] In 1898, the Díaz regime utilized this provision to make Mineral del Chico in Hidalgo a national forest. The government declared that all means should be taken to conserve the forests in this territory.[75] The precedent for a forest reserve system had been established in Mexico.

The 1894 law also contained the first general provisions for the conservation of wildlife. The only animals exempted from protection were "ferocious and dangerous animals," that the government specified could be hunted during any time of the year. Federal authorities prohibited the hunting of young animals and the hunting of females of species that were declining in numbers. They barred hunters from killing or disturbing nocturnal birds and other birds that devour insects in the forests and strictly prohibited the destruction of bird nests and eggs. Nor could hunters set fires, lay traps, take advantage of floods or snow, or use lanterns at night to facilitate the capture of their quarry. The government also outlawed the use of explosives to kill fish. Lastly, hunters and fishers had to obtain permits to conduct their activities.[76] As in the case of the forestry provisions, the Díaz regime never strictly enforced these wildlife conservation measures.

Still, there were members of the Ministry of Public Works committed to wildlife and forestry protection. In 1906, the ministry published excerpts from the conference proceedings on the Exposition of Flowers,

Birds, and Fishes. The conferees stated that while some birds ate fruit, this could not justify killing to the point of extinction beautiful and useful birds that also ate insects.[77] Also in 1906, in response to the Audubon Society's plea to protect the heron in Mexico, the undersecretary of public works wrote a letter to the governor of Oaxaca asking him to protect the bird not only because the bird constituted a benefit to agriculture but also because it represented a public treasure (a national ban on the hunting of the heron, however, was not imposed until 1922).[78]

The Ministry of Public Works also persistently called attention to the grave problem of deforestation in Mexico. The secretary cautioned that, although the use of coal could ease the pressure on forests, reforestation should not stop. To encourage reforestation, the secretary distributed numerous forest publications and tree seeds to many areas of Mexico.[79]

Those concerned about the protection of natural resources within the Ministry of Public Works were fighting a difficult battle. The top officials within the Díaz regime had only a limited interest in conservation, restricted principally to occasional concerns about the availability of natural resources for industrial development. Under such circumstances, pressures for a broader-based conservation policy were difficult to make effective. However, in Miguel Angel de Quevedo, the conservation cause gained an indefatigable and ardent supporter of the natural environment. For the first half of the twentieth century, he would lead a crusade on behalf of the nation's forests. He would encounter considerable opposition to his proposals, but also some tangible successes.

Chapter Four

MIGUEL ANGEL DE QUEVEDO

The Apostle of the Tree

Miguel Angel de Quevedo was born to a prosperous family from Guadalajara on 27 September 1862. According to a whimsical reconstruction, one of the first sights Miguel saw from his nursery was a tree.[1] If so, it was a fitting beginning for a man who would become Mexico's apostle of the tree.[2]

In his youth, Miguel showed no special inclination toward nature. Indeed, his childhood was rather typical for a person of his station. Like other children from the upper class, he enjoyed a variety of privileges, including a classical education at Guadalajara's best schools. Having a keen mind, Miguel began his university education at the seminary in Guadalajara in his early teens. His intelligence, along with his family's wealth, seemed to ensure a secure future for him.[3]

Neither intelligence nor wealth, however, was a guarantee against tragedy. Miguel's mother died when he was ten, the cause of which he attributed to the hardships entailed in taking care of her ailing husband. Seven years later, his father succumbed to the plague.

Custody of the orphaned Miguel was given to an uncle who was a canon in the church at Bayonne, France. Besides coping with the loss of his father and adjusting to a foreign culture, Miguel had to start thinking about a future career. Because of his seminary training and his uncle's position as a canon, many of his relatives thought he would enter the priesthood. Miguel, though, recoiled at the thought of a life of celibacy, and so his uncle discussed with him the possibility of his becoming a doctor, but this idea did not appeal to him either. Although he preferred engineering, primarily because this was the profession of his older brother, he really had no definite plans.

Miguel Angel de Quevedo's future career was as much the product of chance as of choice. It was shaped not only by the education he received in France but by the landscape of France itself, for the years that Miguel spent there were pivotal in the formation of his attitudes toward nature and conservation.

Quevedo's appreciation of nature began in the Pyrenees. After improving his rudimentary knowledge of French at the College of San Luis in Bayonne, he transferred to the College of Resorre, which was located close to the mountains. Here his teachers interspersed their instructions with field trips into the countryside, ending often with a dip in a cool mountain stream. Quevedo's many excursions into the Pyrenees instilled within him a love of forests and mountains.

After Resorre, Quevedo went to the University of Bordeaux, where he received a bachelor of science degree in 1883. With the degree and with a recommendation from Gaston Planté, a member of the French Academy of Sciences, Quevedo went to Paris to further his education. Planté, whose grandmother was Mexican, took a special interest in promising Latin American students who were receiving their education in France. Quevedo had indicated to Planté his interest in studying engineering, but soon after arriving in Paris he became engrossed in the debate surrounding Camille Flammarion's treatise entitled *Plurality of the Inhabited Worlds* and promptly enrolled in Flammarion's Institute of Astronomy and Meteorology, a choice that infuriated Planté. Planté berated his young charge for holding an atavistic attraction to astronomy (sharing the Aztec's fascination with the stars) and for abandoning the interests of his country, which needed engineers not astronomers. Eventually, Planté was able to persuade him to study engineering at the Ecole Polytechnique.

At the Ecole Polytechnique, Quevedo learned about the importance of forest conservation. In a course on hydraulic agriculture, Professor Alfredo Durand-Claye warned his students that a hydraulic engineer not instructed in forestry was "deficient, an ignoramus who will make grave mistakes."[4] In private chats with Quevedo, Durand-Claye stressed that a knowledge of forestry was even more necessary in Mexico than in other nations, since Mexico was a mountainous country that suffered from torrential rains and prolonged droughts. Durand-Claye's advice became an integral part of Quevedo's thinking.

Quevedo also valued the teachings of the prominent French engineer, Paul Laroche. Laroche, who taught a course on maritime works, impressed upon him the importance of modern ports for Mexico's development. Laroche took Quevedo on a tour of various French ports and invited him to visit others on his own. One of the maritime works that most impressed Quevedo was the forested artificial dunes the French had created along the coastline as a buffer against winter storms.

After receiving his diploma in civil engineering (with a specialization in hydraulic engineering) in 1887, Quevedo returned to Mexico eager to apply what he had learned at the Ecole. Through the elemental obstacles that he faced in completing various engineering projects, Quevedo was constantly reminded of Durand-Claye's council about the necessity of forest protection in Mexico.

Quevedo's first job was as a supervisor on the drainage works (the *desagüe* project) in the Valley of Mexico. Beginning in the early seventeenth century, the municipality of Mexico City had undertaken drainage projects to eliminate flooding in the Valley of Mexico through the lowering of lake levels.[5] Quevedo worked on the most massive and the most successful drainage project in Mexican history. He supervised the construction of the Grand Canal and a large tunnel at the northeastern end of the valley that would siphon off thousands of cubic meters of water from the lakes surrounding Mexico City (the *desagüe* project was completed in 1900).

As an offshoot of his job, the young engineer studied the history of drainage projects in the Valley of Mexico. Quevedo cited Humboldt's observation that deforestation of the mountains around Mexico City was responsible for the inundations that the city suffered.[6] He implied that flooding would continue in the Valley of Mexico unless forests were protected, regardless of the *desagüe* project. He also alluded to warnings made by José Antonio Alzate y Ramírez that the lakes surrounding Mexico City should not be completely drained because the poor needed the waters for hunting and fishing. He was also influenced by the Spanish chronicler Juan de Torquemada, who thought that a reduction in the size of the valley's lacustrine zone would produce a higher incidence of disease because of swirling dust and bad vapors (which he argued were diluted by the humid air coming from the lakes).[7] Quevedo believed that the warnings made by Alzate y Ramírez and Torquemada, among others, had been heeded: "Taking into account the view of various doctors and illustrious people, the current drainage project for reasons of health has not sought the complete drainage of Mexico City's lakes, but simply to drain them to levels which would prevent flooding."[8] The *desagüe* project, though, drained more of the valley's lakes than Quevedo had anticipated. By 1920, the *desagüe* project had drained approximately six hundred square miles of former lake beds in the Valley of Mexico.[9] According to Indians in the valley, the drainage of wetlands had resulted in a noticeable decrease in waterfowl populations.[10] Others began to link the desiccation of the region's lakes to the increasingly severe dust storms that buffeted Mexico City and to the heating of the valley floor. Quevedo later downplayed the *desagüe* project's contribution to this meteorological phenomena, arguing that the removal of a forest buffer accounted for the intensity of the dust storms originating from the dry lake beds. He thought that climatic changes in the basin were the result of deforestation rather than the loss of lake water.[11] Quevedo never became as attuned to the ecological problems resulting from the *desagüe* project as he did to the problems resulting from deforestation.

Quevedo's association with the *desagüe* project came to an abrupt end early in 1889, when he was thrown forward from a push cart while inspecting tunnel works (the operator of the cart had carelessly changed tracks). Quevedo lay unconscious as the cart rolled over his back. If he had fallen a few inches to the other side, the cart would have crushed his skull. As it was, Quevedo escaped with injuries that were serious but not permanently disabling. He did, however, have to resign from the drainage project.

After recovering from the accident, Quevedo took a position as a consultant for a railroad company in the Valley of Mexico. While overseeing the construction of lines in the western sector of the valley, Quevedo witnessed firsthand the destructive floods that beset that region. He watched astonished as torrential waters knocked out bridge supports, swept away the freshly washed clothing that had been spread on nearby bushes and rocks to dry, and even carried away goats, sheep, and calves. Thus, besides hampering the development of railroad lines in the valley, these floods had a devastating impact upon the poor, who lost their livestock and sometimes even their lives. In exploring the hillsides and canyons from which the barreling waters had come, Quevedo discovered that they were "entirely bare because of the destruction of the ancient forests and I understood then the absolute necessity of reforestation."[12] He now realized the importance of forests for the public welfare.

The government again called upon Quevedo's services when it appointed him director of port works in Veracruz. For three years (1890–1893), Quevedo's crews toiled under adverse conditions to complete the construction of a large dike at the entrance of the harbor. During the winter months, heavy winds blasted sand into the workers' faces, and many hours were lost removing the dirt from the work site. Then there was the grave threat posed by yellow fever and malaria: Veracruz's swamps provided the perfect breeding grounds for the mosquitoes that transmitted these diseases. A decade later, Quevedo returned to Veracruz to plant trees as a means of reducing the severity of dust storms and the incidence of yellow fever and malaria. For the time being, Quevedo's most permanent tie to the region was provided by his marriage to a Veracruz woman.

In 1893, a French-Swiss hydroelectric company hired Quevedo to investigate the potential for water power in Mexico. He reported back to his employers on how decreased stream flow and sedimentation were reducing the electrical output of dams located near areas in which trees had been heavily cut. During his seven years as a company consultant, he found ample evidence to support his view that forests played a critical role in regulating the hydrological cycle.

In 1901, Quevedo spoke on this matter before the Second National Congress on Climate and Meteorology. He impressed upon the conferees how the destruction of forests negatively affected water supplies: "The lack of vegetation over extensive areas of our country and particularly the lack of forests aggravates in a very harmful manner the irregular rainfall and stream flow so much so that solutions to the problems of agricultural and industrial wealth become impossible if one keeps cutting the forests."[13] He subsequently maintained that deforestation had culminated in droughts in central Mexico and the desertification of once relatively verdant areas of northern Mexico because the remaining forest cover was insufficient to augment precipitation through transpiration and the cooling of the atmosphere.[14] Besides reducing the amount of water available to agriculture and industry, Quevedo asserted that the increased aridity resulting from the destruction of forests constituted a less salubrious climate. He concluded his address by calling for the adoption of strong forestry conservation laws.[15]

Quevedo's message received a mixed response. Several of the delegates rebuffed his appeal for forest conservation laws, asserting instead that the protection of the nation's forest could be achieved through education alone. In the end, though, the congress agreed that in order to regularize surface and ground water, to better the use of these waters, and to ensure public health, it was necessary to restore and conserve forests and that it was imperative to put legislation to accomplish these ends into effect as soon as possible.[16]

The most ardent support for Quevedo's position at the congress came from a coterie of natural scientists and engineers.[17] The members of this group voted for the establishment of a forestry board, the Junta Central de Bosques, to lobby on behalf of Mexico's forests. (Later the Junta Central de Bosques created a journal to publish the results of forestry investigations both in Mexico and in foreign countries and to maintain a permanent forum from which to appeal for the protection of Mexico's forest wealth.)[18] The group chose Miguel Angel de Quevedo as its president.[19] Thus began Quevedo's long career as an advocate for forest conservation.

In 1904, the secretary of the Ministry of Public Works, Manuel González Cosío, solicited the advice of the Junta Central de Bosques on how to mitigate the terrible dust storms that were blasting Mexico City that winter. Quevedo eagerly presented the committee's advice: plant more trees; but González Cosío's departure from the ministry later that year stalled efforts along these lines. Before leaving his post, though, González Cosío took the important step of integrating the Junta Central de Bosques into the Ministry of Public Works. Mexico had its first forestry agency only six years after the creation of the Office of Chief Forester in the United States.[20]

Unlike government conservationists in the United States, however, Quevedo was not working for a president committed to the protection of the nation's resources. He had to seek out government officials sympathetic to his cause wherever he could find them. Administrative changes often robbed Quevedo of valuable allies (as had been the case with Manuel González Cosío). Oftentimes, he lacked the internal support necessary to gain funding for his proposals.

Quevedo was resourceful, however. In 1901, he used his appointment to a commission on public works to successfully promote the creation of parks in Mexico City. Like the great U.S. landscape architect Frederick Law Olmsted, who created Central Park in New York City during the mid-nineteenth century, Quevedo drew upon the European experience to bolster his case for urban parks. He had recently attended the First International Congress on Public Hygiene and Urban Problems (held in Paris in 1900), at which delegates recommended that 15 percent of urban areas be covered by parks as a public health measure. He relied on the conference's findings to convince government officials that the establishment of parks served the public interest.[21]

In 1900, parks and gardens composed less than 2 percent of Mexico City's open urban space. Due to Quevedo's parks program, the ratio had improved to 16 percent by the beginning of the next decade. In numerical terms, Quevedo had increased the number of parks in Mexico City from two to thirty-four. Successful though it was, Quevedo's park creation program had vociferous detractors, among whom, curiously, were parents who lived near the proposed green spots. This group's opposition was based on the fact that they preferred the circuses that had performed in the vacant lots to staid parks. Quevedo attempted to convince disgruntled parents that the piles of trash accumulating in vacant lots presented a serious health threat. In contrast, parks constituted a healthy environment: green grass grew in place of trash heaps; trees oxygenated the air; and children could play safely as their weary parents relaxed on a park bench. Parks provided urban residents some contact with nature.[22]

With the aid of José Yves Limantour, secretary of the Treasury Department and a member of Díaz's inner circle, Quevedo gained funding for another critical project: the expansion of the tree nursery that he had established in Coyoacán (the Viveros of Coyoacán).[23] Limantour, whose friendship with Quevedo dated back to his days as president of the Group for Drainage Works, became an enthusiastic backer of Quevedo's venture after a tour of the *viveros* early in 1907. He was so impressed by the thousands of trees that he saw in the nursery that he prevailed upon Porfirio Díaz to visit the site, after which the president agreed that the project merited government support.[24] The Viveros of Coyoacán was the centerpiece of a nursery system producing 2.4 million trees by 1914.[25] Many trees of the *viveros,* including cedars, pines, acacias, eucalypti, and tamarisks, were planted on the dry lake beds and on the barren hillsides above the city, while others adorned Mexico City's boulevards and the central drainage canal (140,000 trees were planted between July 1913 and February 1914).[26] Quevedo presented Mexico City's tree nurseries, parks, and tree-lined streets as evidence that Mexico was a civilized country. He fondly referred to observations made by North American journalists that Mexico City was a "city of contrasts encircled by poor settlements and unhealthy neighborhoods; it also has the beautiful forests of Chapultepec and the magnificent tree nursery of Coyoacán like no other in America."[27] The admiration of other nations for Mexico's parks and tree nurseries greatly pleased Quevedo.

In the summer of 1907, Quevedo returned to Europe to familiarize himself with forestry practices there and to aid his own forestry objectives in Mexico. At the Second International Congress on Public Hy-

Reforestation work on a hillside south of Mexico City around 1917 and the results two decades later. Mexican Forest Service.

giene and Urban Problems (held in Berlin), Quevedo listened attentively to delegates who recommended that protected forest zones be created around cities and that forests be used to drain swamps. Both measures, the delegates argued, would result in a healthier environment. As part of the conference, Quevedo toured the forest plantations that Berliners had planted to drain swamps around the city.[28]

After the congress in Berlin, Quevedo met with forest service directors from several European countries. The Austrian director arranged a guided tour of reforestation efforts in his country. As part of his working vacation, Quevedo spent a few quiet moments in Vienna's Central Park, which he described as enchanting. Quevedo's next stop was in France, where he visited the forestry schools at Nancy and Lower Charente. He met with Lucien Daubrée, head of the French Forest Service, who promised French aid and staff for a Mexican forestry school. Upon Daubrée's advice, Quevedo traveled to Algeria to observe firsthand the sand dunes the French had stabilized with trees. While in Algeria, he collected pine and acacia seeds hoping to repeat the Algerian success story in Mexico.[29]

He was able to implement some of the European forestry programs in Mexico. In 1908, Díaz accepted Quevedo's proposal to create forested artificial dunes in Veracruz; he was swayed by Quevedo's argument that such dunes would diminish the problems of dust storms, yellow fever, and malaria. The government's patience was tested in this case, as it took several years to raise the land to the necessary level. Government funding was maintained, though, and in 1913 Quevedo had his artificial dune.[30]

In another step forward in 1908, the French government sent the promised aid and teachers to Mexico to start a forestry school.[31] In addition to taking courses in arboriculture and silviculture, Mexican students worked in the tree nurseries and on reforestation projects, all as part of the preparation to become forest rangers. In 1914, the forestry school and its annex had thirty-two students, a modest beginning for the forestry profession in Mexico. Unfortunately, that was the year that political turmoil forced the closing of the school.[32]

As a first step toward providing the knowledge necessary for the proper management of nation's forests, the Junta Central de Bosques completed an inventory of woodlands in the Federal District (Mexico City and its environs) in 1909. The group found that approximately 25 percent of the region was forested. The largest woodlands, which were composed mainly of firs and pines, were located southwest of Mexico City. The Junta Central de Bosques cautioned that the conservation of these already heavily plundered forests was essential, since they contained the region's principal streams. In addition to its own fieldwork, the group provided a forestry questionnaire to the governors and local juntas throughout the republic. The questionnaire, which the central forestry board followed in conducting its survey of woodlands within the Valley of Mexico, asked for the species composition and size of each forest, the climatology and hydrology of the region, the use made of forest products (for firewood, charcoal, construction, industry, etc.), the causes of forest destruction, and reforestation efforts, if any. By 1911, the states had provided the Junta Central de Bosques with information on the types of trees composing their forests and their industrial applications.[33] Although principally qualitative in nature, the Junta Central de Bosques had compiled the first national forestry statistics.

In 1909, Miguel Angel de Quevedo received an invitation from U.S. President Theodore Roosevelt to attend the International North American Conference on the Conservation of Natural Resources in Washington, D.C. Quevedo's existence had been a pleasant surprise for conservationists within the Roosevelt administration. Roosevelt had instructed his chief forester, Gifford Pinchot, to search for a Mexican delegate to the conference, and Pinchot was astonished to learn about Quevedo's reforestation efforts around Mexico City. Neither Roosevelt nor Pinchot had been aware of conservation activities in Mexico.[34]

In many respects, Quevedo was Pinchot's counterpart. Like Pinchot, Quevedo was the chief spokesperson for forest conservation within his country. Though not trained in forestry, Quevedo shared Pinchot's interest in and knowledge of European conservation practices. In their age, upper-class backgrounds, and determination, Quevedo and Pinchot were peers.

Quevedo and Pinchot differed fundamentally, however, on the rationale for forest conservation. Pinchot believed that forest conservation had to be undertaken to prevent a timber shortage in the United States and saw conservation as strictly an economic matter. In contrast, Quevedo, through his education and experience as an engineer in Mexico, had developed an appreciation of the diverse benefits provided by forests.

Quevedo explained to the delegates why forestry concerns were broader in Mexico than in the United States and in Canada:

Because of the ways in which forests aid the general order [by stabilizing soils, alleviating droughts, and impeding floods], it is necessary to prevent further deforestation on Mexican soil; this is a more pressing and serious matter than in the United States and Canada, in whose territory, . . . forestry is merely an economic issue, restricted to providing wood for present and future needs, and the effect which deforestation can have on the hydrological cycle and agricultural productivity is of much less significance than in Mexico.[35]

Quevedo instructed the delegates on the way in which Mexico's hydrological regime and geography differed from the rest of North America. Unlike Canada and the United States, where rain fell on a fairly regular basis, Mexico experienced long dry spells punctuated by brief periods of heavy rains and so was highly susceptible to both droughts and flooding. Forests were a safeguard against both of these disasters. Whereas in the United States and Canada most agriculture was confined to the plains and broad valleys, most of Mexico's agriculture took place in mountainous regions. Flooding and the debris that it spread were much more serious threats to Mexico's cropland than in either Canada or the United States. For Quevedo, lumber was only a small part of the benefits provided by forests. His interest lay less with the establishment of a forest industry based on the principles of sustained yield than it did with the protection of forests because they were biologically indispensable.[36]

Quevedo was neither a strict utilitarian nor a strict preservationist. He approved of the use of forests where such use did not threaten soils, climates, and watersheds. The importance of conservation for people's well-being was always foremost in his thoughts. Thus, in addition to their biological value, Quevedo stressed the scenic and recreational value of forests.[37] In contrast to U.S. preservationist John Muir, Quevedo did not espouse the view that nature had an intrinsic right to exist irrespective of whether that existence served people. Then again, Muir himself promoted tourism to generate support for wild areas. Quevedo's views were utilitarian, but in the broadest sense of the word.

Quevedo included in his speech a list of recommendations he had made to Porfirio Díaz. These recommendations were as follows: protect forests of high biological value on national lands; acquire, through expropriation if necessary, biologically critical private woodlands and lands that could be reforested (Quevedo argued that this step was necessary because so much of the public domain had been sold); place municipal forestlands under an adequate forestry regime; regulate the cutting of forests on private lands; and provide seeds and instructions for reforestation to property owners.[38]

The government followed many of these recommendations. At the end of 1909, the Díaz regime ordered the suspension of the selling of public lands, and the Ministry of Public Works announced that it would not grant concessions for the exploitation of forests on lands that it determined should be conserved for the public good.[39] The government also granted itself the power of expropriation, when necessary, for the reforestation of denuded lands and to maintain springs and streams that supplied water and provided other public health benefits to the cities.[40] Quevedo and Limantour convinced Díaz to use this latter provision in 1910 to create a protected forest zone around the Valley of Mexico in order to prevent floods and safeguard the capital's water supply.[41] Nevertheless, after years of public land sales, so detrimental to the nation's woodlands, Quevedo remained skeptical of Díaz's commitment to forest conservation.[42]

When Francisco Madero's revolution ousted Porfirio Díaz in 1911, Quevedo's conservation goals in Mexico appeared attainable. Madero, who had been educated in agronomy at the University of California, Berkeley, took an avid interest in conservation. He backed Quevedo's efforts to drain swamps by establishing forest plantations. Madero created a forest reserve in the southern Mexican state of Quintana Roo in the first of what promised to be many such decrees.[43] But then in 1913, following a coup d'etat by Victoriano Huerta, Madero was assassinated.

Huerta held a manifest disregard for conservation, and Quevedo despised him. He vehemently opposed Huerta's practice of "transplanting" trees from Mexico City's boulevards to his ranch at Azcapotzalco in the Valley of Mexico and his son-in-law's scheme to convert the Desierto de los Leones forest reserve into a Monte Carlo–style gaming operation. For his part, Huerta considered Quevedo and his colleagues to be subversives. He so seriously threatened the French forestry professors, whom he suspected of supporting opposition forces, that they had to leave the country. When a friend warned Quevedo that he had seen his name on an assassination list, the conservationist, too, reluctantly went into exile in 1914. (Huerta was overthrown later that year.)[44]

Fatigue, illness, and the outbreak of World War I limited Quevedo's forestry studies during his exile in Europe. Shortly before the outbreak of war, he studied French policy toward the forest commons. Quevedo praised the French government for keeping communal forest reserves intact, believing, as he did, that the fractionalization of such lands would have both complicated their administration and led to a greater potential for the individual abuse of the land. Under the French program, peasants sold dead wood and small forest products at public auctions. Ten percent of the proceeds were used to help finance the French Forest Service, among whose most important functions was the restoration and reforestation of damaged lands. Quevedo noted with great satisfaction that not only did people gain financially from the auction arrangement but, at the same time, were helping protect agriculture, climatological conditions, the hydrological cycle, and the beauty of nature.[45]

Quevedo thought Mexico could learn from the French experience. He declared that peasants had been responsible for much of the destruction of Mexico's forests, and he feared that if no limits were placed on the redistribution of land after the Revolution, Mexico's forests were doomed. Quevedo stressed that *campesinos*, who were granted woodlands, must leave such areas undisturbed if they were unsuited for agriculture. Instead of recklessly clearing the land for farming, they should turn to harvests from other parts of the *ejido* (communal lands), make the appropriate use of forest products, and develop other exploitable industries. Mexico had to follow the French example by instilling in the peasantry an appreciation for the value of forests.[46]

As Quevedo studied forestry practices in France, his forestry efforts in Mexico were being undone by the Revolution. In Veracruz, the trees that took several years to plant were destroyed in weeks by soldiers seeking firewood. Other areas had been similarly ravaged. The Revolution, which had been tremendously destructive in human terms, also had a profound environmental impact.[47]

Following the defeat of Huerta's army by the Constitutionalist forces, Quevedo returned to Mexico to resume his lobbying activities for forest conservation. In stark contrast to the Huerta regime, some elements within the new government were receptive to the conservationist's ideas. Working in tandem with the secretary of the Ministry of Public Works, Pastor Rouaix, in 1917 Quevedo convinced President Venustiano Carranza to establish Desierto de los Leones as Mexico's first national park.[48] Quevedo achieved another of his goals when he persuaded delegates to the constitutional convention to include a conservation plank in the constitution.[49] Article 27 of the 1917 Constitution states: "The nation shall always have the right to impose on private property the rules dictated by the public interest and to regulate the use of natural elements, susceptible to appropriation so as to distribute equitably the public wealth and to safeguard its conservation." This clause provided the foundation for Mexico's postrevolutionary conservation legislation.

Fir trees in Desierto de los Leones National Park. Photo by Lane Simonian.

After the death of his wife from the Spanish flu in 1918, a grief-stricken Quevedo temporarily abandoned his conservation activities. Friends sought projects that would keep his mind occupied. After some coaxing, they convinced Quevedo to resume his struggle to protect Mexico's natural resources.[50]

Quevedo worked on behalf of the nation's wildlife, as well as its forests. Most notably, he headed the Mexican Committee for the Protection of Wild Birds during the 1930s (the organization was created in 1931 as an affiliate of the International Committee for Bird Protection). The Mexican committee held that an ethical, economic, aesthetic, and scientific rationale existed for the protection of wild birds. The group lamented the fact that because of unrestricted hunting and deforestation birds had been denied the space needed for breeding. The loss of bird life had not only diminished the charm of the forests but had also led to increased pest damage to orchards, fields, and forests. The committee vowed to educate the country's youth on the value of birds, publish pamphlets, organize conferences and photographic exhibitions, encourage reforestation and the creation of urban parks, push the authorities to create conservation laws, and study the important ecological role of birds.[51]

In its efforts to protect migratory birds, the committee was indirectly aided by Edward Alphonso Goldman, a field biologist for the U.S. Bureau of Biological Survey. Goldman studied waterfowl conditions in the Valley of Mexico off and on over a period of thirty-one years (1904–1935). In 1920, he was accompanied in this endeavor by Valentín Santiago of the Museum of Natural History in Mexico City and the Bureau of Biological Studies.[52] Mexican conservationists took a keen interest in Goldman's field reports. They particularly noted his finding that the waterfowl population had declined sharply in the Valley of Mexico since the turn of the century as the result of the drainage of wetlands and the continuing use of *armadas* (shooting batteries).[53] Goldman was aware that Mexican game officials were concerned about the latter threat to waterfowl: "In recognition of the fact that ducks are being gradually reduced in number through the use of batteries in the Valley of Mexico, game officials are attempting to restrict and ultimately abolish the use of *armadas* altogether."[54] The work of Edward Alphonso Goldman, the Mexican Committee for the Protection of Wild Birds, and Mexican game officials contributed to the government's decision to ban *armadas* in 1932.[55]

Quevedo lent his name and some of his energies to efforts to save birds, but his principal concern was forest conservation. In 1922, he created the Mexican Forestry Society, which was a reincarnation of the Junta Central de Bosques (except for the fact that it remained a private organization). A year later the society published the first issue of *México Forestal*. In this inaugural issue, the forestry society explained its reason for being:

> The Mexican Forestry Society was formed by a group of individuals
> convinced of the important role played by forest vegetation and
> principally by the tree . . . in the maintenance of a climatic equilib-
> rium, in the protection of soils and waters, in the general economy
> and the public's welfare, convinced even more of these beneficial ef-
> fects by the prejudicial actions which are destroying our primevally
> endowed, rich, and beneficial forests.[56]

The society believed that the conscientious citizen must think of the
future and thus must "clamor against the silence of our country against
the national suicide that signifies the ruin of the forest and the scorn of
our tree protector."[57] It saluted the efforts forestry groups were making
in other nations, such as in Spain and in the United States. The Mexican
Forestry Society noted that forest conservation "is not restricted to the
narrow limits of national borders because the forests provide for all of
humanity conserving the climatic equilibrium and biology in general of
the terrestrial globe."[58]

One of the principal goals of Quevedo and the Mexican Forestry Society was the enactment of a strong forestry law. Ministry of Agriculture
officials in the Alvaro Obregón administration (1920–1924) both heard
and heeded the society's request for such a law:

> This Ministry has received daily numerous complaints on how the
> cutting of forests destroys not only wood supplies, but of a graver
> nature results in the drying up of streams and disastrous floods
> which leave a sterile and even a desert-like land in their wake. This is
> why the Ministry with the goal of avoiding such harms is recom-
> mending to the government that they take the means necessary . . .
> to stop these chaotic practices . . . and establish a rational exploita-
> tion of the forest that guarantees the perpetual conservation and use
> of them.[59]

A government appointed commission, with Quevedo as one of its members, produced a draft of a forestry law in 1923.[60] After some modifica-
tions and elaboration on this draft, President Plutarco Elías Calles
(1924–1928) enacted a forestry law in 1926 and an accompanying regulation in 1927.[61]

The forestry law was the archetype for all subsequent forest legislation in Mexico. For the first time on a national level, forestry activities
were regulated on private lands: all entities, whether individuals or corporations, had to submit plans for their forest activities to agriculture

officials for review. The government pledged to carefully manage the use of public lands as well. As part of this effort, federal authorities restricted timber concessions in forest reserves to 50,000 hectares in the tropics and to 5,000 in the temperate regions (a hectare is equivalent to 2.47 acres). Along watersheds and near population centers, the federal executive authorized the creation of forest zones, in which only marked trees could be cut. In addition, the government promised to establish national parks in areas with high biological, scenic areas, and recreational values. Agriculture officials sought to prevent the degradation of rangelands and forests by requiring all livestock owners to obtain a permit for their operations. They further vowed to combat plagues and to enlist the support of the citizenry in the prevention of forest fires. Finally, to provide the underpinnings for the protection and restoration of Mexico's woodlands, the federal executive pledged to create a forestry service, reestablish the forestry school, and establish tree nurseries.[62]

The government's record in regard to the enforcement of the law was mixed. Federal officials did develop a reforestation program and provided aid to state governors for the establishment of tree nurseries.[63] Complementing these initiatives, teachers trained by the Ministry of Education gave practical lessons to *campesinos* on the formation of nurseries and the reforestation of mountain slopes, explaining to them the paramount importance of forests in protecting agriculture, bettering the climate, and in maintaining all of the "phenomena necessary for life of the villages."[64] On another front, the Mexican government recommended that state governments begin an energetic campaign against the use of charcoal for fuel. As part of this campaign, government officials in Mexico City asked the state governors to popularize the use of gasoline, coal, and electricity for cooking and heating.[65] Few of these initiatives, however, became more than pilot projects.

Regrettably, the government did not create any national parks.[66] Nor did it provide adequate funding for the forestry service or for the forestry school. In fact, the forestry school lasted less than a year (1926–1927). After that, a professor in the National School of Agriculture provided the only silviculture courses. Tom Gill, an American who studied forest policy in Mexico during the late 1920s, called into question national priorities: "In cutting down the modest appropriation needed to support the school, the plea used by the Mexican government was economy. It is the same often-repeated plea used by many governments throughout the world when they wish to discontinue appropriations for far-sighted benefits in favor of appropriations that bring more immediate political advancement."[67]

A frustrated Quevedo was even more critical of the government, charging that some members of the Ministry of Agriculture were being less than honest in enforcing the laws.[68] Gill's explanation for the failure of forest conservation programs was more systemic: "One must reluctantly admit that the present forestry law in Mexico has not greatly hindered the vandalization of forests. For laws, of themselves, the history of nations amply proves, possess little force unless behind them stands the alert police power of government and the good will of a nation's people." Gill added, "Forestry still remains a subject of interest only to a small handful of cultured, far-sighted men and women, living for the most part in Mexico City. It has not made itself a part of Mexico's daily living."[69] Charles Sheldon, a U.S. big-game hunter, who lamented the disappearance of the large mammals that had once graced his travels through the wilderness of northern Mexico, likewise observed the lack of government and public backing for one of the nation's most important wildlife decrees: President Obregón's ten-year ban on the hunting of bighorn sheep and antelope (1922). Sheldon exclaimed: "That [the prohibition] is all. No funds for wardens, no plan of actions, accompanies the decree. No sportsmen who will care for its enforcement are at hand, no local sentiment on behalf of saving game exists."[70]

As Gill and Sheldon suggested, the enforcement of conservation laws was weakened by the disinterest of powerful Mexican officials and by a lack of general public support. President Lázaro Cárdenas (1934–1940) corrected the problem of apathy in high political circles as he himself had an abiding interest in the protection of resources, but his administration still faced the difficult task of generating enthusiasm for conservation among the Mexican people.

In the presidential campaign of 1934, Lázaro Cárdenas contacted Quevedo regarding his interest in heading an autonomous Department of Forestry, Fish, and Game. Quevedo modestly turned down the offer at first, replying that he was an engineer not a politician. Cárdenas then invited Quevedo to join him on a campaign stop in Veracruz. After touring and complimenting Quevedo on his work in creating forested dunes (a project to which Quevedo had returned in the late 1920s), Cárdenas asked Quevedo again if he would accept the position, and this time Quevedo said yes.[71]

The 1920s and 1930s were a productive period for conservation in Mexico. By the time Cárdenas became president, many important conservation laws were already on the books. Now, it was time both to enforce the laws and to educate the citizenry on the need for conservation.

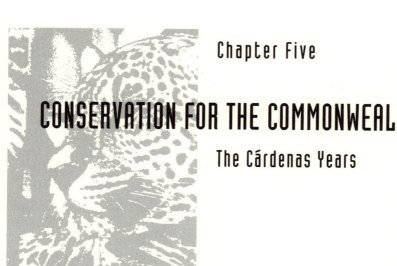

Chapter Five

CONSERVATION FOR THE COMMONWEAL

The Cárdenas Years

Like his U.S. counterpart, Franklin D. Roosevelt (1933–1945), President Lázaro Cárdenas (1934–1940) made the conservation of natural resources one of the top priorities of his administration. Both Roosevelt's New Deal and Cárdenas's populist agenda were predicated upon the belief that the careful use of natural resources was in the public interest. Roosevelt and Cárdenas shared the conviction that the conservation of natural resources was necessary not only to prevent immediate financial losses but also to ensure the future wealth of their nations. This conviction had been forged by the disastrous consequences of environmental abuse in the United States and in Mexico. In the United States, the unenlightened use of the land (particularly the plowing under of the native prairie grasses) had exacerbated the effects of a prolonged drought. The culmination of this process was the Dust Bowl of the early 1930s, a period in which thousands of tons of midwestern topsoil were blown into the atmosphere. The Dust Bowl was a natural and human-made tragedy of enormous proportions.[1] In response, the Roosevelt administration created soil conservation districts staffed by agronomists charged with teaching farmers the techniques necessary to avert another Dust Bowl. Although Mexico did not suffer from a calamity as devastating as the Dust Bowl, many regions within the country were badly eroded and deforested. To conserve Mexico's forests and soils, the Cárdenas administration created forest reserves, protected forest zones, and national parks. Both Roosevelt and Cárdenas recognized the need to take steps to prevent future disasters as well as to restore degraded lands.

They also believed that conservation served the economic needs of the people and of the country. Thus, not only did the Civilian Conservation Corps plant thousands of trees in the United States, the program gave thousands of people jobs during the Great Depression. In Mexico, the government created cooperatives in which it promoted conservation as a means of ensuring a sustained income for the rural poor. Presidents Roosevelt and Cárdenas realized that conservation and development were complementary goals.

Cárdenas's concern for the environment was in part the product of remorse. By his own admission, Cárdenas had been inattentive to environmental issues while governor of his native state of Michoacán (1928–1934). Because of his neglect, many of Michoacán's beautiful forests had been denuded, and once large springs had dried up. During his presidential campaign, Cárdenas conveyed to Quevedo his sadness and disappointment over how his ignorance of conservation had led to such damage. His startling realization was that if he continued in his ignorance as president of Mexico, he would harm not just one state but the entire nation. Cárdenas promised Quevedo and himself that he would not err again on a larger scale.[2]

Cárdenas also had an ideological attachment to conservation, which notwithstanding his mea culpa to Quevedo, was evident even while he was governor of Michoacán. Part of his program, first as governor and then as president, was aimed at improving the conditions of the *campesinos* through the small-scale development of natural resources. Without conservation, these resources would be depleted, and the poor would be deprived of a critical source of income. Thus, as a preview of his actions as president, Cárdenas declared null several concessions given to timber companies in his state and created Indian woodland cooperatives.[3]

Though the phrase had not yet been coined, "small is beautiful" was part of the Cardenista philosophy.[4] Ramón Beteta, a member of the Cárdenas brain trust, contemplated a bounded form of industrialization that would avoid the evils of urbanization, economic insecurity, waste, the triumph of shoddily made goods over fine crafts, and the exploitation of human beings. Speaking on behalf of his colleagues, Beteta proclaimed: "We have dreamt of a Mexico of *ejidos* and small industrial communities, electrified with sanitation, in which goods will be provided for the purpose of satisfying the needs of the people; in which the machinery will be employed to relieve man from heavy toil, and not for so-called overproduction."[5]

In accord with this vision, the Cárdenas administration undertook the largest land reform program in Mexican history, extended irrigation projects to small farmers, experimented with alternative "crops," such as silkworms and sunflowers (for the oil), created rural industries, and established fishing and forestry cooperatives. "Small is beautiful," though, was only one aspect of the Cárdenas economic program. His administration left untouched many of the large agricultural estates in the north, built large dams to provide these estates with irrigation, continued to emphasize the production of export crops, and spurred the development of industry, in part by providing cheap hydroelectric power from dams built in the central highlands. (Mexico had yet to undertake the large-scale multipurpose river development such as was being done in the United States through the Tennessee Valley Authority, but as in the United States, the Mexican government sought to develop hydroelectric power for the benefit of both the poor people and big industry.) Cárdenas maintained a dual economy in Mexico: one "modern" (large-scale) and one "traditional" (small-scale). His uniqueness in the postrevolutionary period lay in his efforts to develop both the "traditional" sector and the "modern" sector simultaneously, rather than favoring the development of the "modern" sector.

Cárdenas's desire to protect natural resources led him to create the first autonomous conservation agency in Mexico: the Department of Forestry, Fish, and Game in 1935.[6] In his speech announcing the creation of the department, Cárdenas stated that the conservation of natural resources was not only beneficial for the economy but also for people's health and well-being, since all human beings depended on the environment. To illustrate his point, he noted that forests were needed to regulate the flow of streams, to maintain the climatic equilibrium, and to prevent soil erosion. He added that in areas denuded of forests, agriculture frequently failed, and some of these lands became deserts. Furthermore, forests provided valuable habitats for Mexico's abundant wildlife. He thereby affirmed that conservation was in the national interests and that the irrational exploitation of the land must come to an end.[7] Cárdenas concluded his message by expressing his confidence that "the Mexican people, conscious of the great benefits provided by forests and fauna, will cooperate enthusiastically and faithfully with this work of salvation and protection of nature, true work of national conservation."[8]

In his speech, President Cárdenas strongly endorsed Quevedo's campaign for forest conservation and clearly enunciated Quevedo's conviction that forests were critical for biological as well as for economic reasons. Cárdenas, though, was not so strong a defender of conservation as was Quevedo. He believed that flexible policies were necessary to ensure the poor an adequate income through the use of forests and other natural resources. Nonetheless, he was the first Mexican president to take an active interest in conservation, and this boded well for the protection of natural resources in Mexico.

Cárdenas directed the Department of Forestry, Fish, and Game to conserve Mexico's forests, to reforest devastated areas, to create tree nurseries, to administer the national parks, to protect the nation's flora and fauna, and to encourage scientific education and investigation.[9]

Members of the department had a keen awareness of the importance of publicity in achieving these goals. In 1935, the department published the first issue of *Protección a la Naturaleza*, a quarterly magazine designed to "extend environmental knowledge to workers and peasants and to make foreign and domestic tourists aware of the nation's beauty."[10] The government distributed the magazine free of charge in an attempt to reach the largest possible audience. Articles in *Protección a la Naturaleza* were written in a nontechnical manner for the benefit of the general populace. The magazine contained informational pieces on Mexico's national parks, the biological diversity of its forests, and Arbor Day plans and celebrations. Also included in the journal were field sketches and descriptions of the nation's rich fauna, often accompanied by a discussion of the value and vulnerability of wild animals to human beings. Thus, writings on various bird species stressed the important role they played in controlling insects. Other wildlife reports explained why, because of the dictates of reproductive biology, the hunting and fishing of certain species had to be curtailed. The common theme in these articles was the importance of exercising stewardship over the nation's natural resources.

Officials within the Department of Forestry, Fish, and Game communicated their conservation ideals directly to the people during Arbor Day celebrations and during visits to fishing and forestry cooperatives. On these and other occasions, they distributed posters and fliers to *campesinos* that emphasized the benefits to be derived from forest protection. One poster showed a peasant family under a tree with the caption reading: "Take care of the tree which gives shelter and valuable food to the people of the fields and the mountains, also beautifying the countryside."[11] The government constantly promoted the idea that the tree was a friend of the people and should be treated as such.

A peasant family flanked by Miguel Angel de Quevedo on the left and Lázaro Cárdenas on the right. The poster contains these words: "Take care of the tree that gives
shelter and valuable food to the people of the fields and the mountains, also beautifying the countryside." Departamento Autónomo Forestal y de Caza y Pesca.

Not surprisingly, Quevedo made forest conservation the principal
work of the department. With Cárdenas's backing, he succeeded in establishing a national system of forest reserves and protected forest
zones. As authorized by the 1926 forestry law, Quevedo established forest reserves in areas where forest cover was determined to be biologically
important. Within the reserves, individuals or groups could engage in
wood cutting only after close consultation with the government. Also
in accordance with the 1926 forestry law, Quevedo created protected
forest zones along watersheds and near cities where forests were considered to be biologically indispensable. Within these zones, only marked
trees could be cut. Quevedo was finally in a position to implement the
provisions of the 1926 forestry law that he had helped draft.

Quevedo sought to restore as well as to protect Mexico's woodlands.
Reforestation became one of the department's most important pro-

grams. During the Cárdenas presidency, two million trees were planted in the Valley of Mexico and four million trees were planted throughout the rest of the republic.[12] In its reforestation efforts, the Cárdenas administration enlisted the support of many groups, including the army.[13] Military trucks transporting soldiers and seedlings became an almost common sight.[14] To meet the need for new trees, the government expanded the system of national, state, and municipal nurseries. The government also created school nurseries to create an appreciation of trees among the young.[15] Small trees began to dot the barren hillsides near Mexican cities and towns.

Along with reforestation, the creation of forest cooperatives was one of the department's top objectives. To provide peasants with an alternative to their one-crop corn economy, forestry officials promoted the investigation and development of new uses for forest products and the establishment of factories to manufacture the finished products of Mexico's forests, such as rare woods, chicle, ixtle fiber, and candelilla wax.[16] In creating forest cooperatives, Cárdenas's intention was to replace the irrational exploitation of forest resources by large domestic and foreign companies with the small-scale use of those resources by indigenous people, who would both derive economic benefits from the forests and conserve them.[17]

Plans for the creation of a forest economy and rural industries in southeastern Mexico provide one illustration of the small-scale development program envisaged by the Cárdenas administration. Quevedo recommended that *campesinos* in the region plant carob and mulberry trees to provide forage for cattle, cocoa palms and sunflowers from which vegetable oils and soap could be processed, coconut trees from which brushes and brooms could be made, and fruit trees. Around coastal communities, fishery and fish-packing industries could be developed. The beaches of Isla Mujeres and Cozumel offered outstanding opportunities for tourism, although Quevedo had in mind a much smaller scale of development than the huge resorts that would eventually be built in the region. Cárdenas and Quevedo were basically seeking sustainable development for the region, a strategy that would once again be embraced by Mexican conservationists during the 1970s.[18]

In his travels through Quintana Roo, Quevedo became acutely aware of the obstacles to a program of sustained resource use in the region. Quevedo's plane rides over the state impressed upon him how vast an area of once lush forests had been converted into chaparral. Forest concessionaires had eagerly exploited the forests of Quintana Roo, disregarding forestry regulations and the dictates of scientific management. Quevedo observed that they undertook "the exploitation of chicle in a form so intense, in trees of insufficient maturity, that it kills the trees, [thus] as happens elsewhere in the Republic, especially with the extraction of resin, the mass of forests disappear rapidly being replaced by secondary species of little or no value."[19]

As Quevedo noted, part of the destruction of Quintana Roo's forests was spurred by foreign companies: "This ruinous exploitation of chicle and precious woods by concessionaires is partly brought about by intermediaries who deal directly with foreign companies which export wood from Quintana Roo; intermediaries and businesses which have no concern for Mexico's national interest; they are indifferent to forestry regulations since they have only their personal interest in mind."[20] Intermediaries continued to operate in the region even after many forest concessionaires were displaced through the creation of *ejidos*. The government sought to eliminate intermediaries and in a closely regulated fashion to allow *ejidos* to sell their forest products directly to foreign companies. Quevedo condemned the *ejiditarios* themselves for persisting in their ruinous practice of slash and burn agriculture. Both foreigners and Mexicans were destroying the nation's forests.[21]

To change the destructive forestry practices of *campesinos*, the government had to ensure an adequate income for members of rural communities. A U.S. Department of Interior report on conservation in Mexico clearly identified the challenge that the Cárdenas administration faced:

> Unless the government can find means whereby they can pay good wages to forest cooperatives and assure better living conditions to the campesinos engaged in agriculture, even a realization of the necessity for preserving the forests will not prevent the Mexican peons from making what profit they can out of illegal or unscientific exploitation of the woods.[22]

Thus, unless peasants could derive more benefits from forest products (many of which could be extracted without killing the tree) than from lumbering or from clearing land for agriculture, they would not conserve the forests.

In the absence of incentives, government conservation programs failed. A perfect example of this was the Department of Forestry, Fish, and Game's campaign to substitute oil and gas for firewood. In the rural areas, wood was the sole source of fuel, and the collection of firewood was one of the chief causes of forest destruction. Though well intentioned, the government's program failed because it did not offset the cost between cheap wood and expensive fossil fuels.[23]

Through the tax system, the government did provide incentives for forest conservation. It annulled taxation on standing stock, taxed dead wood less than cut wood, and taxed trees cut in more remote areas less than trees cut near urban areas.[24] But in an exemption that reflected Cárdenas's concern for the poor, *campesinos* were not taxed on the sale of all forest products. In 1938, the government declared that "the *campesino* who lacks other means of a livelihood than individually using the forests can take forest products to the market (up to fifteen pesos worth weekly) without fear of the tax collector."[25] Cárdenas, if not Quevedo, was willing to ease the economic burden on the poorer segments of society even if this meant a greater exploitation of forest resources.

Cárdenas's conservation program relied upon restrictions as well as incentives. To exercise a more effective vigilance over Mexico's forests, Cárdenas expanded the forest service. During his administration, newly created forestry schools trained over a thousand foresters.[26] Still, the forest service faced a personnel shortage. Another problem was that because of their low salaries, foresters were susceptible to bribery. The forest service was neither well-enough staffed nor well-enough paid to ensure the enforcement of forestry legislation.[27]

Those forest guards who did attempt to enforce forest regulations strictly often were the subject of reprobation by peasant communities. In a confrontation typical of the period, Francisco Barrera, secretary of Agrarian Action for the Committee of Agrarian Communities and *Campesinos* Syndicate of Coahuila, demanded that the government replace a forest ranger, who he identified "as an enemy of the *campesinos*' aspirations for emancipation," with one more sympathetic to the ideology of the peasants' union.[28] Many peasant communities agreed with Barrera that the restrictions upon their use of forest resources were excessive, and they often registered their disapproval by violating regulations.

In his reconnoitering of Mexico, Quevedo was dismayed by the amount of forest destruction he witnessed. It seemed to him that many Mexicans appreciated the value of forests only after they had been removed. In his explorations of rivers in Campeche and Veracruz (states on the Gulf of Mexico), Quevedo related how the heavy cutting of trees upstream had negatively affected the climate and the economy of the region: "The level of the water is very low, there has not been enough rain in this large region, . . . and one sees the erosion caused by deforestation, which has the serious effect of polluting the waters, making them unsuited for fishing, and diminishing the navigability of rivers."[29] Likewise, Quevedo chronicled how deforestation had harmed the rural economy of the state of Mexico, particularly between Desierto de los Leones and Bosencheve, where the barren landscape was broken only by a small forest in the National Park of Nevado de Toluca.[30] Quevedo affirmed that "the previously favorable conditions for agriculture in the valleys, such as Toluca and Lerma, have been lost. *Hacendados* and *campesinos* agree that it is not worthwhile to practice agriculture in these and other valleys of the state [of Mexico] due to alterations in climate and the hydrological cycle produced by the excessive cutting of forests in neighboring mountains."[31] In 1939, Quevedo offered a general summation of the problem:

Each day the Mexican forest problem becomes graver: the large woods are being depleted at an alarming rate, the production of chicle diminishes notably year by year, the hardwoods and even firewood cannot be obtained in regions once classified as heavily forested. Everywhere one observes forests impoverished and ruined by greed and thoughtlessness and almost we can claim that Mexico is heading for disaster.[32]

Quevedo maintained that inadequate funding had shackled his department's efforts to protect Mexico's forests. In 1938, Quevedo requested a budget of 8,397,860 pesos, but he was allotted only 3,200,000 pesos (approximately U.S. $900,000). Between 1935 and 1938, appropriations for the department had increased by a modest 850,000 pesos.[33] Yet Quevedo understood that money was only part of the problem. More than money, a successful conservation program required a commitment from all segments of society. Quevedo believed that Cárdenas's intentions were good but that he had not gone to the heart of the matter, for Quevedo felt that Mexico's forest problem was so complex and so difficult that only a permanent government campaign that enlisted the support of the entire citizenry on behalf of forest conservation could succeed.[34]

John Jernegan and Roger Tyler of the U.S. Department of the Interior offered one of the most astute assessments of the historical significance of conservation during the Cárdenas years:

Mexico's present conservation program is the first scientific attempt ever made to preserve the natural resources of the country. The destruction of the forests in Mexico has been appalling. Even now, in spite of efforts by the Autonomous Department of Forestry, Hunting, and Fishing, the loss in forest resources is still enormous. But a beginning has been made, and by reason of the idea behind it, if not by the results achieved, the conservation program in Mexico is important.[35]

Cárdenas's conservation program was indeed a pioneering effort to design social and economic policies that would maintain an ecological equilibrium in the country for the benefit of both nature and people.

One of the most visible accomplishments of the Department of Forestry, Fish, and Game was the creation of national parks. Prior to 1935, Mexico had only two national parks: Desierto de los Leones (1917) and El Chico (1922). Cárdenas created forty national parks (which by area constitute approximately three-quarters of Mexico's present national park system). Of the national parks Cárdenas created, ten were set aside for their historical or archaeological significance, and twenty-two were less than the size of Hot Springs National Park, the smallest national park in the United States. Still, a few of the areas that Cárdenas set aside were true national parks.[36]

In many respects, the Mexican national park experience paralleled that of the United States.[37] Like their U.S. counterparts, Mexican officials rarely created national parks that incorporated whole ecosystems. They, too, protected coniferous and alpine ecosystems much more frequently than less "scenic" ecosystems. In contrast to the United States, though, Mexican authorities established national parks in areas that contained valuable natural resources, particularly forest resources. The government prohibited commercial lumbering in Mexico's national parks up until 1960 (the 1960 forestry law allowed joint government-peasant timber operations within the parks).[38] At least for awhile, the Mexican government tried to block the exploitation of valuable timberlands within the national parks.

Quevedo, for one, argued that protecting woodlands was justifiable because it benefited farmers: "I ought to correct the belief that parks are a drain on fiscal resources, when one considers the decline in agriculture which can only be remedied through reforestation."[39] From this perspective, preventing the exploitation of one resource was necessary to save another.

The Cárdenas administration selected areas for national parks based on three criteria: scenic beauty, recreational potential, and ecological

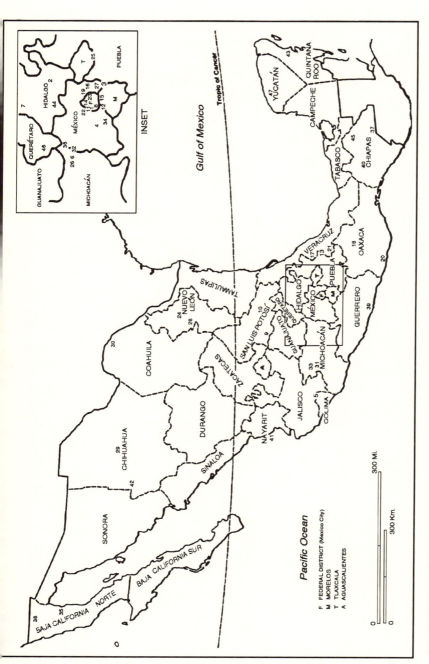

Map 4. National Parks of Mexico. Base map from Robert Jones Shafer, *A History of Latin America* (Lexington, Mass.: D. C. Heath and Company, 1978). Reprinted with permission from Robert Jones Shafer. Location of national parks and most of the information in Table 1 courtesy of Magdalena Juárez for *México Desconocido*.

Table One.
National Parks of Mexico

Park	Location	Date Established	Hectare
1. Desierto de los Leones	Federal District	1917	1,86
2. El Chico	Hidalgo	1922	2,73
3. Iztaccíhuatl-Popocatépetl	México, Morelos, and Puebla	1935	25,67
4. Nevado de Toluca	México	1936	51,10
5. Volcán Nevado de Colima	Colima and Jalisco	1936	22,20
6. Cerro de Garnica	Michoacán	1936	96
7. Los Mármoles	Hidalgo	1936	23,15
8. Cumbres de Ajusco	Federal District	1936	92
9. Gogorrón	San Luis Potosí	1936	25,00
10. El Potosí	San Luis Potosí	1936	2,00
11. Insurgente Miguel Hidalgo y Castilla	Federal District and México	1936	1,75
12. Lagunas de Zempoala	México and Morelos	1936	4,66
13. Pico de Orizaba	Puebla and Veracruz	1937	19,75
14. El Tepeyac	Federal District	1937	30
15. El Tepozteco	Morelos	1937	24,00
16. Zoquiapan y Anexas	México	1937	19,41
17. Cofre de Perote	Veracruz	1937	11,70
18. Lagunas de Chacahua	Oaxaca	1937	14,18
19. Molino de Flores de Netzahualcóyotl	México	1937	5
20. Benito Juárez	Oaxaca	1937	2,73
21. Cañón del Río Blanco	Veracruz	1938	55,69
22. Los Remedios	México	1938	40
23. Cerro de la Estrella	Federal District	1938	1,10
24. El Sabinal	Nuevo León	1938	
25. La Malinche o Matlalcueyatl	Puebla and Tlaxcala	1938	45,71
26. Insurgente José María Morelos y Pavón	Michoacán	1939	1,81
27. Sacromonte	México	1939	4
28. Cumbres de Monterrey	Nuevo León	1939	246,50
29. Cumbres de Majalca	Chihuahua	1939	4,77
30. Balneario de los Novillos	Coahuila	1940	4
31. Pico de Tancitaro	Michoacán	1940	29,31

Table One.
Continued

Park	Location	Date Established	Hectares
32. Bosencheve	México and Michoacán	1940	15,000
33. Lago de Camécuaro	Michoacán	1940	9
34. Desierto del Carmen	México	1942	529
35. Sierra de San Pedro Mártir	Baja California Norte	1947	66,000
36. Rayón	México and Michoacán	1952	34
37. Lagunas de Montebello	Chiapas	1959	6,022
38. Constitución de 1857	Baja California Norte	1962	5,000
39. El Veladero	Guerrero	1980	3,160
40. Cañón del Sumidero	Chiapas	1980	21,789
41. Isla Isabel	Nayarit	1980	194
42. Cascada de Basaseachic	Chihuahua	1981	5,802
43. Tulum	Quintana Roo	1981	664
44. Tula	Hidalgo	1981	99
45. Palenque	Chiapas	1981	1,771
46. El Cimatario	Querétaro	1982	2,447
47. Dzilbilchaltún	Yucatán	1987	539
			768,647

This list does not include the creation of national parks whose designation was later withdrawn. Areas are in hectares; a hectare is 10,000 square meters or 2.47 acres.

value. Because of the importance he attached to forest ecosystems, Quevedo created a national park system whose centerpiece was the high coniferous forests of the central plateau. Quevedo defended this course by arguing that Mexico's highland forests constituted the most scenic, the most accessible, and the most ecologically valuable domain within the country.[40]

As was the case in the United States, Mexican conservationists attempted to create a clientele that would support the national parks. Articles on the national parks in *Protección a la Naturaleza* were accompanied by photographs showing crammed parking lots, happy picnickers by mountain lakes, and relaxed hikers strolling along forest trails. The government was eager to verify the popularity of Mexico's national parks and to entice others to visit them.

Conservationists emphasized the therapeutic value of Mexico's na-

Mexican tourists enjoying outdoor recreation and the natural beauty of La-gunas de Zempoala National Park. Departamento Autónomo de Publicidad y Propaganda.

tional parks. Wild areas provided a perfect escape from the constant noises and pressures of the city. Urban dwellers could go to national parks to relax and delight in the beauty of nature.[41] Quevedo emphasized that people living in rural areas could also benefit from the existence of national parks. He established outdoor camps with potable water so that the peasants who worked so hard in the countryside could enjoy their natural surroundings through recreational outings.[42] Quevedo sought to introduce foreigners as well as Mexicans to the country's natural wonders. Quevedo touted the country's cold, temperate, and tropical forests as containing the most diverse flora in the world. Moreover, their location among towering mountains represented "a marvel of nature not present in other nations." Quevedo argued that Mexico should conserve its forests at all costs for the people's enjoyment and especially for tourists who said that they came to Mexico for its climate, which was moderated by its woodlands, and not for its cities, which had lost their colonial character. More would undoubtedly come in the future to see its national parks with their magnificent mountains and beautiful forests. Quevedo believed that international tourism would further cooperation between Mexico and other countries.[43] He argued that by creating national parks Mexico had placed itself on the level of the most civilized countries.[44]

International cooperation of a more tangible nature occurred in 1935, when a Mexican delegation headed by Miguel Angel de Quevedo and a U.S. delegation met to discuss the creation of an International Parks Commission.[45] The following year, the International Parks Commission, composed of Mexican and U.S. members, convened to advance the establishment of international parks, wildlife refuges, and forest reserves along the U.S.-Mexican border.[46] Mexico and the United States did create wildlife refuges and forest reserves along the border, but Cárdenas never followed through on the creation of an international park in the region.

The Mexican government faced an extraordinarily difficult task in administering national parks. In contrast to the United States, where national parks were created from lands already in public ownership (or in those cases where the land was privately owned, landholders could be bought out or phased out), Mexico's national parks often included areas not owned by the government. Furthermore, since Mexican law prohibited the buying of communal lands, public officials had to enlist the support of peasants in protecting their resources within national parks. Despite a combination of persuasion and fines, cooperation from the *ejidos* was not always forthcoming.[47]

Unfortunately, during the Cárdenas administration, human use threatened flora and fauna in several national parks. One of the most endangered was Cumbres de Ajusco (1936), located near Mexico City. In 1938, Antonio H. Sosa, an official within the National Parks division, commented that the cutting of wood for paper manufacturing and for domestic uses, cattle grazing, and fires had taken a heavy toll on Ajusco's forests. These activities had not ceased simply because Ajusco had become a national park.[48] As in the past, Mexican conservationists faced the difficult task of trying to convince people living on the margin not to exploit all the resources available to them.

Though receiving less of the department's attention than forest conservation, some advances were made in the area of wildlife conservation during the Cárdenas administration. The game division was headed by Juan Zinzer, a respected wildlife manager and an old friend of Quevedo. Under Zinzer's leadership, the division established wildlife refuges, signed a migratory bird treaty with the United States, and fostered the establishment of hunting groups. Game officials also banned the hunting of overexploited species such as the white-tailed deer, the mule deer, wild turkeys, pheasants, and bighorn sheep and antelope (extending the moratorium originally established by President Obregón) and enforced the prohibition against *armadas*, or shooting batteries.[49] Zinzer was building the basis for an effective wildlife conservation policy in Mexico.

One of the bureau's top priorities was the protection of bird populations in Mexico. With assistance from the army, game officials made great strides in eliminating the use of *armadas* to kill ducks in the Valley of Mexico. According to one estimate from the Mexican game division and the Institute of Biology in Washington, D.C., duck populations had increased by 40 percent in the region since the banning of *armadas* in 1932.[50] The prohibition against *armadas* was easier to enforce than most other wildlife regulations because duck hunting by Mexicans was largely confined to the Valley of Mexico.[51]

In its efforts to protect migratory birds, the game service faced a much more difficult task. A small band of game wardens not only had to patrol a large territory, but they also had to rely on cooperation from the United States. The first step toward receiving such cooperation was achieved in 1936, when the United States and Mexico signed the Treaty for the Protection of Migratory Birds and Game Mammals. The treaty established a four-month hunting season for migratory birds, called upon Mexico and the United States to create wildlife refuges, banned the aerial hunting of birds, proscribed the taking of bird eggs and bird nests, prohibited the transportation or sale of mammals and birds (alive or dead) or their products and parts (except when proceeding with proper authorization from private game farms, when possessing a permit, or when used for scientific purposes, propagation, or for museums), and banned the killing of insectivorous birds except for those that did harm to agriculture.[52] Mexican and U.S. conservationists were hopeful that with the treaty they could now curtail the activities of U.S. hunters, which along with habitat destruction, were threatening the existence of several large mammals and game birds in northern Mexico.

They were to be disappointed. Despite cooperation between U.S. and Mexican officials, the U.S. Fish and Wildlife Service estimated in 1948 that U.S. hunters were killing eight hundred ducks per week in northern Mexico.[53] They had also contributed to the near extinction of the Mexican grizzly bear and the Mexican gray wolf.[54] In spite of all of this, though, the 1936 Treaty for the Protection of Migratory Birds and Game Mammals was an important step toward international cooperation between Mexico and the United States on behalf of wildlife.

U.S. and Mexican game officials met on an annual basis at the North American Wildlife Conference. At these conferences, Zinzer informed the U.S. and Canadian delegates on the status of wildlife in Mexico and on the programs that his government was undertaking to ensure the conservation of wild animals.[55] Zinzer expressed his guarded optimism about the game service's ability to ensure the conservation of wildlife in Mexico. In private conversations with the delegates, Zinzer listened to ideas on how Mexico could improve its game management programs and expressed his government's desire to cooperate effectively with the United States in regulating hunting in the borderlands region.[56] By attending the conferences, Zinzer helped form a professional network between U.S. and Mexican game officials.

The game division's decision to foster the growth of sports hunting clubs was inspired in part by the U.S. experience.[57] Mexican conservationists were aware that many sports hunters had actively promoted conservation in the United States. By contrast, in Mexico only a few hunters, cognizant of the decline in game species, voluntarily supported the government's conservation program.[58] Both subsistence hunters who killed animals for food and commercial hunters who killed animals for profit opposed efforts to control their activities. The Cárdenas administration hoped that by creating hunting clubs it could expand the base of affluent and educated hunters, who understood the necessity of conservation, eventually to the point where anticonservation hunters would become a minority group in Mexico. The Cárdenas administration and succeeding governments had only limited success in this area. Unlike the United States, a strong proconservation hunting lobby never emerged in Mexico, in part because most Mexicans did not have the leisure time nor the money to become sports hunters.

As in the case of forestry, the Cárdenas administration granted special hunting privileges to the poor. For instance, the government granted poor communities in the Valley of Mexico and nearby Lerma five free permits for the commercial hunting of ducks by single shots, gave preference to *campesinos* in northern Mexico when granting permits for the capture and exportation of live quail, and recommended that game officials levy the least severe penalty possible against Indians who violated wildlife regulations.[59] These concessions were in line with Cárdenas's pro-Indian orientation, if not strictly in line with his government's conservation objectives.

In the preamble to the 1940 wildlife law, the Cárdenas administration stated its utilitarian objectives: "One declares in the public interest the conservation, restoration, and propagation of wild animals useful to man and the control of harmful animals." The law itself established tariffs for commercial hunting and for the taking of animal parts, with the critical exception of products utilized by industry. To some extent, the administration did take into account the ecological and aesthetic value of wildlife. For example, government officials codified many of the restrictions that the game division had placed on the hunting of threatened species. They also authorized the establishment of reserves and refuges for animals in danger of extinction. Above all, though, the law reflected the growing strength of utilitarian conservationists in Mexico at the end of the Cárdenas presidency.[60]

During the five years of its existence (from January 1935 to January 1940), the game division faced the enormously difficult task of protecting the country's wildlife. Given its limited personnel, the bureau was at a huge disadvantage vis-à-vis hunters. Just as significant, though, was the fact that Mexico finally had high-level officials who were committed to wildlife conservation. They endeavored with limited success to regulate hunting throughout the republic.

Francisco Rubio Castañeda, head of the fisheries division, tried to convince fishers of the need for sustained yield harvests. He stated his case as follows: "By making a rational and methodical exploitation of fish, there exists no danger of exhaustion but on the contrary, one has ensured from time on end a source of production that provides fishermen a source of income."[61] Castañeda's division established fishing cooperatives to encourage the rational use of fisheries for the benefit of the local populations. As in the case of forest cooperatives, the Cárdenas administration attempted to promote the interests of the small producer over the interests of the large producer.[62] By law, the government could not deny concessions to subsistence fishers.[63] On the other hand, the government could and often did deny concessions to large fishing operations.

The fisheries division sought to conserve fish species by prohibiting fishing during spawning season, by enforcing size limits, and by regulating the types of nets and other technologies that could be used to capture fish.[64] Conservation, though, was only part of the agency's program. Almost overshadowing the division's conservation efforts were its efforts to propagate fish species in Mexican waterways. From Cárdenas on down, a consensus existed among government conservationists that Mexico could make better use of its fisheries. From their perspective, fisheries represented a resource of great potential that if properly exploited could reduce Mexico's dependency on agricultural products. In other words, the pressures to open up marginal lands and forests to agriculture could be reduced if Mexicans ate more fish. In order to develop its fisheries, Mexico sought foreign technical assistance. Castañeda used the United States as a liaison to hire Japanese limnologists (the Mexican government knew that the United States had hired Japanese limnologists to teach courses in their schools).[65] After touring Mexico, these experts suggested that Mexico could increase fish production by introducing exotic species within its waterways. They further advised Mexican biologists that, especially within coastal estuaries, there existed a great potential to expand shrimp and oyster beds.[66] In 1939, Quevedo noted that thanks to Japanese assistance many limnology stations had been established in Mexico and that these stations had sought to resolve the production problem by stocking valuable species in interior waters. Quevedo cautioned, however, that the problem had not been completely resolved. He emphasized that the next government would have to maintain these efforts.[67] For better or for worse, Quevedo's plea was not heeded by subsequent governments. The labors of the fisheries division would stand out as the high-water mark in fish propagation efforts in Mexico for several decades to come.

A substantial portion of the fishery division's efforts to conserve and propagate fish species focused on Lake Pátzcuaro, one of the largest natural lakes in Mexico. More significantly, from a political perspective, it is located in Cárdenas's home state of Michoacán. The saga of the lake was closely tied to Cárdenas's political career. While governor of Michoacán, Cárdenas had permitted the introduction of black bass into the lake, not knowing then that one of the fish's favorite prey was the lake's economically valuable white fish. Shortly after becoming president of Mexico, Cárdenas ordered scientists to eliminate the black bass from the lake.[68] Eventually, Mexican conservationists and the Japanese limnologists convinced Cárdenas that while the black bass had led to a decline in the population of white fish, the principal cause of the species' near demise was overfishing. From them, Cárdenas learned that Indians were using nets whose holes were so small that not even tiny fish could pass through. He promptly responded to their reports by establishing a minimum size for the holes in fishing nets.[69] In addition, Cárdenas created a refuge for the white fish at one end of the lake and directed that reforestation efforts be undertaken in the region to prevent soil erosion from contaminating the lake water.[70] The Japanese limnologists informed Cárdenas that an edible Japanese species could be introduced into the lake without harming the white fish.[71] The Pátzcuaro case exemplifies how science, politics, and the desire to conserve and propagate economically valuable fish species shaped Mexico's fishery policies during the Cárdenas era.

Quevedo ceded the conservation of marine fisheries to the Ministry of the Navy, reasoning that his department had neither the human power nor the ships to patrol Mexico's coastal waters.[72] The Ministry of the Navy itself was handicapped in its efforts to protect Mexico's marine life by the absence of an international fishing agreement. In 1925, Mexican and U.S. governments had agreed to the establishment of a joint commission that would set fishing seasons and determine which types of fishing technologies could be used, but Mexico abrogated the convention in 1927 because of conflicts over fishing rights (particularly the U.S. refusal to pay an export tax at the rate set by the Mexican government). In 1931, Mexican and U.S. officials agreed to reestablish the international fisheries commission to preserve marine fish, shellfish, sea turtles, and sea mammals off the Pacific coast of Mexico; many species, the negotiators noted, were in "grave danger of extermination or undue depletion." Yet, once again, the accord collapsed because of economic disagreements.[73] By the mid-1930s, only a powerless fisheries commission composed entirely of U.S. members remained. The fact that the Ministry of the Navy was not disposed to an effective vigilance over marine waters and did not possess an adequate technical corps to ensure the conservation of marine life made a bad situation worse.[74] Hence in 1935, U.S. fishers were taking more than twice as many fish in Mexican coastal waters as were Mexicans (16,865 tons versus 8,388 tons).[75] And the United States was only one of the countries exploiting Mexico's marine fisheries.

While collecting marine specimens in the Sea of Cortez in 1940, the U.S. novelist John Steinbeck observed the plundering of marine life by foreign fishers:

> In addition to the shrimps, these boats kill and waste many hundreds of tons of fish every day, a great deal of which is sorely needed for food. Perhaps the Ministry of Marine [Navy] had not realized at the time that one of the good and strong resources of Mexico was being depleted. If it has not already been done, catch limits should be imposed, and it should not be permitted that the region be so intensely combed. Among other things, the careful study of this area should be undertaken so that its potential could be understood and the catch maintained in balance with the supply. Then there might be shrimp available indefinitely. If this is not done, a very short time will see the end of the fish industry.[76]

Steinbeck, who was a keen observer of both humanity and nature, stated the crux of the matter:

> The Mexican official and the Japanese captain were both good men, but by their association in a project directed honestly or dishonestly by forces behind and above them, they were committing a true crime against nature and against the immediate welfare of Mexico and the eventual welfare of the whole human species.[77]

Several Mexicans shared Steinbeck's insights, but the regulation of marine fisheries proved beyond their control.

During the 1920s and 1930s, the government paid insufficient notice to the loss of soils as well.[78] From 1926 to 1940, district agronomists were charged with teaching farmers good agriculture practices, but this program was underfunded.[79] The Cárdenas administration focused most of its attention on preventing soil erosion in forested regions rather than on rangelands and farmlands. In 1939, Cárdenas did instruct the National Irrigation Commission to survey soils in irrigation districts to assess more accurately the need for erosion control measures. The head of the survey, Lorenzo Patiño, stated that in some parts of the country farmers had to abandon their previously fertile lands because erosion had left only barren subsoils that could barely support plants of any value. Patiño declared that soil erosion was a grave problem requiring immediate government attention.[80] Patiño's warning presaged the emergence of soil conservation as a national issue in Mexico.

In January 1940, Lázaro Cárdenas announced the closure of the Department of Forestry, Fish, and Game. He cited budgetary constraints as the overriding factor in his decision. Quevedo challenged Cárdenas's reasoning, noting that through fines, taxes, and licensing fees, the department was one of the few government agencies that took in more money than it expended.[81] Apparently, Cárdenas's decision to close the department was based on factors other than the budget.

During his presidency, Cárdenas had received many complaints about the manner in which Quevedo had operated the Department of Forestry, Fish, and Game. At the same time, the Ministry of Agriculture kept pressing its claim that it was the proper agency to manage Mexico's forests and wildlife.[82] Among the charges brought by Mexican citizens against Quevedo were that he failed to ensure that his subordinates enforced the law, failed to give proper pay and direction to the forest service, and failed to allow for the proper development of natural resources.[83] Because of his aristocratic background and his "service" to Porfirio Díaz, Quevedo was particularly vulnerable to criticisms that he held antirevolutionary beliefs.

The wildlife conservationist Rodolfo Hernández Corzo provided a retrospective summary of the mood of many peasant and workers groups during the period when he stated that: "Quevedo acted against the agrarian reform and the utilization of the woods for the benefit of the *campesino* and continually disputed the Secretary of Agriculture in the development of the national territory. Quevedo was a social conservative or better yet a reactionary opposed to all institutions and programs of the Revolution."[84]

Some of these criticisms rang true. Quevedo did not favor Cárdenas's land reform program because he believed the peasants would expand their fields at the expense of the forests.[85] He also looked askance upon Cárdenas's decision to weaken forestry and wildlife conservation regulations for the immediate economic benefit of the *campesino*. Cárdenas and Quevedo did not share an identical conservation philosophy. Cárdenas considered the conservation of natural resources to be a component of his larger program of rural development. His allegiance was ultimately with the small producer. Quevedo was sympathetic to the needs of the *campesinos* as well, but he believed that when necessary the protection of natural resources had to take precedence over the claims of resource users. This philosophical difference at times created strains between the two men (such as over how rigidly the use of natural resources by the rural poor should be controlled). It may even have contributed to Cárdenas's decision to transfer responsibility for the conservation of natural resources back to the Ministry of Agriculture.

A number of Mexican conservationists rued Cárdenas's decision to shut down the department. Quevedo was obviously disappointed. He anticipated that the closure of the department would result in the destruction of the forests that he had worked so hard to protect.[86] Juan Zinzer also expressed his disapproval of Cárdenas's decision. A year after the department's closure, Zinzer charged that "the Game Service was undertaken by a group of men who never before had had the slightest contact with wildlife problems, and due to their lack of knowledge and interest, intense persecution of the fauna was permitted."[87] To bear out his point, Zinzer noted that *armadas* (the battery shooting of ducks) had resumed in the central plateau, the drying up of reservoirs for irrigation had contributed to a sharp decline in duck populations, the regulations prohibiting the trading of deer hides had ceased to be enforced, and the hunting of bighorn sheep and antelopes was being pursued without restriction.[88]

Concerned individuals outside government bemoaned Cárdenas's decision as well. In an editorial entitled "Return to Barbarism," forestry society member Carlos González Peña reminded his readers that before the Cárdenas administration, the Ministry of Agriculture had failed to conserve Mexico's natural resources. Cárdenas had to create an autonomous department to accomplish this end. To bolster his point, González Peña compared the records of the two agencies. Before 1934, only two nurseries existed in Mexico; 294 nurseries were established between 1934 and 1940.[89] Before 1935, there were no school nurseries; 4,000 school nurseries were created over the next five years. In 1934, the secretary of the Ministry of Agriculture had directed the planting of only a thousand trees; between 1935 and 1939, 6,337,464 trees were planted in Mexico. Therefore, González Peña rejected the argument that the department had to be closed because it was not meeting its objectives.[90] He then eulogized Quevedo: "The Department of Forestry, Fish, and Game constituted the synthesis and crowning achievement of the great work in defense and propagation of our natural resources that the wise investigator, the noble apostle, the pure spirit, Miguel Angel de Quevedo has undertaken during his life."[91] González Peña predicted that returning control of the nation's forests to the Ministry of Agriculture would result in disaster.

Others applauded Cárdenas's decision to reestablish the ministry's jurisdiction over natural resources. The agronomist Ramón Fernández y Fernández reasoned that forestry, hunting, and fishing were integrally related to agriculture and livestock and therefore were properly the province of the Ministry of Agriculture.[92] Fernández thought that the clearing of forests for agriculture should be permitted under most circumstances and that only when forests were needed for special ends and where reforestation was difficult should limitations be established. He charged Quevedo with establishing limitations that were too rigorous and without reason. He then rejected Quevedo's rationale for forest conservation: "The benefits provided by forests have been exaggerated: they do not produce or increase rainfall nor change climate, they [forests] are simply a part of the wealth of the country due to the utility and value of their product."[93] In effect, Fernández was claiming that forests had only an economic value and that conservation could only be justified on economic grounds. His philosophy would become the predominant one in Mexico after the Cárdenas years. With the push for heavy industrialization that began during the 1940s, conservation ceased to be a concern among most high-level government officials and was promoted by government conservationists mainly on economic grounds. Only a few retained Quevedo's conviction that forests should be protected for their biological value.

The preponderance of scientific evidence supported the claims of utilitarian conservationists that forests had little or no effect on rainfall or climate (at least not on a regional basis). On the other hand, their presumption that forests had no biological value appeared to be contradicted by the facts. Most scientists agreed that forests curbed flooding and maintained springs by keeping soils friable. Observations also indicated that forests impeded erosion by shielding the ground from heavy rains (which also reduced flooding) and by anchoring soils. Trees maintained the humidity of the air through transpiration, while simultaneously reducing evaporation and the baking of soils by deflecting solar radiation. With the possible exception of the effects of forests on rainfall and climate, Quevedo's conservation policy was based on good science.[94]

Quevedo continued his campaign on behalf of Mexico's forests until his death in 1946. In 1941, the government adopted his proposal to make it obligatory for the forest service and local authorities to establish and maintain forest zones around port cities. As he had done many times in the past, Quevedo drew attention to the harmful chain of events that deforestation unleashed. In the case of the port cities, marshes, which were perfect breeding grounds for mosquitoes carrying malaria and yellow fever, were being formed because of the overflowing of drainage ditches clogged by detritus eroded from deforested hillsides. Moreover, deforestation was destroying the beauty and tourist value of Mexico's port cities. Quevedo was incensed by the failure of government officials to protect the newly created forest zones.[95] The port cities episode was a microcosm of what was happening throughout Mexico: the national system of forest reserves and protected forest zones created by Quevedo were becoming meaningless because the government was not enforcing regulations.

Quevedo was further disheartened by the closure of several forestry schools, which he knew would lead to the decline in the size and the effectiveness of the forest service.[96] Quevedo perceived that some of the major accomplishments of the Cárdenas administration were being undone by the succeeding government.

In one of his last public speeches, Quevedo reflected on his life and career.[97] He concluded his speech by urging all people to give part of their lives to protecting the forests, since all generations and all of humanity owed part of their well-being to the tree.[98]

Mexican conservationists during the Cárdenas era did not achieve all that they had wanted to nor had they laid an unalterable foundation for the perpetuation of conservation efforts in Mexico. But in the trees above several Mexican cities and in sustainable development plans could be found the tangible and philosophical legacy of the Cárdenas conservation program.[99] Quevedo's lifework had not been completely in vain.

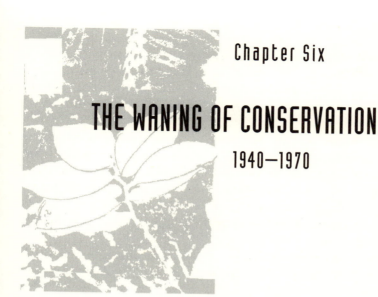

Chapter Six

THE WANING OF CONSERVATION
1940—1970

During the 1940s, Mexico began an era of rapid demographic growth, urbanization, and industrialization that vastly accelerated the deterioration of the environment. Between 1940 and 1970, Mexico's population exploded from twenty million to forty-eight million. During that same period, the number of Mexicans living in urban areas rose from four million to twenty-four million.[1] In concert with these demographic changes, the industrial sector's contribution to the nation's economic output expanded from 25 percent to 34 percent.[2] The excessive concentration of people and factories in Mexico City and in other urban areas culminated in massive pollution problems.

Tragically, as well, the confluence of rapid demographic growth and the government's promotion of industrialization resulted in a relentless exploitation of the nation's soils, waters, forests, and wildlife. Government officials not only channeled natural resources into the industrial sector but also industrialized the use of natural resources themselves. By providing subsidies (mostly to the prosperous farmers of northwestern Mexico) for the use of heavy machinery, inorganic fertilizers, pesticides, and high-yielding plant varieties, by constructing large hydroelectric dams, and by consolidating forest tracts in order to encourage their rational and efficient exploitation, the Mexican government was in effect subjecting natural resources to the same large-scale, mechanized production process that characterized the industrial sector. Through its development programs, the Mexican government was a principal agent in the country's environmental decline. Partly because of apathy and partly because of the tremendous obstacles to the enforcement of conservation laws, government officials also failed to check the environmental damage done by private citizens. As participants and as bystanders, Mexican politicians oversaw the destruction of their nation's natural resources.[3]

By the 1970s, government officials reluctantly began to acknowledge that their policies had contributed to Mexico's environmental crisis. But what of the period between 1940 and 1970 when the commitment of government officials to industrialization was unshakable? What type of conservation policies emerged out of a period in which one of the government's highest priorities was to provide natural resources for industrial development?

Not surprisingly, most high-level government officials placed little emphasis on conservation. Mexican presidents still spoke of the need for conservation, but their actions routinely belied their words. Conservation programs were underfunded and conservation agencies were understaffed. Though the government passed some strong conservation laws during the period, it rarely initiated strong conservation programs. In an era in which the government's main objective was rapid industrialization, the political elite were not willing to strictly enforce laws that either prohibited or restricted the use of natural resources.

Government conservationists themselves held positions consistent with the overall strategy of industrial development. Luis Macías Arellano, head of various conservation agencies in Mexico between 1946 and his death in 1962, spoke for many of his colleagues when he asserted that conservation and industrialization were compatible goals. After acknowledging that conservation was necessary for Mexico's future development, Macías Arellano asserted:

Unquestionably the establishment of new industries will affect natural resources, however, they [new industries] are being oriented in such a manner that they aid rather than hinder conservation. . . . I firmly believe that Mexico in the near future will be working effectively and will be able to solve its conservation problems without detriment to industrial expansion by balancing the supply to meet the needs.[4]

Conservation officials believed that through a wise use of resources industries would be guaranteed an adequate supply of raw materials in perpetuity.

Within government circles, economic utility became the primary rationale for conservation. Conservation officials, such as Luis Macías Arellano, pejoratively labeled as romantics those who advocated the strict protection of forests and wildlife on aesthetic, ethical, or biological grounds. Though restrictions still existed on the exploitation of natural resources, the operative word became "use."

The balance that Cárdenas had maintained between the small-scale development of resources in the traditional sector and the development of "modern" agriculture and industry was largely undone by his successor, Manuel Avila Camacho (1940–1946). He promoted the expansion of agribusinesses to provide the underpinnings for industrialization itself. By producing cash crops, these enterprises would generate export revenues that the government could use to purchase industrial equipment from abroad. He cautioned, however, that Mexico was not in a position to compete on the international market as an industrial country. Instead, Mexico should industrialize to meet its domestic needs so that it could break its cycle of dependency in which it exported cheap raw materials and imported expensive manufactured goods. Avila Camacho concluded, then, that to prosper in a system dominated by foreign economic powers that "Mexico must not seek to be an exclusively industrial country. It must, on the contrary, strive to be a preeminently agricultural country."[5]

Avila Camacho's pronouncement was important, for if Mexico were to be a preeminently agricultural country it would have to conserve its soils. From government reports and from his own travels, he had come to appreciate the extent of soil erosion in Mexico. He recognized that erosion was a serious problem tied to, but not limited to, deforestation. Reforestation was necessary, particularly along watersheds, but more critically, conservation techniques had to be taught to the nation's farmers. In his emphasis on forest conservation, Miguel Angel de Quevedo had addressed only a part of the soil erosion problem. Avila Camacho sought to rectify this situation by expanding the scope of soil conservation efforts in Mexico. He declared that soil erosion represented "a cause of national impoverishment that has been underestimated, but it is now time for corrective work well-established and rationally planned."[6]

Avila Camacho took the first step along these lines when he created the Department of Soil Conservation within the National Irrigation Commission. He implored government soil conservationists to devote particular attention to the prevention of soil erosion in river basins and irrigation districts where siltation was filling in reservoirs and clogging irrigation canals. The department's overall mission was to publicize the problem and to instruct Mexican farmers on means of caring for the land.[7]

To accomplish this mission, the Department of Soil Conservation created soil conservation districts—the same unit that had been created in the United States after the Dust Bowl. In 1943, the Mexican government established the first two soil conservation districts in the central Mexican states of Mexico and Tlaxcala. Despite the fact that Avila Camacho earmarked only nine million pesos for the maintenance of arable lands during his six-year term, the Department of Soil Conservation managed to establish eight more soil conservation districts by the end of his presidency.[8]

In 1946, Avila Camacho obtained the passage of a landmark soil and water conservation law. The legislation was the first of its kind in Mexico and has remained as Mexico's principal document on soil and water conservation. The central premise of the statute is that soil and water conservation are basic to the country's agriculture. The Avila Camacho administration expressly declared that the public interest was served by the prevention of soil erosion and flooding. To accomplish these goals, the government called for the diffusion of conservation techniques to farmers, the establishment of conservation districts, and the development of conservation education for the young, the *campesinos*, and for the entire nation. The Ministry of Agriculture pledged to study and to foster the adoption of the best means for conserving the nation's soils and waters. Among the methods mentioned in the law itself were terraces, dams, dikes, contour ploughing, revegetation with trees and grasses, crop rotation, drainage controls, and adequate irrigation.[9]

Mexican officials wanted to learn more about conservation techniques being applied in the United States. The Soil and Water Conservation Law established a scholarship fund so that agronomy students and scientists within the Department of Soil Conservation could study at U.S. colleges.[10] Not all Mexican agronomists, however, believed that their country should unquestionably adopt U.S. conservation practices. José Navarro Samano, for one, maintained that the peasants had rejected the conservation techniques being promoted by the government because of their unfamiliar nature. He warned that "one should use experiences obtained in similar labors in the United States as only a guide to our work, but never thinking that being good there, it will also be good here."[11] The proper balance between technical borrowing and indigenous innovation was not one that Mexican agronomists could easily agree upon.

In 1946, the new president, Miguel Alemán (1946–1952), transferred responsibility for the protection of the nation's soils to the Ministry of Agriculture. A number of conservationists lost their jobs in the shuffle.[12] Some of those who left the government lent their efforts to civic projects for soil conservation. Avila Camacho himself became an honorary president of Amigos de la Tierra, a private conservation organization dedicated to the dissemination of soil conservation techniques to Mexico's farmers.[13]

Those agronomists who obtained jobs within the Ministry of Agriculture continued to push for the development and enlargement of soil conservation programs, but only a few of their superiors shared their enthusiasm. Furthermore, working funds did not permit an expansion of conservation activities. Instead, the government unveiled a scaled-back program for soil conservation. Agriculture officials encouraged the creation of state commissions for soil and water conservation. The government placed other regions in the hands of local conservation boards.[14]

As yet another cost-saving measure, the Alemán administration created motorized brigades of agronomists. Traveling along Mexico's principal highways, these brigades provided information and demonstrations on soil conservation techniques to farmers living in the vicinity. At each stop, the agronomists tried to establish local conservation boards. Through this shoe-string operation, government agronomists annually visited around thirty towns and villages in each state of the republic. Creative policymaking, however, was no substitute for a strong national program of soil conservation.[15]

The Soil Conservation District of Saltillo provides one example of how the soil conservation programs developed during the Avila Camacho and the Alemán administrations affected local communities. During the mid-1940s, soil conservationists in the Saltillo District (located in the northern Mexican state of Coahuila) had promoted the practices of crop rotation and contour ploughing, the planting of grapevines and walnuts on lands with limy soils, the use of walnut and quince trees as windbreaks, the planting of wheat in the valleys and apple orchards on the sides of the mountains, and the formation of soil conservation propaganda boards.[16] A decade later, Philip Wagner, a U.S. geographer, produced a study of resource use in Parras, Coahuila, which was part of the Saltillo District. Wagner noted how the soils around Parras had been disturbed by plowing, goat raising, woodcutting, the greatly increased use of water, and the continued planting in one place of crops like maize and cotton (as opposed to crop rotation).[17] Wagner was struck by the *campesinos'* ironical fate: "It is in regions like the Parras country, where large numbers of people live close to the bare margins of survival, that resource depletion constitutes a life-and-death matter. Unfortunately, it is in this same kind of poor community that the strongest influences are at work to increase the intensity and rapidity of resource use."[18]

The *campesino*, though, was not the only culpable party in the degradation of the land. As Wagner noted, prosperous farmers often mistreated the land as well: "The large farming enterprises . . . are sometimes more considerate of the soil, but this is one of those lands of opportunity where wealth comes first and wisdom last, and many large operators are frankly and enthusiastically mining their soil."[19] Government soil conservationists had made a modicum of headway in the Parras region:

> Some of the citizens of Parras have founded local organizations to improve farming methods, and have applied improved techniques on their own lands. The Mexican federal government has also taken an interest in some of the problems of the area, most notably those of forestry and water supply, and has set up agencies for scientific study and education. But the resource problem is still extremely grave, and no measures yet instituted are radical enough to prevent continuing deterioration.[20]

At least farmers in the Parras region had received assistance from government soil conservationists. The vast majority of Mexican farmers had never met a soil conservationist. Gonzalo Blanco Macías, a Mexican agronomist working for the Pan American Union, wrote in 1950 about the many Mexican farmers who were ignorant of soil conservation techniques:

> Because Mexico suffers from a scarcity of arable land, even the slopes are used for agricultural purposes, and this necessitates special agricultural techniques such as contour ploughing, terracing, strip cropping, and other means. However, few of the small farmers have heard of these practices and have been accustomed to growing their crops on whatever land was available, sometimes on slopes even up to 45°. In this manner, they have been destroying the one thing that made their existence possible.[21]

Government rhetoric often identified the protection of the nation's soils as a pressing necessity. In 1955, President Adolfo Ruiz Cortines affirmed that soil erosion was the "great enemy of our economic progress."[22] Nevertheless, the amount of public funds directed to the rehabilitation and conservation of soils remained practically nil. After taking into account the 33 percent devaluation in the peso that occurred during Ruiz Cortines's presidency, the Bureau of Soil and Water Conservation's actual budget remained at the same level or actually decreased between 1953 and 1958. Agronomists within the bureau were disheartened by Ruiz Cortines's lack of attention to soil conservation at a time when burgeoning populations were exposing vast tracts of land to erosion.[23]

President Adolfo López Mateos (1958–1964) conformed to the same pattern. During his campaign for the presidency in 1958, López Mateos declared that "soil erosion is one of the most serious problems confronting Mexico, and it is necessary to avoid with much effort each day, the destruction to the patrimony of each generation."[24] Yet in 1960, only eighty soil specialists were enrolled in the National School of Agriculture at Chapingo. The scholarship program (established by the 1946 Soil and Water Conservation Law) that sent Mexican agronomists abroad to study soil and water conservation techniques was basically defunct. According to government estimates, farmers were applying soil conservation techniques on only 300,000 hectares out of 16 million hectares of cultivated lands (the actual figure may have been higher, since the government apparently overlooked those *campesinos* who utilized traditional conservation practices).[25]

During the presidency of Gustavo Díaz Ordaz (1964–1970), agronomists attained the application of soil conservation techniques on an additional 240,000 hectares. Yet this accomplishment was more than offset by the amount of arable land lost to soil erosion, which totaled nearly a million hectares during Díaz Ordaz's presidency. At the beginning of Díaz Ordaz's administration, only 1.1 percent of the Ministry of Agriculture's budget was being devoted to soil and water conservation. By the end of Díaz Ordaz's presidency, this figure had slightly more than doubled to 2.3 percent, a statistical change that gave little comfort to soil and water conservationists.[26] Government rhetoric on the necessity of soil conservation may have been sincere, but it had not been backed up by substantial financial resources or human power. Government officials decried soil erosion as a national tragedy but were not willing to make the prevention of soil erosion a national priority.

As during the past, the government was partly responsible for the *campesinos'* exploitation of natural resources because it forced the peasantry to enter into a market economy for the benefit of an economic elite. This time, the state promoted the interests of industrialists at the expense of the peasant. Specifically, the government instituted agricultural price controls to maintain low industrial wages and urban peace and raised tariff barriers to protect domestic industries from foreign competition. As a result of these policies, many *campesinos* had to produce more food for sale to earn the income needed to purchase various consumer goods and farm inputs (others entered into the urban labor force, which drove industrial wages down even further). Along with rural population growth and the take of moneylenders and middlemen, the government's development program exacerbated the problems of deforestation and soil erosion by forcing peasants to open up marginal lands to production. As a final repudiation of the subsistence economy, the government allocated most of its agricultural aid to wealthy landowners rather than to *campesinos*.[27]

As might be expected, then, Avila Camacho's most lasting stamp on Mexican agriculture was not in the area of soil conservation but in the area of agricultural "modernization." In a momentous agreement in 1943, Avila Camacho approved a Rockefeller Foundation program to improve wheat and corn varieties, control pests destructive to plants, and increase soil productivity. Avila Camacho's secretary of agriculture, Marte Gómez, added his endorsement to the Rockefeller Foundation's program, stating that it would "undoubtedly be favorable to the development of agriculture in Mexico."[28] Though members of the Avila Camacho administration may not have been aware of all the details of the foundation's program, they along with many Mexican scientists were eager to increase agricultural production by whatever means possible.[29]

The Rockefeller Foundation's approach to agricultural production, with its reliance on plant breeding, soon became an integral part of agricultural research and education in Mexico. In 1961, the Mexican government took over full operation of the foundation's program. In practice, the Green Revolution, as the Rockefeller Foundation's program was called, required heavy machinery, extensive irrigation, inorganic fertilizers, and pesticides to ensure the success of the new hybrids.

The cornerstone of the Green Revolution was the development of dwarf varieties of grains that could assimilate large quantities of chemical fertilizers without toppling over. Farmers heavily irrigated their fields so that plants could absorb even greater doses of the artificial nutrients. They also applied pesticides to control the insects, fungi, and weeds that flourished in the wet microenvironment and to combat the plant-specific pests that threatened Green Revolution monocultures (in some

Table Two.
Newly Irrigated Lands in Mexico, 1926–1955

Years	Hectares Newly under Irrigation	Average per Year
1926–1946	816,224	38,868
1947–1952	565,512	94,252
1953–1955	576,967	192,322

cases, plant geneticists developed grains resistant to various diseases, but because of mutations the pests were often able to attack the plants anew. Over time, insects and other plagues developed resistance to pesticides as well). The new technologies served their function in terms of increasing yields, but they produced consequences that extended beyond the realm of agriculture. The Green Revolution resulted in pesticide poisonings, the runoff of inorganic fertilizers into streams and rivers, and the loss of soil fertility and soil moisture (because of the application of inorganic fertilizers), thus, harming both people and the natural world.[30]

Mexico sought to modernize farming techniques without considering the impacts of modern agriculture upon the environment. Furthermore, the Ministry of Agriculture regarded increasing agricultural productivity to be a more important task than conservation, despite the fact that crop yields ultimately depended on an adequate layer of topsoil. The promise of greater and greater production through modern science may have in fact eased the government's anxiety over the accelerated pace of soil erosion within the country. Similarly, many planners felt that the delivery of inexpensive water to farmers through irrigation projects mitigated the need for water and soil conservation measures. From their vantage point, water could be delivered to areas where it was scarce, and new lands could be opened up to cultivation to offset those lost to soil erosion.

As the figures in Table 2 indicate, there was a sharp increase in the acreage brought under irrigation during the 1940s and 1950s.[31] Most of the irrigation projects built during the period were directed toward the prosperous agricultural estates of northwestern Mexico.[32]

Not all government officials approved of the stress being placed on the expansion of irrigation projects. Gonzalo Andrade Alcocer, a scientific investigator for the Mexican Soil and Water Conservation Service during the Alemán administration, warned that the construction of irrigation projects was not a panacea for Mexico's agricultural problems. He noted that in many areas wind and water erosion had left only a thin layer of topsoil. Andrade Alcocer urged Mexicans to embark on a huge conservation program to ensure the people a future food supply.[33] Gonzalo Blanco Macías shared his colleague's belief in the importance of conservation. Blanco Macías insisted that Mexico had to maintain a balanced equilibrium between agriculture and industry. He believed that the ability to support industry depended on a prosperous rural sector and that a prosperous rural sector was impossible without soil and water conservation.[34]

U.S. conservationist William Vogt, who headed the conservation section in the Pan American Union's Division of Agricultural Cooperation, sounded the same theme at the Second Congress on the Mexican Social Sciences held in Mexico City in 1945. Vogt reasoned that the lands suitable to irrigation could be irrigated any time in the future, but the land that washed away and disappeared each rainy season could not wait. Mexico's future was dim if its people continued to destroy the productivity of the land for short-term economic gain.[35]

In retort to Vogt, Adolfo Orive Alba, director of the National Irrigation Commission, claimed that the extensive irrigation works undertaken by the Mexican government would actually reduce soil erosion in the country because many peasants would migrate to the new agricultural zones rather than continue their exploitation of marginal lands.[36] Orive Alba's vision was naive, however, because the large irrigation projects built in northern Mexico were never intended to benefit the *campesino.*

On a more basic level, Orive Alba disagreed with his colleagues over the importance of agriculture for Mexico's posterity. As Alemán's secretary of water resources, Orive Alba maintained that before any water was used for irrigation, it should be used to generate electricity. He reasoned that because of its topography and lack of rainfall, Mexico could never become a great agricultural country. Therefore, Mexico should direct its efforts toward industrialization, and one of the keys to industrialization was the development of cheap hydroelectric power.[37]

Orive Alba's top priority was the construction of dams in humid areas to control floods and generate hydroelectric power. In 1947, he appointed a commission to study the potential for hydroelectric power development in the Papaloapan River basin (located in the tropical regions of Oaxaca, Puebla, and Veracruz). Soon, engineers were constructing dams in the basin. The Papaloapan project began to be referred to as the tropical TVA (Tennessee Valley Authority) because it entailed the large-scale, multipurpose development of a river basin.[38]

Another similarity between the Tennessee Valley Authority and Alemán's dam projects was the treatment of watersheds as a unit. Both Franklin Roosevelt and Miguel Alemán created legal protection for forests along watersheds that fed storage reservoirs and directed reforestation efforts along watersheds whose ground cover had already been disturbed.[39] They undertook these steps to reduce the buildup of silt behind dams. In both Mexico and the United States, forest conservation was an important part of water resource development. Orive Alba argued that the multipurpose use of water was in itself a conservation measure. As others noted, though, dams do not save water but channel it for human use. In fact, more water evaporates from reservoirs than from free-flowing rivers because of the increased surface area, and therefore dams are more properly an aspect of water resource development than of water conservation.

From the perspective of Mexican water officials, however, any water that was not put to productive use was wasted. José Hernández Terán, secretary of water resources during the Díaz Ordaz administration, aptly defined the agency's mission as fostering the "rational distribution of water in order that it be used where the highest economic and human benefit may be obtained."[40] The ministry's principal objectives were to conduct large volumes of water to areas where it was most needed and to reduce its drainage to the sea. Water officials acknowledged that some conservation measures were also needed, such as the lining of canals, the collection of rainwater, and the careful reuse of wastewaters, so as to avoid the contamination of streams and groundwater. In addition, they sought to restore lands that had become saline because of poor drainage practices (salinization is caused by the evaporation of irrigation water that has picked up salts from the soils).[41] These initiatives, however, received much less attention from the Ministry of Water Resources than the construction of dams and irrigation projects.

Forestry policies in the post-Cárdenas era were yet another reflection of the shifting attitudes toward resource conservation and resource use. Though acknowledging the biological value of the nation's forests, the Avila Camacho administration stressed the importance of developing Mexico's forest resources wisely and efficiently for the advancement of industry. In a speech given in 1941, President Avila Camacho indicated that his interest in forest conservation was largely economic in nature:

> The government has appealed for conservation to prevent their [the forests] wasteful destruction by excessive felling of trees and fires which ravage our already insufficient timber reserves. The destruction of forests has an unfavorable effect on weather and rainfall, thus contributing to higher prices on important industrial raw materials, and causes the rapid destruction, by erosion, of agricultural soils built up by Nature in thousands of years.[42]

The administration's emphasis on forest conservation as a complement to economic development is even more apparent in a 1942 Arbor Day speech given by Fernando Quintana, head of the Bureau of Forestry and Hunting:

> Mexico will find itself in an advantageous position if it utilizes its forest resources rationally, promoting the establishment of forest industries which benefit the country, by means of the use of conifers in temperate zones and of priceless species which until today, in large part have been subject to exploitation with great harm to the national economy.[43]

During the 1940s, Mexican officials began to view forests as storehouses of raw materials critical for the development of an industrial economy (such as gums and resins). The Allies' demand for wood during World War II made Mexican officials keenly aware of the potential value of their forests.[44]

In its quest to ensure an adequate supply of forest products for industry, mining, pulp manufacturing, transportation, construction, and war materials, the Avila Camacho administration created an important new entity, the industrial forest exploitation unit.[45] The government placed small contiguous properties under a single management plan. Officials believed that such a consolidation would eliminate the irrational development of forests that had resulted from land reforms (under which forests had been divided into small parcels). By schooling the owners of industrial forest exploitation units on the principles of sustained yield and by requiring timber companies to engage in reforestation, the government was confident that it could guarantee industries a steady flow of products. Since forestry officials could veto any sales agreement between forest owners and timber companies, theoretically they could block forestry operations by companies that had bad track records in terms of conservation. In fact, though, no such careful screening was done and consequently deforestation continued at a rapid pace.[46]

Miguel Alemán adopted a more cautious tone in regard to forest exploitation. Alemán's "conviction" was that forest areas should be cleared for farm use or for industrial use only when this constituted the best use of the land. He established forest reserves and protected forest zones in river basins to safeguard the irrigation and hydroelectric power systems and placed a total ban on the use of woodlands in the states of Mexico, Querétaro, Morelos, and the Federal District of Mexico to ensure their recuperation.[47]

In 1948, Alemán approved a forestry law that on paper embodied much of the spirit of the Cárdenas years. Herein, the federal executive stated that in addition to ensuring a perpetual source of forest products, a forest cover was necessary to avoid soil erosion, facilitate the recuperation of already eroded lands, aid the formation of fertile soils where they no longer existed, prevent floods and aid water storage, conserve and beautify tourist centers, preserve and improve climatic conditions throughout the republic (by dampening winds and moderating the climate), convert unhealthy marshes and swamps into lands that people could use, protect cities against dust storms, beautify urban centers and provide a place of rest for its tired inhabitants, and preserve wildlife habitats.

The law required companies operating in industrial forest exploitation units to plant ten trees for every cubic meter that they cut, called for the maintenance of tree nurseries, and authorized lumbering only when it did not harm the productive capacity of the forests.[48] Evidently, Alemán wanted to protect the nation's forest wealth.

In a 1951 Arbor Day speech, Alemán evoked the words of Miguel Angel de Quevedo: "Trees are a source of wealth in wood and in fruit, they conserve the land and give home to animals, they moderate climate, enrich the springs which feed rivers, protect against the wind, give shade, and beautify the countryside."[49] Alemán boasted that his government had strengthened its efforts to protect the nation's forest wealth by adopting the most energetic measures permitted by the law, but that conservation required the cooperation of everyone. In particular, he called upon the citizens of Mexico to plant trees on each piece of land and to respect the limits that had been set on the use of woodlands. Alemán promised that his administration would proceed with its efforts to enforce sanctions against the undue exploitation of forests, establish tree nurseries, distribute seeds and seedlings, and reforest the country. He also expressed his determination to stop the exportation of unprocessed timber and to eliminate the use of charcoal. Alemán emphasized that all Mexicans had a solemn responsibility to protect the nation's forests, whose value to agriculture, the economy, and society was incalculable.[50]

Alemán implicitly acknowledged in his Arbor Day speech that many of the administration's goals had not been met. The 1948 forestry law had not been rigorously enforced. The destruction of forests in river basins proceeded unchecked.[51] The campaign to end the use of charcoal had produced disappointing results.[52] In 1950, there were only twelve forestry students in Mexico.[53] Thus, the country lacked a sufficient technical corps to maintain vigilance over its forests.

The Alemán forestry program did produce some qualified successes. In 1947, Mexican tree nurseries were producing twenty-five million trees, many of which were subsequently planted throughout the country.[54] Unfortunately, however, Mexican officials did not adequately care for many of the forest plantations (this was not a failure confined to the Alemán administration).[55] The government successfully banned the cutting of Christmas trees in 1951, but this removed only a minor threat to Mexico's forests.[56] The Alemán administration never succeeded in establishing an effective program of forest conservation.

Like the Cárdenas administration, the Alemán administration faced a daunting task in attempting to protect the nation's forests. The Alemán government, though, appeared to lack a certain amount of will as well when it came to the enforcement of forestry regulations. Conservation officials, convinced that industrial development and conservation were compatible goals, failed to properly assess the pressures that industrial expansion were placing upon the nation's forests. Luis Macías Arellano, head of the Bureau of Forestry and Hunting, spoke for the Alemán administration when he said that Mexico was less concerned with the taxonomic classification of trees than it was in learning what forest products could be obtained from trees.[57] The Alemán administration embraced some of the elements of the Cárdenas conservation program, but like other governments in the post-Cárdenas era its principal goal was the expansion of the forest industry.

The government of Adolfo Ruiz Cortines (1952–1958) retained many of the restrictive forestry policies of Miguel Alemán but, at the same time, offered special concessions (principally to railroad companies)

Message from a government poster around 1960: "To plant a tree is to make the country." Secretaría de Agricultura y Ganadería, Subsecretaría Forestal y de la Fauna.

that had resulted in the despoliation of large tracts of forests.[58] Ruiz Cortines's public works programs coincided with a forestry campaign aimed at dissuading peasants from their wasteful and irrational use of forests. In a publication entitled *Campesino: Defend Your Forests!*, government officials warned the peasants that unless they protected their forest resources the accomplishments of the government's public works programs—the roads, railroads, bridges, and hydroelectric plants—would be for naught.[59] The irony, of course, was that these projects themselves had contributed to the destruction of Mexico's forests. By chastising peasants for their wasteful use of forest resources needed by the government, Ruiz Cortines was sounding a familiar complaint in Mexican history.

The administration of Adolfo López Mateos (1958–1964) set forth the most comprehensive forestry program and the most well-defined forestry goals since the Cárdenas era. When López Mateos instructed his undersecretary of forestry and fauna, Enrique Beltrán, to develop a forestry policy "which was neither romantic nor demagogic, but rational and scientific," Beltrán enthusiastically complied.[60] Beltrán believed that past administrations had committed a grave error by placing severe restrictions on forest use:

> Another negative aspect of the period [the Alemán presidency] was the notorious restrictions on forest activities, believing foolishly, as since the beginning of this century unfortunately with the possibly well-intentioned but unjustified campaigns of the engineer Miguel Angel de Quevedo, that the best means of conserving forests is to avoid using them.[61]

Beltrán believed that such an approach to forest conservation was wrong for several reasons: the government denied the *campesinos* a valuable source of income; the government itself lost a valuable source of revenue; and the government could not enforce the restrictions. According to Beltrán's gospel, the use of forests not only benefited the peasantry and the nation, it also encouraged conservation because people would want to maintain a resource that had become economically valuable.[62] In the introduction to a review of his agency's activities, Beltrán provided a succinct statement of his conservation philosophy:[63]

1. A clear recognition that forests at the same time that they protect other resources of enormous value are also a natural resource that can benefit the national economy.

2. An explicit recognition that the proper exploitation of forests results not in their destruction but, on the contrary, contributes to their conservation.

3. The consequent necessity of abandoning the exclusively restrictive and punitive approach that laws and authorities have taken toward the forestry industry, substituting for it a policy of promotion.

4. The promotion of large forest exploitation units because, by reason of the quantity of their investments, the owners of such units are more interested in the care of the forests.

5. The necessity of spurring the industrialization of forest products to the greatest extent possible, so much as to ensure a more complete use of wood as to increase its value and to generate employment.

6. The necessity of giving a truly scientific base for the management of forests.

7. The necessity of focusing on the socioeconomic aspect of the problem, particularly the needs of small proprietors and *ejidatorios* in forest zones, who traditionally have received the least use of forests.

Beltrán had translated these "imperatives" into several policies: he allowed small proprietors and *ejidatorios* to sell their forest products to any individual or company, permitted government-peasant timber operations in national parks, eliminated many of the absolute restrictions on forest use, conducted an inventory of the nation's forests, tested the effectiveness of both chemicals and natural predators in combating forest pests and plagues, and experimented with different plants in the revegetation of semiarid and arid regions.[64] Beltrán's defenders argued that only the lack of strong government backing had limited the successful implementation of his programs and the validation of his conservation philosophy.[65]

The Díaz Ordaz administration continued to focus on the use of the nation's forests. Díaz Ordaz told delegates at the Third National Forestry Convention that he wished to avoid both the extreme exploitation of forests and their extreme conservation.[66] The delegates themselves discussed the incentives, technologies, and management techniques that could be used more effectively to exploit the nation's forest resources. Absent from the presentations was a recognition of the biological value of forests.[67]

Throughout his tenure, Díaz Ordaz's undersecretary of the Bureau of Forestry and Fauna, Noé Palomares, stressed the importance of providing adequate forest resources to industry. According to Palomares, Mexico could no longer afford to squander its forest wealth through misplaced conservation efforts: "If we do not adopt silviculture practices [such as sustained yield forestry], then we will lose harvests. . . . Preserving this [forest] wealth means exposing it to many risks, leaving without use millions of mature trees which ought to be incorporated into the national economy."[68] He deferred to other members of the Ministry of Agriculture and Livestock a discussion of the role played by forests in maintaining soils and water supplies.[69] Most government conservationists advocated forest conservation on strictly utilitarian grounds.

Though forest conservation received greater or lesser attention by the various administrations that followed Cárdenas's, the one constant was the emphasis on the economic value of Mexico's forests. Yet even a narrowly economic justification for forest conservation did not find much favor among high-level government officials. Most Mexican politicians failed to appreciate the diverse benefits provided by their nation's forests.

Mexico's forests provided invaluable products for industry, and its soils and water were essential for agriculture. This reality helped spur some conservation activities. In contrast, Mexico's wild lands and wildlife rarely seemed to have an economic value that would justify their conservation; in fact, they appeared to be an obstacle to Mexico's agricultural and industrial expansion. Not surprisingly, the protection of wilderness and wildlife received scant attention between 1940 and 1970.

Mexico was a signatory to the 1940 Convention on Nature Protection and Wild Life Preservation in the Western Hemisphere.[70] Mexico thereby pledged to ensure the survival of its native flora and fauna and to preserve lands of great scenic beauty by establishing national parks and other protected areas.[71]

Mexican presidents, though, created only seven national parks between 1940 and 1970.[72] In 1944, in accordance with the government's industrial policies, the Mexican Congress altered the boundaries of Colima National Park to exclude nearly all of the forested areas so as to allow their exploitation by a paper factory.[73] Other national parks, such as Cumbres de Monterrey, underwent a de facto reduction in size because of urban expansion.[74] In still others, livestock, farmers, loggers, and hunters decimated the natural flora and fauna. In fact, most of Mexico's national parks suffered some degree of damage.[75]

Mexican policymakers did not provide conservation agencies with enough human power to enforce land use restrictions in nature reserves.[76] Enrique Beltrán, for one, argued that Mexico could not afford to create new national parks, since it could not effectively administer the ones it already had.[77] He eliminated areas that were not true national parks and redrew boundaries to exclude lands converted to other uses. He also sought the expropriation of private lands within national parks (a goal that he could not attain).[78] Sadly, Beltrán's efforts marked the zenith in national park policy between 1940 and 1970.

Mexico's wildlife populations also suffered from a lack of legal protection, notwithstanding the passage of a new game law in 1952 at the end of the Alemán administration. By this statute, game officials proscribed the use of poisons to kill animals, prohibited commercial hunting and the exportation of animal parts, and restricted the granting of hunting permits to hunting clubs and associations only. In addition, they banned hunting in all national parks (previously hunting had been allowed in some parks) and reiterated the need to create wildlife refuges, especially for the protection of endangered species.[79] However, because Mexico lacked an overall management plan and because the government allocated neither the funds nor the human power necessary to enforce the law, the persecution of Mexican wildlife continued unabated.[80]

In some cases, the Mexican government itself played a critical role in the near demise of a species. Beginning in 1950, the Pan American Union in conjunction with the U.S. Fish and Wildlife Service assisted Mexican livestock associations and the government in the development of predator control programs. In 1954, Mexican and U.S. officials began to lace dead carcasses with 1080, a highly toxic poison, in order to kill coyotes and wolves (in violation of the 1952 law).[81] Even after the program was discontinued, individual ranchers continued to use 1080. In 1981, the U.S. Fish and Wildlife Service estimated that only thirty gray wolves remained in northern Mexico.[82]

In addition to hunting and predator control programs, population pressures, grazing, and agricultural expansion were threatening Mexican wildlife.[83] According to Luis Macías Arellano, nature sometimes had to be sacrificed for development to occur. For instance, he argued that lakes and swamps had to be drained so that agricultural production could be increased, or in other words, these habitats had to be destroyed so that Mexico could feed its burgeoning population. On the other side of the ledger, Macías Arellano maintained that irrigation projects and dams in northern Mexico had created new habitats for waterfowl and other birds.[84]

Macías Arellano stated his conviction that Mexico was less interested in wildlife from a purely aesthetic perspective than it was in harvesting game populations. As he put it: "The modern ideology on which the technical administration of wildlife must rest cannot longer be based on a romantic feeling for conservation, but must be directed toward increased production, setting the rules in accordance with the potential reproduction rate of the species."[85] Enrique Beltrán believed in this philosophy as well. He promoted the establishment of hunting clubs, reasoning that sports hunters best appreciated the need for conservation. Additionally, he established an experimental hunting season for bighorn sheep (one part of his goal was to remove absolute restrictions on game hunting), created experimental stations and laboratories, part of whose mandate was to propagate game species, and conducted scientific studies of wildlife habitats and migratory bird patterns in order to develop better game management plans.[86]

Mexican wildlife officials, such as Beltrán and Macías Arellano, wanted to manage game populations scientifically for the enjoyment of conservation-minded sports hunters. Also, the government profited from this arrangement in the form of licensing fees that could be used to fund conservation programs. The tenet of government wildlife conservationists was that Mexico could financially benefit from the recreational hunting of its game populations while still ensuring a future supply of the same.

Rodolfo Hernández Corzo, who served as director of the Bureau of Wildlife from 1962 to 1970, thought that outdoor recreation could potentially become a big business in Mexico. Fishing and hunting expeditions would create jobs for guides, generate tourist dollars (from both Mexicans and foreigners), and stimulate the growth of the sports equipment industry in Mexico. Thus, the conservation of wildlife was merited on monetary grounds.[87]

In addition to its economic value, Hernández Corzo emphasized the physical and health benefits that recreation provided. For instance, he observed that the value of fishing in terms of health, rest, recuperation, liberation from tensions, and the calming of the spirit was inestimable. In a position that was considered heretical by members of Mexico's development agencies, Hernández Corzo concluded that the use of water for recreational activities, such as fishing, might be more valuable economically and socially than its use for irrigation and power.[88]

He also insisted that the government consider the effects of water development on flora and fauna and unsuccessfully pleaded with water officials not to build a large dam on the Grijalva River (in southeastern Mexico) because it would destroy thousands of hectares of priceless tropical trees and irreplaceable wildlife.[89] He regarded the preservation of wild animals to be a moral issue as well as an economic one: "It is the duty of a culture to conserve animals so that they do not disappear, because the extinction of wildlife before the progress of the human species, as the irreversible act that it is, is an unpardonable deed."[90]

Hernández Corzo's concern for endangered species did not translate into strict regulations on the use of wildlife. Like his predecessor, Luis Macías Arellano, and his one-time superior, Enrique Beltrán, Hernández Corzo was a staunch advocate of wildlife management.[91] In fact, he offered an even more ambitious plan for the "harvesting" of wild animals than did his peers. His goal was the utilization of all fauna rather than just game species.[92] Hernández Corzo noted that, while much of the country was unsuited for agriculture or cattle grazing, it did contain abundant wildlife (including fisheries). According to the conservationist, Mexico had to exploit these resources to ensure its prosperity.[93] Believing that, in the final analysis, human beings were the central interest and not nature itself, Hernández Corzo maintained that it was necessary to seek "the best habitat for man, without the destruction or degradation of nature, but also without conservation that was either dogmatic or obsessive."[94] Like his colleagues, Hernández Corzo was optimistic that Mexico could extensively develop its resources without depleting them.

Progress toward conservation had been made during the Cárdenas presidency because of the existence of a strong conservation agency and presidential support. Between 1940 and 1970, the conjunction of these two factors did not occur again, and consequently Mexico's natural resources were not adequately protected.[95] A few officials struggled to promote conservation, mainly using economic arguments, but in general Mexican governments abandoned conservation altogether, mesmerized by the potential of industrialization and the Green Revolution. A few private individuals and groups were left to carry the banner for conservation.

Chapter Seven

AGAINST THE TIDE

The Conservationists'

Crusade

As government interest in conservation waned, a few individuals dog-
gedly worked for the protection of Mexico's natural resources. They directed their efforts toward making both government officials and the
public aware of the consequences if Mexico continued to exploit its
lands without limits. Mexico's leading conservationists of the post–
World War II era, Enrique Beltrán, Miguel Alvarez del Toro, and Gertrude Duby Blom, tried to make conservation a civic cause that would
incorporate a wide spectrum of Mexican society. Despite their varying
backgrounds, philosophies, and efforts, each shared the conviction that
the conservation of natural resources was the most important task facing the nation.

Generating a concern for the protection of nature has been a more
difficult task in Mexico than in the United States. Admittedly, U.S. conservationists have not always gained immediate acceptance for their
causes. For instance, Aldo Leopold's (1887–1948) call for a land ethic
passed into obscurity until discovered by the environmental movement
of the 1960s.[1] Rachel Carson (1907–1964) was more fortunate in that
her powerful description of the dangers posed by pesticides coincided
with a growing concern about how pollution was affecting human
health.[2] Nevertheless, the major thrust of environmental legislation
would not come until nearly a decade later. Twentieth-century U.S. conservationists, though, have always worked with some level of public and
government support. Their Mexican brethren have not been so fortu-

nate. Both the government's and the people's recognition of the need for environmental action, though it has been increasing in recent years, remains low. Many Mexican politicians and private citizens still view conservation as an unwarranted obstacle to the nation's economic development. Whereas the ideas of Aldo Leopold and Rachel Carson have now reached a mass audience, the ideas of Enrique Beltrán, Miguel Alvarez del Toro, and Gertrude Duby Blom have reached only a small portion of the Mexican public. Yet Beltrán, Alvarez del Toro, and Blom have profoundly influenced the views of many of Mexico's new generation of conservationists and in a smaller, but perhaps no less significant manner, they have changed the way that thousands of Mexicans think about the natural environment.

Enrique Beltrán (b. 1903) first became interested in conservation while a student of biology at the National Autonomous University of Mexico (1922–1926). His teacher, Alfonso Herrera, had distinguished himself as a naturalist in Mexico through his campaign to protect insectivorous birds (1898), his direction of the Bureau of Biological Studies since its inception in 1915 (under Herrera's leadership the bureau created botanical gardens and a zoo in Chapultepec Park), and his role in convincing President Obregón to establish a ten-year moratorium on the hunting of bighorn sheep and pronghorn antelopes (1922).[3] Though his leanings were toward one of Herrera's other interests, protozoology, Beltrán learned about conservation from this professor whom he held in such high regard. Herrera, appreciative of his student's talents and energies, appointed Beltrán to head two marine commissions (in 1923 and 1926), that were established to study and improve the use of Mexico's coastal fisheries. Both of these commissions were short-lived: the first did not survive the armed rebellion of 1923; the second was a victim of budget cuts. Beltrán had his first taste of how scientific research could be adversely affected by political turmoil or by a decision to cut off government funding.[4]

Beltrán continued his research on Mexico's marine fisheries after his graduation in 1926. In 1929, he published the results of his research in an article entitled "Fish in the Gulf of Mexico and the Necessity of Marine Biology Studies in Order to Develop This Wealth." As the title of the article suggests, Beltrán called for the rational development of Mexico's marine resources.[5] In 1931, he received a Guggenheim fellowship to consult oceanographic archives in the United States and to study protozoology at Columbia University. Two years later, Beltrán graduated from Columbia with a doctorate in zoology.[6]

Upon returning to Mexico, Beltrán became the first director of the Instituto Biotécnico (Biotechnical Institute), which was created partly to centralize in one government agency the investigations relating to the conservation of natural resources. At the institute, scientists conducted applied research into soils, flora and fauna, and oceanography.[7]

Beltrán rapidly became disenchanted with the direction that Mexico's new president, Lázaro Cárdenas, gave to the agency. He was particularly irritated by Cárdenas's meddling in the activities of the institute's limnology station at Lake Pátzcuaro. When Cárdenas ordered Beltrán to remove the predatory black bass from the lake, Beltrán balked. In the heated conversation that followed, Beltrán tenaciously argued that it was impossible to eliminate the intrusive fish from the lake.

Ultimately, Cárdenas conceded that the extermination of the black bass was impractical, but he continued to interfere with the research agenda of the limnology station.[8] When Cárdenas turned over operation of the station to the Department of Forestry, Fish, and Game, Beltrán bitterly complained: "The carefully planned program for the limnology station was not achieved because the government substituted for it a white elephant—that had the same name and the same location as the old station but very different direction—which was underfunded and accomplished practically nothing." As Cárdenas prepared to dole out the rest of the functions of the institute to various agencies, a frustrated Beltrán resigned.[9]

Beltrán's disdain for the Department of Forestry, Fish, and Game extended well beyond its operation of the limnology station at Lake Pátzcuaro. He sharply disagreed with Miguel Angel de Quevedo's approach to conservation, contending that his restrictive policies had contributed to the destruction of Mexico's forests. Beltrán later remarked that Quevedo's implementation of romantic conservationism was the worst thing that could have happened to the nation's woodlands. Beltrán had developed an opposing philosophy: the best conservation policy was one that encouraged the wise utilization of natural resources rather than imposing regulations from above. According to Beltrán, laws barring the rational development of forests were foolish not so much because Mexico lacked the resources or personnel to accomplish the task (although this certainly was a problem), but rather that the Mexican nation and the Mexican people would not allow themselves to be deprived of such a valuable economic asset. The failure of Quevedo to stem the tide of deforestation convinced Beltrán that a just conservation policy entailed use.[10]

In fact, Beltrán and Quevedo's philosophies regarding conservation were not poles apart. Quevedo, after all, did not believe in a complete prohibition against timber use, and Beltrán acknowledged that some restrictions on timber use were necessary. Both men, however, were extremely proud and were convinced that their approach to conservation was the right one. Only Beltrán's status as a relatively minor conservation figure within the Cárdenas administration prevented a direct clash with Quevedo, such as that which had occurred between the preservationist John Muir and the utilitarian conservationist Gifford Pinchot in the United States.

Despite his dispute with Cárdenas and his differences with Quevedo, Beltrán continued to serve the administration. As an employee of the Ministry of Education (1935–1938), he sought to integrate conservation into the school curriculum at all levels, using civics, geography, and biology courses as the chief conduits. In 1934, he drafted a textbook for a college course on zoology and oceanography that covered basic ecological notions and stressed that the conservation of natural resources "meant not the lack of utilization, but a permanent use that permitted a sustained supply."[11]

In a 1939 article, Beltrán expressed his view that the use of natural resources had to be based on sound ecological principles. Resources, he argued, had to be viewed in their totality rather than as separate entities, for, after all, forests, soils, water, and wildlife were all interrelated. Moreover, people had to recognize that ecological processes were not confined by national boundaries. Indeed, the misuse of resources in one nation often adversely affected other countries.[12]

Beltrán was angered by the short-sightedness of resource use in Mexico. Mexicans still clung to the age-old belief that their country could become an agricultural paradise. Because of their steadfast insistence that all lands were suitable for agriculture, farmers turned regions that could have been used for hunting, forestry, or grazing into deserts, for after the winds swept across fields of exposed topsoil, areas once covered by marshes, meadows, and forests became rocky wastelands. Mexico's land use policies and traditions were short-sighted because they ignored ecological reality.[13]

In 1939, Beltrán became head of the Department of Protozoology of the Institute of Health and Tropical Diseases, a post he held for thirteen years (1939–1952). During this period, Beltrán's interest in conservation intensified rather than abated. He was struck by the irony that while he was struggling to reduce the incidence of fatal diseases in the Mexican tropics, population growth in the region was undermining the ability of people to survive. Beltrán became convinced that population growth was the root cause of all environmental problems from pollution to the destruction of natural resources.[14]

While head of the Department of Protozoology, Beltrán continued to work on projects related to conservation education. In 1945, he designed a course on the conservation of natural resources for the Escuela Normal Superior, the school that trained Mexico's future teachers. The course emphasized the critical need for resource conservation and environmental education. Specific segments of the class focused on ecology, the means of protecting forests and pasturelands, the rational use of woodlands, the causes of and the remedies for soil erosion, soils adequate and inadequate for agriculture, the conservation of wildlife, the use of freshwater and marine fisheries, the aesthetic value of nature, and population growth. Beltrán's hope was that once Mexico's future teachers had learned the importance of conservation they could train Mexico's future citizens to value the natural world.[15]

During the mid-1940s, Beltrán began to campaign for the creation of a conservation organization to promote the rational development of natural resources. He did not seriously consider establishing such an institute himself, though, until his friend and fellow conservationist Tom Gill persuaded his colleagues at the Charles Lathrop Pack Forestry Foundation (Gill was the group's secretary) to help fund the generally conceived project. On 25 January 1952, the foundation granted Beltrán $100,000 to be used for education, research, and development in the field of conservation, with the stipulation that the money be matched by Mexican sources (which it was). Thus, with the support of the Charles Lathrop Pack Forestry Foundation and from Mexican business and civics groups, Enrique Beltrán began his directorship of the Instituto Mexicano de Recursos Naturales Renovables (the Mexican Institute of Renewable Natural Resources, or IMERNAR).[16]

Beltrán's carefully delineated program for IMERNAR was "to form an inventory of natural resources, to investigate the potential and possibility of sustained development of these resources, to study their maximum possible use without endangering conservation, to study the factors which threaten to diminish or to completely exhaust natural resources, . . . to promote conservation education."[17] This program has not changed over the course of four decades.

The dissemination of information has been a key part of the organization's activities. Between 1952 and 1990, the institute sponsored twenty-eight roundtable conferences in which Mexican conservation-

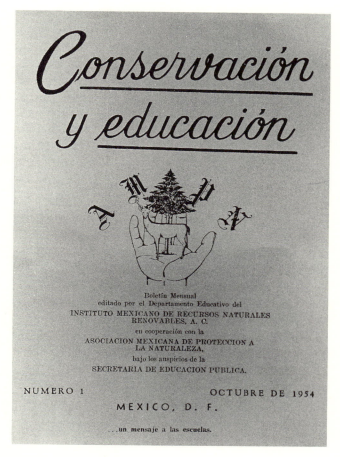

Conservación y educación

Boletín Mensual
editado por el Departamento Educativo del
INSTITUTO MEXICANO DE RECURSOS NATURALES
RENOVABLES, A. C.
en cooperación con la
ASOCIACION MEXICANA DE PROTECCION A
LA NATURALEZA,
bajo los auspicios de la
SECRETARIA DE EDUCACION PUBLICA.

NUMERO 1   OCTUBRE DE 1954
          MEXICO, D. F.
          ...un mensaje a las escuelas.

An early publication of the Mexican Institute of Renewable Natural Resources Courtesy of Enrique Beltrán, Director, Instituto Mexicano de Recursos Naturales Renovables, A.C.

ists gathered to discuss environmental problems and offer recommendations for regions such as the tropics, the arid zones, the southeast, the Valley of Mexico, Chihuahua, Puebla, Chiapas, and Veracruz and on topics such as population growth, rural industries, sports hunting and fishing, water and air pollution, soil conservation, fisheries development, and forestry. IMERNAR has printed fifty-four pamphlets covering a similarly wide range of topics and published a series of bibliographies on natural resources. Beltrán himself has written over a hundred articles and more than a dozen books on conservation issues.[18] The institute's library is the oldest of its kind in Mexico and contains one of the best collections on ecology and conservation in all of Latin America. Many Mexicans, students and nonstudents alike, have benefited from its existence.

When the International Union for the Conservation of Nature awarded Enrique Beltrán its medal in 1966, the presenter offered words of praise that are even more appropriate today: "To Enrique Beltrán, distinguished professor and international scientist, who put aside his personal interests and research to become the leader in resource and nature conservation in Mexico. Through his wisdom, courage, and integrity he has had a major influence not only on national well-being and wildlife protection, but also on conservation thought and practice throughout the Western Hemisphere."[19] Although he trained only a handful of students, Beltrán has affected the perspectives of many of Mexico's younger conservationists through his writings.[20] His ideas on conservation have thus been extremely important.

Beltrán condemned both the exploiters of Mexico's resources and Mexican preservationists. Those who irrationally exploited the nation's forests, he said, revealed a "total ignorance of ecology and a scorn for the human necessities that cannot be satisfied with money." Beltrán observed that forests produced not only diverse economic benefits that were very important, they were also critical from an ecological perspective: producing oxygen, regulating stream flow and absorbing runoff, protecting against the nefarious effects of erosion, and providing an irreplaceable habitat for a rich and varied fauna. Apart from their biological value, the woodlands held an enduring charm. As Beltrán averred "not only the ecologist . . . , but the most elevated of the human spirit can never consider obsolete the unmatched beauty of the forests, nor will it ever become passé the pleasure that one experiences walking under the leafy canopy and enjoying the contemplation of the thousand and one organisms that live there."[21] On the other hand, Beltrán thought that those who intended to protect all of nature from human intervention were naive, since natural resources had to be consumed in the production of clothing, food, shelter, and many of the other necessities of daily life.[22]

Beltrán declared that the conflict between conservationists and preservationists was unfounded, since conservationists favored the rational use of resources to serve all human needs, including the need for aesthetic beauty.[23] Thus, he could hold the position that national parks should be appreciated for the escape that they provided from the noise and antisocial attitudes of the cities while at the same time approving of forest projects (albeit carefully planned) in Mexico's national parks. Mexicans could enjoy the natural beauty of the land, while the country obtained economic benefits from the wise use of its resources.[24]

Beltrán regarded the supposed conflict between tourism and the protection of flora and fauna in national parks to be another red herring. As a biologist, Beltrán expressed his sympathy for the position that national parks should preserve wild areas for scientific studies.[25] Beltrán questioned, though, whether the populace could be convinced to "voluntarily deprive itself of the economic or recreational use of land only to have it serve as a tract for scientific studies . . . whose value the majority of the public does not know or is not capable of evaluating adequately."[26]

At the First World Conference on National Parks held in Seattle in 1962, Beltrán suggested that the conflict between preservation and use could be avoided through a zoning system. For the majority of tourists who disliked inconvenience and were searching for maximum comfort, Beltrán proposed a zone for general relaxation that would contain parking lots, restaurants, hotels, and campgrounds. A second zone would be open to the public, but would contain no roads, hotels, or other "amenities." The third zone would be used exclusively for scientific study and investigation. This zone would be open only to qualified groups and individuals.[27] Beltrán was one of the early contributors to discussions on the zoning of wild areas. A decade later, zoning had become the dominate approach to wilderness protection in the Third World.

Enrique Beltrán concurred with Aldo Leopold that the critical finding of ecology is that people and nature are interdependent.[28] He did not, however, endorse the outcome of Leopold's land ethic: nature has a right to exist separate from the needs of humankind, since human beings are a part of nature and not the owner of it. Rather, he believed that ecology directed people to use resources wisely for their own benefit. Furthermore, he insisted that ecology was a science and not an environmental philosophy. Beltrán pejoratively labeled as "instant ecologists" those who promoted environmental causes without an understanding of ecological science.[29] He charged that cultured and educated people, through their misguided efforts at conservation, were just as responsible for the destruction of Mexico's natural resources as were the ignorant and the greedy. From Beltrán's vantage point, the main defect of the instant ecologists was their inability to understand that the preservation of nature was both unecological and unrealistic. By trying to protect the forests, Beltrán charged, preservationists were preventing their renewal, thus making them ripe for fires and plagues. He also chastised preservationists for failing to understand that without fishing and hunting, wildlife populations would exceed their natural limits.[30]

In his emphasis on the wise use of natural resources, Beltrán was a disciple of Gifford Pinchot. Unlike Pinchot, however, he clearly recognized that forests had an aesthetic and biological value as well as an economic value. Beltrán sought a middle road for resource use in Mexico that rejected preservation on economic and "scientific" grounds and rejected the anarchic use of natural resources on aesthetic, ethical, and particularly ecological grounds. Beltrán was confident that he had found the proper balance in regard to the use of natural resources, but not all Mexican conservationists agreed.

At its creation, Beltrán rightfully touted the Mexican Institute of Renewable Natural Resources as a pioneer institution in the history of conservation in Mexico.[31] Through dint of hard work, Beltrán succeeded in establishing IMERNAR as a prominent spokesgroup for the rational use of resources in Mexico.[32] In fact, in terms of longevity and impact, the institute became one of Mexico's premier conservation organizations. It was not, however, the only environmental group that began during the 1950s.

In 1951, Gonzalo Blanco Macías and a few of his colleagues founded a group called the Amigos de la Tierra (Friends of the Earth).[33] Like the Mexican Institute of Renewable Natural Resources, the Amigos de la Tierra sought "to conserve the soils, water, flora, and fauna of Mexico with the end not only to conserve them but to increase their development for the well-being of the people of the country." Members considered their work to be a patriotic endeavor and encouraged all those "who shared a love and veneration of nature" to participate in the organization. The ambitious goal of Blanco Macías and his colleagues was to form local chapters of the Amigos de la Tierra in all the cities, towns, and villages of Mexico.[34]

The group endeavored to protect and restore the land. In pursuance of this goal, the Amigos de la Tierra assisted many municipalities in the formation of tree nurseries and the planting of orchards and trees in urban areas. In the countryside, its members planted trees along roads, steep banks, and property boundaries and constructed small dams to collect water and trap eroded soil particles. The Amigos de la Tierra aided

Amigos de la Tierra avows that its work to protect and restore the nation's renewable natural resources—its soils, waters, flora, and fauna—is grandly patriotic. Amigos de la Tierra.

farmers through the establishment of special pilot projects used to demonstrate the value of soil conservation techniques. The group stressed that people's survival depended upon the careful use of the land.[35]

For slightly more than a decade (1953–1964), the Amigos de la Tierra published a journal on soil and water conservation called *Suelo y Agua*. The editors had two basic goals. The first was to appraise government conservation efforts. Though giving the government credit for the establishment of successful soil and water conservation programs in various parts of the country, the editors of *Suelo y Agua* focused on the many regions of Mexico that had not received the benefits of government assistance. Blanco Macías and his compatriots used the pages of the journal to plead with the government for a significant expansion of its conservation programs. The editors' second goal was to disseminate knowledge of soil and water conservation techniques to Mexico's farm-

Amigos de la Tierra informs farmers and ranchers that it can develop plans for the rational use of their natural resources. Amigos de la Tierra.

ers. Through its pilot projects and its journal, the Amigos de la Tierra was attempting to provide extension services to regions neglected by the government.

Without explanation, Blanco Macías ceased publication of *Suelo y Agua* in 1964. Although the Amigos de la Tierra continues its efforts for conservation today, the absence of a printed forum has reduced the group's visibility and influence.[36] At one time, though, Amigos de la Tierra was a major voice for conservation in Mexico.

In addition to his commitment to soil conservation, Blanco Macías was an ardent advocate for Mexico's national parks. Like the U.S. naturalist John Muir, Blanco Macías sought to instill in his country a mystical attitude toward nature. As he observed:

> Mexicans have been accustomed to thinking in terms of pesos rather than the intangible long-term value that its national parks provide in terms of pure streams and a refuge for wildlife. . . . The idea of a national park implies the renunciation of material gains creating in its place the conviction that the moral and spiritual values of people are magnified when they can enjoy intimate contact and silent communion with nature. The conservation of a forest for aesthetic and healthy diversion constitutes exactly the measure of a people.[37]

Blanco Macías was cognizant of a tragic Catch-22 in nature preservation efforts in Mexico: population growth and urbanization intensified people's needs for the solitude and the openness of wild places, but the same forces that made wilderness essential for people's physical and mental well-being were also leading to its ruin.[38] One area in which the destruction of nature has been most evident is the state of Chiapas. It is also the state where two of Mexico's finest conservationists have concentrated their efforts.

The ecological diversity of Chiapas is unmatched by any other region in North America. Chiapas, located in southwestern Mexico, contains the last tropical rain forest and the last cloud forests in North America. Chiapas "houses" over eight thousand species of vascular plants, which constitute two-fifths of the plant species in Mexico. The state also provides habitats for two-thirds of the country's bird species. Though one-third the size of California, Chiapas contains twice as many bird species as exist in the United States (641 bird species in all) and more than twice as many butterfly species as exist in Canada and the United States combined (1,200 species). Many unique groupings of reptiles, amphibians, fish, and invertebrates are also found in Chiapas. Because of habitat destruction and unregulated hunting, many of Chiapas's species are now endangered.[39]

The flora and fauna of Chiapas began to be threatened fifty years ago. Before then several logging operations had taken place in the region, but all on a modest scale.[40] During the 1940s, landless peasants began to colonize the state. In the years that followed, a flood of immigrants drawn by government colonization programs or by their own initiative

have come to Chiapas. In more recent years, Guatemalans fleeing repressive military governments (or military-dominated governments)
have entered the region. The new arrivals lacked the traditional ecological knowledge held by some of Chiapas's indigenous groups. Rather
than planting fruit trees or keeping some vegetation on the milpa plots,
they simply denuded the forests to plant their crops.[41]

During the 1960s, the Mexican government undertook a massive
road construction program to facilitate the extraction of the region's remaining mahogany, cedar, and ceiba trees. At the same time that the
forest industry was booming in Chiapas, immigrants unable to support
themselves on soils being rapidly depleted of their nutrients sold their
lands to cattle ranchers who, supported by local politicians, rapidly expanded their operations, converting much of the jungle into range-
land.[42] Statistics give some sense of the magnitude of the destruction. In
1940, the Lacandón Jungle in Chiapas covered 1.3 million hectares; in
1990 only 300,000 hectares remained.[43] A number of Mexican conservationists warn that unless the Mexican government takes strong action soon, the Lacandón Jungle will disappear by the beginning of the
twenty-first century.

To round out the picture of environmental destruction in Chiapas,
game hunters have decimated many of Chiapas's unique species. If the
Mexican government had abided by the Convention on Nature Protection and Wild Life Preservation or had enforced the 1952 game law,
then the status of wildlife in Chiapas today would have been quite different. As it is, however, many of Chiapas's species are threatened with
extinction.[44]

Miguel Alvarez del Toro is a towering figure in the conservation
movement of Chiapas. Though not a native of Chiapas, he became one
of its most devoted citizens. His fascination and love of the natural
world originated from his childhood in the state of Colima, where he
was born in 1917. One of his most cherished activities was collecting
the plants, insects, birds, and animals that lived around his family's
property. Through his wanderings and observations as a youth, he not
only increased his scientific knowledge of nature but also learned the
importance of humility and respect toward nature.

Miguel Alvarez del Toro's parents patiently lent their support to the
hobbies and collections of their child naturalist.[45] On one particularly
joyful occasion, Miguel's mother bought him his first taxidermy book,
exacting from him a solemn pledge to attend catechism and never to
miss Sunday mass. Finally, he would be able to prevent the decomposi-
tion of the animals in his collections.[46]

In 1939, Miguel and his family moved to Mexico City after losing their property as a result of agrarian reform. Although in those days the city had clean air and open spaces, Alvarez del Toro felt enslaved in this urban setting so far removed from the tropical beauty of Colima. Determined to maintain some kind of connection with the natural world, he contacted Angel Roldán, the director of the National Museum of Flora and Fauna, about possible employment opportunities. No official positions were open, but after inquiring into Alvarez del Toro's background, Roldán found a spot for him as a taxidermist. Miguel soon discovered that his immediate supervisors resented his knowledge of taxidermy and his suggestions on how to improve the museum. They did not provide him with the tools necessary to practice his craft, so instead of preparing animals, he taught himself English. During Roldán's absence on an official trip, Alvarez del Toro's superiors relegated him to washing floors, except when they needed a translator during visits by North Americans. Upon his return, Roldán promoted Alvarez del Toro to deputy director of the museum, but his change of fortune was short-lived. With the passage of functions of the museum from the Department of Forestry, Fish, and Game to the Ministry of Agriculture in 1940, Alvarez del Toro lost his benefactor for good and was once again assigned to menial tasks. Shortly thereafter he resigned, taking from the experience an abiding distaste for bureaucrats.[47]

After the fiasco at the National Museum of Flora and Fauna, Alvarez del Toro accepted a position as scientific collector with the Academy of Natural Sciences of Philadelphia. Although he detested the commerce in wild animals, he felt compelled to take the new job in order to help support his family. His first task was to collect birds near Mexico City, but the academy soon requested specimens from more distant regions. Alvarez del Toro chose the virgin jungle of the Isthmus of Tehuantepec for his explorations. On the Coatzacoalcos River, Miguel and his companion almost perished when their boat capsized in a whirlpool near a waterfall.[48] This was the first of many journeys into the wild areas of southern Mexico, which were frequently punctuated by drenching rains, searing heat, insect scourges, and encounters with jaguars and crocodiles, along with views of some of the most enchanting, but fleeting, places in the hemisphere.

Shortly after his return to Mexico City in 1942, Alvarez del Toro read a newspaper story about the plans of the governor of Chiapas, Rafael Pascacio Gamboa, to create a natural history museum in his state. His friends at the National Museum of Flora and Fauna, then, belatedly informed him that the governor's collaborator on the project, Eliseo Palacios, had made repeated attempts to recruit a taxidermist from among their ranks, but that no one wanted to work in such a remote and wild part of Mexico. Alvarez del Toro, on the other hand, viewed the job as a marvelous opportunity to explore a naturalist's paradise. His only fear was that someone else had already taken the position.[49]

As it turned out, the job as a taxidermist was still open, and only one other person had applied. Palacios hired Alvarez del Toro on the basis of his superior qualifications and his willingness to let the government set his salary, which would be the equivalent of two dollars a day (his rival had insisted that danger pay be included as part of his earnings). Alvarez del Toro arrived in Tuxtla Gutiérrez, the capital of Chiapas, eager to begin his new job, only to discover that the museum did not exist. Palacios had not taken very seriously his mandate from Governor Pascacio Gamboa to create a natural history museum, perhaps because he anticipated that future governors would withdraw their support for the institution. Until a new structure could be built, Palacios and Alvarez del Toro stored the few existing collections in a large old house. Such was the humble beginnings of one of Mexico's oldest conservation institutions.[50]

Because of a lack of transportation, Alvarez del Toro had to make his first collecting trips in the company of hunters. These were not particularly pleasurable outings for the naturalist, who abhorred the wasteful exploitation of wildlife. He had no qualms about shooting animals for exhibits, however. To those who saw a contradiction between his killing of animals for scientific ends and his dedication to conservation, Alvarez del Toro answered that people could utilize natural resources so long as they did not destroy them. He emphatically rejected the view, though, that nature existed only to serve human beings.[51]

Upon the death of Palacios in 1944, Alvarez del Toro became director of the Department of Tropical Nurseries and the Museum of Natural History (later known as the Institute of Natural History of Chiapas). In addition to the natural history museum, which was completed in 1943, he inherited a small dismal zoo. The first captured animals lived in intolerable conditions. Most of them were kept in tiny wooden cages covered with wire mesh, which became "perfect ovens" during hot weather. People passing by on the streets that bordered the zoo would throw stones at the animals or poke them with sticks to make them move. During political campaigns, the setting off of fireworks near the zoo terrified the animals to such a degree that some of them died while battering themselves against the walls of their pens in a desperate attempt to escape. One of Alvarez del Toro's most ardent desires was to construct a new zoo.[52]

Two jaguars (one partially obscured) in the Miguel Alvarez del Toro Zoo in Tuxtla Gutiérrez, Chiapas. Lane Simonian.

In 1948, the governor of Chiapas, General César Lara, proposed the creation of a new zoo on the outskirts of town at Parque Madero, now home to the institute's botanical gardens. Lamentably, however, the Department of Public Works bulldozed all the trees, depriving the animals of any shade. Alvarez del Toro and his staff devised artificial shade structures and sprayed many of the species with water to keep them alive. Another three decades would pass before Alvarez del Toro could gain government backing for a zoo that would meet his specifications.[53]

In developing plans for a new facility, Alvarez del Toro deliberately avoided the safari model; that is, a zoo that displays in tightly boxed cages animals taken from all over the world. The present zoo at El Zapotal contains only animals from Chiapas (of the zoo's 213 species, 90 percent are in danger of extinction). The animals live in surroundings that closely mimic their native habitats. Though Alvarez del Toro was not able to dispense with cages altogether, he used "natural" barriers, such as stone walls and ravines, to separate many of the compounds. The tropical canopy and running water in the zoo provide a natural setting that attracts birds, squirrels, and other animals that roam freely. Many experts consider the zoo to be one of the finest in Latin America.[54]

Conservation is the zoo's primary mission. Signs indicate the habitats, behavior, and threats to the survival of each of the species. Along the path meandering through the zoo are stone plaques containing quotes, from the Aztec to Aldo Leopold, emphasizing the importance of preserving the beauty and integrity of the natural world.[55] One empty exhibit contains a mirror, with a sign inside saying: "Here you can see the most dangerous species, destroyer of nature and probably of itself." It is a message that Alvarez del Toro fervently believes.

Admission to the zoo is free so that all Chiapans can come to see it, and over a half-million people visit each year.[56] Miguel's daughter, Rebecca Alvarez del Toro, has developed innovative educational programs for the young visitors to instill in them an appreciation for the flora and fauna of Chiapas.[57] On "Cultural Saturdays," for instance, preschoolers learn about the life history of one of the species in El Zapotal and why its survival is threatened. They draw pictures and make models of the animal. At summer classes, students from ages four to fifteen spend five days learning about the behavior and habitats of different species. Rebecca Alvarez del Toro and her aides take the older children on a field trip to a nearby natural area. The cost of the program is seven dollars, but students from poor families are supported by donations from other participants. Teenagers can spend another three weeks aiding the staff. Many of those who participate in the summer program leave with a greater concern for the animals of Chiapas.[58]

The Alvarez del Toro family knows that a love of nature is innate in children, but also something that needs to be developed. As Miguel Alvarez del Toro notes: "Every child has an interest in nature and every child should be taught to develop this interest. But they aren't. Children are taught how to live in society, but they aren't taught how to live with nature. They aren't taught how to protect it or to respect it." Although he believes that some children will learn to protect nature from their contact with the zoo, he wonders if it is not already too late. He worries about what will be left for them to protect when they are adults.[59]

While Alvarez del Toro is pleased by the support that Chiapans have given to his efforts, his relationship with the government and the private sector has brought him little but discouragement. The government and the private sector have been apathetic to his work and, when not apathetic, actively hostile.[60] For many years, the shortage of financial resources and the lack of moral support from the government prevented Alvarez del Toro from expanding his conservation activities.

With the creation of the Miguel Alvarez del Toro Foundation (FUNDAMAT) in 1987, a parallel organization that raises money for the Institute of Natural History, and with recent support from the government, the institute has been able to take a more active role in the management of natural resources in Chiapas.[61] At the invitation of Governor Patrocinio González Garrido, the group assisted in the drafting of a development plan for the state during the late 1980s. The governor later placed a moratorium on the clearing of new lands and appointed Alvarez del Toro to head the Commission of Forests and Environment.[62]

The Institute of Natural History runs six of the eleven nature reserves in Chiapas, including El Triunfo, which the federal government raised to the level of a biosphere reserve in 1990.[63] In addition, the group has participated in efforts to create an international park that would incorporate the rain forest regions of Guatemala, Belize, and Mexico. But Alvarez del Toro has reservations about the outcome of this project: "Even if an area is set aside for conservation, some future president could still give it to one of his relatives."[64] His past relations with the Mexican government have made him wary of its commitment to conservation.

Alvarez del Toro supports the creation of national parks because he believes they fulfill a legitimate function by protecting areas of great scenic beauty for the enjoyment of tourists. However, he is equally adamant that some areas should never be subjected to human influence. As he argues, zones should exist that "are not national parks but natural areas that one should protect jealously against all types of exploitation or use; no more than for scientific studies. That is to say they should remain in their original states, conserving for itself with a minimum interference of man, the dynamics of ecosystems. Whether they are of easy access or not is of little importance."[65] He knows that the survival of Chiapas's endangered species depends on the creation and protection of these zones. In its management of natural resources, Alvarez del Toro's Institute of Natural History has sought above all else to protect the region's diverse flora and fauna.

Among both Mexicans and foreigners, Alvarez del Toro is acknowledged as an expert in the field of zoology. His books *Los animales silvestres de Chiapas* (1952), *Los reptiles de Chiapas* (1962), *Las aves de Chiapas* (1971), and *Los mamíferos de Chiapas* (1977) are a natural scientist's bible of the region. Even more important, he is the voice of conscience for conservation not only in Chiapas but throughout Mexico. He has a deeply rooted ethical concern, not unlike that of Aldo Leopold, for the natural world. He also knows that humankind's survival depends upon a reevaluation of its relationship with the environment: "The basic beliefs of society rest on the idea that this world was created for their benefit and that they could do whatever they wanted without worrying about the consequences. It's a very mistaken view. . . . People must realize that their actions will finish off humanity just as they finished off many other species."[66] According to Alvarez del Toro, the Mexican government has perpetuated the notion that nature is expendable:

> Unfortunately, in Mexico, officials have convinced the public that reserves are a luxury. . . . If they see a piece of forest they say, "Ah, that should be cultivated. People need to eat." Very well, people should eat, but if we look at what people are going to die of—a lack of food, lack of water or lack of air—we see the forests are not just fallow land. Forests are working to retain clean water and purify the air.[67]

If the forests are lost, farmers will not be able to grow their crops because of diminished water supplies, leading Alvarez del Toro to conclude: "Saving the forests isn't a romantic vision. It's a necessity for those farming. The people are already seeing this. There's less rain. The answer would be for people to do what they used to do—farm the valleys and conserve the forested mountains."[68]

Humankind is constantly simplifying ecosystems to the point at which complete restoration becomes impossible. Although he supports efforts at environmental restoration such as reforestation, he also knows that such restoration can never re-create the richness and diversity of natural ecosystems. Even if they survive, replanted trees because of their shallow root systems and scant foliage cannot protect soils or retain rainfall as well as old growth. Nor can forest plantations match the grandeur of the ancient forests. This is in itself a tremendous loss, for, as Alvarez del Toro observes, people need not only clean water and clean air, they also need natural beauty. Ecologically and aesthetically, Mexico's pristine forests are irreplaceable.[69]

The destruction of Chiapas's mangroves (a colony of trees and shrubs that grow in coastal waters) provides another example of Alvarez del Toro's observation that "man always has the eagerness of modifying that which he considers inconvenient in nature for his own egoistic interests and if he has the opportunity, he does it, even though it produces negative and worse yet irreversible consequences." Many of Chiapas's mangroves have been destroyed for agriculture, for new houses, and for firewood. As he notes, these mangroves provide multiple benefits for Mexico, including protection against typhoons and hurricanes and an important food resource for the country. In addition, Mexico's mangroves are the breeding grounds for 96 percent of the fish captured along Mexico's coasts; they also provide a niche for many crustaceans and mollusks. The immediate gains brought by the destruction of the mangroves is more than offset by the long-term loss of an important habitat.[70]

The long-term consequences of Mexico's poorly conceived program of development have never been far from Alvarez del Toro's mind: "Frequently Chiapas has been called the sleeping giant loaded with natural resources. Probably this is true, but when the sleeping giant awakes it will find that its wealth has been taken leaving it indigent with all its resources gone, pillaged, used in the most anarchic way possible." Then the citizens of Chiapas would lament the wasteful use they had made of their inheritance, which includes their obligation to the survival of their descendants.[71] According to Alvarez del Toro, human beings have a fateful optimism in their ability to alter nature for their own purposes: "We have an excessive confidence in modern technology. . . . People believe that technology can resolve all our needs without the help of nature. The ancient pact that man made with nature has been broken. Man thinks he is powerful enough to liberate himself from nature, that vast biological complex of which he has always been a part."[72] His admonition is that people must abandon their quest to dominate the environment in order to ensure the perpetuation of life. Both ethics and self-survival require humankind to restore the ancient pact with nature. Mexico has had few finer advocates for the natural world than Miguel Alvarez del Toro.

Another defender of nature in Chiapas, Gertrude "Trudi" Duby Blom, was born far away from Mexico in Switzerland in 1901.[73] Not atypical of schoolchildren, Trudi preferred the outdoors over the classroom. Unlike many other children, though, her love of nature would be lifelong.

When playing Indians with her friends in the Swiss forests, she adopted the exotic Aztec name Popocatépetl, for at an early age, Trudi had taken an interest in the mysterious land of Mexico. She had also developed an interest in the native inhabitants of the Americas. As a child, she was captivated by Carl May's novels of the Indians.

Blom received degrees in horticulture from a college in Niederlenz and in social work from the University of Zurich. After graduation, she became a journalist and a member of the Swiss Social Democratic Party. In 1927, she went to Germany to work on behalf of the socialist movement and to write articles on German politics for the Swiss press. When Hitler came to power in 1933, opponents of the Nazi regime were forced to work underground. Blom herself was placed on Hitler's blacklist in 1934, a "status" that forced her to change apartments every night to avoid arrest by the secret police. Finally, after four months of this terrifying routine, she escaped to Britain on a passport given by a friend. Five years later, she returned to Continental Europe, proceeding to Paris to join an international movement against fascism and the impending war. Blom became one of the many antifascists arrested by French agents in 1939. After spending five months in a detention camp, Blom was freed thanks to the lobbying efforts of the Swiss government. Soon afterward, she left Europe for the United States. She passed eight months in New York City, where she helped resettle French refugees who were fleeing Nazi persecution.

On the ship to the United States, Blom had read Jacques Soustelle's book *Mexique: Terre indigène*. She was particularly captivated by Soustelle's description of the Lacandón Indians. When Blom arrived in Mexico in 1940, she did not have enough money to go to the Lacandón Jungle. Instead, she spent her time working alongside the textile and tobacco workers in the states of Jalisco, Nayarit, and Sinaloa. She also produced a photojournal of the women who had fought in the Zapatista army, a photographic essay that received critical acclaim. Though without formal training, Blom had a talent for capturing the human spirit through photography.

In 1943, Blom received a small inheritance from Switzerland that she used to complete her dream of seeing the Lacandón rain forest. Upon arriving in Chiapas, she learned that the first government commission to investigate the Lacandón Indians was about to depart. Never a shy person, Blom convinced the governor of Chiapas, Rafael Pascacio Gamboa, to allow her to join the expedition as a photojournalist. She felt an immediate sense of kinship with the jungle, for this was her element. Her efforts to protect the Lacandón Indians and their jungle would occupy most of the rest of her life.

On another expedition in 1943, she met U.S. anthropologist Frans Blom, who had begun his archaeological research in southern Mexico in 1919. Trudi and Frans were aware of each other's work, and even be-

Frans and Gertrude Blom chose the jaguar motif for their scientific center in San Cristóbal de las Casas, after recalling how Lacandón Indians had once confused the name Blom with their word for jaguar (*barum*). The Tzotzil called the center Na-Bolom—House of the Jaguar—after the tiles that adorn its entrance. Courtesy of Na-Bolom.

fore meeting, a mutual admiration existed between them. On the expedition, Frans Blom contracted malaria, and Trudi ferried him to a camp where he could receive help. After this experience, the two became fast companions and were married in 1950. In 1951, the Bloms bought a house in San Cristóbal de las Casas, a picturesque town in the highlands of Chiapas. Immediately, they began to convert the house into a center for scientific studies. As part of this effort, they established the Fray Bartolomé de las Casas Library, which today contains twenty-five hundred specialized works on Chiapas and over eight thousand works on subjects related to Mexico and Mesoamerica. Over the years, many visitors, ranging from regional Indians to foreign researchers, have come to the house. Also, the center has conducted numerous scientific expeditions into the jungles and highlands of Chiapas.[74]

At first, the Bloms' interest in Chiapas was largely anthropological and sociological: they collected artifacts from various Indian cultures to prevent their loss; they inoculated the Lacandón in an attempt to protect them from outside diseases; they tried to shelter them from the influences of the outside world; and Trudi photographed the Lacandón people. As the deforestation of the Lacandón Jungle accelerated, though, the Bloms recognized that it would be impossible to protect the Indians without protecting the forests. Trudi and Frans sent numerous petitions and letters to the Mexican government asking for the creation of national parks in the Lacandón region.[75] After the death of her husband in 1963, Blom became even more committed to the task of saving the jungle. As one biographer noted: "Over the last twenty years, Gertrude Blom has become more and more concerned, lately to the point of obsession, with this ongoing ecological disaster. Since 1970, she has practically abandoned photographing people in favor of documenting the destruction of the ancient trees. . . . Her religion is the trees that for years have sustained and protected the Lacandón, and her message: to stop the destruction."[76]

In her battle to save the Lacandón Jungle, Blom has concluded that government decrees to protect the jungle can never succeed without the people's support. In the early 1970s, she praised President Luis Echeverría's decision to give the Lacandón Indians their own reserve, but the destruction of the forests continued.[77] In 1978, Blom and other conservationists persuaded the government to create the Montes Azules Biosphere Reserve in the Lacandón Jungle, but the trees still fell.[78] Even if the government intended to preserve the Lacandón Jungle, it could not prevent the people from exploiting the forests. In Blom's words: "The government is incapable of solving ecological problems without the civic support of the people."[79] Most important, teachers had to awaken in their youngest students "a love of nature and a consciousness for conserving the future."[80]

In recent years, Blom has directed her efforts toward the creation of a conservation consciousness among the highland peoples of Chiapas. She has chosen this focus out of a recognition that the destruction of the lowland jungles is inextricably linked to the ecological deterioration of the highlands. Because of the loss of soil fertility and soil erosion in the highlands, Indians have migrated into the jungle to clear new lands for their cornfields. In 1975, as part of her campaign to reforest the highlands of Chiapas, Blom created a tree nursery from which she provided trees free of charge to the people of Chiapas. Many of the indigenous people of Chiapas responded favorably to the program, planting thousands of trees in the highlands. By doing so, they protected not only their farmlands from wind and soil erosion but also preserved a part of the Lacandón Jungle.[81] In addition to planting trees, she had advocated that highland farmers use terraces, organic fertilizers, and crop rotation to save their lands.[82]

Blom maintains that the destruction of forests will continue until people are presented with valid alternatives. Instead of engaging in slash and burn agriculture, cattle grazing, and lumbering, she suggests that the people of Chiapas plant fruit trees, coffee, and other crops that can grow under the forest canopy, expand their local handicrafts industry, carefully use wood for a furniture industry, grow vegetables for self-consumption and sale, establish small industries, and promote tourism.[83]

Blom is less enthusiastic about tourist development in wild areas than in towns and cities: "I want to declare emphatically that I would like to leave these places as I knew them the first time without people, without homes, peace and silence. . . . I don't like the tourism solution, but the economists don't want to leave a place without gains. If it helps the neighboring people of these places, the project will have its positive side. This course would be better than total destruction."[84] Her overall prescription for Chiapas is unequivocal: "We can save Chiapas if we don't fall into the error of imitating the super-industrialized nations. They suffer today from those errors. We have time to avoid them. Progress does not mean super-industrialization, it means the struggle for a healthy environment where we all have to eat and be clothed. Progress today means saving our country and our planet from destruction."[85]

The survival of Chiapas also depends upon recognizing the true nature of its wealth. Chiapas's tropical forests are a source of great beauty and ecological diversity. As Blom has said many times, their existence is a benefit to all of humanity.[86] Yet farmers practicing slash and burn agriculture daily participated in the destruction of this irreplaceable resource. The ultimate irony was that once the forests were removed agriculture failed. Blom said: "I saw that the land of the tropical rain forest was not at all suitable for agriculture, and that the richness of the region lay in its forests, that the people could live well by exploiting forests rationally and scientifically, that cutting down trees meant destroying the future."[87] She contended that "the politician's dream to incorporate the rain forest into the national economy will soon bear fruit on eroded hillsides, and in weeded, wasted valleys."[88] And to the question often asked her, "What will people eat?" Blom responded, "What will they eat tomorrow?"[89]

The disappearance of the Lacandón Jungle has greatly saddened Blom:

In 1943, I rode on a horse from Catasajá to Palenque through a gorgeous forest full of Howler monkeys, birds of all kind, tapirs, peccaries, and jaguars. All that is left now are cattle who have trampled the once delicate soil to stone-hard earth.

I knew Chancala when it was a lush, high jungle. Now there is not a tree left. Gone are the mahoganies, cedars, and rich nut palms, . . . Now, even the majestic ceiba, sacred tree of the Mayans, is under the relentless attack of the chain saw to be turned into paper and plywood.[90]

The culprits in the destruction of the rain forest are many:

Indians, ranchers, cattle grazers, the corn growers, brutes, and intelligent people, illiterates and the educated, a few because of a lack of instruction, for hunger, because they have no other options, others not excusable because of rapacity and all destroy the future of their children. Hunger, ignorance, weakness, and rapacity turn to smoke, ashes, and stone the marvelous Lacandón Jungle.[91]

Even some of the Lacandón themselves contributed to the destruction of their forests by selling concessions to outsiders in return for material goods: "Old Chan K'in [a Lacandón leader and long-time friend of Blom's] is saddened to see how little the religious ceremonies mean to most of the young people. He once said to me, 'The car is their new god. When the jungle is gone, we will be gone. When a tree falls, a star falls.' "[92]

Blom's failure to prevent the destruction of the Lacandón Jungle has left her despondent and self-tormented. In a recent interview, she said: "I was a fighter all my life, but that's a sad story. I tried to change the world without much success. The Nazis came; then we tried to avoid the war and the war came. I fought for the Lacandón and the forest and that's lost too."[93]

Blom's despair has also been shared by Miguel Alvarez del Toro and Enrique Beltrán. For each of them, the obstacles to the conservation of natural resources in Mexico have often seemed overwhelming. And when matters of great importance are at stake, it is almost impossible to accept failure. Despite all their speeches, all their writings, all their projects, Gertrude Duby Blom, Miguel Alvarez del Toro, and Enrique Beltrán could not generate a national crusade for conservation in Mexico. Yet, due largely to their efforts, Mexico today does have a modest conservation movement. The writings and works of Blom, Alvarez del Toro, and

Beltrán have been a source of inspiration and wisdom to a new generation of Mexican conservationists. By the 1970s, new conservation groups and conservation leaders had joined in the search for a program of development that would take into account both the needs of the people and the needs of the land.

Chapter Eight

FOR HUMANKIND AND NATURE

The Pursuit of Sustainable

Development

During the early 1970s, the Mexican conservation movement was affected by two developments on the international level. The first was the United Nations Educational, Scientific, and Cultural Organization's (UNESCO) initiation of Man and the Biosphere Program in 1971. The second was the United Nations Conference on the Human Environment held in Stockholm in 1972. Through the auspices of the United Nations, a new perspective on the relationship between conservation and development began to emerge.

The United Nations Man and the Biosphere Program was based on a recognition that humankind had modified landscapes throughout the world. UNESCO's goal was to "provide the knowledge, skills, and human values" necessary to attain a harmonious relationship between people and the environment. Because of the impoverished conditions in which many people lived, the use of natural resources could not be avoided. UNESCO, though, held that less disruptive means of land use could be found. The main instrument the U.N. organization used to promote a new human-environment relationship was the biosphere reserve. Each reserve contained a core area that was strictly protected for scientific studies and for the maintenance of ecological stability. Outside the core area, resource managers encouraged local people to adopt economic activities that were less harmful to the environment.[1]

One year after the initiation of the Man and the Biosphere Program, the United Nations Conference on the Human Environment was held.

This conference was a landmark event in the history of the international environmental movement. Although some of the issues discussed at Stockholm had been addressed previously, the meeting was unique because it attracted delegates from so many different parts of the world and because it received considerable international attention. The most significant aspect of the conference, though, was its legacy: it established the framework under which the issues of conservation and development were dealt with thereafter.

Delegates at Stockholm redefined development to encompass the rights of people to food, shelter, a clean environment, political and social freedom, and human dignity rather than simply in terms of economic growth or industrial output.[2] Furthermore, the conference served to erode the commonly held belief that conservation and development were inherently contradictory goals. According to U.N. officials, conservation and development were in fact inseparable goals: the maintenance of a resource base (water, soil, forests, etc.) was essential for long-term development, and economic options had to be provided so that the peasantry could survive without exploiting the land. The key, then, was for countries to find development programs that would provide an income to the poor without undermining the long-term capacity of the land.[3]

The emerging philosophy of sustainable development or ecodevelopment was not warmly embraced by all of the delegates to the United Nations Conference on the Human Environment. Many delegates from Third World countries considered the demands of industrialized countries for pollution control and environmental protection in the Third World to be yet another attempt by the rich nations to keep the poor nations nonindustrialized, underdeveloped, and in a state of dependency. As Pakistan's representative, Mahbub ul Haq, proclaimed: "Poverty is the worst form of pollution."[4] The Mexican response was more equivocal. Mexicans had witnessed the detrimental effects of several decades of industrialization on the environment without achieving many of the promised economic benefits. However, the Mexican government, while admitting that serious environmental problems existed in the country, was not yet ready to jettison its program of rapid industrialization for a program of sustainable development. As the government's preparatory commission for the conference stated: "We believe that the path of industrial expansion is the most effective means for now of meeting the growing demands for goods and services. On the other hand, industrialization has produced serious environmental problems.

Steps must be taken to combat these problems."[5] These steps would not entail a radical reevaluation of the country's development policies. The Mexican government did not accept the position that development had to be accompanied by strict environmental protection.

In contrast, Mexican conservationists embraced the concept of sustainable development. For many of them, biosphere reserves offered a preferable alternative to Mexico's traditional system of nature protection—national parks. The United Nations Conference on the Human Environment fueled the determination of Mexican conservationists to alter their country's destructive development programs. Mexican conservationists were attracted to ecodevelopment because they believed it represented a viable strategy for protecting the land while ensuring social justice.

Gonzalo Halffter, a scientist who was instrumental in the creation of Mexico's first biosphere reserves, was one of the chief critics of Mexico's national park system. He thought that national parks were a model inappropriately borrowed from the United States without contemplation of Mexico's needs and that national parks could be successful only in countries that faced few demographic pressures, could afford the luxury of taking one or more areas out of production, had a tradition of concern for nature, and had the administrative capability to ensure the protection of the land. According to Halffter, the United States met these criteria, but Mexico did not.[6] Halffter rued the fact that Mexico's national parks had failed to protect representative ecosystems. Most national parks were established to preserve pretty places for scenery and recreation rather than to protect critical gene pools.[7] Thus, despite high plant endemism, scrublands and grasslands were rarely set aside as national parks.[8] In contrast, coniferous forests whose species diversity is relatively low, were repeatedly protected.[9] Halffter was further disturbed that most conservation officials did not conduct ecological studies before creating national parks and that ecological research was not an integral part of the park service's mission. The creation of national parks resulted in neither the protection of representative ecosystems nor in the advancement of ecological knowledge.[10]

Halffter found Mexico's national parks wanting in another important regard: they failed to address the social needs of the local population. With the exception of tourism, local people derived no economic benefits from national parks. According to Halffter, the government's failure to restrict hunting, lumbering, and grazing within national parks was

due less to lax enforcement than the failure to address the issue of economic needs.[11] He concluded that when people were left without viable
economic alternatives they had no choice but to exploit the land. Halffter framed his "attack" on national parks in the form of questions:

(1) Is it worthwhile and possible for the intertropical developing
countries of today to achieve their goals with any kind of park or reserve destined to protect ecosystems, plants, and animals that does
not include the people of the area as part of its structure or form?
(2) In these countries, is there moral, political, and economic justification for protecting areas from exploitation when the lack of food
is a reality and production must be increased?[12]

Halffter's answer was tacit, but unmistakable nonetheless: development
must accompany conservation.

Halffter did not advocate the elimination of the national park system
in Mexico. Any type of land protection system would be better than
none at all. Nor did he argue for the conversion of all national parks
into biosphere reserves. He acknowledged that national parks served an
extremely important function by providing solace and contact with
nature to an increasingly urban population.[13] Halffter maintained,
though, that "today the great challenge for world conservation is not to
open new national parks, but to find solidly-based ecological, social, and
economic answers to the apparent dichotomy between protected areas
and regional development."[14] According to Halffter, biosphere reserves
offered the best strategy for maintaining genetic diversity while meeting
the economic and social needs of local populations.

A pivotal event for the Biosphere Reserve Program in Mexico occurred in 1974, the year the VI Latin American Zoological Conference
and a United Nations Environment Program/UNESCO conference on
the Man and the Biosphere Program were held concurrently in Mexico City. This fortuitous circumstance provided representatives from
UNESCO a chance to speak to Latin American zoologists on the importance of establishing biosphere reserves throughout the continent. Afterward, the governor of Durango, Dr. Hector Mayagoitia, invited the
conferees to join him on a tour of his state's diverse ecosystems. Among
those accompanying Mayagoitia was Gonzalo Halffter, Mexico's principal representative to conferences on the biosphere program and director
of the recently created Instituto de Ecología (Institute of Ecology).[15]

Mayagoitia's political support for biosphere reserves in Durango and Halffter's organizational resources made for an auspicious beginning for the biosphere reserve program in Mexico.[16]

Halffter and Mayagoitia established two biosphere reserves in Durango: Mapimí and La Michilía. The two reserves incorporate different natural and human environments: Mapimí is a sparsely inhabited desert ecosystem, whereas La Michilía is relatively densely populated dry forest. In recognition that human beings had a dissimilar impact upon the environment in the two regions, Halffter designed two different strategies for managing the reserves. Because of Mapimí's small human population, he decided that ecological studies should take precedence over the search for environmentally sound economic alternatives for its inhabitants.[17] The principal threat that humans presented to the environment within the reserve was the hunting of the Bolsón (desert) tortoise. After ecologists presented them with information on the slow reproductive rate of the tortoise, many of the region's hunters voluntarily limited their killing of the animal. Basic ecological research rather than applied ecological research, however, was the norm at Mapimí.[18]

At La Michilía, Halffter's emphasis was on finding alternatives to destructive land use practices. Ecological damage in the region was the result of two factors: the extension of agricultural production onto marginal lands and overgrazing. Halffter thought that the solution to the *campesino* problem was not to bring marginal lands under cultivation but to increase the harvest per hectare on good agricultural lands, optimize the use of forests and pastures, and establish agro-industries. Halffter and his colleagues attempted to reduce the pressures for agricultural expansion at La Michilía by promoting apiculture (beekeeping), strawberry production, production of jams, wood-packing, and vegetable processing. As an alternative to overgrazing, they promoted the idea of game ranching. By providing cattle ranchers with an additional source of income and food, game ranching would reduce the pressures upon cattle ranchers to expand the size of their herds. Ranchers could profitably exploit a number of species, including wild boars, wild turkeys, peccaries, and deer. Ecologists at the reserve discovered that deer could be raised without detriment to cattle, since the two species occupied complimentary niches. They also studied the potential of the prickly pear as a source of fodder for cattle so that the destructive impact that livestock had on the native vegetation could be curtailed. Scientists sought to enlist the support of cattle ranchers by doing research that would indicate how they could optimally use the land.[19]

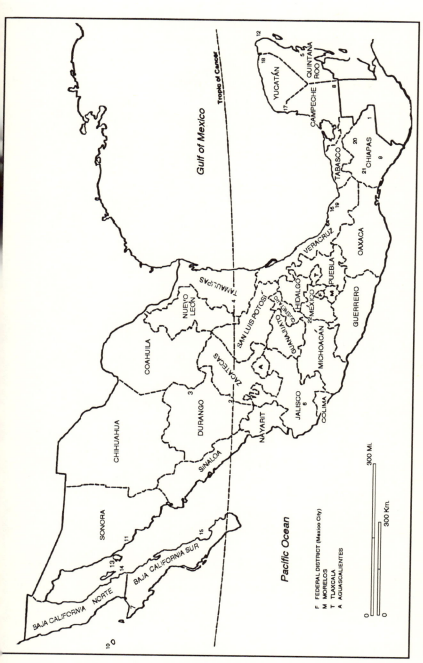

Map 5. Biosphere Reserve System of Mexico. Base map from Robert Jones Shafer, *A History of Latin America* (Lexington, Mass.: D. C. Heath and Company, 1978). Reprinted with permission from Robert Jones Shafer. Location of biosphere reserves and most of the information in Table 3 courtesy of Magdalena Juárez for *México Desconocido*.

Table Three.
Biosphere Reserve System of Mexico

Biosphere Reserve	Location	Date	Hectares
1. Montes Azules	Chiapas	1978	331,200
2. La Michilía	Durango	1979	35,000
3. Mapimí	Durango	1979	20,000
4. El Cielo	Tamaulipas	1985	144,530
5. Sian Ka'an	Quintano Roo	1986	528,147
6. Sierra de Manantlán	Jalisco	1987	139,577
7. El Vizcaino	Baja California Sur	1988	2,546,790
8. Calakmul	Campeche	1989	723,185
9. El Triunfo	Chiapas	1990	119,177
			4,587,606

Special Biosphere Reserve

10. Isla Guadalupe	Baja California Norte	1922	25,000
11. Cajón del Diablo	Sonora	1937	Not defined
12. Isla Contoy	Quintana Roo	1961	176
13. Isla Tiburón	Sonora	1963	120,800
14. Isla Rasa	Baja California Norte	1964	6.9
15. Islas del Golfo de California	Baja California Sur and Sonora	1978	150,000
16. Volcán de San Martín	Veracruz	1979	1,500
17. Ría Celestún	Campeche and Yucatán	1979	59,130
18. Río Lagartos	Yucatán	1979	47,840
19. Sierra de Santa Martha	Veracruz	1980	20,000
20. Cascadas de Agua Azul	Chiapas	1980	2,580
21. Selva del Ocote	Chiapas	1982	48,140
22. Mariposa Monarca	México and Michoacán	1986	16,110
			491,282.9

The special biosphere reserves are generally smaller and contain less species diversity than biosphere reserves, but they are managed in a similar manner. The category of special biosphere reserve was created by the 1988 General Law on Ecological Equilibrium and Environmental Protection. Many of the special biosphere reserves were previously wildlife refuges.

Part of the original mission of the Biosphere Reserve Program was to promote cooperation between foreign scientists. Halffter enthusiastically backed this mission by forming close ties with his counterparts abroad and by inviting foreign scientists to do research in Mexico. U.S., Argentine, French, and Soviet scientists collaborated with Mexican graduate students and senior scientists on important research projects within the Mapimí and La Michilía Biosphere Reserves.[20]

Halffter made a unique contribution to the Biosphere Reserve Program by encouraging local participation in the development of programs for Mapimí and La Michilía. The Institute of Ecology consulted with both community leaders and the general public before undertaking any significant action at the reserves. Halffter concluded, though, that it was simply not enough to solicit community support for projects designed from above. Instead, local people had to have a direct say in the operation if the reserves were to be successful. Thus, many times research activities were requested by the residents of Mapimí and La Michilía themselves.[21]

Halffter's aspirations for the Biosphere Reserve Program in Mexico have been partially met. Today, biosphere reserves constitute nearly 85 percent of the protected natural areas in Mexico.[22] On paper, these reserves protect a number of diverse ecosystems, including deserts, dry forests, temperate forests, tropical rain forests, subhumid and humid lands. Biosphere reserves have contributed to the recovery of the Bolsón tortoise, the Ridley turtle, and the crocodile in Mexico.[23] On the other hand, some conservation organizations and agencies have struggled to develop and implement management plans for biosphere reserves under their aegis. The program as a whole can be deemed neither a success nor a failure since each reserve has produced different results.

The Sian Ka'an Biosphere Reserve, founded in 1986 in Quintana Roo, is a good example of a well-managed natural area based on local participation. Representatives from fishing cooperatives, farmers, plantation owners, and other economic groups have collaborated with government officials, academics, and conservationists in the development of programs for the reserve.[24]

In the small village of El Ramonal, federal and state officials and the conservation group Amigos de Sian Ka'an encouraged farmers to raise food through drip irrigation and intercropping (growing several different crops in one field) rather than extensively through slash and burn agriculture and cattle grazing. By producing more food per hectare, the people of El Ramonal were able to conserve nearly all of their forests.[25]

In response to concerns by lobster fishers, the government conducted a biological study of the species that resulted in a two-month closed season on lobster catching in late winter when they laid their eggs (fishermen turned to other activities, such as hunting and equipment repair, during this period). The National Autonomous University of Mexico (UNAM) subsequently designed a trap that would harvest live lobsters so that females carrying eggs could be returned to the sea. In addition, university researchers advocated fishing diversification, including the harvesting of other shellfish, such as crabs. As a consequence of these measures, lobster numbers began to stabilize.[26]

At times, the participating groups faltered in their administration of the reserve. For instance, the government scrapped a promising sea turtle protection program in 1986, after which poaching began anew. Along with inadequate funding, the operation of the reserve was hindered by bureaucratic wrangling and inertia. A general management plan for Sian Ka'an was delayed for several years because the various institutions, agencies, and organizations could not agree on their roles and jurisdictions. Because of an inadequate education and public relations effort, many surrounding communities were unaware of the reserve's existence, let alone the value of its programs. Nevertheless, important progress has been made at Sian Ka'an.[27]

The Río Lagartos Special Biosphere Reserve in Yucatán offers another example of some of the difficulties entailed in implementing programs for protected areas. The managing agency for Río Lagartos, the Center for Graduate Studies of the University of Yucatán (CINVESTAV), faced the unenviable task of reconciling competing interests. The main conflict was between fishers and salt factory owners and workers. Fishers charged that the operation of the salt factory was destroying fisheries, including the mangrove swamps that provide breeding grounds for fish and protection for fish fry. Ill feelings reached such a point that frustrated fishers began to joke about dynamiting the salt factory. During the summer of 1990, the Ministry of Urban Development and Ecology (SEDUE) came to the aid of fishers and the coastal ecosystem when it halted the plant's expansion by locking the pumps to its evaporation ponds. The factory owners retaliated by closing off the local community's water supply (the pipes ran across the plant's property). Members of the local community, Las Coloradas, blamed SEDUE for threatening their jobs and water supply.[28]

This was the unfavorable setting in which CINVESTAV had to work. After the summer of 1990, fishers, the owners of the salt factory, and labor leaders from the salt factory met with park administrators and conservation biologists in an attempt to resolve their conflicts. During the course of these talks, CINVESTAV became aware that everyone had a different concept of what sustainable development meant. Thus, a "solution" that satisfied all parties appeared unlikely. Nonetheless, CINVESTAV presented a series of options to local communities within the reserve that were designed to alleviate overfishing and to provide economic alternatives to the salt factory. CINVESTAV's recommendations included aloe plantations for cosmetics and for first aid products, crocodile ranching for meat and leather products, *kuca* (palm) plantations to supply decorative vegetation to hotels in Cancún, production of crops using composted seaweed on sand bottoms (an ancient Maya technique), crab aquaculture for use in baiting octopuses, craft production using local shells, and ecotourism.[29]

CINVESTAV believed that ecotourism would provide local people with an incentive to conserve nature. Some residents, however, fretted that tourism would result in their exclusion from beaches and fishing areas. Outside consultants working for CINVESTAV noted a series of other potential problems: higher food prices, crime, cultural clashes, control of profits by a few villagers and outsiders, limited employment opportunities (in resort areas residents have been relegated to such low-paying jobs as dishwashing and janitorial work), and the economic costs of developing an adequate sewage system and a clean water supply. Ideally, ecotourism would have little negative impact on either the environment or the local people. Tourists would hike along narrow boardwalks in the mangroves, take canoe trips to Maya archaeological sites, use cheaply made solar cookers (as opposed to scarce firewood), and lodge in accommodations run by local descendants of the Maya. Despite the potential benefits of ecotourism for other areas within the reserve, CINVESTAV limited its ecotourism plans to the area surrounding Las Coloradas in recognition that ecotourism presented risks as well as opportunities.[30]

Notwithstanding the fact that SEDUE allows the public to visit only one of the five monarch butterfly sanctuaries in the states of Michoacán and Mexico, the ministry promotes ecotourism as the principal means to ensure the monarch's survival. Over the years, the number of butterflies who return each fall from east of the U.S. and Canadian Rockies to their wintering grounds in the highland forests has declined dramatically. SEDUE and the conservation group Pro-Mariposa Monarca realize that unless they find viable alternatives to woodcutting in the region the species will perish from a lack of shelter and water. Conservationists understand, too, that the pressures for deforestation are great. Loggers receive the equivalent of up to 150 U.S. dollars for each tree they cut, and peasants must collect wood for income as well as for fuel, since their rocky hillside plots yield only enough corn and beans to meet their subsistence needs. To alter this reality, SEDUE is overseeing the construction of facilities that will bring more tourists to the El Rosario Reserve. Besides building a campground and two parking lots, the agency plans to improve the dirt road to El Rosario, a road whose steep grade and loose traction wear truck gears and brakes (as well as the nerves of passengers) and the sawdust supply of local drivers. Despite the wear and tear on their vehicles, the operators of the shuttle service already run a profitable business. A number of peasant families have at least marginally bettered their standard of living by operating a string of food stands at the reserve. Others are employed by SEDUE as guides and game wardens. Community leaders from the nearby town of Angangueo welcome the influx of tourist dollars into an economy reeling from the decline of the regional mining and flower industries. In addition to the town's one hotel, some residents profit from the tourist trade by renting out guest rooms. The fifty thousand or so people who visit the reserve each year add thousands of dollars to the regional economy. Some conservationists are encouraged by the manner in which tourism is reshaping community attitudes toward the butterflies. They point to the fact, for example, of peasant participation in tree-planting programs. As Jaime Oca, a SEDUE official noted: "The people now don't see the butterfly as their enemy. They understand that protecting the monarch's forest benefits them." Others are less sanguine about the possibility that tourist dollars will ever replace logging revenues. Indeed, more and more loggers are migrating out of the region. More seriously, for the future of the monarchs, woodcutting continues to destroy their habitat. Already, two of the reserves have been completely deforested. Ecotourism by itself may not ensure the preservation of these beautiful insects.[31]

Several international environmental organizations have assisted Mexican conservation groups in their efforts to protect unique ecosystems.[32] The efforts of the World Wildlife Fund and Conservation International stand out in this regard. Since its inception in 1961, the World Wildlife Fund has striven to protect wildlife and natural habitats globally. In Mexico, the fund has supported a number of conservation organizations ranging from private groups to state agencies. It has provided training to Mexicans interested in conservation (including scholarships), assisted in the development of resource management plans for biosphere reserves and other natural parks, and attempted to foster a conservation ethic through pamphlets, books, and audiovisual materials. The World Wildlife Fund's creed is that conservation and development are compatible goals.[33]

Conservation International subscribes to this philosophy as well. In 1987, the group split off from the Nature Conservancy because it opposed the conservancy's strategy of buying land for wilderness preservation. Conservation International concluded that political, social, and economic realities made wilderness preservation unfeasible in developing countries. Instead, the organization held that the proper course of action was to help conservation groups abroad improve their knowledge and management of nature.[34]

In Mexico, Conservation International has focused its efforts on two biotically rich ecosystems: the Sea of Cortez and the rain forests of Chiapas. During the mid-1980s, the group helped finance research conducted by Dr. Bernardo Villa and Enriqueta Velarde of UNAM's Institute of Biology into the population ecology of birds that nest on the Midriff Islands in the Sea of Cortez. Conservation International subsequently worked with the institute in the design and implementation of a conservation management plan for the islands. For the region as a whole, the organization emphasized the sustained development of fisheries and planned tourism.[35] In Chiapas, Conservation International provided funding for the Institute of Natural History's Conservation Information Center (the center tracks the condition of Chiapas's ecological resources) and assisted in the development of an ecosystem management plan for the region's tropical forests.[36] The group induced a further investment in conservation in Chiapas by negotiating the first debt for nature swap in Mexico. In 1991, Conservation International bought four million U.S. dollars of Mexico's foreign debt (at a discount rate of close to 1.8 million dollars) in return for a pledge by the Mexican government to spend 2.6 million dollars on environmental projects. The federal executive earmarked more than half of this money for the protection of the Lacandón Jungle, including a grant to the Institute of Natural History's data center and the rehabilitation of a scientific field station in the Montes Azules Biosphere Reserve.[37] Through a variety of channels, the World Wildlife Fund and Conservation International contributed not only money but also technical support to Mexican conservation groups.

The Biosphere Reserve Program is a utilitarian approach to the protection of nature, albeit one that tries to minimize the impact of human use on the environment. Mexico has produced conservationists, such as

Miguel Alvarez del Toro, who believe that the preservation of wild areas is justified on aesthetic and ethical grounds. Yet, many conservationists sympathetic with the aesthetic and ethical position agreed that biosphere reserves constituted the best means of protecting ecosystems in Mexico. As the conservationist Carlos Alcérreca Aguirre couched it:

> We ought to recognize implicit in the concept of management is a marked anthropocentric criteria and an end tinted by a certain utilitarianism that goes beyond the limits of metaphysics—that is to say, with the enjoyment of man for the beauty manifested by nature, toward the search for economic benefits, . . . [However] in this anthropocentric focus is where we find the arguments for justifying, before the common man, the need to conserve the quality of his surroundings and each of its components, in order to procure for us in the immediate future a sustained use of the same.[38]

Alcérreca and others concluded that nonanthropocentric arguments were simply unsellable in a country where many people must intensely utilize the environment for their survival. The best that could be achieved was to find means of using the land that were less destructive to the environment.

The flip side to finding conservation programs that included development was to find development programs that fostered conservation. In Mexico, the growing conservation movement publicized the failures of the country's land use system from the pesticide poisoning of agricultural workers in the north to the clearing of forests by timber operators, cattle ranchers, and land hungry peasants in the south. In their search for alternatives, conservation groups looked both to modern techniques and to ancient Indian practices.

The Green Revolution was one of the programs censured by Mexican environmentalists. In 1971, Norman Borlaug, one of the fathers of the Green Revolution, spoke at the United Nations Food and Agriculture Organization's conference, blasting the environmental community: "If one prohibits the use of fertilizers in agriculture because of senseless legislation that is promoted by a powerful and hysterical interest group [environmentalists] that arouse fear by predicting the poisoning of people by chemical products, then the world will be condemned by death not through poisoning but through starvation."[39] Mexican environmentalists (together with those from other countries) rejected the proposition that the poisoning of nature and people through the use of inorganic fertilizers and pesticides offered the only alternative to starvation.

Mexican ecologists examined both the economic and environmental limitations of the Green Revolution. Between 1945 and 1970, agricultural production on farms using Green Revolution technologies increased by 22 percent. Most of the increases were due to the Green Revolution's higher yielding corn and wheat varieties rather than to the expansion of lands devoted to grain production. In fact, despite a 54 percent increase of lands brought under cultivation near the border between 1960 and 1979, the land dedicated to grain production did not substantially change (in some years it actually dropped). Most of the new areas were devoted to the growing of fruits, horticulture, forage for cattle, and other products, such as sugar, cotton, garlic, safflower, and tobacco.[40]

Most Green Revolution farmers were more interested in expanding production of profitable export crops than in expanding grain production. Furthermore, Mexico's chief grain producers, the peasantry, rarely had access to new technologies. Between 1965 and 1990, agricultural production in Mexico as a whole grew by less than 1 percent a year (in 1990, it actually dropped). During the same period, Mexico's population grew at a rate of 3 percent a year.[41] In sum, agricultural production in Mexico did not keep up with population growth. Today, Mexico is a major importer of grain.[42]

The Green Revolution itself contributed to Mexico's agricultural woes by showcasing a new system of farming that was based on the heavy use of chemical inputs and extensive irrigation. In northwestern Mexico, the "home" of the Green Revolution, thirsty crops, such as alfalfa and cotton, depleted ground water supplies.[43] Poor drainage techniques produced waterlogged and saline soils incapable of supporting agriculture.[44] The delivery of cheap water encouraged the wasteful use of that precious resource. The excessive use of fertilizers burned the soils, killing microorganisms that break down organic material into a form usable by plants (i.e., the natural fertility of the soil was destroyed). In short, the productive capacity of the land itself was sapped by agricultural technologies whose widespread use by prosperous Mexican farmers began with the Green Revolution.[45]

The Green Revolution (as well as its derivatives) produced a series of environmental problems, not the least of which was the pesticide poisonings of Mexican fieldworkers. In 1974, scientists reported that pesticide poisonings in the Comarca Lagunera region of Durango had resulted in four deaths and 847 illnesses.[46] The study offered one of the few statistical accounts of pesticide poisonings, since both the federal government and agribusinesses tried to suppress information on the subject. On top of pesticide spraying, the runoff of inorganic fertilizers into Mexican streams and rivers killed fish and contaminated water supplies.[47] Mexican ecologists argued that from the perspective of environmental health, the Green Revolution had failed.

Critics of the Green Revolution contended that organic fertilizers and integrated pest management techniques (IPM) offered a viable alternative to chemically dependent agriculture. The use of animal wastes and plant stubble (so-called green fertilizers) would restore the natural fertility of the soil and would not contaminate water supplies. Integrated pest management techniques, such as the use of natural predators, the release of sterile male insects, trapping insects, intercropping (which reduces the impact of plant specific pests and provides a natural barrier to pest movement), and the selective use of chemical pesticides, would reduce crop damage while protecting the health of both workers and environment.

Some progress has been made toward the adoption of integrated pest management techniques. During the early 1970s, the Mexican government used IPM techniques to control a screwworm epidemic.[48] Currently, in the grain fields of Sonora and Sinaloa (in northwestern Mexico) and in the sugarcane fields in the Culiacán Valley of Sinaloa, agricultural officials are assisting private farmers in the use of IPM techniques. On some farms, the use of biological methods of control reduced pesticide applications from twelve to two per year. In truth, though, neither agricultural officials nor private farmers are enthusiastic about the use of IPM techniques. Large-scale farmers (many of whom are absentee landlords) are sold on the quick fix furnished by pesticides. They are unwilling to provide the careful management that IPM techniques require. Furthermore, they prefer the known effectiveness (in the short term) of pesticides to the uncertainty of biological methods of control. Even farmers who wish to try biological control techniques often are precluded from doing so because their neighbors' heavy use of pesticides would likely kill any introduced pest predators. The application of IPM techniques requires regional planning and cooperation. Most agricultural officials, though, are more comfortable with the old system. Mexican agricultural education and credit systems have long been geared toward pesticide use. At best, the conversion to IPM techniques will come slowly.[49]

Many of the proposed changes for land use in Mexico are based on ancient Indian practices. For the semiarid and arid lands of northern Mexico, Mexican scientists avow that the diverse utilization of plants and animals made by the ancient Indians is a positive alternative to monoculture agriculture and extensive cattle grazing. As an example of the botanical possibilities, the Seri collected seventy-five plant species, and the Pima and Papago based their food supply on fifteen different types of legumes. The harvesting of drought resistant plants would reduce the burden that agriculture currently places on the region's scarce water supply. Native plants could also be cultivated as forage, making cattle raising more intensive and less damaging to the environment.[50]

In central Mexico, scientists rediscovered the merits of the *chinampas* as a highly productive and ecologically sound form of agriculture. Before the Conquest, *chinampas* (the growing of crops on fields of mud and decayed organic materials) made an important contribution to the Nahua's food supply. *Chinampas* could once again produce large quantities of food and in so doing reduce the burden that corn production places on the stability and fertility of the soils of the central plateau.[51] Mexicans could reduce their overreliance upon corn itself by increasing their consumption of nutritious crops of pre-Hispanic origin, such as beans, squash, amaranths, lime-leafed sage, and maguey. Maguey is a particularly versatile crop, as it can be used for food, drink, fiber, forage, and terracing.[52] The ancient system of terracing itself, which was abandoned by the Spanish because they did not want to allocate the labor necessary for its upkeep, could be revived to retain the thin topsoil of the badly eroded central highlands.

Botanist Arturo Gómez-Pompa and his colleagues suggest that modern-day farmers in southern Mexico could correct the destructive aspects of slash and burn agriculture by adopting the techniques of their Maya ancestors. They could (as some farmers in the region still do) leave perennial grasses and legumes as well as trees on their milpas to restore soil fertility and to reduce soil erosion while at the same time providing food. Farmers could produce additional foodstuffs without harming the environment by adopting Maya silviculture practices. Fruit trees, such as pineapples, mangoes, bananas, peaches, lemons, and avocados, would provide a valuable cash crop while maintaining forest ecosystems. The adoption of other techniques apparently utilized by the Maya, such as kitchen gardens, terraces, and raised fields, would also result in a more sustainable system of agriculture.[53] As anthropologist James Nations and resource management specialist Ronald Nigh observe, populations in southern Mexico are too large to permit the wholesale adoption of Maya practices. However, they, like Gómez-Pompa believe that the retrieval of ancient knowledge is a positive step toward achieving an ecologically sound system of food production in the tropics.[54]

Some Mexican conservationists propose that the nation should make a greater use of its wildlife and fisheries. They note that the ancient Indians of Mexico consumed small mammals, reptiles, fish, and insects in much larger quantities than modern Mexicans, inferring that if they could alter their diets to include more native plants and animals, less land would have to be cleared for agriculture and cattle grazing.[55]

During the twentieth century, Mexican limnologists and government officials have attempted to spur greater utilization of both freshwater and saltwater fisheries. Not since the ancient coastal Indians inhabited the region have Mexicans fully valued the importance of aquatic life as a food source.[56] Through aquaculture, Mexicans have combined new techniques (new techniques for Mexico) with the ancient use of fisheries. Mexican officials have promoted aquaculture on the basis that it can generate employment, feed people, and create a more harmonic regional development. Between 1982 and 1988, the amount of fish and shellfish harvested through aquaculture increased from 122,000 to 188,000 tons. This impressive increase, notwithstanding, the aquaculture industry in Mexico is still in its infancy. Mexico uses only 4.6 percent of the 3.6 million hectares suitable for aquaculture and harvests only 26 of 126 commercially exploitable species. Fishery officials project a substantial increase in both figures during the course of the 1990s. Aquaculture is a small, but growing industry in Mexico.[57]

In addition to aquaculture, the Mexican Foundation for the Development of Fisheries (a government agency) has promoted polyculture: the combining of agriculture with fish farming and animal husbandry.[58] The recycling of wastes is an important part of the system: organic material is used both for fertilizers and foraging.[59] Thus, readily available green fertilizers and night soil can be used in the place of expensive inorganic fertilizers. In fact, all aspects of the polyculture operation can be undertaken with a minimum investment, using indigenous resources. Furthermore, polyculture provides work for the elderly, children, and women. Also, all members of the household benefit from more protein in their diet. Some supporters of the model argue that it even creates a love of the land. Fishery officials believe that polyculture, like aquaculture, has enormous potential.[60]

In point of fact, though, the government has not yet given substantial backing to this experiment. During the early 1980s, public officials instructed the National Institute for Research on Biotic Resources (INIREB was created by the government in 1975) to assist farmers in the adoption of polyculture techniques, but then failed to provide funding for the program. INIREB was able to continue with the project only after receiving aid from the U.S. Inter-American Foundation. Although several hundred polyculture farms were established during the 1980s, many of them did not survive because of the absence of government support.[61]

Inadequate government funding was not the only obstacle to the success of ecodevelopment techniques in Mexico. Lack of technical assistance was also a factor. In the mid-1970s, INIREB, aided by a traditional farmer from Xochimilco, established experimental *chinampas* in the Gulf of Tabasco. The experiment was a tremendous success, so successful that abundant crops saturated local markets. For farmers taking part in the project, high yields were, ironically, a liability because they did not have the capabilities to sell the produce in regional and national markets. Then, after the departure of the *chinampero* from Xochimilco, farmers discarded his suggestions regarding techniques and species for making the *chinampa*. Eventually, because of the heavy labor requirements involved, farmers abandoned the *chinampas* altogether.[62]

Arturo Gómez-Pompa, who headed INIREB during this period, drew several conclusions from this unsuccessful experiment. According to Gómez-Pompa, the project failed largely because INIREB did not have the technical capacity to answer farmers' questions or to help them market their products. In addition, it was INIREB and not the rural Tabascan who decided that intensive agriculture was needed in the region. If farmers were to undertake the risks and extra labor requirements of *chinampa* production, they had to be convinced that the result would be more income. In fact, the promoters of the Green Revolution faced the same problem, but here the capital of large-scale farmers combined with generous assistance from the state overcame resistance to the project. As Gómez-Pompa concluded, the obstacles to the adoption of traditional agricultural methods were economic and political, not technological (i.e., the indigenous techniques themselves were viable).[63]

In 1987, Mac Chapin, an anthropologist and program director for Cultural Survival (an advocacy group for the rights of indigenous peoples), visited fifteen ecodevelopment projects in southern Mexico, including the abandoned *chinampas* and polyculture farms in Tabasco and Veracruz.[64] He located only two projects that were working well, both in the state of Oaxaca.

In the Yodocono region, north of Oaxaca City, World Neighbors (a U.S.-based organization engaged in small-scale development projects in the Third World) and the Center for Appropriate Technology Studies in

Mexico (CETAMEX) collaborated with farmers on improving agriculture techniques. They introduced furrow agriculture to reduce plant over-crowding and experimented with different combinations of chemical and organic fertilizers (some of which were obtained through compost-ing). Participants in the program rejected proposals by outsiders to grow exotic crops because they deemed the market to be too risky. Some local farmers who were trained as extension agents by World Neighbors and CETAMEX personnel persuaded their fellow cultivators to build terraced fields, bordered by fruit trees and crossed by canals that followed the contours of the land. Children gathered seedlings for local tree nurser-ies, whose staff distributed them free of charge to the *campesinos*.

In San Pedro Quiatoni, a region south of Oaxaca City, peasants played an even more central role in developing ecodevelopment projects. In response to local concerns about the growing scarcity of water in the area, Eucario, a Zapotec Indian employed by the Ministry of Education, organized the building of a catchment basin to store spring water for irrigation. When someone placed minnows in the pool, the community became interested in a more ambitious program—the building of fish ponds. People in San Pedro had heard of fish farming in other regions of Mexico, but they had no technical knowledge on which to proceed. Eu-cario solicited advice from fishery officials in Oaxaca City, but they re-sponded by setting specifications for pools that were incompatible with the local terrain. From the information Eucario garnered on his own and from their own observations, the people of San Pedro became successful fish farmers. They learned what types of food the fish liked and how they spawned in the shallow waters (which meant the ponds had to be built with a gentle slope). Members of the community took turns main-taining the flow of springs to the pools, fending off predators, and feed-ing the fish. Chapin concluded that the programs in Oaxaca worked be-cause they were based on local participation (rather than on directives from outsiders) and because organizers appreciated that ecodevelop-ment was a social, political, and economic endeavor rather than just the transfer of technology.[65]

Most studies on ecodevelopment in Mexico centered on defining the requirements for successful programs. In contrast, almost no analysis has been done of the environmental effects of alternative food produc-tion systems. The proposals made by Mexican ecologists are generally presumed to be environmentally benign. Some ecodevelopment strate-gies, however, present serious risks. The attempt to produce more food through the utilization of wild plants and animals rather than through agriculture and grazing may simply result in a shift from the exploitation of the land to the direct exploitation of wildlife and native plants. Disposing of the wastes produced from aquaculture and preventing the nutrients pumped into the "farms" from threatening the surrounding environment may prove to be a herculean task. The impact as well as the potential for ecodevelopment projects is uncertain. For most Mexican conservationists, these are distant concerns, as perhaps they should be. Mexican conservationists may not have a master plan for the future, but they agree that the current direction of "development" is a blueprint for disaster. Mexico, they observe, is in the process of impoverishing its land and its people. By 1970, even the Mexican government was grudgingly admitting that environmental problems had become so severe that they could no longer be ignored.

Chapter Nine

RECONSIDERING

Mexican Environmental

Policy

The development of Mexican environmental policy has followed a definite pattern. Over the past two decades, successive Mexican presidents have expressed a greater commitment to environmental protection, have enacted stronger laws, and have implemented bolder programs. Typically, however, the rhetoric and the laws have been stronger than the actions. During the early 1970s, President Luis Echeverría placed environmental issues onto the political agenda, but was steadfast in his commitment to industrialization. A decade later, Miguel de la Madrid made environmental issues an important part of the political discourse, but economic issues were of paramount importance in his estimation. Environmental policies have become progressively stronger over time, but the changes have not been revolutionary, as Mexican leaders neither consistently placed environmental concerns above industrial interests nor required a thorough transformation in personal life-styles.

President Luis Echeverría (1970–1976) rather reluctantly placed environmental issues on the political agenda. Unlike President Richard Nixon (1968–1974) in the United States, Echeverría did not enact legislation in response to an increasingly powerful environmental movement. In fact, only a small group of academics, engineers, health officials, and private citizens pressured the president to curb pollution.[1] Echeverría acted principally because he feared that the severity of environmental problems in Mexico would result in political and social unrest. In 1973, he voiced his concerns to the Mexican Chamber of Deputies:

> The development of technology and industry along with demo-graphic pressures have given rise to great urban concentration without services; moreover erosion, the deterioration of the atmo-sphere, the contamination of water, the depletion of flora and fauna, malnutrition, low productivity, and illness produce political instability and social unrest. This reality obliges us to avoid danger.[2]

After three decades of championing industrial and technological growth, the Institutional Revolutionary Party (PRI) began to question the cost of this progress. The party still believed, however, that industri-alization was the best development strategy for the country. Further-more, the PRI asserted that through the installment of antipollution technology, environmental protection and industrialization could oc-cur simultaneously.[3]

Echeverría adamantly defended his economic programs before inter-national bodies that were critical of the social and environmental dis-locations produced by industrialization. In a 1971 speech before the United Nations, Luis Echeverría defiantly declared that industrialization was the only viable option for Third World countries: "Industrialization has often produced pollution, but one should not try to stop the process of development nor even accept some means for stopping the advance of industrialization in poorer countries."[4] In 1975, Echeverría offered his perspective on the root causes of environmental problems before the Club of Rome, a group that had sponsored an influential study on the limits to future growth.[5] He identified "underdevelopment" rather than "overdevelopment" as the chief cause of the Third World's environmen-tal woes. In particular, he contended that it was the economic system that the "developed nations" had organized with the exclusive objective of monetary gain and not industrialization and technological growth, in and of themselves, that were the cause of resource scarcity and the degradation of the environment. According to Echeverría, the bulk of Mexico's environmental problems were caused by multinational corpo-rations and by the poverty that originated from Mexico's inability to benefit from the international system of trade.[6] The point that he failed to make was that many multinational corporations invested in Mexico because they were not subjected to the nation's environmental laws.[7]

Echeverría vociferously argued that the Third World should not have to limit its growth so that rich countries could have greater access to its resources. As part of his program to gain control over natural resources for the benefit of Mexicans, Echeverría in 1976 declared an exclusive economic zone of two hundred miles off the Mexican coasts.[8] Not surprisingly, he was an ardent supporter of the Law of the Sea Treaty, which sanctioned the expansion of national control over marine resources and granted Third World countries an equal share of the profits accruing from the mining of undersea minerals.[9]

Echeverría complained that industrialized countries were making unreasonable demands on Third World countries in the area of pollution control as well as in the use of the earth's raw materials. According to Echeverría, the preservation of the environment was a common responsibility, whose costs had to be distributed according to the financial possibilities of each country. He was piqued that the same industrialized countries that had impeded the development of the Third World nations were now demanding that these same nations invest more of their resources in environmental protection.[10]

At home, Echeverría expressed greater sympathy for the cause of environmental protection. He acknowledged that the land and water had limits that could not be transgressed without harmful repercussions, and he promised to attack the problem of pollution without delay.[11] In 1971, Echeverría enacted the first piece of antipollution legislation in Mexico—the Law for the Prevention and Control of Pollution. This law embodied his palliative approach to environmental problems. In particular, it proposed technological remedies for Mexico's environmental ills. From Echeverría's perspective, this approach had obvious advantages. He could be seen as taking steps to control pollution without having to disrupt industrial production or without having to require a change in people's life-styles.

Like their counterparts in the United States, Mexican officials had traditionally envisioned pollution as a public health problem. The U.S. Clean Air and Clean Water Acts (1970 and 1972) and the Mexican Law for the Control and Prevention of Pollution only partially broadened this perspective to include the threat that pollution posed to the natural world. The regulation for the Mexican law stated that "the pollution of the environment constitutes a grave threat to public health and provokes degradation of ecological systems in detriment to the national economy and to the harmonious development of society" and "it is necessary to control pollution because it endangers the life and well-being of humans, plants, and animals."[12] But the fact that the government placed the newly created Sub-Ministry of Environmental Improvement within the Ministry of Health and Welfare was a strong indication that public officials were primarily concerned about the danger that pollution posed to human health rather than the threat it posed to ecosystems. Furthermore, the Ministry of Agriculture and Livestock and the Ministry of Water Resources retained control over the exploitation of the country's natural resources. These ministries were more concerned with the expansion of agriculture than with the integrity of the environment. Echeverría's environmental initiatives were limited to pollution control.[13] He did not combine environmental protection and the conservation of natural resources together in a single program for ecological maintenance.[14]

Mexico and the United States enacted quite similar pollution control laws. Both countries set emission standards for point sources of air and water pollution, required industries to install antipollution devices, mandated that automobile manufacturers produce better engines, allocated moneys for sewage treatment plants, and set fines for those who violated the laws. The Mexican law required new industries to obtain a license for operation and required all industries to register with the government. In addition, it established a procedure by which Mexican citizens could report polluters to the government, a leverage that became significant after the emergence of an environmental movement during the 1980s. Mexico's anticontamination law also offered tax breaks and other incentives for the relocation of industries and civil servants in Mexico City to smaller cities throughout the republic. Few manufacturers and bureaucrats, though, were willing to leave the center of political and economic power.[15] In a sense, decentralizing industry and population was yet another technological solution to Mexico's pollution problems, in this case relying upon social engineering rather than upon civil engineering.[16]

Many aspects of the Mexican Law for the Prevention and Control of Pollution were poorly enforced. Like their U.S. counterparts, Mexican officials granted extensions to industries that claimed they could not afford or did not have enough time to install antipollution technology. For a variety of reasons, though, the enforcement of pollution control laws was much more problematical in Mexico than in the United States. Relative to the United States, the development of certain technologies, such as catalytic converters, lagged behind in Mexico. Because of budget constraints, the Mexican government lacked the personnel to inspect polluting industries. Public officials often had to rely on an industry's goodwill to register with the government. As might be expected, many industries either did not register or gave inaccurate information. Some industries apparently bribed government officials to falsely report that they had installed the pollution control devices.[17] Members of the Sub-Ministry of Environmental Improvement had to share responsibility for the enforcement of the air pollution regulations with the Ministry of Industry and Commerce and water pollution regulations with the Ministry of Water Resources. In comparison to these development-oriented industries, the subministry was underfunded and bureaucratically weak. Thus, even when officials within the subministry wanted to enforce pollution control laws rigorously, they often could not obtain the necessary support from other ministries. All of these factors added to the lack of enforcement of environmental regulations. According to the findings of one investigator, as of the early 1980s, only 2 percent of fifteen hundred polluting factories had actually installed antipollution technology.[18] Industry was confident in the knowledge that the government was not going to "sacrifice" economic growth to control pollution.[19]

Echeverría's lackluster enforcement of pollution control laws produced some public outcry. His undersecretary of environmental improvement, Francisco Vizcaíno Murray, reacted angrily to charges that the government had reneged on its promise to clean up the environment. He insisted that because of scarce fiscal resources and a precarious economy, Mexico could not afford to adopt more stringent environmental measures. He also rebuffed the suggestion that Mexico should seek foreign technical assistance in dealing with its environmental problems. He retorted that Mexico would deal with its environmental problems in its own way. Vizcaíno Murray proclaimed that by abating pollution without arresting development, the Echeverría administration had accomplished a true revolution.[20]

Mexico's next president, José López Portillo (1976–1982), shared Echeverría's perspective on environmental issues. Echoing his predecessor's credo, López Portillo declared that it was "all hysterical exaggeration that pollution is the result of our development process itself." Like Echeverría, his assertion was that "man had the genius to both grow and preserve the environment." During the first half of his presidency, López Portillo had an opportunity to test the validity of this thesis, as skyrocketing oil prices produced an economic boom in Mexico. López Portillo amplified the revenues produced from oil exports by borrowing billions of dollars from foreign banks. He proceeded to funnel this wealth into large-scale public works projects, such as dams and highways, which further accelerated deforestation and soil erosion in Mexico. When oil prices plummeted at the beginning of the 1980s, the Mexican economy went into a tailspin. Faced with billions of dollars in outstanding loans, López Portillo began implementing austerity measures. He pleaded that he could not institute stronger pollution control measures because such action would force up the price of goods and further erode Mexico's competitive position on the international market. During both boom and bust times, López Portillo found it inopportune to apply stricter environmental measures.[21]

López Portillo did institute some minor changes in environmental policy and administration. In 1977, the federal executive gave the Ministry of Health and Welfare responsibility for planning and directing the nation's environmental policy. A year later, the president created an intersectoral commission (i.e., composed of representatives from different agencies) for environmental health to coordinate environmental programs. These changes strengthened the hand of environmental policymakers within the Mexican government. On the other hand, environmental officials faced a powerful adversary to the enforcement of pollution control regulations in the newly created Ministry of Agriculture and Water Resources. Although the Ministries of Health and Welfare and of Agriculture and Water Resources did improve the monitoring of water quality in Mexico, they did not adopt bold measures to reduce water pollution. Environmental education programs also advanced incrementally. The Ministry of Education introduced environmental materials into the curriculum of primary schools and announced a similar program for secondary schools. Most Mexican students, however, remained uneducated about the environmental crisis within their country. For the most part, López Portillo had adhered to the narrow environmental remedies of his predecessor.[22]

Late in his term, López Portillo appointed one of his relatives, Manuel López Portillo y Ramos, to head the Sub-Ministry of Environmental Improvement. Manuel López Portillo y Ramos advocated and obtained a stronger environmental law: the Federal Law for the Protection of the Environment (1982). The new statute gave the government the power to shut down industries that did not install pollution control devices and to sentence to prison (from six months to five years) corporate executives who violated the law. The government could suspend industrialization and urban development when such development could be shown to have a harmful effect on the environment and on ecological processes. Both government agencies and industries had to file environmental impact statements (this provision was stronger than the 1970 National Environmental Policy Act in the United States, which required environmental impact statements for federally funded projects only). The law held the promise of greater government intervention on behalf of environmental protection.[23]

Though not trivial, the environmental measures undertaken by Echeverría and López Portillo had done little to arrest Mexico's environmental decline. As the government itself acknowledged: "There is no doubt that after ten years of environmental preoccupation of legislation and attitude, we have not made substantial advancement in improving the quality of the environment."[24]

During the presidential campaign of 1982, Miguel de la Madrid announced his intention to address Mexico's environmental ills. For the first time in Mexican history, a presidential candidate had made the environment a campaign issue.[25] During his bid for the presidency, de la Madrid made the following statement:

We have defended our natural resources from the ambition of foreigners, but not from ourselves. The irregular human settlements, the irrational exploitation of forests and jungles, the industrial pollution of the air, land, and water require an action not only of the government but by all of society. We ought to develop a national ecological consciousness and a respect for the norms and criteria necessary for the conservation of our natural resources.[26]

De la Madrid appeared eager to enlarge the scope of Mexico's environmental programs and to spur citizen participation in environmental protection and restoration. He partially fulfilled his pact with the Mexican people to integrate ecological concerns into government programs.[27]

A few cases illustrate the expansion and the continued limitations of environmental policy under de la Madrid. In 1985, the government closed down one fertilizer plant in the state of Mexico and temporarily closed down two others.[28] In January 1988, during a particularly severe thermal inversion (an atmospheric condition in which cold air and pollutants became trapped under warm air), the government suspended 50 percent of the industrial activity in Xalostoc and 30 percent of the principal factories in Tlalnepantla (both northern satellite communities of Mexico City) for five days (the ban was lifted when the government said meteorological conditions had improved).[29] In these cases and in several others, the de la Madrid administration enforced the 1982 Federal Law for the Protection of the Environment.

In other cases, de la Madrid's commitment to environmental protection was more equivocal. During his term, public and private groups planted over sixty-five million trees, but for every tree planted another one hundred were cut.[30] Within the Valley of Mexico, many of the tree seedlings died from pollution or were chopped down to make way for street expansion. The de la Madrid administration created an interministerial commission for the protection of the Lacandón Jungle. Nevertheless, 143,000 hectares of the Lacandón rain forest were cut during his term.[31] De la Madrid had adopted some positive environmental measures, but had not effectively regulated harmful environmental activities, some of which the government itself had perpetrated.

De la Madrid's treatment of Pemex, the government's oil monopoly, marked only a slight change from the past. During the 1970s and 1980s, Pemex, despite being one of the most polluting industries in Mexico, was never fined by the government (although after the 1981 Ixtoc oil spill in the Gulf of Mexico, the government required Pemex to establish a clean-up fund and to take preventative measures to avoid future oil spills).[32] In 1983, *campesinos* from the state of Tabasco (along the Gulf of Mexico) protested against Pemex for allowing oil to leak from its derricks. The *campesinos* complained that the oil that washed up along the coast of the Gulf of Mexico was killing their cattle and destroying their lands. The government responded to these protests by signing an accord with Pemex in which the company agreed to restore the lands affected by the spills. The government, however, rejected the peasants' request for collective compensation. Peasants in Tabasco responded to this decision by stealing cars and damaging Pemex property. Eventually the government reached an agreement with the peasants based on individual compensation.[33]

The de la Madrid administration was similarly lenient with Pemex after the 1984 explosion of its refinery in San Juan Ixhuatepec (a small community north of Mexico City), which resulted in the deaths of at least 452 people. Pemex blamed the explosion on a nearby Unigas plant, but no one in San Juan accepted this explanation, since the Unigas installation was still standing while the Pemex plant was completely destroyed. Moreover, for years before the disaster, residents in the vicinity of the refinery had complained about the smell of gas. Citizen's frustration with the unresponsiveness of public officials to their grievances reached its height a few weeks after the explosion when a government commission refused to assess the cause of the blast or to investigate reports of missing relatives. Graffiti appeared in the community accusing Pemex of murder.[34] A month after the explosion, the de la Madrid administration finally held the state-run oil monopoly responsible for the disaster at San Juan Ixhuatepec. De la Madrid called upon Pemex to pay reparations, but he brought no criminal charges against its officials. Pemex could no longer act with impunity, but the government was still highly protective of its interests.[35]

The creation of the Ministry of Urban Development and Ecology (SEDUE) was potentially the most important environmental action taken by de la Madrid. SEDUE promised to be an effective agency for dealing with environmental matters because it had ministerial status (SEDUE was Mexico's first cabinet-level environmental agency) and because it was granted jurisdiction over most conservation and environmental protection programs. On paper, at least, SEDUE had the principal responsibility for the formulation and implementation of the nation's environmental policy.

Many Mexican conservationists and environmentalists became disappointed with SEDUE's performance. The Mexican botanist Arturo Gómez-Pompa was among those who joined the chorus against the agency. His terse assessment of SEDUE was that it had not accomplished much.[36] He urged ecologists to become involved in the development of the country's environmental programs rather than abdicating this role to ill-equipped lawyers, architects, and public accountants.[37] Reportedly, Arturo Gómez-Pompa himself had expected to be appointed the first head of SEDUE. He was certainly well qualified for the post. As director of the National Institute for Research on Biotic Resources (INIREB), Gómez-Pompa had worked tirelessly to advance the knowledge of Mexico's tropical ecosystems and in particular the heavily altered ecosystems of Veracruz. He demonstrated the value of his expertise when he wrote a comprehensive environmental plan for the de la Madrid administration. In choosing SEDUE's first secretary, though, Miguel de la Madrid, passed over Gómez-Pompa for a career politician. De la Madrid's choice convinced many conservationists that the new administration did not want SEDUE to become a powerful advocate for environmental protection.[38]

Some SEDUE officials acknowledged the limitations of their agency. The undersecretary of ecology, Alicia Bárcena Ibarra, noted that officials in ministries traditionally responsible for management of resources resented and resisted SEDUE's attempts to define priorities because they viewed the department's environmental orientation to be a brake on development. The response of the Ministry of Agriculture and Water Resources to SEDUE's efforts to regulate pesticide use illustrates Bárcena Ibarra's point. After initial discussions, agricultural officials agreed to maintain a "polite working relationship" with SEDUE over the application of pesticides, but turned down the agency's proposal for scheduled meetings and refused to cede any of their authority over pesticide use.[39] The rural environment was further neglected because many high-level Mexican officials were concerned only about improving the quality of life within urban areas. This bias was manifest in the de la Madrid administration's creation of SEDUE, which oversaw both urban development and environmental protection (the ministry became even more preoccupied with urban problems after Mexico City was devastated by an earthquake in 1985). As in the past, the government's efforts to maintain ecosystems were principally restricted to the creation and management of protected natural areas and to the conservation of flora and fauna. With the exception of a few small programs, such as the promotion of game ranching, aquaculture, and horticulture, government support for sustainable development in rural areas was lacking.[40]

Bárcena Ibarra's general conclusion was that SEDUE's effectiveness depended on an expansion of intersectorial planning and agreements with private enterprises. She asserted, therefore, that in the short term, the environmental education of powerful officials was even more important than the education of the nation's youth. In addition, Bárcena Ibarra argued for the inclusion of state and municipal authorities and civic groups in the campaign for environmental improvement. The backing of local governments and community organizations as well as the upper echelons of the federal government was essential for the restoration of the natural world.[41]

Despite its weak position, SEDUE modestly advanced the cause of environmental protection in Mexico. In 1987, the National Ecology Commission, an interdepartmental body that included representatives from SEDUE, announced one hundred actions that were being—or would be—taken to protect the environment. Some of these actions repeated the traditional technological responses to pollution control, such as employing the most advanced technologies for reducing automobile emissions, developing better fuels, installing antipollution devices in factories, requiring all cars to have mufflers, and building or upgrading sewage systems throughout the country. For instance, in 1987 SEDUE expended over 10 percent of its 200-million-dollar budget on water pollution control projects.[42] The commission, however, acknowledged that pollution could not be significantly diminished until people and businesses changed their behavior.

Among the changes advocated by the commission were car pooling, reducing the number of automobiles in circulation, improving public transportation, changing deliveries to nonrush hours, and recycling. The commission placed attention on the importance of environmental education and participation in dealing with Mexico's environmental crisis. It promised to make "conservation activities a permanent part of the lives of school age children and society." Among the conservation measures outlined in the one hundred actions were the creation of natural reserves for the monarch butterfly and the sea turtle, a ban on the hunting of toucans, black bears, and jaguars (all of which are endangered species in Mexico), the creation of biosphere reserves and wildlife refuges, and the stiffening of penalties for the killing of and trafficking in various species.[43]

SEDUE addressed transboundary environmental problems, too. In 1983, the de la Madrid administration dictated that industries return any imported hazardous materials left over from the production process back to the country of origin.[44] In an agreement aimed principally at stopping U.S.-based companies from transporting and dumping toxic waste into Mexico, the Mexican and U.S. governments pledged in 1986 to notify each other about the transshipment of hazardous wastes across the border and to respect each other's national laws on the matter.[45] Mexican and U.S. officials also embarked on the control of air and water pollution on the borderlands. Mexico built sulfur dioxide treatment plants for two of its copper smelters in northwestern Sonora and the United States shut down a foundry in southern Arizona as part of a cooperative effort to eliminate the dispersal of pollutants and acid rain in a region that had become known as the "Gray Triangle."[46] Assisted by a three-million-dollar investment from the United States, the de la Madrid administration improved Mexicali's drainage, sewerage, and garbage disposal systems to prevent the runoff of wastes into the New River and via the New River into the United States.[47] Mexican authorities also took unilateral steps to control transboundary pollution, including the building of a new waste treatment plant at Tijuana.[48] At least some of the borderland problems became part of the environmental agenda in Mexico and in the United States.[49]

Yet despite SEDUE's efforts, the treatment plants, landfills, and other facilities necessary to mitigate pollution problems along the border remained inadequate. As a U.S. waste disposal expert noted in 1990: "Protecting the environment has become a political priority in Mexico. But the infrastructure is totally missing, and building it will involve astronomical costs and a lot of time."[50] Many new sewage treatment plants in border cities were quickly overburdened. In addition, millions of gallons of sewage flowed into local waterways and seeped into the groundwater because many residents lacked indoor plumbing. Because of a shortage of personnel, SEDUE was also ill equipped to oversee the proper disposal of toxic wastes. Thus, U.S. companies on both sides of the border continued to poison the Mexican environment. The magnitude of the pollution problems in border cities combined with the scarcity of financial and human resources to deal with them dimmed hopes of reversing environmental damage in the region.

In some cases, SEDUE was remiss in its enforcement of environmental regulations. This was particularly true of the agency's failure to control the illegal trade in endangered species, despite its pledge to do so. SEDUE only occasionally prosecuted violators of national laws against the possession of threatened animals. Furthermore, Mexico was the only country in the Western Hemisphere not to sign the Convention on the International Trade in Endangered Species (CITES) and for this reason became a major entrepôt for animal traffickers. The smugglers' merchandise included live species of such distant origin as Indonesian cockatoos, Brazilian macaws, African monkeys, and South American boa constrictors. In addition, the traffickers' trade in feline furs is contributing to the disappearance of the jaguar, puma, and ocelot in Mexico. During the late 1980s, U.S. and Mexican conservationists estimated that hundreds of thousands of species were smuggled across the border each year and that the annual value of the trade was 400 million dollars. The reluctance of the Mexican government to sign CITES drew sharp protests from Mexican conservationists and from environmentalists abroad.[51]

Many SEDUE officials were concerned about the future of environmental protection in Mexico. They strove to establish a legal framework that would make it difficult for de la Madrid's successor to disregard environmental issues.[52] Their efforts culminated in the promulgation of the General Law on Ecological Balance and Environmental Protection in 1988. Herein, the federal executive declared: "The control and prevention of environmental pollution, the proper utilization of natural resources, and the improvement of natural settings within human communities are fundamentally important to the betterment of human life."[53] According to the law, the government had to address environmental matters in its national plans and review any proposed project that exceeded federally set environmental threshold levels. Equally important, the General Law on Ecological Balance and Environmental Protection delegated more authority to state and municipal officials to deal with environmental problems. The de la Madrid administration called on governments at all levels to "regulate, control, and when possible, prevent all forms of pollution."[54]

The legislation outlined a program for the control of air, water, noise, and soil pollution, hazardous wastes and materials, and nuclear energy. Among its most noteworthy provisions, the statute prohibited the importation of pesticides, fertilizers, and other toxic substances that were banned in the countries where they were produced, authorized the establishment of smog inspection stations, and empowered the government to suspend traffic during periods of severe pollution.[55] The General Law on Ecological Balance and Environmental Protection incorporated many of SEDUE's past programs as well as many of the elements from previous laws. The act was more than a compendium of past policies and legislation, though; it was a strong statement that the control of pollution required the concerted action of government officials at all levels and by all members of society.

In another major section of the law, the federal executive presented a series of proposals to conserve Mexico's natural resources. These included the reuse of wastewater, the application of soil conservation techniques, and a shift away from the slash and burn method to ecologically sound forms of agriculture.[56] The de la Madrid administration also presented a broad-based rationale for the establishment of protected areas that had roots in the country's conservation history. In a passage reminiscent of the expositions of Miguel Angel de Quevedo, Miguel Alvarez del Toro, Enrique Beltrán, Gertrude Duby Blom, and Gonzalo Halffter, the federal executive pronounced that the creation of natural reserves was justifiable and necessary to preserve the genetic diversity upon which the continuity of evolutionary processes depended, to ensure the survival of representative ecosystems for their own value and for scientific research, to foster the rational use of natural resources as well as their preservation, and to protect roads, industrial plants, and farms in mountain zones where floods originate and the hydrologic cycle in river basins. In regard to the creation of national parks, the de la Madrid administration tendered the same anthropocentric arguments (scenery, recreation, and tourism) and biocentric arguments (the protection of flora and fauna) that Miguel Angel de Quevedo had offered a half century earlier.[57] At least on paper, the PRI was adopting some of the ideas of Mexico's pioneer conservationists.

The General Law on Ecological Balance and Environmental Protection was an extensive piece of legislation. Yet even the secretary of SEDUE, Manuel Camacho Solís, acknowledged that the law was not a panacea for Mexico's environmental problems. Alfonso Ciprés Villarreal, an environmental leader in Mexico, adopted an incredulous attitude toward the law. As Ciprés Villarreal noted, part of the problem in Mexico was that past laws had not been enforced. He was troubled by the vague language regarding the development and implementation of "technical norms," that would define unacceptable levels of environmental degradation. He called upon the government to establish standards expeditiously to ensure "that the law is applied and does not remain a declaration of good intentions."[58] The fate of this new law depended on the course chosen by de la Madrid's successor, Carlos Salinas de Gortari.

Salinas's rhetoric indicated that he was committed to the cause of environmental protection. In 1982, he stated that: "Traditionally it has been affirmed that we ought to be preoccupied with generating employment and later we can begin to resolve environmental problems. This thesis is as false as the thesis that we ought to grow first and redistribute later. . . . What good is employment if the health of the worker is affected by air pollution, food contamination, and deafening noise?"[59] More recently, in a speech in which he promised to end the plundering of the Lacandón Jungle, Salinas declared: "Mexico is committed to making progress and progress does not mean more degradation and destruction of [Mexico's] natural resources."[60] Salinas apparently did not consider environmental protection to be an obstacle to development nor did he appear to conceive of industrialization and economic growth as sacred cows. Instead, he professed to believe that the care of the environment was essential for the well-being of all Mexicans.

During his presidential campaign in 1988, Salinas promised to make environmental protection and restoration one of the top priorities of his administration. He was particularly concerned about the ecological collapse of the Valley of Mexico:

Few problems in the city have produced such a preoccupation so broad and shared by all sectors of society as the deterioration of the environment. The resources that permitted the rapid development

of the region have come to the limits of their exploitation. Our valley has lost its ecological equilibrium. It will be the task of several
generations to restore it until once again we will have a clear hori-
zon to see our volcanoes and contemplate.[61]

The Salinas administration has taken measures to begin the process
of ecological restoration in the Valley of Mexico. One project involves
the rescue of Xochimilco. Xochimilco's famous waterways, along which
flower- and tourist-laden boats ply, have become clogged with vegetation because of the "introduction" of wastewaters containing phos-
phates. Increased evaporation, drainage projects, and water drafts have
led to the desiccation of many lakes and canals. The ecological equilibrium of Xochimilco began to be broken in 1909, when an aqueduct was
built to divert water that fed into the lakes. By the 1950s, most of the
springs in the region had dried up. Wells were then dug, but this led to
the subsidence of the soil. Annual average rainfall in the region has
dropped by 30 percent since the beginning of the century.[62] Salinas's
plan to rescue Xochimilco entails stopping the march of urbanization
in the region, preserving existing springs and recharging aquifers, preventing pollution from entering into waterways (through the collection
and treatment of wastes), and creating new green spaces and recreational areas.[63] Though not yet complete, the government's program to
protect the waters of Xochimilco has received praise from environmental groups.[64]

Other government efforts have focused on water conservation and
reforestation in the Valley of Mexico. Between 1990 and 1992, the government raised water fees by 400 percent in an effort to stimulate conservation (prior to this series of price hikes, Mexico City's residents paid
one of the lowest water rates in the world).[65] Mexican officials understand that water conservation is the only alternative to pumping water
into the Valley of Mexico from increasingly distant river basins. As they
readily admit, the economic and ecological costs of water importation
are becoming unbearable.[66]

In regard to reforestation, the Salinas administration has sought to
enlist the support of the valley's 20 million residents in civic tree-
planting programs. In the summer of 1990, the government put up posters throughout the city exhorting each family to plant a tree. As part
of this campaign, public officials distributed 750,000 saplings free of
charge to families who wanted to plant them in their gardens and pa-
tios. In addition, they recruited volunteers to plant one million trees in

public areas.[67] In 1990, SEDUE began a companion program in which parents of newborn children were given a tree to grow and care for as they cared for their children.[68] These programs were meant to complement the government's own reforestation program.

Salinas's boldest programs were directed against Mexico City's staggering air pollution problems. In November 1989, Salinas began the no traffic campaign: motorists were barred from driving their cars one day during the workweek through the winter months, when air pollution is at its worst. This program took approximately 500,000 cars out of circulation each weekday. The fine for driving on a prohibited day, as determined by a color-coded and numbered registration sticker, was 115 U.S. dollars—the equivalent of one month's salary at minimum wage. Some recalcitrant motorists bribed police officers to avoid paying the penalty. Still, the majority of car owners complied with the new regulation, despite encountering a public transportation system overburdened with new riders. The main opposition to the program came from business people who claimed that they had fewer customers as a result of the reduction in car traffic and more problems in making deliveries. The Salinas administration, though, referred to polling data indicating widespread support for the day without a car to justify the continuation of this aggressive pollution control effort. In fact, Mexico's no traffic campaign is one of the most restrictive measures undertaken in any country against the use of automobiles. In part because of the campaign, levels of carbon monoxide, hydrocarbons, sulfuric dioxide, lead, and nitrogen oxide dropped by 15 percent between November and March. During its first winter, the day without a car program was at least a partial success.[69]

After this, however, the effectiveness of the program declined because car ownership increased. In the year following the initiation of the no traffic campaign, residents in Mexico City bought 300,000 new automobiles. Some were purchased as second vehicles by wealthy Mexicans in order to guarantee themselves a car to drive every day of the week. Soon the number of new cars added to the road exceeded those taken out of circulation by the no traffic campaign. Thus, the program could only lessen the rate of increase in automobile generated air pollution rather than reduce it.[70]

During the winter of 1991, the government implemented tough measures to cope with one of the worst periods of air pollution ever in Mexico City. The government cut commercial fuel oil supplies by 80 percent, thereby compelling businesses to switch to diesel fuel or to natural gas to make up for the deficits.[71] Public officials pledged to expend

1.3 billion dollars on new taxis and buses that would have catalytic converters and that could use unleaded gasoline; the new vehicles are to replace Mexico City's aging and polluting ground fleet (this program was in large part financed by a one-billion-dollar loan from the Japanese).[72] They also developed contingency plans to close down schools, cancel public events, and eliminate highly polluting industries if air pollution levels exceeded certain levels.[73] The Salinas administration soon applied this strategy in dramatic fashion by closing down Pemex's 18th of March refinery. The refinery, a major polluter, supplied fuel to 15 million residents in the valley (the government increased imports to meet the demand for gasoline) and employed over three thousand workers. The refinery, which is slated to be reconstructed outside the Valley of Mexico, was dismantled at a cost of 500 million U.S. dollars. A park and other green space now exist in its place.[74] The mayor of Mexico City, Manuel Camacho Solís (the past head of SEDUE), declared that the closure was a warning to other industries: "If it could be done with the refinery, it can be done with any industry."[75] Indeed, the government permanently or temporarily shut down eighty factories for violating air quality standards in the Valley of Mexico between February and May 1991.[76]

Salinas's actions seemed to redress the complaint from his secretary of urban development and ecology, Patricio Chirinos, that SEDUE lacked "the funds to check pollution levels and enforce Mexico's toothless anticontamination laws."[77] Yet even though President Salinas increased the number of SEDUE inspectors from nine to fifty (in April 1991) and stepped up factory closures, many industries continued to gamble that the administration had neither the capacity nor the will to shut them down. Indeed, only 5 percent of the 1,150 factories SEDUE inspected in the Valley of Mexico in 1991 were meeting air quality standards. Many companies correctly gauged the reluctance of the government to close their operations, for Salinas cracked down on only a few of the worst offenders.[78]

Bracing for yet another winter of severe pollution, Camacho Solís announced his plans in November 1991 to remove old cars from the road more quickly, reduce the use of government vehicles by 30 percent, in part by conducting official business via telefaxes and bicycle messengers, cut operations at thermoelectric plants, eliminate the use of high sulfur fuels by factories, and impose stricter emission standards on cars and industries. Alfonso Pérez Contreras, director of the Autonomous Institute of Ecological Research, criticized Camacho Solís's antipollution package for being too modest: "The city needs big solutions, and these are small solutions gathered together." The mayor responded by spotlighting the government's most impressive environmental programs in Mexico City: "It is no small thing that the government has switched the city's microbuses to unleaded fuel, put all the cars out of circulation one day a week, shut down the area's biggest refinery, and planted 12.6 million trees a year."[79]

Yet neither small nor big programs could counteract the increase in car ownership and the failure of industries to install new pollution control devices. Moreover, many government antipollution programs entailed long lead times. For instance, trucks, buses, and taxi owners had until 1996 to convert their engines to burn alternative fuels or buy new vehicles with catalytic converters.[80] Not surprisingly, then, Mexico City's air pollution problems worsened. On 16 March 1992, ozone levels (a pollutant formed by the interaction of nitrogen oxides and hydrocarbons with sunlight) reached .45 parts per million, more than four times the maximum acceptable level set by the World Health Organization. Government officials responded by imposing a second-stage emergency that entailed a second day without a car, including weekends (taking 40 percent of the automobiles out of circulation), the closure of two thousand schools, and a reduction in the operations of 192 industries by 50 to 75 percent.[81] Salinas lifted the emergency after one day but had to reinstitute it later in the week as pollution levels soared again.

In the midst of this second emergency, Salinas announced a new ecological pact that gave Mexico City's two hundred worst polluters two years to reduce sulfur dioxide emissions by 90 percent and levels of nitrogen oxide by 50 percent or else move out of the Valley of Mexico. To facilitate the retrofitting, Salinas offered factories a 300-million-dollar loan package. While most industrialists supported the plan, some such as Vicente Gutiérrez, president of the National Manufacturing Chamber, complained that industry was being asked to shoulder too great of the burden for air pollution control, since automobiles were responsible for 75 percent of the problem in the Valley of Mexico (factories, however, emitted most of the sulfur dioxide and heavy metals). On the other side, some environmentalists were disappointed that Salinas did not announce plans to shut down some of the city's worst polluters immediately. Despite criticisms, the administration seemed intent on taking the middle road.[82]

In trying to portray pollution control measures in Mexico City as extraordinary, Fernando Menéndez Garza, director of Environmental Projects for the Federal District, said, "We've got a 4.68 billion dollar environmental program in a Third World city emerging from ten years of its worst economic crisis. If that's not commitment to the environment, what is?"[83] Increasingly, though, Mexico City's residents began to wonder whether it was enough. In a radical alternative to current environmental policies, the director of the city's clean air program suggested a 1,000 percent tax on gasoline, barring all automobile traffic, distributing hundreds of thousands of bicycles, and making public transportation available to everyone.[84] For now, though, the government is largely counting on the use of new technologies to improve air quality in Mexico City.[85]

Salinas has demonstrated less commitment to the resolution of many of Mexico's other environmental problems. A few months after coming to office, he declared a three-month moratorium on cutting in the Lacandón Jungle and banned new settlements in the region.[86] However, Salinas failed to enforce these measures, raising doubts among conservationists about his dedication to preserving Mexico's rain forest. The World Bank's environmental division, for one, somberly adjudged that "the absence of protection [for the Lacandón Jungle] . . . lends little credibility to the government's resolve to promote conservation."[87] With funding from the World Bank and Conservation International (as part of the debt for nature swap), Salinas initiated programs during the early 1990s to study the biological diversity of the rain forest and to promote sustainable development in the region. The outcome of the latter program is particularly critical, for if the region's inhabitants do not adopt alternatives to the destruction of the forest soon, it will disappear.[88]

The Lerma River–Lake Chapala basin is another degraded ecosystem in need of immediate remediation. The Lerma River, which passes through a long industrial and agricultural corridor in west-central Mexico, is a cesspool for human and animal wastes, heavy metals, and toxic chemicals, including pesticides and inorganic fertilizers. Furthermore, because of the expansion of cities, factories, and farms, only one-sixth of the flow of the Lerma River reaches Lake Chapala as it did a decade ago. Coupled with the river's reduced volume, the use of Lake Chapala's waters by farmers and by Guadalajara (Mexico's second largest city) has produced a two-thirds drop in the level of the lake since 1960. Ecologist warn that unless this process is reversed, the region will soon become a desert.

In 1989, Salinas allocated fifty-two million dollars to the construction of sewage treatment plants, collector systems, and reclamation projects (such as the lining of open ditches) intended to halve the river's pollution and to raise the level of Lake Chapala by 10 percent. Construction on many of these projects, however, is proceeding slowly, and in some cases, not at all. Even if all the systems are eventually completed, it is doubtful that the promised improvements in water quality and quantity will be met given the tremendous demands that are placed on the Lerma River and Lake Chapala.[89]

One of Salinas's most definitive conservation acts came in 1990, when he banned the commercial exploitation of sea turtles. Prior to this edict, only the rare Kemps Ridley turtle was officially protected, even though seven other species were also endangered. The turtle's skin and shell provided a lucrative export trade in clothing products and jewelry. Apart from its export value, some poachers collected turtle eggs and killed the animal for its meat. One of the unlikely threats to the turtle, though, came from the government itself. In 1989, crews in officially approved slaughterhouses killed approximately 35,000 turtles. At least, Salinas's ban has removed the government as an accomplice in the marine turtle's demise.[90] Environmentalists hope that Salinas's decision to sign the CITES treaty in 1991 reflects his commitment to eliminating the trade in all endangered species.[91]

The Salinas administration moved less decisively to reduce the number of dolphins killed in the nets of Mexican tuna fishers (one member of the Delphinidae family, the vaquita porpoise, is an endangered species). In 1989, the U.S. environmental group Earth Island Institute obtained a court order forcing a reluctant Bush administration to impose a tuna embargo against Mexico because its fleets exceeded the level of dolphin kills permitted by an amendment to the Marine Mammal Protection Act. Mexican fishery officials strenuously objected to the use of a U.S. environmental law to restrict access to one of their resources.[92] In their campaign to have the embargo removed, the Mexican government employed two strategies: first, they asked a special GATT (General Agreement on Tariffs and Trade) panel to rule that the sanction violated the principle of free trade, and second, they began to develop a dolphin protection program. In August 1991, the GATT committee ruled in Mexico's favor, stating that "a member-nation has no right to obstruct trade detrimental to the environment beyond its borders." If enshrined as a tenet of GATT, this decision threatened to undo many international conservation treaties.[93] Mexico, though, did not request a ratification of this ruling by the full GATT, perhaps fearing an environmental backlash that might jeopardize the North American Free Trade Agreement (NAFTA). Instead, the Ministry of Fisheries presented its dolphin protection program that included the placement of foreign observers on all Mexican tuna boats and a one-million-dollar project to develop techniques that would reduce dolphin kills.[94] In 1992, Mexico agreed not to set nets around schools of tuna that included dolphins, perhaps resolving this long-standing dispute between the Salinas administration and the international environmental community.[95]

Despite Salinas's promising rhetoric, from the beginning Mexican environmentalists questioned his commitment to environmental protection. When in the fall of 1989, Mexican writer and environmental leader Homero Aridjis was asked by a journalist if Carlos Salinas had kept his promise to make the environment a top priority of his administration, he responded:

> Not yet. His ecological policy has been very weak. SEDUE has failed to take a stand with respect to almost all our environmental problems—pollution, the forest fires in Quintana Roo last summer, radioactive leaks in the Laguna Verde nuclear power plant. We are very concerned about the lack of a concrete environmental policy because there are many ecological crises here.[96]

Since then, Salinas's environmental record has received mixed reviews from Aridjis and other environmentalists. When the U.N.-backed United Earth Association honored Carlos Salinas de Gortari for his "valiant environmental actions that will benefit both Mexico and the world," Aridjis reflected that, through Salinas, Mexico could potentially become a model for the rest of Latin America in the field of environmental protection. Yet he also noted that Salinas received the award in the same year (1991) that air pollution had reached dangerous levels in the Valley of Mexico, forest fires (95 percent of which had been deliberately set) had destroyed 150,000 hectares of vegetation, more than 370,000 hectares had been deforested, wildlife had perished because of hunting, trafficking, and habitat destruction, and water sources had been further depleted and contaminated.[97] In implementing environmental laws, any Mexican government faces a daunting task because of the staggering nature of the problems themselves, the chronic shortage of revenues, and the job of policing so many manufacturers and such a large territory, but no obstacle would be more serious than a government which lacked the will or the desire to restore environmental quality. On the one hand, Salinas has taken some dramatic steps to diminish the destructive impact of human beings upon the environment, particularly within the Valley of Mexico. On the other hand, he is ideologically committed to a program of privatization and foreign investment which he feels is necessary to revitalize the Mexican economy. The two goals are not mutually exclusive, but the question still remains: To what degree will Salinas sacrifice his commitment to environmental quality in order to pursue his economic goals?

The course of negotiations on the free trade agreement between Mexico and the United States will likely reveal the extent of Salinas's commitment to environmental protection. Environmentalists on both sides of the border are concerned that in its eagerness to attract outside investment, the Salinas administration will not enforce pollution laws against foreign companies.[98] SEDUE officials, anxious to allay this fear, expressed their determination to prevent multinational corporations from "dumping pollution" on Mexican citizens. They added that the country's goal "was not to attract polluting industries but to use the free-trade agreement to substitute clean industries for dirty ones."[99] Mexican authorities insisted that they could shape the direction of foreign investment.

The recent experience with free trade in northern Mexico, however, raises serious doubts as to whether the Mexican government can effectively regulate foreign companies. In 1965, Mexico and the United States reached an agreement that not only permitted U.S. businesses to operate on the Mexican side of the border but exempted them from most tariffs and trade barriers. Today, the *maquiladora* industry (predominantly, U.S.-based multinational corporations that assemble raw materials imported from the United States and then export the finished products back across the border) consists of nearly two thousand enterprises, many of which generate air pollutants and toxic wastes. The General Law on Ecological Balance and Environmental Protection included strict regulations for the disposal of hazardous substances, which applied to both domestic and foreign corporations.[100] Nevertheless, only 30 percent of the *maquiladora* plants that handle toxic chemicals have registered with the government and only 19 percent have properly disposed of their wastes.[101]

As an adjunct to the free trade agreement, the U.S. Environmental Protection Agency (EPA) and SEDUE have agreed to assess the environmental risks posed by the *maquiladora* plants operating on the border.[102] In a continuing effort to woo environmentalists on both sides of the border in support of the free trade agreement, the Salinas and Bush administrations announced environmental cleanup plans for the borderlands.[103] In 1990, the U.S. and Mexican governments agreed to jointly fund a 192-million-dollar San Diego–Tijuana sewage plant to be located just north of the Mexican border (12 million gallons of sewage and chemicals run into the Tijuana River each day, some of which flows into the Pacific Ocean and then washes up onto Imperial Beach near San Diego).[104] Mexico has allocated 460 million dollars over three years (1992–1994) to tackle pollution problems along the frontier. As part of this effort, Salinas pledged to increase the number of SEDUE inspectors on his country's border from fifty to two hundred.[105] The U.S. program entails the expenditure of 379 million dollars over two years (1992–1993), principally to deal with environmental problems on the U.S. side of the border.[106] EPA head William Reilly acknowledged, however, that it will take 3 billion dollars just to address waste water problems alone.[107]

In any case, the U.S.-Mexican plan did not mollify environmentalists opposed to the free trade agreement. Not only did they consider the cleanup effort to be inadequate, but they also were perturbed by the refusal of President Bush and President Salinas to conduct a complete environmental assessment as part of the free trade pact.[108] Given Bush's and Salinas's placement of environmental issues as secondary and considering the largely futile efforts of the Mexican government to regulate the *maquiladora* industry, Mexican and U.S. environmentalists are understandably worried about the ecological consequences of opening Mexico to foreign investment. They fear that, along with more industry, Mexico's pollution problems will be exacerbated by the expansion of commerce.[109] If the free trade agreement does result in a substantial deterioration of the Mexican environment, it would be a bitter legacy left by two presidents who claimed to be concerned about environmental issues.[110]

In addition to the free trade agreement, two other unfolding events may impinge upon the future of environmental policy in Mexico: the aftermath of the gas explosion in Guadalajara that killed 192 people and the planned termination of SEDUE.

The immediate events surrounding the explosion at Guadalajara in 1992 were uncannily similar to those at San Juan Ixhuatepec eight years earlier. Once again, Pemex tried to blame the disaster on another industry, this time a cooking oil plant, despite the fact that the plant's hexane (a volatile liquid) tanks were full a day after the explosion. Moreover, for several days before the explosion, people had complained about the smell of gas coming from the city's sewer—gas that had leaked out of a Pemex pipeline. The difference this time was that official investigators quickly implicated the oil monopoly, along with state and local authorities, in the disaster. A few days after the blast, the government charged four Pemex officials, three functionaries from the municipal water company, the mayor of Guadalajara, and the Jalisco state secretary of urban development with negligent homicide. On the other hand, the explosion revealed the failure of government officials to enforce health, safety, and environmental laws. The Salinas administration could take the tragedy as an opportunity to review the safety of all Pemex installations in Mexico and to repair the unsafe ones. Manuel Camacho Solís has already announced that he will have all of Mexico City's sewerage systems checked for gas leaks. Unfortunately, though, the tragedy at Guadalajara may not linger long in the minds of public officials.[111]

Some Mexican environmentalists are disconcerted by Salinas's proposal to replace SEDUE with a new superministry of social development that will administer his antipoverty public works program known as Solidarity, promote indigenous rights and education, and subsume the functions of the Ministry of Housing and Planning, Ministry of Forestry and Land Management, and the National Ecology Commission. Homero Aridjis said that Salinas's decision to dismantle SEDUE makes "it look like he is trying to marginalize ecology or bury the political risks." Martin Goebel, the head of Conservation International's Mexican program, noted that including environmental and forestry officials in the same ministry would likely lead to a direct showdown, since "the forestry service has fought the environmental movement in Mexico every step of the way. Foresters are trained in crop management, not in managing a forest as an ecosystem." On the other hand, Federico Estévez, a political scientist at the Autonomous Technological Institute of Mexico, believes that if the new National Ecology Commission "has teeth and it's run by technical experts, not politicians, then a decentralized, depoliticized agency will do a better job than a ministry of ecology." Indeed, the critical question is whether ecological concerns would perish or flourish in a social development ministry.[112] Like the free trade agreement, the answer to this question may depend on the president's commitment to environmental protection.

Seemingly, an important change in the political leadership's perception of environmental problems occurred during the 1980s. The rhetoric of Miguel de la Madrid and Carlos Salinas de Gortari indicated a shift away from Luis Echeverría's and Jose López Portillo's interpretation of pollution as a public health threat that could be resolved through limited government action. Miguel de la Madrid and Carlos Salinas instead identified pollution as part of a set of ecological problems that could only be resolved through concerted governmental and societal action. While Echeverría and López Portillo spoke of resolving environmental problems without significantly altering industrial development, de la Madrid and Salinas spoke of altering economic plans to take into account the needs of the environment. In rhetoric, at least, de la Madrid and Salinas had placed environmental considerations on the same level as economic considerations. Whether such a fundamental shift had indeed occurred was vigorously contested by most Mexican environmentalists. The impact of a complex environmental movement on Mexican politicians and society is a story in its own right.

Chapter Ten

THE GREEN REVOLUTION

The Mexican Environmental

Movement

Like their U.S. counterparts, a growing number of Mexicans have become concerned about how pollution and the destruction of natural resources is affecting the quality of their lives. As in the United States, concerns for human health and the health of the natural world led to an environmental movement in Mexico.[1] The Mexican environmental movement, however, is still in its infancy. Mexico has over one thousand ecological organizations, but none of them has a mass membership.[2] In fact, not much public support exists for environmental causes in Mexico. Nevertheless, the Mexican environmental movement has become a vocal and periodically successful advocate for the protection of the natural world, in part because political leaders are beginning to share their belief that the country is facing an ecological crisis.

The creation of the Mexican environmental movement was spurred by the dissatisfaction that people felt living in an increasingly polluted environment and by the attention that the media brought to bear on environmental issues. It is these same two factors that are now leading to the expansion of the movement.

The ecological nightmare in Mexico City has been a focal point for environmental concerns in Mexico. By the 1980s, pollution had become a familiar topic of conversation among the residents of the capital. Scores of *capitalinos* suffer from pollution-caused irritations, such as burning eyes, throbbing ears, chronic coughs, and constant fatigue. For many residents, the conditions in Mexico City seem less tolerable because of their recollections of a different time and a different place.

For tens of thousands of *capitalinos*, pollution is more than a nuisance. In slum areas, contaminated water supplies have resulted in a particularly high incidence of dysentery, typhoid, and hepatitis. The six hundred tons of fecal dust that blow into the air each year carry deadly microorganisms, such as *Salmonella typhosa*, *Streptococcus*, and *Staphylococcus*. Mexico City is one of the few places in the world where it is possible to contract typhoid and hepatitis just by breathing the air.[3] The Federal District of Mexico produces eleven thousand tons of garbage daily, fifteen hundred tons of which are not adequately disposed, providing another source for disease transmission.[4] During the course of a year, 4.35 million tons of pollutants are emitted into the air.[5] Concentrations of ozone, carbon monoxide, nitric oxides, sulfur dioxide, hydrocarbons, cadmium, and lead regularly exceed international health standards, sometimes by alarming amounts. For instance, the average lead level in the blood of Mexico City residents is nearly four times that of the residents of Tokyo.[6] In March 1987, U.S. toxicologist Tom Dydek found that nitrogen dioxide and hydrocarbon levels at his monitoring sites in Mexico City were comparable to those found in the Lincoln tunnel, which connects New Jersey to New York City. Dydek's understated conclusion was that "exposure to these concentrations of these chemicals could be expected to cause adverse health effects. No one should be exposed to these levels of air pollution."[7] Physicians in Mexico City attribute many cases of skin anomalies, nervous disorders, mental retardation, respiratory problems, cardiac difficulties, and cancer to the city's heavily polluted air.[8] Medical records from the mid-1980s indicated that thirty thousand children and seventy thousand adults in the city annually died from air and water pollution.[9] Through deaths to family members or through serious illness to loved ones or to themselves, some of Mexico City's twenty million inhabitants became acutely aware of the effects of contamination on public health. From these ranks, the environmental movement drew some of its support.

The health of the natural world is also seriously threatened in Mexico. Three-quarters of Mexico's soils suffer from some degree of erosion;[10] 95 percent of its rivers are contaminated;[11] and 470,000 hectares of forests disappear each year.[12] These are distant problems for Mexico's urban population. Still, an increasing number of urbanites have come to the conclusion that their survival depends on the health of the land. José Sarukhan, a Mexican ecologist and rector of the National Autonomous University of Mexico, observed that formerly technical terms like "ecology," "environment," and "conservation" had become part of the common language. As each year people heard more about the shortages of potable water, clean air, and fertile soil, they began to link human behavior to the damage of the natural environment that sustains life.[13]

As Sarukhan implied, the Mexican media played (and continues to play) an important role in raising the level of ecological awareness in Mexico. The coverage of environmental issues by newspapers was particularly important, since most Mexicans receive their news from this source. By the late 1970s, Mexico's largest newspapers were regularly reporting on environmental matters. Mexican journalists chronicled the pollution of entire river systems, the desiccation of lakes, the rapid destruction of forests, and the heavy levels of pollution in urban areas. They also exposed scandals, such as gross negligence in the management of toxic wastes and Pemex's polluting of the Mexican southeast.[14] Newspapers became an invaluable source of information on Mexico's environmental woes.[15]

Unomásuno (Mexico City) and the *Mexico City News* provided some of the most extensive commentary on the nation's environmental problems.[16] During the mid-1980s, Fernando Césarman, a Mexican psychologist and environmentalist, became a regular contributor to *Unomásuno*. In a series of editorials ranging from soil erosion to pesticide poisonings, Césarman constantly reminded his readers of humankind's dependence upon the natural world.[17] With *Unomásuno* as his forum, Césarman could communicate his ideas to a mass audience. In August 1989, the newspaper began a monthly supplement on the environment. This special section contained features that not only elucidated the destructive nature of industrial and agricultural development in Mexico but that also told of experiments in alternative techniques, such as agroforestry, solar energy, and hydroponics.[18] *Unomásuno*'s articles increased the public's awareness of the need for ecological maintenance and restoration.

The *Mexico City News* was particularly aggressive in its coverage of Mexico's environmental crisis. In 1988, the paper began its pollution watch that consisted of statements from Mexican citizens and foreign tourists on the state of the Mexican environment (editors placed the quotations on the front page). In both a serious and comic vein, several Mexican citizens questioned where "progress" had led them.

What good are medical breakthroughs which will help us live longer if our technological advances are killing us?[19]
                                        —Robert Suárez, Accountant, Mexico City

I've often wondered how much we are willing to sacrifice for a life of leisure and comfort—and now I know.[20]

—Arturo Villalobos, Environmentalist

Hell isn't hot, it's polluted.[21]

—Hugo Escalante, Student, Mexico City

Some of those quoted in the *Mexico City News* expressed the opinion that the city's pollution problems had been exaggerated. In response to this attitude, Manuel Torres Fuentes, a Mexico City accountant said, "What really frightens me is that we are beginning to accept it even though it is poisoning us."[22]

Fuentes's fear was shared by the editors of the *Mexico City News*. The paper's pollution watch and environmental articles were an attempt to keep pollution and resource degradation in the public's mind. The paper was also trying to pressure government officials into tackling the nation's environmental problems. According to the paper's editors:

Our object is twofold: to alert the authorities to industries and other operations that are polluting the environment so that these activities can be quickly stopped; and to keep the authorities constantly on their toes and aware that they are under continuous scrutiny of citizens and residents of Mexico—and the entire world for that matter, since the Valley of Mexico has become an environmental laboratory.[23]

The Mexican press not only chronicled the country's environmental problems but also demanded action to resolve them.

Though reaching a smaller audience, books also played a role in heightening of environmental concerns. In *The Mexican Metropolis and Its Agony* (1973), Arturo Sotomayor wrote of future space travelers who landed in the Valley of Mexico only to find it uninhabitable. Sotomayor, then, went on to chronicle how his fellow citizens were daily making this bleak future a reality.[24] In *Ecocide: A Psychoanalytical Study of the Destruction of the Environment* (1972), Fernando Césarman examined the suicidal nature of human beings. He coined the term "ecocide" to describe how people were destroying life by destroying the environment.

In his book, Césarman analyzed the roots of the human species' callous treatment of nature. According to Césarman, a critical transition occurred when the vision of nature as paradise was replaced by the vision of nature as an unmitigated obstacle to human welfare and happiness: "The environment is seen as something we must struggle against, struggle against the land to make it produce, struggle against the rivers, the sea, the air, the wild animals. In this aggressive fantasy we imagine the world as sadistic, before which we are victims, against which we must fight."[25] Another fantasy that humankind engaged in was believing that through science and technology we could force nature to provide whatever we wanted. Science and technology had created the dangerous illusion that human beings were superior to nature. In spite of the growing severity of environmental problems, we still refuse to recognize our dependence upon the natural world, for to do so would undermine our myth of superiority over nature. Another impediment to environmental restoration is that we cannot face the fact that our actions are leading to the destruction of the species. If humankind is to avoid ecocide, however, we must radically reconceive of our place in the natural world.[26]

Ecocide became a part of the Mexican vocabulary,[27] even entering into political parlance. At least in rhetoric, President Carlos Salinas de Gortari has used Césarman's idea of ecocide.[28] Recently he said: "Civilization has transformed nature into a habitat devastated by man—who is constantly battling to gain control and use her as an instrument for progress while forgetting her well-being."[29] At the very least, Césarman, Sotomayor, and others helped stimulate a debate over the consequences of environmental degradation.

Mexican conservationists, too, raised the level of ecological awareness in Mexico. Between the early 1970s and early 1980s, the number of conservation groups in Mexico proliferated. Among the most important organizations forming during this period were the Centro de Ecodesarrollo (1972), Pro-Mariposa Monarca (1980), Pronatura (1981), and Biocenosis (1982).[30] Many of the groups designed educational programs to teach young people about the value of nature.[31] By raising the ecological consciousness of young and old alike, conservationists helped build the foundations for the environmental movement.

Ironically, though, many conservationists scorned the new upstarts. Enrique Beltrán claimed that environmentalists "only add confusion and offer absurd solutions."[32] Arturo Gómez-Pompa shared Beltrán's sentiment. He warned that the proliferation of "ecological" associations was a dangerous development. Because of their naïveté, environmentalists misled the public by offering overly pessimistic (and nonscientific) assessments of the state of the Mexican environment.[33] What should have been a natural alliance between conservationists and environmentalists was obstructed by the disagreement over whether science had to inform environmental activism.

Not surprisingly, divisions exist within the environmental movement itself. When broadly defined, the movement consists of a wide spectrum of groups, including squatter communities, fishers, Indians, and "hippies" as well as neighborhood associations, political pressure groups, and political parties.

For the urban poor, the struggle for a healthier environment is part of a larger struggle for better living conditions. Community leaders from poor settlements have persistently demanded from the government improved services, including running water and some kind of sewage treatment system. Squatters have attempted to help themselves by constructing cisterns to collect water and by gathering discarded materials to build shelters. For the urban poor, water conservation and recycling are a matter of survival. In many neighborhoods, petitioning the authorities to curb industrial pollution has become another part of the fight for health and life. Although most activists in the barrios do not perceive of themselves as environmentalists per se, their goal is to improve the quality of the environment within their communities.[34]

Likewise, Indian groups struggling to protect their resources from outside exploitation do not regard themselves as conservationists. Yet their goal is to protect the land. On several occasions, Indians have formed organizations in an attempt to stop the government and private companies from cutting local forests. When President José López Portillo (1976–1982) granted a paper company rights to exploit forests in the states of Mexico and Morelos and in the Federal District, affected communities promised to prevent it "cost what it may."[35] Also during the López Portillo presidency, twenty-six Indian communities in Oaxaca created an organization that vowed to "defend together our natural resources, principally our forests, to develop our people and defend our organization from the political and educational apparatus of the state."[36] In 1983, fifty-six Indian groups formed a supreme council that pressed President de la Madrid to "take energetic action to end unlimited concessions to lumber companies who without scruples exploit and contaminate the land."[37] The council also urged native peoples to retake their knowledge of agriculture and the environment and transmit it to a new generation, so that they would not become party to the destruction of their own resources.[38] Despite external and internal pressures, some Indian communities did protect their forests and soils by planting kitchen gardens and constructing terraces, among other traditional practices. In addition, they adopted pre-Conquest systems of labor allocation for new tasks, such as reforestation and garbage collection.[39] On both a local and national basis, Indians had organized themselves in defense of the environment.

Fishers, too, attempted to maintain their livelihood by rallying against the exploitation of resources. At Lake Pátzcuaro, fishers joined a local ecology group to seek an end to the pollution of the lake and an end to the diversion of streams and rivers that feed the lake.[40] Their compatriots in Lázaro Cárdenas, Michoacán, opted for a more confrontational approach. They blockaded the port for seventy-two hours before industrial polluters agreed to help fund a program to restock coastal waters with fish, lobster, and shrimp and to stop the ocean dumping of wastes.[41] Through both persuasion and protest, fishing cooperatives in Mexico sought to protect aquatic ecosystems.

Reminiscent of the 1960s counterculture in the United States, a few people established communes in Mexico. The counterculture in the United States rebelled against many aspects of mainstream U.S. society: materialism, competitiveness, "rigid" social mores, and an unquestioning acceptance of authority. One of the ways in which the hippies of the 1960s dropped out of mainstream society was by forming communes. Those who joined the communes were seeking a mellower and simpler life-style. In Mexico, the communes are more explicitly an ecological experiment. The Mexican communes are attempting to demonstrate the value of appropriate technologies. For instance, the Huehuecóyotl commune in Morelos (in central Mexico) has employed dry latrines, terraces, and gray water recycling systems to conserve soils and water.[42] Communes, such as Huehuecóyotl, are protesting against the unsustainable demands being placed on the Mexican environment. More than that, they are attempting to demonstrate that an eco-revolution is possible in Mexico.[43]

During the presidential campaign of 1982, Miguel de la Madrid astutely observed that "the quality of the environment affects the quality of human life; it is a problem that affects each and every one of us; it is not a matter of class. The entire nation finds itself in grave danger because to degrade nature is to degrade human beings."[44] Wealthier Mexicans could lessen their exposure to certain forms of pollution, but they could not escape the problem altogether. For instance, they could buy a house in one of the nicer districts of Mexico City and be guaranteed clean water and relative peace, but all of Mexico City's twenty million residents have to breath the same polluted air. The fact that many of Mexico's better educated and politically more powerful citizens suffer from pollution just like everyone else has been an important factor in the development and the potential of the Mexican environmental movement.

The predominantly middle-class makeup of the Mexican environmental movement has not resulted in a uniform strategy or philosophy. One of the most marked divisions among environmental groups concerns the question of whether they should act as an apolitical community organization, as a pressure group, or as a political group.

A number of Mexican environmental groups have ruled out the option of forming a Green Party. Alfonso Ciprés Villarreal, head of the Mexican Ecologist Movement (MEM), has said that the only thing MEM would accomplish by becoming a political party would be "to confuse and betray the confidence of millions of Mexicans that have invested in us because of the deterioration, lack of prestige, and erosion of existing political parties."[45] Others agreed that the creation of an environmental party would be counterproductive, since it would take votes away from parties sympathetic to environmental causes. Homero Aridjis, head of the environmental organization the Group of 100, has remarked in this regard: "I don't think it's necessary for them [the Green Party] to exist. By forming another party, you ensure that you and others lose. It makes no sense."[46] Jorge González Torres, president of the Green Party, has responded to these criticisms as follows: "They are totally wrong. You can't force change when you don't participate. You only create the appearance of change, and that's dangerous."[47]

Some groups have attempted to avoid political conflict altogether, believing that communities can improve their environments without having to beseech the support of unsympathetic bureaucrats. One such organization is Tierra Madre of San Miguel de Allende (San Miguel de Allende is a community of about 100,000 located in the central Mexican state of Guanajuato). Tierra Madre's objective is to gain acceptance for alternative technologies that will raise people's living standards and improve the quality of their environment. The group's main project has been the promotion of a household source separation system (separating organic from inorganic garbage) for composting and recycling. Tierra Madre is selling this project to the people of San Miguel de Allende as a means of earning more income rather than as an environmental measure. The association's basic philosophy, though, is that the quality of people's lives is directly tied to the quality of their environment. In addition to its recycling program, Tierra Madre is developing a simple filtration sewage system to stem the runoff of sewage into a nearby lake and is encouraging the reuse of wastewater. On the outskirts of San Miguel de Allende, the group is constructing a small ecological village that will demonstrate the practicality of solar distillers, passive solar energy, hydroponic greenhouses, and other ecotechnics. In conjunction with the Audubon Society in San Miguel de Allende, Tierra Madre has encouraged the use of solar energy and gas to reduce the consumption of fuel wood.[48] Tierra Madre is hopeful that its efforts in San Miguel de Allende will serve as a model for the rest of Mexico.[49]

Two of Mexico's most influential environmental organizations, the Mexican Ecologist Movement (MEM) and the Ecological Association of Coyoacán, function both as neighborhood associations and as political pressure groups. With ten thousand members and two hundred affiliates, the Mexican Ecologist Movement (organized in 1981) is the largest environmental group in the country. MEM describes itself as a nongovernmental group without help from religious associations, political parties, or multinational corporations. The organization has utilized television and radio spots, bumper stickers, videos, and posters to conduct a permanent campaign for the protection of Mexico's endangered species and threatened ecosystems and for the improvement of the human environment. MEM's campaigns have included the placement of litter bags in cars, the use of bicycles, a day without a car program, the exchange of recycled materials for tree seedlings, eliminating the abuse of pesticides, support for the General Law on Ecological Balance and Environmental Protection, and scholarships for ecological studies. MEM asserts that to be successful in its defense of the country's natural resources, ecology, and environment, it must act as a pressure group on private and public industries that are so destructive to the environment. At the same time, MEM's local affiliates improve the quality of life in neighborhoods by planting trees and collecting litter. The group has sought to improve the quality of life for all Mexicans. As MEM puts it, "Our struggle is not for class, but for life."[50]

In 1983, the Ecological Association of Coyoacán formed for the specific purpose of saving the grand tree nursery of Coyoacán (which they did). Since then, the association has broadened its activities to include reforestation, recycling, and environmental education. Like MEM, the association has become a prominent voice on national environmental issues. Through community solidarity, the Ecological Association of Coyoacán is attempting to create a new manner of living that is politically, economically, and environmentally superior to the undemocratic, mercantile-oriented, ecologically destructive regime under which Mexicans currently live.[51]

Unlike MEM and the Ecological Association of Coyoacán, the Group of 100 acts exclusively as a political pressure group. The body formed in 1985, when a hundred writers and artists published a declaration against pollution.[52] In this manifesto, the Group of 100 implored the government "to stop its speeches and plans which it never carries out and immediately act to defend and protect the inhabitants of this city from the slow death to which corruption and negligence have condemned us year after year."[53] Members of the Group of 100 have skillfully utilized the media and public forums on environmental issues to arouse public concern about pollution and to pressure the government into taking stronger actions.[54]

Homero Aridjis, the head of the Group of 100, argued that his organization's tactics had contributed to Carlos Salinas de Gortari's recent decision to close the 18th of March refinery: "With this decision the government of Mexico and the authorities of the Federal District place themselves at the head of the concrete struggle to reduce pollution in the Valley of Mexico, and show that they have heard the voices of civil society."[55] Pressures from environmental interest groups may have indeed prompted this drastic action.

In addition to pollution, the Group of 100 has called attention to the destruction of the natural world. Reflecting upon his own state of Michoacán, Homero Aridjis has said, "I've noticed that animals that used to live in the mountains are no longer there. Our mountains and forests are becoming silent. Our rivers and lakes are drying up."[56] Even the monarch butterflies, which, Aridjis recalled, once set the entire fall sky aflame with red, black, yellow, and orange are vanishing because of deforestation.[57]

Both meditations upon the past and the future of his birthplace have unsettled Aridjis:

> The images that had fed my childhood were being destroyed and I felt that it was my childhood that was being killed, that my memory of natural beauty that had once overwhelmed me was being ravaged. The possibility of my village becoming a wasteland, a silent country without wind in the trees or animal sounds or bird songs, makes me feel desperate. Such disrespect for nature humiliates me as a human being; it makes me a stranger in the place of my birth.[58]

For Aridjis, the degradation of nature is a social as well as an environmental crime, for it yields a desolate land that can provide people with neither food nor joy. This conviction has motivated Aridjis and other members of the Group of 100 in their fight for the protection of the wild places and animals of Mexico.[59]

Other groups sought to change governmental policies from the inside. During the early 1980s, the United Socialist Party of Mexico (PSUM) attempted to become Mexico's first environmentally oriented party.[60] Party member Víctor Manuel Toledo maintained that socialism and environmentalism were symbiotic movements. According to Toledo: "The exploitation of the worker and the destruction of the environment—the only sources from which capital extracts wealth—are not but two dimensions of the same process."[61] Under the capitalist system, a few people enriched themselves through the exploitation of nature, thus destroying the long-term ability of the land to support people. Toledo held that the origins of Mexico's environmental crisis lay in colonialism, neocolonialism, and imperialism. The liberation of nature and people depended upon the creation of a socialist state.[62]

Toledo condemned the reactionary nature of Mexican environmentalism. He lamented that, due to its domination by politically neutral scientists, the ecological movement had not become a radical movement against capitalism, and he chided Mexican ecologists for displaying the same apolitical character as their counterparts in the United States. He complained that even in Europe, where philosophers and sociologists rather than scientists were at the forefront of the environmental movement, Green Parties had ignored the oppression of the workers. In addition, he criticized traditional leftist political organizations for ignoring environmental issues. Toledo envisioned PSUM as being the first legitimate leftist environmental party.[63]

Arturo Gómez-Pompa responded in kind to Toledo's charge that Mexican ecologists were apolitical by admonishing PSUM for its late and lukewarm embrace of environmentalism.[64] Indeed, Toledo never was able to convert PSUM into a socialist-environmental party.

The Mexican Green Party has assumed PSUM's mantle as an environmental party. The party evolved from one of Mexico's first ecological groups, the Brigade for Social Liberty and Justice, which began as a neighborhood association in Mexico City in 1979 and which then joined with other environmental groups in the country to become the Ecologist Alliance in 1984.[65] After several years of attempting to raise people's consciousness about pollution and garbage, the group decided that it was time for a new tack. In 1987, the alliance chose to form a Green Party because it was convinced that environmental problems and solutions were basically political. Without pressure from the inside, the alliance believed that the government would continue to make verbal concessions to environmental pressure groups but balk at making real change.[66]

Until they could gain a foothold within the government, members of the new party acted as watchdogs over public officials. At its bimonthly press conferences, the Green Party took the government to task for inadequately enforcing Mexico's antipollution laws. The party charged that the government had used outdated technology to certify that cars had met exhaust standards and that the government had deliberately underreported pollution statistics. The Green Party sharply criticized government claims that its policies had resulted in lower concentrations of sulfur dioxide, carbon monoxide, and lead in Mexico City. The Greens considered the falsification of pollution statistics to be highly condemnable because it was difficult to arouse public concerns about pollution when the government hid the true scope of the problem from the people.[67]

The Green Party has taken a number of unpopular stands. Many Mexicans have particularly disliked the party's forceful advocacy of animal rights; however, it has articulately defended its position: "Sports hunting, bull fights, cock fights, dog fights, the capturing and caging of animals are practices cruel and treacherous by means of which people enjoy the suffering of innocent beings. While they continue being accustomed and entertained by such cruelty, human beings cannot live in harmony with nature or with themselves."[68] The party is advocating nothing less than the extension of respect to all parts of the natural world.

In addition, the Mexican Green Party favors environmental education at all levels and the adoption of a form of economic development that "respects the natural harmony of life and contributes to the restoration of the environment." The party is sympathetic to a variety of social causes as well. Unlike PSUM and the Green Parties in Europe, however, the Mexican Green Party has not committed itself to a broader social agenda, such as nuclear disarmament, feminism, or workers' rights. Instead, the party has concentrated on what it considers to be Mexico's most serious problem: the destruction of the environment.[69]

During the midterm elections in 1991, the Mexican Green Party had the opportunity to test the resonance of its message among the Mexican public. In a comment indicating the limits to environmental concerns in Mexico, a refrigerator repairman told one of the party's candidates in Mexico City: "I understand, señora, that you are trying to correct things. But I have to worry about my kids. I can't worry about trees."[70] Others, however, were more receptive to the party's platform, which calls for the conservation of ecosystems, the protection of wildlife, the cleanup of the environment, and ecodevelopment.[71] In all, the Green Party received 330,799 votes, finishing seventh among ten parties nationwide and fifth in Mexico City. The Greens, however, fell .06 percent short of the 1.5 percent of the vote necessary to gain permanent status as a party. It must now sit out one election before running again.[72] Despite this setback and persistent criticism from other environmental groups, the Mexican Green Party will continue to seek environmental change by entering into the political process.

Several Mexican environmental leaders accused the government of seeking to block the expansion of the environmental movement by fomenting dissent within its ranks. Alfonso Ciprés Villarreal, the head of MEM, contended that the government feared "a real ecology movement" and therefore attempted to divide and co-opt environmental groups. The ruling elite did incite rivalries between ecological associations by periodically restricting participation and consultation on environmental programs to groups most supportive of its actions. Environmental activists, who had regularly been excluded from the decision-making process because of their outspoken positions, sharply criticized their counterparts for cooperating with the regime. Homero Aridjis accused the PRI of attempting to create dissent not only between groups but also within them. He recalled that on several occasions government officials had contacted members of the Group of 100 to solicit their opposition to the organization's stance. According to Aridjis, the authorities sometimes resorted to more repressive measures, such as personal harassment and press censorship, to limit the group's effectiveness. The government's strategy of co-option and repression underlay the debate within the environmental community over how best to achieve their goals.[73]

The fragmentation of the Mexican environmental movement can easily be exaggerated. A broad spectrum of the environmental movement successfully worked together to gain government acceptance for the day without a car program in Mexico City. This type of cooperation is the rule rather than the exception.

The environmental movement's most celebrated campaign was

against the Laguna Verde Nuclear Power Plant. The outcome of this campaign indicates that environmental groups are limited in their ability to affect government decisions.

The Laguna Verde Nuclear Power Plant has had a long and accident-prone history. Construction on the plant began in 1972, but because of a series of delays, it was not ready for operation until the late 1980s. On 20 June 1988, General Electric, which produced the plant's Mark II reactor (a reactor that because of its flaws has been discontinued in the United States), and the Mexican Federal Electricity Commission announced that they were beginning final tests on the plant. According to G.E. and the Mexican Federal Electricity Commission, these tests were supposed to last no more than 188 days. As it turned out, they conducted tests for 785 days before finally opening the plant on 14 August 1990. On 25 November 1989 and 27 April 1990, radioactive steam containing Cesium 137 and Strontium 90 escaped due to a fissure in the prime circulation tube. In December 1989, 130,000 liters of radioactive water were discharged into a nearby saltwater lake. Veracruz fishers alleged a drop in the production of shrimp from the lake.[74]

On 27 January 1987, ten thousand people and twenty-five environmental groups participated in a symbolic closure of the plant.[75] Environmentalists questioned the wisdom of spending 3.5 billion dollars on a plant that would last thirty years at most.[76] Of even greater consequence, they questioned the sanity of government officials in locating Laguna Verde on a geological fault in one of the most densely populated regions in Mexico.[77] Then, there was the nettlesome issue of how to dispose of the radioactive wastes. According to government officials, the wastes could be safely stored in a specially constructed cave. Environmentalists doubted that any secure storage system could be found and called upon the government to abandon nuclear energy in favor of safer and cheaper sources of energy, such as solar and wind power.[78]

Local fishers joined environmentalists in the struggle against Laguna Verde. Eduardo Gómez Téllez, the representative for a group of fishing cooperatives in Veracruz, said that the plant was monthly discharging ten million liters of contaminated water, which was killing fish and destroying the small organisms that formed the base of the food chain. According to Téllez, when the plant went into full operation one thousand fisher families would be adversely affected. Members of the fishing cooperatives threatened to blockade the drainage channel and close the workers' access to the plant. Téllez acknowledged that "we know that they will repress us. But it is worse that they are removing our source of work and bread from our mouths."[79]

Another group protesting against the plant was the Mothers of Veracruz. These women drew attention to the threat that the plant posed to human and nonhuman life in the region.[80] Carlos Salinas de Gortari promised the Mothers of Veracruz that he would have an impartial audit done of the plant to determine whether it should be put into full-scale operation or be permanently shut down. However, to do the audit, Salinas chose Manuel López Rodríguez, whose impartiality was compromised by three factors: he was a promoter of nuclear energy in Spain; he was a friend of Juan Eibenshutz, who was the father of Laguna Verde Nuclear Power Plant; and he had connections with Hidroeléctrica Española S.A., one of the contractors for Laguna Verde. Not surprisingly, López Rodríguez pronounced Laguna Verde safe for operation. The Mothers of Veracruz had pressured Salinas into doing an audit, but they could not force him to make an honest one.[81]

The most unexpected opponent to the Laguna Verde Nuclear Power Plant were the bishops of Veracruz. The church has assiduously avoided political issues in Mexico and has been silent on environmental issues. But in their Christmas message of 1989, the bishops of Veracruz spoke out against the destruction of the environment in general (and in the process recast the biblical injunction for man to dominate the earth) and against the plant specifically:

Jesus Christ loves nature, he is respectful of it, he is its admirer. When man was called to dominate the earth, he was not called to dominate it in a despotic manner but to humanize it, putting it into service through his works. . . . Returning to our day and looking at our environs, we have to deplore the use men are making of nature. How we are dirtying it! How we are making aggression against human life! How in the altar of said progress, modernity, industrial civilization, development, we are offering and sacrificing human life, nature, the creation! . . . We understand and share the sentiments of the people and groups who have directed pronouncements to the government and to public opinion [on Laguna Verde] calling attention to the grave risks of mortal accidents and genetic consequences for all living species.[82]

But neither the church, fishers, mothers, or environmental groups could persuade the government to scrap Laguna Verde. The government had invested too much money and prestige to turn back. Ironically, while many countries, in the wake of the nuclear accident at Three Mile Island in the United States and after the meltdown at Chernobyl in the Soviet

Union, were turning away from nuclear power, Mexico was dashing blithely into the nuclear age.[83] The environmental movement may have helped delay Mexico's arrival into this brave new world (the many tests may have been as much to allay public concern as to actually test the plant), but it could not prevent it.

While the Mexican government moved closer to the environmentalists' position on some issues, political leaders pursued policies counter to ecological maintenance when they considered other goals to be more important. At this point, the environmental movement lacks the political clout to force politicians to take strict measures to protect the environment. They have, however, been able to exercise some influence over the course of Mexican environmental policy, and just as important, ecological associations made progress on a societal level during the 1980s. They raised public consciousness about environmental issues, which is a prerequisite for the resolution of environmental problems on both national and local levels. In addition, they attained community participation in ecological restoration projects, improving the quality of life in several areas without government support. Gradually, the environmental movement is emerging as an important political and social force in Mexico.

Conclusion

When, in 1982, Carlos Salinas de Gortari rejected the thesis that Mexico should develop first and worry about the environment later, he was expressing an opinion that had historical antecedents.[1] Even as Spanish and Mexican rulers promoted the relentless exploitation of natural resources, a few public officials warned against the dire consequences of resource scarcity. In truth, most of these officials condemned colonists, Indians, or *ejiditarios* rather than the government for the wasteful use of natural resources. Furthermore, their interest in conservation rarely extended beyond a desire to ensure a supply of raw materials for future economic development. Strict utilitarian arguments for conservation, though, never completely eclipsed other perspectives. Public servants, as well as private citizens, drew attention to the multiple benefits accruing from conservation, including the role that stable ecosystems played in safeguarding people's livelihoods and health and the importance of wild places for recreation and mental health. During the Cárdenas administration, this broad-based rationale for conservation actually gained ascendancy over the strict utilitarian perspective. Cárdenas was the first Mexican president to discern that conservation and development had to occur simultaneously.

Nearly a half-century of unrestricted growth passed before another political leader, Carlos Salinas de Gortari, reinvoked this idea. Unlike Cárdenas, though, Salinas has not made sustainable development a top priority of his administration. In fact, he has allowed many serious ecological problems, such as the destruction of the Lacandón rain forest and the contamination of the Lerma River, to go virtually unchecked. He has implemented bold measures to reduce the unbearable levels of pollution in Mexico City, but even there the administration was reluctant to hinder economic development for the sake of a cleaner environment. Furthermore, Salinas's eagerness to conclude a free trade agreement with the United States and Canada without an ironclad guarantee to keep "dirty" industries out of the country seems to indicate his willingness to place environmental considerations aside for the sake of foreign investment. Salinas's commitment to the prevention of ecological degradation appears to be qualified.

A number of Mexican public figures do not share Salinas's limited enthusiasm for environmental restoration. Despite the fact that deforestation and soil erosion are destroying the productive capacity of the land and that pollution is reducing the productivity and life spans of the Mexican people, prominent Mexicans continue to assert that economic advancements must precede environmental protection. As former President Luis Echeverría said recently: "People in developing countries cannot afford the luxury of worrying about the quality of the air they breathe."[2] According to Echeverría (and others), the Mexican under class cannot be concerned about environmental problems, since their livelihood often depends on the strength of the industrial sector or on the exploitation of natural resources. Furthermore, the government is incapable of funding ambitious environmental programs because of a huge foreign debt, limited revenues, and an array of more pressing social problems. Hence, from this perspective, Mexico must first generate revenues and raise living standards through rapid economic development before it can afford to redress environmental problems. Ironically, such a strategy would put Mexico in the position of destroying its environment first in order to save it later.

Mexico does need development, but in a form that does not further erode the resource base or further exacerbate pollution. The emergence of strong environmental policies and a broad environmental consciousness are not wholly contingent upon future development, though. Absolute revenues are limited, but Mexican politicians can reallocate more money to environmental programs. In the case of community projects, such as garbage collection, recycling, and tree planting, the government can make a major contribution in materials and publicity with small outlays. International conservation organizations, foreign governments, and international governmental organizations further allay the problem of scarce resources by providing Mexican agencies with technical and foreign aid for environmental programs. Ultimately, the success of Mexico's environmental policies depends more on political will than the size of the Mexican treasury.

Most important, the success of Mexican environmental efforts hinges upon the level of public support (or demand) for such efforts. Mexican environmental groups are composed nearly exclusively of members from the middle class. Support for environmental causes in Mexico, however, is not restricted to a small (though potentially powerful) class of people. In recent years, subsistence fishers have protested against water diversion projects and against the pollution of aquatic ecosystems; Tabascan peasants have demonstrated against Pemex oil spills; and squatter communities have demanded better services, including sewage systems and clean water, and the enforcement of industrial health and safety regulations. For these groups, environmental protection is not perceived as an obstacle to their well-being. In fact just the opposite; they regard a nonpolluted environment to be essential for their economic and physical survival. A larger environmental movement with broad-based support is within the realm of possibility in Mexico, as more Mexicans become aware of how ecological damage negatively affects the quality of their lives.

In 1940, John Steinbeck and Edward Ricketts saw how Japanese fishers were decimating the shrimp population in Mexico's coastal waters. Steinbeck was moved to write:

Fifty miles away the Japanese shrimp boats are dredging with overlapping scoops, bringing up tons of shrimp, rapidly destroying the species so that it may never come back, and with the species destroying the ecological balance of the whole region. That isn't very important in the world. And thousands of miles away the bombs are falling and the stars are not moved thereby. None of it is important or all of it is.[3]

The number of Mexicans holding the position that all of it is important has been increasing in recent years. Upon their ability to convince politicians and ordinary citizens to restore the natural balance that has been lost, lies the hope of a land and its people.

Appendix One

The Political History of Mexico from Independence to Revolution

1821	Mexico gained its independence from Spain
1822–1823	The Imperium of Agustín Iturbide
1824	The execution of Iturbide
1836	The loss of Texas
1846–1848	Mexican-American War
1848	Mexico ceded its northern territories of California and [greater] New Mexico to the United States through the Treaty of Guadalupe Hidalgo
1856–1857	The passage of the Liberal Reform Laws
1857	The Liberals enacted a new constitution
1858–1861	Civil war between the Liberals and the Conservatives
1861	First presidential term of Benito Juárez
1862–1867	The French Intervention
1864	The French install Austrian Archduke Maximilian as emperor of Mexico
1867	The execution of Maximilian
1867–1872	Second and third presidential terms of Benito Juárez
1876–1911	Porfirio Díaz ruled Mexico
1910	The beginning of the Mexican Revolution

Appendix Two

Mexican Presidents, 1911–1994

1911	Francisco León de la Barra
1911–1913	Francisco Madero
1913	Victoriano Huerta
1914–1920	Venustiano Carranza
1920	Adolfo de la Huerta
1920–1924	Alvaro Obregón
1924–1928	Plutarco Elías Calles
1928–1930	Emilio Portes Gil
1930–1932	Pascual Ortiz Rubio
1932–1934	Abelardo Rodríguez
1934–1940	Lázaro Cárdenas
1940–1946	Manuel Avila Camacho
1946–1952	Miguel Alemán
1952–1958	Adolfo Ruiz Cortines
1958–1964	Adolfo López Mateos
1964–1970	Gustavo Díaz Ordaz
1970–1976	Luis Echeverría Alvarez
1976–1982	José López Portillo
1982–1988	Miguel de la Madrid
1988–1994	Carlos Salinas de Gortari

Appendix Three

Chronology of Conservation

in Mexico

Thirteenth century   Nopaltzin, a Chichimec prince, restricted the setting
of fires in the mountains and in the countryside.

Fifteenth century   King Nezahualcóyotl of Texcoco created a forest
reserve.

Nezahualcóyotl and other monarchs directed the formation of
forested parks, botanical gardens, zoos, aviaries, and fishing
ponds for their enjoyment.

Nahua rulers prohibited their subjects from catching any more
fish than they could eat or sell.

Sixteenth century   Kings Carlos I and Felipe II established ordinances to
conserve oysters for their pearls.

1539   King Carlos I ordered *encomenderos* to plant trees for the benefit
of the community.

1541   King Carlos I declared that all forests, pasturelands, and waters
in the Indies were held in common.

1550   Viceroy don Antonio de Mendoza forbade the setting of forest
fires near the mining community of Taxco.

Ca. 1550   Viceroy Mendoza advised his successor don Luis Velasco to rigorously enforce the forestry laws of the Indies.

1559   King Felipe II reaffirmed that the Indians had free access to the
forests, but added that they should not cut trees in a manner
that prevented them from growing or regenerating.

1579   Viceroy don Martín Enríquez prohibited the setting of forest
fires and the cutting of trees at their base in the Chalco region

near Mexico City. He required licenses to cut trees above their trunks.

1592	Viceroy don Luis de Velasco, the younger, dedicated the central alameda (a beautiful park with trees) in Mexico City, for the recreation of the city's residents.
1765	King Carlos III required licenses to cut trees on private as well as on public lands throughout the realm and ordered that for every tree cut three more had to be planted.
1803	King Carlos IV issued an ordinance to conserve coastal hardwoods.
1813	The Spanish Cortes announced its plans to convert almost all of its common forests on the Iberian peninsula and in the New World to private property.
1813	The Cortes indicated that it would transfer responsibility for the conservation and repopulation of the remaining common forests to local officials.
1824	The Mexican government forbade nonnationals from hunting and trapping fur-bearing animals.
Ca. 1826	Governor José María Echeandía of California introduced a clause into hunting licenses that prohibited the killing of sea otter pups.
1833	The National Institute of Geography and Statistics, later known as the Mexican Geographical and Statistical Society, was established.
1834	The territorial commission of California prohibited the exportation of timber and required a license for woodcutting and for the transportation of timber from port to port.
1839	To reduce the occurrence of prolonged droughts, Interior Minister José Antonio Romero called upon Mexico's governors to protect their region's forests and to restore those that had been destroyed.
1845	The governor of Veracruz, Antonio María Salonio, created tree protection boards to protect and restore woodlands in his state.
1845	Officials from Los Angeles mandated that all timber cut on public lands be used for the common good.
1853	The Ministry of Public Works was created.
1854	The Ministry of Public Works prohibited crew members loading guano onto either domestic or foreign ships from shooting coastal or island birds.
1854	The Ministry of Public Works required a permit for the export on either domestic or foreign ships of woods used in cabinet-making or construction.

1854	The Ministry of Public Works directed mining commissions throughout Mexico to conduct forest surveys.
1856	The Mexican government set aside Desierto de Carmelitas, later named Desierto de los Leones, as a forest reserve.
1861	President Benito Juárez enacted the first national forestry law in independent Mexico.
1862	The governor of Baja California, Teodoro Riveroll, enacted a law requiring government approval for cutting trees on public and private lands.
1865	The scientific commission of Pachuca appealed for the conservation of natural resources in the state of Hidalgo.
Ca. 1866	Leopoldo Río de la Loza, a chemistry professor, drafted a broad forestry ordinance.
1866	Emperor Maximilian ordered the planting of trees along all the public roadways in Mexico City.
1868	The Mexican Natural History Society was established.
1870	The Ramírez commission issued its report on forest conservation in Mexico.
1880	A government circular drew attention to the critical role that forests played in maintaining a stable environment.
1892	Jesús Alfaro published his medical thesis in which he expounded upon the many ways in which forests contributed to the health of human beings.
1894	President Porfirio Díaz enacted a new forestry law that also contained provisions for the conservation of wildlife.
1895	Mexican natural scientists discussed the need for conservation and reforestation at the First Concourse of Mexican Scientists.
1898	Díaz set aside Mineral del Chico in the state of Hidalgo as a forest reserve.
1898	Alfonso Herrera, a biology professor, published a proposal calling for the protection of useful birds.
1901	Miguel Angel de Quevedo spoke on the biological value of forests before the Second National Congress on Climate and Meteorology.
1901	The members of the congress voted to create the Central Forestry Board (the Junta Central de Bosques), with Quevedo as its president.
1901	Quevedo began his campaign to create more public parks in Mexico City.
1908	Quevedo received public funding for his tree nursery at Coyoacán (the Viveros de Coyoacán). Many of the nursery seedlings were subsequently planted in and around the Valley of Mexico.

1908	Quevedo established the first forestry school in Mexico City, which he staffed with professors from France.
1908	Quevedo embarked upon the creation of forested artificial dunes in Veracruz.
1909	Quevedo addressed the International North American Conference on the Conservation of Natural Resources, Washington, D.C.
1909	The Central Forestry Board completed its survey of woodlands within the Valley of Mexico.
1909	Díaz suspended the selling of public lands.
1910	Díaz established a protected forest zone around the Valley of Mexico.
1911	State officials presented the Central Forestry Board with some basic statistics on the nation's woodlands.
1915	Alfonso Herrera became the first director of the Bureau of Biological Studies.
1917	Article 27 of the Mexican Constitution allowed for the expropriation of land when necessary for conservation purposes.
1917	President Venustiano Carranza created Mexico's first national park: Desierto de los Leones.
1919	The Bureau of Biological Studies established botanical gardens in Chapultepec Park in Mexico City.
1922	Quevedo founded the Mexican Forestry Society.
1922	President Alvaro Obregón created Mexico's first wildlife refuge: Isla Guadalupe.
1922	Obregón placed a ten-year moratorium on the hunting of bighorn sheep and antelope.
1923	The first issue of *México Forestal* was published.
1923	The Bureau of Biological Studies began construction of a zoo in Chapultepec Park.
1926	President Plutarco Elías Calles enacted a sweeping forestry law that served as the archetype for later forestry laws.
1931	The Mexican Committee for the Protection of Wild Birds was established.
1932	The Mexican government banned the use of shooting batteries (*armadas*) to kill waterfowl.
1934	Enrique Beltrán became the first director of the Biotechnical Institute.
1935	President Lázaro Cárdenas created the Department of Forestry, Fish, and Game.
1935–1939	The department published the conservation magazine *Protección a la Naturaleza*.
1935–1940	The Cárdenas administration created forty national parks.

1936	An International Parks Commission consisting of Mexican and U.S. members met to discuss the possibility of creating protected areas across both sides of the border.
1937	The United States and Mexico signed the Treaty for the Protection of Migratory Birds and Game Mammals.
1939	Cárdenas instructed the National Irrigation Commission to survey soils in irrigation districts to assess more accurately the need for erosion control measures.
1940	Cárdenas abolished the Department of Forestry, Fish, and Game.
1940	Cárdenas enacted a game law.
1942	The Mexican Congress ratified the 1940 Convention on Nature Protection and Wild Life Preservation in the Western Hemisphere.
1942	President Manuel Avila Camacho created the Department of Soil Conservation.
1942	Eliseo Palacios and Miguel Alvarez del Toro created the Department of Tropical Nurseries and the Museum of Natural History, later known as the Institute of Natural History of Chiapas.
1944	William Vogt published *El hombre y la tierra*.
1946	Avila Camacho enacted the Soil and Water Conservation Law.
1946	The Mexican Geographical and Statistical Society published the proceedings from a conference on the conservation of natural resources in Mexico.
1948	Governor César Lara supervised the construction of a zoo at Parque Madero in Tuxtla Gutiérrez, Chiapas.
1951	Tom Gill published *Land Hunger in Mexico*.
1951	Gonzalo Blanco Macías founded Amigos de la Tierra.
1951	Frans and Trudi Blom established a center for scientific studies in San Cristóbal de las Casas, Chiapas.
1952	President Miguel Alemán enacted a new game law.
1952	Enrique Beltrán founded the Mexican Institute of Renewable Natural Resources.
1952	Miguel Alvarez del Toro published *Los animales silvestres de Chiapas*.
1953–1964	Amigos de la Tierra published the journal *Suelo y Agua*.
1970	President Luis Echeverría created the National Council of Science and Technology.
1971	Echeverría enacted the Law for the Prevention and Control of Pollution.
1972	Fernando Césarman published *Ecocido: Estudio psicoanalítico de la destrucción del medio ambiente*.
1972	The Center for Ecodevelopment was established.

1973	Arturo Sotomayor published *La metropolí mexicana y su agonía*.
1974	Gonzalo Halffter founded the Institute of Ecology.
1974	Halffter and the governor of Durango, Dr. Héctor Mayagoitia, discussed plans for the creation of the Mapimí and La Michilía biosphere reserves.
1975	Arturo Gómez-Pompa became the first director of the National Institute for Research on Biotic Resources.
1978	President José López Portillo created Mexico's first biosphere reserve: Montes Azules.
1979	López Portillo created the Mapimí and La Michilía biosphere reserves.
1980	Alvarez del Toro oversaw the completion of the zoo at El Zapotal in Tuxtla Gutiérrez, Chiapas.
1980	Pro-Mariposa Monarca was established.
1981	Pronatura was established.
1981	The Mexican Ecologist Movement was established.
1982	Biocenosis was established.
1982	López Portillo enacted the Federal Law for the Protection of the Environment.
1982	President Miguel de la Madrid created the Ministry of Urban Development and Ecology.
1983	The Ecological Association of Coyoacán was established.
1984	The Ecologist Alliance was established.
1985	Homero Aridjis organized the Group of 100.
1986	The Pact of Ecologist Groups (Pacto de Grupos Ecologistas) was established.
1986	Amigos de Sian Ka'an was established.
1986	De la Madrid created five monarch butterfly reserves.
1987	Ten thousand people and twenty-five environmental groups participated in the symbolic closing of the Laguna Verde nuclear power plant.
1987	FUNDAMAT (The Miguel Alvarez del Toro Foundation) was established.
1987	The Ecologist Alliance formed the Green Party.
1988	De la Madrid promulgated the General Law on Ecological Balance and Environmental Protection.
1988	De la Madrid created the expansive El Vizcaíno Biosphere Reserve on the Baja California peninsula.
1988	President Carlos Salinas de Gortari abolished the National Institute for Research on Biotic Resources.
1989	Salinas initiated the day without a car program.
1990	Salinas banned the commercial exploitation of sea turtles.
1991	Salinas closed down the 18th of March Pemex oil refinery.

1991   Mexico signed the Convention on the International Trade in
            Endangered Species.
1991   The Mexican Green Party ran its first candidates in a national
            election.
1992   Salinas abolished the Ministry of Urban Development and
            Ecology and transferred responsibility for the administration of
            environmental programs to the newly created Ministry of So-
            cial Development.
1992   Salinas eliminated the Center for Ecodevelopment.
1993   Salinas created a marine sanctuary in the Sea of Cortez in part
            to protect the endangered vaquita porpoise.
1993   The U.S., Mexican, and Canadian governments ratified the
            North American Free Trade Agreement.

Notes

Epigraphs

The quote from the *Huehue Tlatolli* is inscribed on a wall in the inner courtyard of the National Museum of Anthropology in Mexico City. For a partial Spanish rendition of the original document, see *Huehue Tlatolli*, trans. of the ancient conversations or discourses by Fray Juan de Torquemada and Dr. don Alonzo de Zurita. The Aztec made a drink out of the maguey and ate the fruit and leaves of the nopales.

For the quote from Edilberto Ucan Ek, see Partido Revolucionario Institucional and Instituto de Estudios Politicas, Económico y Sociales, *Medio ambiente y calidad de vida*, 82.

Carlos Fuentes, "Asphyxiation by Progress," *New Perspectives Quarterly* 6 (Spring 1989): 44.

Fernando Benítez quoted in Juan M. Vásquez, "Mexico City Is Strangling on Its Growth," *Los Angeles Times*, 8 December 1983, A16.

Introduction

1. Miguel Alvarez del Toro, "Chiapas, gigante saqueado," *Numero Uno* [Tuxtla Gutiérrez, Chiapas], 24 June 1982, 9. The author translated all quotations taken from Spanish-language sources.

2. For a bibliographic essay on the various schools of thought regarding the Indians' treatment of the land, see J. Baird Callicott, "American Indian Land Wisdom," *Journal of Forest History* 39 (January 1989): 35–42.

3. Texcoco is located in the eastern part of the Valley of Mexico.

4. Mesoamerica encompassed central Mexico, southern Mexico, and Central America.

1. The Magical and the Instrumental: Nature in the Pre-Hispanic World

1. "Earth Day Celebrated across the Globe," *The News* (Mexico City), 23 April 1990, 1.

2. Interview with Natalia Grieger of the Mexican Green Party, Mexico City, 25 October 1989. Meeting with Homero Aridjis, president of the Group of 100, Mexico City, 27 October 1989.

3. Carmen Aguilera, *Flora y fauna mexicana: Mitología y tradiciones*, 6.

4. George A. Collier, *Fields of Tzotzil: The Ecological Bases of Tradition in Highland Chiapas*, 109–116.

5. Gonzalo Blanco Macías, "Realizaciones y perspectivas en la conservación del suelo en México," in Instituto Mexicano de Recursos Naturales Renovables, *Mesas redondas sobre utilización y conservación del suelo en México*, 89; Michael C. Meyer, *Water in the Hispanic Southwest: A Social and Legal History, 1550–1850*, 19; Gary Paul Nabhan and Thomas Edward Sheridan, "Living Fencerows on the Río San Miguel, Sonora, Mexico: Traditional Technology of Floodplain Management," *Human Ecology* 5 (June 1977): 97–111; and Secretaría de Agricultura y Recursos Hidráulicos, Subsecretaría de Infraestructura Hidráulica, *Agua y sociedad: Una historia de las obras hidráulicas en México*, 51–60, 70–71.

6. Meyer, *Water in the Hispanic Southwest*, 19.

7. William E. Doolittle, *Canal Irrigation in Prehistoric Mexico: The Sequence of Technological Change*, 80.

8. Woodrow Borah and Sherburne Cook made this estimate based on Aztec tribute rolls. They extrapolated the populations for groups, such as the Tarascan and Zapotec, which remained independent of the Aztec empire. Woodrow Borah and Sherburne F. Cook, *The Aboriginal Population of Central Mexico on the Eve of the Spanish Conquest*, 5, 79–89.

9. Aguilera, *Flora y fauna mexicana*, 7; C. A. Burland, *The Gods of Mexico*, 63.

10. *Chilam Balam de Chumayel*, ed. Miguel Rivera Dorado, 25.

11. Partido Revolucionario Institucional, *Medio ambiente*, 4.

12. Fray Toribio de Benavente [Motolinía], *Historia de los indios de la Nueva España*, ed. Claudio Esteva Fabregat, 229.

13. The Tzotzil are usually included as part of the highland Maya.

14. Fray Francisco de Burgoa, *Geográfica descripción*, 1:274, 412; Cecelia F. Klein, *The Face of the Earth: Frontality in Two-Dimensional Mesoamerican Art*, 144.

15. Cited in Collier, *Fields of Tzotzil*, 119.

16. Gary H. Gossen, *Chamulas in the World of the Sun: Time and Space in a Maya Oral Tradition*, 21, 86–87.

17. Sahagún completed the Florentine Codex during the 1570s. Fray Bernardino de Sahagún, *Florentine Codex: General History of the Things of New Spain*, trans. from Aztec into English with notes and illustrations by Charles E. Dibble and Arthur J. O. Anderson, 11:105.

18. Ibid., 106.

19. *Chilam Balam*, 18.

20. Antonio Mediz Bolio, *La tierra del faisán y del venado*, 111.

21. Arturo Gómez-Pompa, "On Maya Silviculture," *Mexican Studies/Estudios Mexicanos* 3 (Winter 1987): 7.

22. Sahagún, *Florentine Codex*, 11:105.

23. Francisco Hernández, *Antigüedades de la Nueva España*, ed. Ascensión H. de León-Portilla, 78.

24. Klein, *Face of the Earth*, 144.

25. *Chilam Balam*, 95.

26. Mediz Bolio, *La tierra del faisán*, 112.

27. Gómez-Pompa, "On Maya Silviculture," 7.

28. "The Death of the Lacandón Culture and Rain Forest: An Interview with Gertrude Duby Blom," *Mexico City News*, 18 March 1983, 16.

29. Hernando Ruiz de Alarcón, "Tratado de supersticiones y costumbres gentílicas que oy viuen entre los indios naturales de esta Nueva España," in *Tratado de las idolatrías, supersticiones, dioses, ritos, hechicerías y otras costumbres gentílicas de las razas aborígenes de México*, notes, commentaries, and a study by don Francisco del Paso y Troncoso, 2:66–67.

30. Jacinto de la Serna, "Tratado de las supersticiones, idolatrías, hechicerías y otras costumbres de las razas aborígenes de México," in *Tratado de las idolatrías, supersticiones, dioses, ritos, hechicerías y otras costumbres gentílicas de las razas aborígenes de México*, notes, commentaries, and a study by don Francisco del Paso y Troncoso, 1:231–232.

31. Karl Lumholtz, *Unknown Mexico: A Record of Five Years' Exploration among the Tribes of the Western Sierra Madre; in the Tierra Caliente of Tepic and Jalisco; and among the Tarascos of Michoacán*, 1:356.

32. Serna, "Tratado de las supersticiones," 1:234–236, 239.

33. Lumholtz, *Unknown Mexico*, 1:356.

34. See, for example, Peter N. Carroll, *Puritanism and the Wilderness: The Intellectual Significance of the New England Frontier, 1629–1670*.

35. *Relación de las ceremonias y ritos y población y gobierno de los indios de la provincia de Michoacán (1541)*, facsimile reproduction of the manuscript at El Escorial with transcription, prologue, introduction, and notes by José Tudela; revision of the Tarascan voices by José Coruña Nuñez; foreword by Paul Kirchoff, 174.

36. Ibid., 188.

37. Ibid., 241; *The Chronicles of Michoacán*, trans. and ed. Eugene R. Craine and Reginald C. Reindorp, 66.

38. Ruth M. Underhill, *Papago Indian Religion*, 15–16, 285. Today the Papago inhabit the far southern reaches of Arizona and are closely related to the Pima of Sonora. They engage in hunting and gathering to supplement the food they produce through irrigated agriculture.

39. Miguel del Barco, *Historia natural y crónica de la antigua California*, ed. Miguel León-Portilla, 217.

40. For a treatise on the spiritual separation of people from animals provoked by the transition from a hunting and gathering to an agricultural society, see Calvin Luther Martin, *In the Spirit of the Earth: Rethinking History and Time*.

41. Fray Diego de Landa, *Relación de las cosas de Yucatán*, ed. Miguel Rivera Dorado, 116–117.

42. *Popul Vuh*, trans. Dennis Tedlock, 182. The territory of the Quiché Maya of Guatemala once extended into Chiapas.

43. The Toltec migrated to the central highlands of Mexico around A.D. 900.

44. Gregorio Torres Quintero, *Mitos aztecas: Relación de los dioses del antiguo México*, 70–74.

45. Lumholtz, *Unknown Mexico*, 2:196.

46. Burgoa, *Geográfica descripción*, 1:412.

47. Aguilera, *Flora y fauna mexicana*, 15. The Olmec occupied the gulf regions of Tabasco and Veracruz. They reached the height of their development between 700 and 400 B.C.

48. Ibid.; Gossen, *Chamulas*, 86.

49. Rosa Brambila Paz et al., *El animal en la vida prehispánica*, 8; Sahagún, *Florentine Codex*, 11:7.

50. Aguilera, *Flora y fauna mexicana*, 9.

51. Gossen, *Chamulas*, 86; *Popul Vuh*, 254.

52. Gossen, *Chamulas*, 86–87; Lumholtz, *Unknown Mexico*, 1:308; Lic. Constantino J. Rickards, "Zoolatría entre los Zapotecas," *Memorias y Revista de la Sociedad Científica "Antonio Alzate"* 35 (September 1921): 333–334.

53. Lumholtz, *Unknown Mexico*, 1:331.

54. Ibid., 308–309.

55. Ibid., 310.

56. Ibid., 331.

57. Rickards, "Zoolatría," 334.

58. Michael D. Coe, *The Maya*, 17–27.

59. Gómez-Pompa, "On Maya Silviculture," 5–7.

60. Peter D. Harrison, "So the Seeds Shall Grow: Some Introductory Comments," in Peter D. Harrison and B. L. Turner II, eds., *Pre-Hispanic Maya Agriculture*, 16–17; Mary Pohl, "Interdisciplinary Research in Lowland Maya Archeology," in Mary Pohl, ed., *Prehistoric Lowland Maya Environment and Subsistence Economy*, 3.

61. B. L. Turner II and Peter D. Harrison, "Implications from Agriculture for Maya Prehistory," in Harrison and Turner, eds., *Pre-Hispanic Maya Agriculture*, 349–350, 368.

62. Arturo Gómez-Pompa, José Salvador Flores, and Victoria Sosa, "The 'Pet Kot': A Man-made Tropical Forest of the Maya," *Interciencia* 12 (January–February 1987): 10–15; Landa, *Yucatán*, 161–162.

63. Gómez-Pompa, "On Maya Silviculture," 1–14;; Rodolfo Lobato González, "Terrazas prehispánicas en la Selva Lacandona y su importancia en sistemas de producción agrícola," *Alternativas para el uso del suelo en areas forestales del trópico húmedo*, 3:11–12, 25, 34; James D. Nations and Ronald B. Nigh, "The Evolutionary Potential of the Sustained-Yield Tropical Forest Agriculture," *Journal of Anthropological Research* 36 (Spring 1980): 2; B. L. Turner II, "Ancient Agricultural Land Use in the Central Maya Lowlands," in Harrison and Turner, eds., *Pre-Hispanic Maya Agriculture*, 168–173.

64. Turner and Harrison, "Implications from Agriculture," 368.

65. For a theoretical discussion of the Maya collapse, see T. Patrick Culbert, ed., *The Classic Maya Collapse*.

66. See, for example, Don S. Rice, Prudence M. Rice, and Edward S. Deevey, "Paradise Lost: Classic Maya Lacustrine Environment," in Pohl, ed., *Prehistoric Lowland Maya Environment and Subsistence Economy*, 91–105.

67. Elliot M. Abrams and David J. Rue, "The Causes and Consequences of Deforestation among the Prehistoric Maya," *Human Ecology* 16 (1988): 388–391.

68. Anthony Andrews, *Maya Salt Trade and Production*, 16.

69. Julian C. Lee, "Creatures of the Maya," *Natural History* 99 (January 1990): 47–50.

70. Mediz Bolio, *La tierra del faisán*, 108.

71. Pedro Reyes Castillo, *La fauna silvestre en el plan Balancán-Tenosique*, 2–3.

72. Landa, *Yucatán*, 54, 165, 177.

73. Sherburne F. Cook, *Soil Erosion and Population in Central Mexico*, 14–32, 36–44, 44–48, 81, 86.

74. Ibid., 10.

75. Sherburne F. Cook, *The Historical Demography and Ecology of the Teotlalpan*, 52, 54.

76. Borah and Cook base this figure on estimates of agricultural yields and on the caloric consumption of people in the region. Borah and Cook, *Aboriginal Population*, 91.

77. Sahagún, *Florentine Codex*, 10:78.

78. Ibid., 81; Juan Bautista Pomar, *Relación de Tezcoco*, facsimile of the 1891 edition with a foreword and notes by Joaquín García Icazbalceta, 60; Bernal Díaz del Castillo, *Historia verdadera de la conquista de la Nueva España*, ed. Miguel León-Portilla, 1:331.

79. Sahagún, *Florentine Codex*, 11:106.

80. Díaz del Castillo, *Historia verdadera*, 1:332.

81. *Códice Mendocino o Colección de Mendoza*, Mexican manuscript from the sixteenth century that is preserved in the Bodleian Library in Oxford, ed. José Ignacio Echeagry, 25, 88–161.

82. Emily McClung de Tapia, *Ecología y cultura en Mesoamérica*, 36.

83. S. L. Cline, *Colonial Culhuacan, 1580–1600: A Social History of an Aztec Town*, 132; Ross Hassig, "The Famine of One Rabbit: Ecological Causes and Social Consequences of a Pre-Columbian Calamity," *Journal of Anthropological Research* 37 (Summer 1981): 178–180.

84. Borah and Cook, *Aboriginal Population*, 79.

85. Henrico Martínez, *Reportorio de los tiempos e historia natural de Nueva España*, introd. Francisco de la Maza, bibliographic appendix by González de Cossío, 180.

86. Fernando de Alva Ixtlilxóchitl, *Historia de la nación chichimeca*, ed. Gérman Vázquez Chamorro, 66. The Spanish generically referred to the Indians of northern Mexico as Chichimec.

87. *Chronicles of Michoacán*, 13; Helen Perlstein Pollard and Shirley Gornstein, "Agrarian Potential, Population, and the Tarascan State," *Science* 209 (11 July 1980): 276.

88. Ixtlilxóchitl, *Historia de la nación*, 165.

89. Fray Bartolomé de Las Casas, *Los indios de México y Nueva España*, 2d ed., ed. Edmundo O'Gorman with the collaboration of Jorge Alberto Manrique, 9.

90. Ixtlilxóchitl, *Historia de la nación*, 154.

91. In some areas, the pursuit of wild animals was, itself, a religious ceremony. In Oaxaca, hunting and fishing were steeped in ritual. The Spanish bishop Gonzalo de Balsabore described how Indians lit candles and burned copal to gain success at fishing. Hunting and fishing expeditions took on a festive air. Gonzalo de Balsabore, "Relación auténtica de las idolatrías, supersticiones, vanas observaciones de los indios del obispados de Oaxaca," in *Idolatría y superstición entre los indios de Oaxaca*, 2d ed.,

112; Heinrich Berlin, "Los antiguas creencias en San Miguel Sola, Oaxaca, México," in ibid., 63–87.

92. *Relación de las ceremonias*, 27, 28, 175; Edward S. Deevey, Jr., "Limnological Studies in Middle America, with a Chapter on Aztec Limnology," *Transactions of the Connecticut Academy of Arts and Sciences* 39 (February 1957): 224.

93. Sahagún, *Florentine Codex*, 10:188.

94. Pomar, *Relación de Tezcoco*, 59; Benavente, *Historia de los indios*, 229.

95. Díaz del Castillo, *Historia verdadera*, 1:331; Hernández, *Antigüedades,* 103–105; Las Casas, *Los indios*, 45, Sahagún, *Florentine Codex*, 10:80.

96. Aguilera, *Flora y fauna mexicana*, 10.

97. Las Casas, *Los indios*, 82.

98. *Códice Mendocino*, 25, 88–101.

99. Ixtlilxóchitl, *Historia de la nación*, 137.

100. Cook, *Historical Demography*, 29–30.

101. Cook, *Soil Erosion*, 86.

102. Pomar, *Relación de Tezcoco*, 59; Benavente, *Historia de los indios*, 229.

103. For an exposition of this theory, see Michael Harner, "The Ecological Basis for Aztec Sacrifice," *American Ethnologist* 4 (February 1977): 117–135.

104. Borah and Cook conclude that the Aztec still had access to many hectares of unused arable land. Hassig argues that during the mid-fifteenth century the inhabitants of the Valley of Mexico were not living dangerously close to the carrying capacity of the land, since it took four years of agricultural failures before they experienced a large-scale famine. Borah and Cook, *Aboriginal Population*, 91; Hassig, "Famine of One Rabbit," 175.

2. The Spanish Resolve: Conserving Resources for the Crown

1. Julio Caro Baroja, *Ritos y mitos equívocos*, 100–110, 339–351.

2. Instituto Mexicano de Recursos Naturales Renovables, *Mesas redondas sobre utilización y conservación del suelo en México*, 89, 111–112, 128; Secretaría de Agricultura y Recursos Hidráulicos en México, Subsecretaría de Infraestructura Hidráulica, *Agua y sociedad*, 70–71.

3. Martínez, *Reportorio de los tiempos*, 180. In 1607, Martínez became the chief engineer on the first drainage projects in Mexico City. The siphoning off of the valley's lakes eventually reduced flooding, but in its stead produced a desiccated landscape prone to dust storms. In addition, Mexico City lost a valuable source of water.

4. The Spanish colony of New Spain included the present-day territory of Mexico, Texas, the U.S. Southwest, and much of California.

5. Meyer, *Water in the Hispanic Southwest*, 30, 36, 50, 68, 78, 89, 166.

6. Charles H. Harris III, *A Mexican Family Empire: The Latifundio of the Sánchez-Navarros, 1766–1867*, 47.

7. In their legal battles for water rights with the Indians, the Spanish colonists often prevailed. Meyer, *Water in the Hispanic Southwest*, 58.

8. For the Arabic legacy regarding the management of water resources on the Iberian peninsula, see S. M. Imamuddin, *Muslim Spain, 711–1492 A.D.: A Sociological Study*, 78–79, and Jan Read, *The Moors in Spain and Portugal*, 235.

9. *Novísima recopilación de las leyes de España*, 3:639–642, 651–652; *Recopilación*

de las leyes destos reynos, libro 7, título 8. The two editions differ slightly in regard to factual information.

10. Decreed by King Carlos I and Queen Juana in 1542.

11. Quoted in Luis Urteaga, *La tierra esquilmada: Las ideas sobre la conservación de la naturaleza en la cultura española del siglo XVIII*, 123.

12. *Colección de documentos inéditos para la historia de España*, ed. Marquis de Pidal and Miguel Salvá, 26:314; "No se pegue fuegos en los montes, campos ni caunas," Ordenanzas de Mesta para ganados mayores y menores 81, Ramo de Ordenanzas I, Archivo General de la Nación, Mexico City; "Ordenanza sobre pastos de ovejas," 19 November 1603, 109v–110, Ramo de Ordenanzas I, Archivo General de la Nación, Mexico City; *Recopilación de leyes de los reynos de las Indias*, facsimile of the 4th ed. printed in Madrid in 1791, libro 4, título 17, ley 10; *Las siete partidas del Rey don Alfonso el Sabio*, reproduction of the Madrid 1807 edition, partida 7, título 15, leyes 10, 24, 28.

13. Julius Klein, *The Mesta: A Study in Spanish Economic History, 1273–1836*, 36–38, 316–326.

14. David E. Vassberg, *Land and Society in Golden Age Castile*, 39–40.

15. *Novísima recopilación*, 3:510; *Recopilación de las leyes destos reynos*, libro 7, título 7, ley 7.

16. *Novísima recopilación*, 3:510–511; *Recopilación de leyes destos reynos*, libro 7, título 7, ley 15.

17. Vassberg, *Land and Society*, 36–38, 54.

18. Miguel de Cervantes Saavedra, *Don Quijote de la Mancha*, 5th ed., ed. Francisco Rodríguez Marín, 1:250–251.

19. For example, an ordinance requiring a license to hunt within two leagues of Veracruz and a similar restriction on the use of firearms around Monterrey. "Se confirme el mandamiento expedido por el corregidor de Veracruz, para que sin licencia no se pueda salir a cazar en dos leguas de contorno de la ciudad," 12 August 1611, 138, Ramo de Ordenanzas I, Archivo General de la Nación, Mexico City; "Que se guarda la ordenanza hecho por el conde de Monterrey, tocante a cacería con arcabuz," 23 December 1603, 145, Ramo de Ordenanzas II, Archivo General de la Nación, Mexico City.

20. Don Alonso de la Mota y Escobar, *Descripción geográfica de los reinos de Nueva Galicia, Nueva Vizcaya, y Nuevo León*, introd. Joaquín Ramírez Cabañas, 54.

21. *Recopilación de leyes de los reynos*, libro 4, título 25, leyes 26, 32, 33.

22. Barco, *Historia natural y crónica*, 141–143.

23. Francisco Javier Clavigero, *The History of [Lower] California*, trans. from the Italian by Sara E. Lake, ed. A. A. Gray, 74–75.

24. Benavente, *Historia de los indios*, 250.

25. Clavigero, *The History of [Lower] California*, 79–80.

26. Barco, *Historia natural y crónica*, 217–218.

27. Alejandro de Humboldt, *Tablas geográficas políticas del reino de Nueva España y correspondencia mexicana*, 57.

28. *Recopilación de leyes de los reynos*, libro 4, título 17, ley 16.

29. William Vogt, *Los recursos naturales de México: Su pasado, presente, y futuro*, 46.

30. *Los virreys españoles en América durante el gobierno de la Casa de Austria: Mexico*, ed. Lewis Hanke with the collaboration of Celso Rodríguez, 273:40.

31. The Hapsburgs ruled Spain from 1516 to 1700.

32. *Ordenanzas de tierras y aguas*, 5th ed., abridged by Mariano Galván Rivera, 26.

33. "Ordenanzas de 27 de agosto de 1803.—Para el gobierno de los montes y arbolados," in *Código de colonización y terrenos baldíos de la República Mexicana años de 1451 a 1892*, comp. Francisco F. de la Maza, 50–145.

34. *Recopilación de leyes de los reynos*, libro 4, título 17, ley 5.

35. Ibid., ley 14.

36. Ibid., ley 19.

37. *Real ordenanzas para la dirección, régimen y gobierno del importante cuerpo de la minería de Nueva España y de su real tribunal general de orden de su magestad*, título 13, articulos 12, 14.

38. Mota y Escobar, *Descripción geográfica*, 51.

39. Some Indian communities filed lawsuits to maintain control over their lands, but the courts rarely ruled in their favor. Charles Gibson, *The Aztecs under Spanish Rule: A History of the Indians of the Valley of Mexico, 1519–1810*, 285–288.

40. William Taylor, *Landlord and Peasant in Colonial Oaxaca*, 1–2, 7–17, 35–110.

41. Enrique Beltrán, "El Virrey Revillagigedo y los bosques de San Luis Potosí," *Revista de la Sociedad Mexicana de Historia Natural* 17 (1956): 128–129.

42. Ibid., 128.

43. "Sobre la orden del cortar en los montes de Yaleo (Chalco)," 21 March 1579, 225v–226, Ramo de Ordenanzas II, Archivo General de la Nación, Mexico City.

44. John Perlin, *A Forest Journey: The Role of Wood in the Development of Civilization*, 128.

45. Beltrán, "El Virrey Revillagigedo," 128.

46. Ibid., 126.

47. Ibid., 125.

48. Anonymous Conqueror, *Narrative of Some Things of New Spain and of the Great City of Temestitan, Mexico*, trans. into English and annotated by Marshall H. Saville, 15.

49. Benavente, *Historia de los indios*, 243.

50. For example, Landa, *Relación de las cosas de Yucatán*, 177–181; El P. Joseph de Acosta, *Historia natural y moral de las Indias*, ed. Edmundo O'Gorman, 129; and Mota y Escobar, *Descripción geográfica*, 54–55, 187.

51. Acosta, *Historia natural y moral*, 129.

52. Father Juan Cavallero Carranco, *The Pearl Hunters in the Gulf of California, 1668*, summary report of the voyage made to the Californias by Captain Francisco de Lucenilla, transcribed, translated, and annotated by W. Michael Mathes, 81.

53. Quoted in Ernest J. Burrus, S.J., "Rivera y Moncada, Explorer and Military Commander of Both Californias, in the Light of His Diary and Other Contemporary Documents," *Hispanic American Historical Review* 50 (November 1970): 684.

54. Joan Corominas, *Diccionario crítico etimológico de la lengua castellana*, 2:2.

55. Roderick Nash, *Wilderness and the American Mind*, 1–2.

56. Anonymous Conqueror, *Narrative*, 15.

57. Mota y Escobar, *Descripción geográfica*, 139–140.

58. Beltrán, "El Virrey Revillagigedo," 124–125.

59. Gibson, *Aztecs under Spanish Rule*, 303.

60. D. José Antonio Alzate y Ramírez, *Gacetas de literatura de México*, 2:43. Alzate y Ramírez felt that the region's climate was also affected by the amount of water re-

tained in its lakes. Joseph Antonio Alzate y Ramírez, "Proyecto para desaguar la Laguna de Tescuco y por consiguente las de Chalco y San Cristóval, según las circunstancias, assequible y por el poco costo, apreciable, fundado sobre varias obserbaciones phisicas que comprueban so no difícil execución," 1767, pp. 18–19, volumen 17, expediente 12, Ramo de Desagüe, Archivo General de la Nación, Mexico City.

61. Alexander de Humboldt, *Political Essay on the Kingdom of New Spain*, trans. from the original French by John Black, 2:23–25, 87–88.

62. Humboldt, *Political Essay*, 2:24. Don Luis de Velasco, the younger (1590–1595) was the first viceroy to direct the planting of a park with trees (alameda) for the recreation of Mexico City's residents. Juan de Torquemada, *Los veyente y un libros rituales y monarchia yndiana con el origen y guerras de los Yndos Occidentales de sus poblaçones, descubrimiento, conquista, conuersión y otras cosas marauillosas de la mesma tierra*, 1:328.

63. Although the amalgamation process reduced the need for wood, it created another environmental danger: mercury poisoning. The debilitation and deaths resulting from mercury poisoning is a fascinating subject that had been briefly researched. Robert C. West cites a report from Solorzano y Pedeyra, a Peruvian colonial official, on the paralysis and death of workers in the Huancavelica mercury mines. Those involved in the amalgamation process were less severely affected because their contact with mercury was less pronounced, but even here some workers suffered from paralysis. See Robert C. West, *The Mining Community in Northern New Spain: The Parral Mining District*, 54–55. Mercury lost during the process of silver extraction probably contaminated the surrounding environment as well.

64. Humboldt, *Political Essay*, 3:235.

65. Humboldt, *Tablas geográficas*, 137.

66. Tom Gill estimates that 85 percent of Mexico was forested during the time of the Conquest. Robert C. West and John P. Augeli arrive at a figure of 60 percent. See Tom Gill, *Tropical Forests of the Caribbean*, 168, and Robert C. West and John P. Augeli, *Middle America: Its Lands and People*, 340. One method of estimating forest depletion is by calculating how much wood was used in various processes (such as mining).

67. Gill, *Tropical Forests*, 168.

68. Miguel Angel de Quevedo, "El problema de la deforestación en México.—Solución práctica del mismo," *México Forestal* 2 (July–August 1924): 65–66.

69. "Decreto de 4 de enero de 1813.—Sobre reducir los terrenos baldíos y otros terrenos comunes á dominio particular: Suertes concedidas á los defensores de la patria y á los ciudadanos no propietarios," in *Código de colonización y terrenos baldíos de la República Mexicana años de 1451 a 1892*, comp. Francisco F. de la Maza, 148–152.

70. Manuel Payno, "Bosques y arbolados," *Boletín de la Sociedad de Geografía y Estadística de la República Mexicana*, 2ª época, 2 (1870): 79.

3. Conservation during Unfavorable Times: Independent Mexico until the Revolution

1. Mexican political history during the nineteenth century yields a complicated mosaic. After the execution of Mexico's first ruler, Agustín de Iturbide, Liberals and Conservatives competed against each other (and against themselves) for control over the country. The Liberals ruled the country between 1855 and 1858, during which time they enacted a constitution (in 1857) and a series of reform laws that in part

were designed to end the privileges of the military and the church. Between 1858 and 1861, Liberals and Conservatives engaged in a civil war. In 1861, the Liberals triumphed, only to be toppled a year later by the French with the blessing of the Conservatives (ostensibly the French invaded Mexico because the Mexican government had declared a moratorium on the payment of the country's foreign debt). In 1864, the French made Austrian Archduke Maximilian emperor of Mexico. In 1867, the Liberals executed Maximilian, an event that not only marked the end of the French Intervention but also the end of Conservative rule in Mexico. Liberal politicians still plotted against each other, but the power of the party itself was now secure.

2. Fernando Ortiz Monasterio et al., *Tierra profanada: Historia ambiental de México*, 232.

3. Pedro Blazquez, *El cazador mexicano o el arte de la caza en México y en sus relaciones con la historia natural*, 14, 18–19.

4. José M. Santos Coy, *Hay bosques porque llueve; o. ¿Llueve porque hay bosques . . . ? (El interés individual)*, 36.

5. José M. Romero, "Memoria sobre el Distrito de Pachuca," in Ramón Almaraz,ed., *Memoria de los trabajos ejecutados por la comisión científica de Pachuca en el año de 1864*, 112.

6. Blazquez, *El cazador mexicano*, 11.

7. Ibid., 11–12.

8. *José María Velasco, 1840–1912*, exhibition, Philadelphia Museum of Art and the Brooklyn Museum, note on Velasco's paintings by Henry Clifford, 15.

9. Ibid.

10. McKinley Helm, *Modern Mexican Painters*, 7.

11. For an excellent discussion of conservation thought in eighteenth-century Spain, see Urteaga, *La tierra esquilmada*.

12. See, for example, Blazquez, *El cazador mexicano*, and Manuel Villada, "Estudios sobre la fauna de Pachuca, Real del Monte, Mineral del Chico y Barranca Honda," in Almaraz, ed., *Memoria de los trabajos*, 265–334.

13. Adele Ogden, *The California Sea Otter Trade, 1784–1848*, 106, 113–114; David J. Weber, *The Mexican Frontier, 1821–1846: The American Southwest under Mexico*, 148.

14. "G. Pedraza a los Comandantes de la Marina," 26 y 28 de enero de 1825, *Ordenes y circulares espedidas por el supremo gobierno desde el año de 1825 hasta la fecha para arreglo y legitimidad del comercio marítimo nacional*, 1–3.

15. "Victoria al Ministerio de Relaciones," 1831, *Departmental Records*, 9:136–137, Archives of California, Manuscript Collections, Bancroft Library, Berkeley, California.

16. Ogden, *California Sea Otter Trade*, 114, 123, 142.

17. "1834—mayo 13—Diputacional sesión del día de la fecha," 1834–1835, *Legislative Records*, 2:68–69, Archives of California, Manuscript Collections, Bancroft Library, Berkeley, California; "1834—noviembre 3—Diputacional territorial sobre estracción de maderas, California," ibid., 2:207.

18. "1845—mayo 16—Angeles (sesión de esta día)," 1841–1846, *Legislative Records*, 4:152.

19. Theodore H. Hittell, *History of California*, 2:364.

20. "1839, México.—Romero a Gobierno de Californias—Villa de Los Angeles,

junio 12," 1839, *Superior Government State Papers. Decrees and Dispatches*, 15:128, Archives of California, Manuscript Collections, Bancroft Library, Berkeley, California.

21. A person could hire a substitute to do work for him or her.

22. Antonio María Salonio, "Reglamento para la conservación y aumento de bosques," *Boletín de la Sociedad de Geografía y Estadística de la República Mexicana*, 2ª época, 1 (1869):14–20.

23. Leopoldo Río de la Loza, "Tala de bosques y exportación de maderas," in *Escritos de Leopoldo Río de la Loza*, comp. Juan Manuel Noriega, 329–332.

24. "Disposición para todos los buques nacionales o extranjeros deban tener permiso para explotar maderas de construcción de ebanistería," 1854, Serie: Decretos, Circulares, y Leyes, Fondo: Fomento y Obras Públicas, Archivo General de la Nación, Mexico City.

25. "Noviembre 25 de 1854.—Se piden á las diputaciones de minería noticias de los bosques y su extensión," in *Código de colonización y terrenos baldíos de la República Mexicana años de 1451 a 1892*, 582.

26. Río de la Loza, "Tala de bosques," 330.

27. "Setiembre 24 de 1856.—Resolución de Ministerio de Hacienda—Sobre adjudicación de Desierto de Carmelitas," in *Legislación mexicana o colección completa de las disposiciones legislativas expedidas desde la independencia de la República*, comp. Manuel Dublán and José María Lozano, 8:251–252.

28. "Circular de 15 de abril de 1857.—Para que los gobernadores de los estados eviten la destrucción de los bosques y cuiden de su conservación," *Código de colonización y terrenos baldíos de la República Mexicana años de 1451 a 1892*, 662–663.

29. "Abril 18 de 1861.—Reglamento expedido por el Ministerio de Fomento á que deben sujetarse los cortadores de árboles en terrenos nacionales," in *Legislación mexicana o colección completa de las disposiciones legislativas expedidas de independencia de la República*, comp. Dublán and Lozano, 9:160–162.

30. Río de la Loza, "Tala de bosques," 333.

31. Romero, "Memoria de Pachuca," 112.

32. Ibid., 86.

33. Río de la Loza, "Tala de bosques," 331–332.

34. Ibid., 332.

35. *Reglamento de huertas y sembrados para el territorio de la Baja California, 18 de agosto de 1862*, 9.

36. Those who owned less than 33.3 acres had to plant a proportional amount of trees.

37. Leopoldo Río de la Loza, "Proyecto de ordenanzas de bosques, de arbolados y de exportación de maderas," in *Escritos de Leopoldo Río de la Loza*, 335–341.

38. H. Romero Gil, "Selvicultura," *Boletín de la Sociedad de Geografía y Estadística de la República Mexicana*, 2ª época, 1 (1869): 9.

39. The other members of the commission were Gumesindo Mendoza, Luis Malanco, and Ignacio Cornejo. "Bosques y arbolados," *Boletín de la Sociedad Geografía y Estadística de la República Mexicana*, 2ª época, 2 (1870): 23–24.

40. Ibid., 23.

41. Ibid., 19. Druidism refers to the worship of nature by members of an ancient Celtic priesthood. Naturalism in this context signifies a romantic exaltation of the natural world.

42. Ibid., 19, 23.

43. Ibid., 21–22.

44. Ibid., 19.

45. Ibid., 20.

46. Ibid., 24.

47. Río de la Loza, "Tala de bosques," 329–330.

48. Ibid., 333.

49. Matías Romero, "Railways in Mexico," *International Review* 13 (1892): 491.

50. The *carboneros* were people who burned wood to make charcoal. Payno, "Bosques y arbolados," 87–88.

51. Ibid., 87.

52. Evelyn Hu-Dehart, *Yaqui Resistance and Survival: The Struggle for Land and Autonomy, 1821–1910,* 81, 99, 155.

53. "Nuevos prejucios a la agricultura," *El Tiempo* (Mexico City), 9 June 1905. Some students of the period theorize that the *hacendados'* expropriation of Indian land contributed to a rapid growth in the Indian population as Indian laborers needed more children to produce more income. This population growth, set in motion during the Porfiriato, meant a greater exploitation of natural resources not only then but for years to come. Interview with Ronald Nigh, Asociación de Dana, Mexico City, 16 October 1989.

54. Payno, "Bosques y arbolados," 85.

55. At the end of Porfirio Díaz's first term as president in 1880, Mexico had only 478 miles of railroads. When the Díaz regime finally collapsed in 1911, Mexico had a railroad system totaling 15,360 miles. Frank William Powell, *The Railroads of Mexico,* 1.

56. Letter from Robert Anderson Marshall to his nephew Charles A. Gauld, Circleville, Ohio, 29 December 1936, concerning his stay in Mexico, 1906–1907, letterhead, Rio Grande, Sierra Madre, & Pacific Railway, enclosed [in Marshall's missive], Manuscript Collections, the Bancroft Library, Berkeley, California. For wide-eyed accounts of the abundance of wildlife in Chihuahua during the middle of the nineteenth century, see John Russell Bartlett, *Personal Narrative of Explorations and Incidents in Texas, New Mexico, California, Sonora, and Chihuahua, Connected with the United States and Mexican Boundary Commission during the Years 1850, 1851, 1852, and 1853,* 1:236, and George Frederick Augustus Ruxton, *Adventures in Mexico and the Rocky Mountains,* 155.

57. John Locke, *The Second Treatise of Government,* ed. Thomas P. Peardon, 25.

58. Auguste Comte, *A General View of Positivism,* trans. J. H. Bridges, 1–226, 355–444.

59. Leopoldo Zea, *El positivismo en México: Nacimiento, apogeo y decadencia,* 147, 294–299, 371, 403–406.

60. Secretaría de Agricultura y Fomento, *Colección de leyes sobre tierras y demas disposiciones con las mismas,* 26.

61. The Indian communities bore the brunt of vacant lands/positivistic thought. Díaz and the *científicos* viewed the Indians as an obstacle to the development of the nation's wealth. They disdained them as a backward group producing food for their own basic needs rather than for the national economy. By doing so, the Indians had forfeited the land to the state that could now dispose of it to more "progressive"

elements in society. Two centuries before, Puritans in the English colonies had cleared the lands left "vacant" by Indians and had converted them to "productive" agriculture. The Puritans and the *científicos* shared basically the same notion of progress, although the Puritans built theirs on religious grounds (God wanted humankind to advance civilization), whereas the *científicos* constructed theirs upon the supposedly scientific foundations of positivism.

62. Enrique Beltrán, "Forestry and the Public Domain: A Mexican Viewpoint," *American Forests* 75 (December 1969): 59.

63. Alfred Mordecai Papers, vol. 4 (1860–1867), Letter from Alfred Mordecai to Ellen Mordecai, 27 May 1866, Manuscript Division, Library of Congress, Washington, D.C.

64. Mexico National Railway Company, *Mexico National Railway: Confidential [Report]*, 22.

65. Romero, "Railways in Mexico," 489–490.

66. Benjamin Anthony Micallef, "The Forest Policy of Mexico," Master's thesis, University of California, Berkeley, 1955, 23–24.

67. "Circular de 15 de febrero de 1880.—Exitando á los gobernadores de los estados á que dicten las medidas á evitar la destrucción de montes y arbolados," in *Código de colonización y terrenos baldíos de la República Mexicana años de 1451 a 1892*, 857–858.

68. In addition to Jesús Alfaro's published thesis, see Manuel M. Villada and Eduardo Armendaris, "Necesidad de la conservación de los bosques," in Sociedad de Historia Natural, *Primer concurso científico mexicano*, 1–18, and Fernando Altamirano, "Necesidad de la repoblación de bosques," in ibid., 18–41. All three were members of the Natural History Society of Mexico.

69. Jesús Alfaro, *Algunas palabras acerca de la influencia higiénica de las arboledas y necesidad de reglamantar su uso entre nosotros*, 12.

70. Ibid., 12–35.

71. Santos Coy, *Hay bosques*, 3–4, 15, 19, 25–27.

72. Ibid., 36.

73. Ibid., 32, 35–37.

74. *Reglamento para la explotación de los bosques y terrenos baldíos y nacionales*, 7–8.

75. Secretaría de Fomento, Colonización, é Industria, "Monte vedado del Mineral de Chico," *Diario Oficial*, 22 June 1898, 3–4.

76. *Reglamento*, 22–24. In contrast to the situation regarding forests and wildlife, few regulations guarded the use of soils and water. The adoption of soil and water conservation techniques continued to be left to the discretion of private property owners. One of the exceptions was a regulation that permitted the drainage of water only if this did not lower river flow or lake size and that required a permit for the mining of riverbeds. "El aprovechamiento de las aguas y la agricultura," *El Tiempo*, 23 October 1905; *Ley sobre aprovechamiento de aguas de jurisdicción federal de 13 de diciembre de 1910 y reglamento de la misma de 31 de enero de 1911*, 15.

77. "La protección a las aves útiles a la agricultura," *Boletín de la Secretaría de Fomento*, 3ª época, 5 (July 1906): 3.

78. Secretaría de Fomento, Dirección de Bosques, Departamento de Administración, "Comisión de Parasitología Agrícola, denuncia caza inmoderada de garzas en

Tehuantepec, Estado de Oaxaca," 22 February 1906, caja 3, expediente 29, Serie: Bosques, Archivo General de la Nación, Mexico City; Rodolfo Hernández Corzo, *La administración de la fauna silvestre en México*, 13. The Audubon Society was not the only U.S. organization interested in wildlife in Mexico. The Bureau of Biological Survey, the forerunner to the Fish and Wildlife Service, began conducting investigations in Mexico in 1892. "Mexico Also Owns the Ducks," ca. 1949, Records of the Fish and Wildlife Service, Record Group 22, National Archives, Washington, D.C.

79. Mariano Bárcena, *Ensayo práctico de repoblación de bosques*, 3–4.

4. Miguel Angel de Quevedo: The Apostle of the Tree

1. M. E. Musgrave, "The Apostle of the Tree," *American Forests* 46 (May 1940): 204.

2. The sobriquet "apostle of the tree" was given to Miguel Angel de Quevedo by his friend and fellow admirer of trees, the engineer Felix Fulgencio Palavicini in the newspaper *El Universal* (Mexico City) in 1919. Felix Fulgencio Palavicini, *Grandes de México*, 134.

3. The biographical information on Quevedo's early life and career comes from Miguel Angel de Quevedo, *Relato de mi vida*, 1–29.

4. Ibid., 6.

5. For a history of the *desagüe* projects, see Louisa Schell Hoberman, "Technological Change in a Traditional Society: The Case of the *Desagüe* in Colonial Mexico," *Technology and Culture* 21 (July 1980): 386–407.

6. Miguel Angel de Quevedo, *Memoria sobre el Valle de México, su desagüe y saneamiento*, 37.

7. Joseph Antonio Alzate y Ramírez, "Proyecto para desaguar la Laguna de Tescuco y por consiguiente las de Chalco y San Cristóval, según las circunstancias, assequible y por el poco costo, apreciable, fundado sobre varias obserbaciones phisicas que comprueban so no difícil execución," 1767, p. 17v, volumen 17, expediente 1, Ramo de Desagüe, Archivo General de la Nación, Mexico City; Torquemada, *Los veyente y un libros rituales*, 1:341.

8. Quevedo, *Memoria sobre el Valle de México*, 53.

9. Edward Alphonso Goldman, "Observations Concerning Waterfowl in Mexico, with Special Reference to Migratory Species, January 20 to April 10, 1920," Fish and Wildlife Reports of Edward Alphonso Goldman, Smithsonian Institution Archives, Washington, D.C., 14.

10. Edward Alphonso Goldman, "Mexico. Mexico, City of Mexico and Vicinity, January 17–19 and June 22–30; Lerma, July 1–11, 1904," ibid., 22–30.

11. Miguel Angel de Quevedo, "Los desastres de la deforestación en el Valle y Ciudad de México," *México Forestal* 4 (May–June 1926): 67–82.

12. Quevedo, *Relato de mi vida*, 11.

13. Miguel Angel de Quevedo, *Conveniencia de estudiar todas las circunstancias en que se distribuye el agua pluvial que cae en las varias cuencas del territorio, de coordinar las observaciones pluviométrica con las de hidrometría en las mismas cuencas, así como también de que se expidan las leyes conducentes á la conservación y repoblación de los bosques*, 6.

14. Miguel Angel de Quevedo, "La influencia de los bosques en la precipitación

pluvial: Su aplicación al territorio mexicano," *Memorias y Revista de la Sociedad Científica "Antonio Alzate"* 43 (January–February 1924): 47–63. For a debate between Quevedo and a colleague on whether any causal relationship existed between forest cover and precipitation, see Gabriel M. Oropesa, "Las lluvias en Necaxa no han disminuido," ibid., 65–69, 79–89, and Miguel Angel de Quevedo, "Nota sobre la precipitación pluvial en la región de Necaxa," ibid., 71–77, 91–93.

15. Quevedo, *Conveniencia de estudiar,* 6.

16. Ibid., 8–9; Quevedo, *Relato de mi vida,* 38.

17. This group included Dr. José Ramírez; Professor Mariano Leal; the Director of Public Works, Guillermo Beltrán y Puga; and the Director of the Central Meteorological Observatory, Manuel E. Pastrana. Miguel Angel de Quevedo, "La Junta Central de Bosques," *Revista Forestal Mexicana* 1 (July 1909): 4–5.

18. "Nuestra Revista Forestal," *Revista Forestal Mexicana* 1 (July 1909): 1–2.

19. Quevedo, "La Junta Central," 5.

20. Ibid., 7.

21. Quevedo, *Relato de mi vida,* 45.

22. Miguel Angel de Quevedo, *Espacios libres y reservas forestales de las ciudades: Su adaptación a jardines, parques y lugares de juego,* 5–6, 23, 36.

23. Coyoacán is a southern suburb of Mexico City.

24. Díaz provided the first public moneys for the *viveros* in 1908. Quevedo, *Relato de mi vida,* 43; José García Martínez, "La legislación forestal como base de un mejor administración de los recursos naturales de los bosques de nuestro país," in Secretaría de Agricultura y Fomento, Dirección General Forestal y de Caza, *Memoria de la Primera Convención Nacional Forestal,* 239.

25. Secretaría de Fomento, Dirección de Bosques, Departamento de Administración, "Informe de los trabajos llevados a cabo por la Sección 3a del Departamento de Bosques, desde el 1° de julio de 1913 al 16 de febrero del año de 1914," caja 14, expediente 3, Serie: Bosques, Archivo General de la Nación, Mexico City. Quevedo created four other nurseries around the Valley of Mexico: Volantes in Santa Fe, Nativitas in Xochimilco, Aragón in Guadalupe, and the Viveros of Desierto de los Leones. Tereso Reyes e hijos, *México está en peligro de perecer, por la perdida de su agricultura, a causa de la destrucción de los bosques,* 29.

26. Secretaría de Fomento, "Informe de los trabajos"; Miguel Angel de Quevedo, "Informe sobre los principales trabajos emprendidos por la Junta Central de Bosques y Arbolados durante el año fiscal 1909–1910, rendido al C. Secretario de Fomento por el Presidente de la Junta, el 30 de junio de 1910," *Revista Forestal Mexicana* 1 (June 1910): 259–260; Miguel Angel de Quevedo, "Las polvaderas de los terrenos tequezquitosos del antiguo lago de Texcoco y los procedimientos de enyerbe para remediarlas," *Memorias y Revista de la Sociedad Científica "Antonio Alzate"* 40 (October–December 1922): 533–548.

27. Quevedo, *Relato de mi vida,* 50.

28. Miguel Angel de Quevedo, *La iniciación de la Campaña de Protección Forestal del Territorio Nacional y sus desarrollos sucesivos y tropiezos,* 7–8.

29. Quevedo, *Relato de mi vida,* 43–46; idem, "La Junta Central," 9–10; Reyes, *México está en peligro,* 28.

30. Samuel Solís S., "La labor del Ingeniero Miguel A. de Quevedo en Veracruz," *México Forestal* 24 (July–September 1946): 60–61.

31. Quevedo, *La iniciación de la Campaña,* 8–9.

32. Secretaría de Fomento, "Informe de los trabajos"; Quevedo, "Informe sobre los prinicipales trabajos," 261–263.

33. "Cuestionario relativo á los bosques y montes existentes en la República propuesta por la Junta Central de Bosques á las juntas locales de los estados," *Revista Forestal Mexicana* 1 (December 1909): 119–124; Miguel Quevedo, "Breve reseña de los fundamentos y métodos que han servido para la formación del catálogo forestal de la República," *Revista Forestal Mexicana* 2 (October 1911): 124–131 and attached tables; idem, "Informe sobre los principales trabajos," 256.

34. Musgrave, "Apostle of the Tree," 203.

35. Miguel Angel de Quevedo, "Conferencia Internacional Norteamericana sobre Conservación de Recursos Naturales celebrada en Washington durante los días del 18 al 24 de febrero de 1909," *Revista Forestal Mexicana* 1 (October 1909): 81.

36. Ibid., 78, 81.

37. Daniel F. Galicia, "Mexico's National Parks," *Ecology* 22 (January 1941): 107–110.

38. Quevedo, "Conferencia," 83–85.

39. Miguel Angel de Quevedo, *Algunas consideraciones sobre nuestro problema agrario,* 103–104.

40. García Martínez, "La legislación forestal," 239.

41. Quevedo, *Relato de mi vida,* 46.

42. Quevedo, *Algunas consideraciones,* 102–103.

43. Ibid., 104.

44. Quevedo, *Relato de mi vida,* 50–52.

45. Quevedo, *Algunas consideraciones,* 13–14.

46. Ibid., 15–16.

47. Solís, "La labor del Ingeniero Quevedo," 61.

48. Fernando Vargas Márquez, *Parques nacionales de México y reservas equivalentes: Pasado, presente y futuro,* 45; Secretaría de Fomento, Poder Ejecutivo, 15 de noviembre de 1917, Records of the Foreign Agricultural Service, Narrative Reports, Record Group 166, National Archives, Washington, D.C.

49. Quevedo, *Relato de mi vida,* 39–40.

50. Ibid., 55–56.

51. "Comite Nacional para la Protección de las Aves Silvestres," under the theme of *selvicultura* in the Archivo Fernández y Fernández, Biblioteca del Colegio de Michoacán, Zamora, Michoacán.

52. To a certain extent, the Mexican Department of Biological Studies (created in 1915) was modeled after that of the U.S. Bureau of Biological Survey. In particular, the Mexican agency "adopted" its U.S. counterpart's emphasis on the study of natural history.

53. The *armadas* were a line of guns that hunters simultaneously set off with a triggering mechanism to kill the largest number of ducks at one time. A typical shooting battery consisted of around 110 guns. Goldman, "Observations Concerning Waterfowl," 1–23.

54. The government had limited permits for the operation of *armadas* to about seventy licensees. Ibid., 22–23.

55. Edward Alphonso Goldman, "Migratory Waterfowl Conditions in Mexico,

December 20, 1934, to May 7, 1935," Fish and Wildlife Reports of Edward Alphonso Goldman, Smithsonian Institution Archives, Washington, D.C., 50.

56. "México Forestal," *México Forestal* 1 (January 1923): 1.

57. Ibid.

58. Ibid., 2.

59. Secretaría de Agricultura y Fomento, Dirección Forestal y de Caza y Pesca, Circular 17 de mayo de 1922, Serie: Obregón y Calles, Fondo: Presidentes, Archivo General de la Nación, Mexico City.

60. "Proyecto de Ley Forestal y Arbolados," *México Forestal* 1 (February 1923): 1–8.

61. Mexican laws usually consist of statements of objectives (the "law") followed later (most often the following year) by more specific regulations.

62. Secretaría de Agricultura y Fomento, "Reglamento de la Ley Forestal," *Diario Oficial*, 27 October 1927, 1–24.

63. Excerpt from "Quarterly Review of Commerce and Industries, December Quarter 1930," American Consulate General, Mexico City, American Consul Dudley G. Dwyre, 20 January 1931, Records of the Foreign Agricultural Service, Narrative Reports, Record Group 166, National Archives, Washington, D.C.

64. Reyes, *México está en peligro*, 37.

65. "Quarterly Review of Commerce and Industries, September Quarter, 1930," American Consulate General, Mexico City, Consul Dudley G. Dwyre, Mexico, D.F., Mexico, 18 October 1930, Records of the Foreign Agricultural Service, Narrative Reports, National Archives, Washington, D.C.

66. Mexico's second national park, El Chico, was created in 1922, but another national park was not established until 1935. Angel Roldán, "Movimiento forestal mexicano," *Memorias y Revista de la Sociedad Científica "Antonio Alzate"* 51 (1929): 425; "Relación de los parques nacionales que han sido declarados desde la creación del Departamento Forestal y de Caza y Pesca hasta el 24 de noviembre de 1939," *México Forestal* 17 (July–December 1939): 67–74.

67. Gill, *Tropical Forests*, 179–180.

68. Miguel Angel de Quevedo, "La organización del Servicio Forestal por el Departamento Autónomo Forestal de Caza y Pesca y su programa y labores," *México Forestal* 13 (January–February 1935): 4.

69. Gill, *Tropical Forests*, 184.

70. Charles Sheldon, *The Wilderness of Desert Bighorns and Seri Indians*, 167–168.

71. Quevedo, *Relato de mi vida*, 63–64.

5. Conservation for the Commonweal: The Cárdenas Years

1. For a history of the Dust Bowl, see Donald Worster, *Dust Bowl: The Southern Plains in the 1930s*.

2. Quevedo, *Relato de mi vida*, 63.

3. Carlos M. Peralta, *Estudio sobre los bosques de Uruapan*, 3–5, 27. Lázaro Cárdenas's natural resource policies often did not make a sharp distinction between the rural poor or *campesinos* and native populations. In fact, there was a considerable overlap between these two groups.

4. The environmental philosopher E. F. Schumacher coined the term "small is

beautiful." E. F. Schumacher, *Small Is Beautiful: A Study of Economics as if People Mattered.*

5. Quoted in Tom Clark Call, *The Mexican Venture: From Political to Industrial Revolution in Mexico*, 21. For a homage to the work, spirit, and play of the "machineless people" of Mexico, see Stuart Chase, in collaboration with Marian Tyler, *Mexico: A Study of Two Americas*, 1–13, 168–207, 304–327.

6. The literal translation for the department is the Department of Forestry, Hunting, and Fishing, but I have chosen the more familiar Department of Forestry, Fish, and Game.

7. "Mensaje del C. Presidente de la República, General Lázaro Cárdenas, radiado al pueblo mexicano el 1o de enero de 1935, en lo concerniente a la creación del Departamento Autónomo Forestal y de Caza y Pesca," *Boletín del Departamento Forestal y de Caza y Pesca* 1 (September–October 1935): 36.

8. Ibid., 38.

9. "Decreto que crea el Departamento Autónomo Forestal y de Caza y Pesca, 31 de diciembre de 1934," in Departamento Forestal y de Caza y Pesca, *Código de Pesca de los Estados Unidos Mexicanos*, 3–4.

10. "Protección a la Naturaleza," *Protección a la Naturaleza* 1 (October 1935): 3.

11. Quevedo, *Relato de mi vida*, 88.

12. Carlos González Peña, "El retorno a la barbarie," *El Universal* (Mexico City), 4 January 1940, 3.

13. "Mensaje del Presidente," 37.

14. Musgrave, "Apostle of the Tree," 225.

15. González Peña, "El retorno a la barbarie," 3.

16. John D. Jernegan and S. Roger Tyler, Jr., American vice consuls, "Mexico's Conservation Program," 30, prepared on behalf of the National Park Service of the Department of the Interior, 23 May 1938, Records of the Foreign Agricultural Service, Narrative Reports, Record Group 166, National Archives, Washington, D.C.

17. In a famous article entitled "The Tragedy of the Commons," Garrett Hardin, a professor of human ecology at the University of California, Santa Barbara, argued that resources held in common were ripe for abuse because nearly everyone maximized their own exploitation of the land without consideration of the cumulative impact. The predominant philosophy was: "Why shouldn't I be able to better my lot like everyone else?" Garrett Hardin, "The Tragedy of the Commons," *Science* 162 (1968): 1243–1248. Private property owners, though, also exploited the natural resources on their lands without taking into account the environmental consequences. Private landownership did not guarantee a benign use of the land; likewise the degradation of communal holdings was not a foregone conclusion.

18. Miguel Angel de Quevedo, "Informe que rinde el Ciudadano Jefe del Departamento Forestal y de Caza y Pesca al Ciudadano Presidente de la República, sobre la exploración forestal y de caza y pesca, a la región sureste," 1937, 1–14, Serie: Lázaro Cárdenas, Fondo: Presidentes, Archivo General de la Nación, Mexico City. The documents from the Archivo General de la Nación cited in this chapter are filed under the card catalog heading of Departamento Forestal y de Caza y Pesca.

19. Ibid., 16.

20. Ibid.

21. Ibid., 15–20.

22. Jernegan and Tyler, "Mexico's Conservation Program," 32.

23. Ramón Fernández y Fernández, "El retorno a la Secretaría de Agricultura," 1940, 6, under the theme of *selvicultura*, Archivo Fernández y Fernández, Biblioteca del Colegio de Michoacán, Zamora, Michoacán.

24. H. Arthur Meyer, "Forestry in Mexico," *Chronica Botanica* 6 (November 1941): 397.

25. Departamento Forestal y de Caza y Pesca, "Decreto que reforma el Artículo 87 de la Ley Forestal," *Diario Oficial*, 21 January 1938, 10.

26. Letter from Miguel Angel de Quevedo to Lázaro Cárdenas, 9 November 1939, 3, Serie: Lázaro Cárdenas, Fondo: Presidentes, Archivo General de la Nación, Mexico City.

27. Jernegan and Tyler, "Mexico's Conservation Program," 8–9.

28. Letter from Ing. Salvador Guerrero to Luis I. Rodríguez, 14 February 1936, 1, Serie: Lázaro Cárdenas, Fondo: Presidentes, Archivo General de la Nación, Mexico City.

29. Mexicans had not yet undertaken the large-scale exploitation of coastal mangroves. Miguel Angel de Quevedo, "Informe sobre la exploración forestal y de caza y pesca llevado a cabo en la región del sureste del territorio mexicano," *Boletín del Departamento Forestal y de Caza y Pesca* 4 (June–August 1939): 16–17.

30. Miguel Angel de Quevedo, "Informe sobre la exploración forestal llevado a cabo por el jefe del ramo en la región del camino México-Morelia-Guadalajara y en la region norte de Jalisco," 1939, 1, Serie: Lázaro Cárdenas, Fondo: Presidentes, Archivo General de la Nación, Mexico City.

31. Miguel Angel de Quevedo, "La creación de los parques nacionales y sus ventajas," *Boletín del Departamento Forestal y de Caza y Pesca* 4 (December 1938–February 1939): 62.

32. Miguel Angel de Quevedo, "Anteproyecto del plan sexenal para el período 1941–1946 en los ramos forestales," *Boletín del Departamento Forestal y de Caza y Pesca* 4 (March–May 1939): 1.

33. Jernegan and Tyler, "Mexico's Conservation Program," 31, 33; Meyer, "Forestry in Mexico," 398.

34. Quevedo, "Anteproyecto del plan sexenal," 1–2.

35. Jernegan and Tyler, "Mexico's Conservation Program," 1.

36. "Relación de los parques que han sido declarados desde la creación del Departamento Forestal y de Caza y Pesca hasta el 24 de noviembre de 1939," *Mexico Forestal* 17 (July–December 1939): 67–74; Enrique Beltrán and Rigoberta Vázquez de la Parra, *En defensa del Parque Nacional Desierto de los Leones*, 30–31, 33.

37. For policies and attitudes toward national parks in the United States, see Alfred Runte, *National Parks: The American Experience*.

38. *Ley Forestal y su reglamento*, 15.

39. Quevedo, "La creación de los parques nacionales," 63.

40. Quevedo, *Relato de mi vida*, 65.

41. Miguel Angel de Quevedo, "Informe de los principales trabajos desarrollados por el Departamento Forestal y de Caza y Pesca en cumplimiento del plan sexenal desde mayo de 1937," *México Forestal* 16 (July–September 1938): 40.

42. Quevedo, *Relato de mi vida*, 76.

43. Quevedo, "La creación de los parques nacionales," 62.

44. Letter from Quevedo to Cárdenas, 1939, 3.

45. Gonzalo Blanco Macías, "El Parque Internacional de las Naciones Amigas y la Presa Falcón," *Suelo y Agua* 1 (16 November 1953): 2.

46. American Embassy, Mexico City, 16 February 1951, Records of the Foreign Agricultural Service, Narrative Reports, Record Group 166, National Archives, Washington, D.C.

47. Jernegan and Tyler, "Mexico's Conservation Program," 25.

48. Antonio H. Sosa, "Parque Nacional Cumbres de Ajusco," *México Forestal* 16 (April–June 1938): 32–33.

49. Departamento Forestal y de Caza y Pesca, "Acuerdo que establece las vedas para los diferentes especies de caza," *Diario Oficial*, 24 January 1938, 11–12; Juan Zinzer, "Informe de los principales trabajos desarrollados por la Jefatura del Servicio de Caza de acuerdo con lo establecido por el plan sexenal," *Boletín del Departamento Forestal y de Caza y Pesca* 4 (December 1938–February 1939): 94–95.

50. Ibid., 94.

51. Goldman, "Migratory Waterfowl Conditions in Mexico," 50.

52. "Convenio entre los Estados Unidos Mexicanos y los Estados Unidos de Norteamérica para la protección de aves migratorias y de mamíferos cinegeticos," *Boletín del Departamento Forestal y de Caza y Pesca* 1 (February–April 1936): 153–157.

53. Letter from Jesse F. Thompson and Gustav A. Swanson to Chief Office of Foreign Activities, Fish and Wildlife Service, Proposed Trip of the Director to Discuss Waterfowl Conditions with Mexico, 4 August 1948, Records of the U.S. Fish and Wildlife Service, Record Group 22, National Archives, Washington, D.C.

54. Sheldon, *Wilderness of Desert Bighorns,* 161, f. 166; U.S. Fish and Wildlife Service, *Mexican Wolf Recovery Plan,* 8–10.

55. Juan Zinzer, "The Mexican Wildlife Situation," in the *Proceedings of the First North American Wildlife Conference,* 6–11; idem, "A Message from Mexico," in the *Transactions of the Third North American Wildlife Conference,* 10–15.

56. Zinzer, "Informe de los principales trabajos," 96.

57. For the role of sports hunters in the U.S. conservation movement, see John F. Reiger, *American Sportsmen and the Origins of Conservation.*

58. "Mexico Also Owns the Ducks," ca. 1949, Records of the Fish and Wildlife Service, Record Group 22, National Archives, Washington, D.C.

59. Zinzer, "Informe de los principales trabajos," 95–96.

60. Secretaría de Agricultura y Fomento, "Ley de Caza," *Diario Oficial*, 13 September 1940, 4–5.

61. "Vedas pesqueras," *Protección a la Naturaleza* 1 (October–December 1936): 25.

62. Miguel A. Quevedo, "Informe sobre los principales trabajos desarrollados por el Departamento Forestal y de Caza y Pesca durante el año de 1936," *México Forestal* 15 (January–February 1937): 8.

63. "Ley de Pesca de 26 de agosto de 1932," in Departamento Forestal y de Caza y Pesca, *Código de Pesca de los Estado Unidos Mexicanos,* 13.

64. Reglamento de la Ley de Pesca de 20 de enero de 1933," in Departamento Forestal y de Caza y Pesca, *Código de Pesca de los Estados Unidos Mexicanos*; "Vedas pesqueras," 25.

65. Quevedo, *Relato de mi vida,* 77.

66. "Es incalculable la riqueza de México dentro de los mares: Comisión especial

exploradora de la fauna y flora acaba de regresar a la capital, tras recorrer el sureste de la República y opina que industrializada en forma debida la pesquería, sería un renglón de ingresos," 10 June 1938 [from *El National* (Mexico City)], under the theme of *pesca* in the Archivo Fernández y Fernández, Biblioteca del Colegio de Michoacán, Zamora, Michoacán.

67. Quevedo, "Anteproyecto del plan sexenal," 3–4.

68. Interview with Enrique Beltrán, Mexico City, 7 September 1989.

69. Letter from Miguel Angel de Quevedo to Lázaro Cárdenas, "Informe sobre la exploración de los lagos de Pátzcuaro y Zirahuén, Michoacán," 3 April 1936, 2, Serie: Lázaro Cárdenas, Fondo: Presidentes, Archivo General de la Nación, Mexico City.

70. Ibid.; Quevedo, "Informe sobre la exploración forestal," 3–4.

71. Letter from Quevedo to Cárdenas, 1939, 3–4.

72. Quevedo, *Relato de mi vida*, 79.

73. "Draft Convention Regarding Game and Fishing," 21 May 1925, Records of the Fish and Wildlife Service, Records of the U.S.- Mexican International Fisheries Commission, 1925–1937, Record Group 22, National Archives, Washington, D.C.; "Convention between the United States of America and the United States of Mexico for the Preservation of Marine and Aquatic Resources," December 1931, ibid.

74. Miguel Angel de Quevedo, "Se informe sobre el estado actual de la organización de la pesca y sus beneficios a la nación," 8 February 1939, 12–13, Serie: Lázaro Cárdenas, Fondo: Presidentes, Archivo General de la Nación, Mexico City.

75. Enrique Beltrán, *La pesca en México: Su estado actual y un proyecto para impulsarla*, 26–27.

76. John Steinbeck, *The Log from the Sea of Cortez*, 297.

77. Ibid., 298.

78. Rómulo Escobar, *Economía rural y administración*, 46–47. Escobar, a professor at the National School of Agriculture in Chapingo, was one of the earliest crusaders for soil conservation in Mexico.

79. Tom Gill, *Land Hunger in Mexico*, 30.

80. Lorenzo R. Patiño was a delegate of the National Irrigation Commission of Mexico to the VI Scientific Congress of the Pacific. Lorenzo R. Patiño, *A Few Observations on Soil Erosion Control in the Central Plateau of Mexico*, 3.

81. Letter from Quevedo to Cárdenas, 1939, 1–2.

82. Hernández Corzo, *La administración de la fauna*, 33.

83. "Cargos contra Jefe Miguel Angel de Quevedo," Serie: Lázaro Cárdenas, Fondo: Presidentes, Archivo General de la Nación, Mexico City.

84. Hernández Corzo, *La administración de la fauna*, 33.

85. Quevedo, *Relato de mi vida*, 63.

86. Ibid., 87–89.

87. Juan Zinzer, "Greetings from Mexico," in *Transactions of the Sixth North American Wildlife Conference*, 11.

88. Ibid., 11–12.

89. Other accounts indicate that González Peña underestimated the first figure.

90. González Peña, "El retorno a la barbarie," 3.

91. Ibid., 5.

92. Fernández y Fernández, "El retorno a la Secretaría," 2–3. Responsibility for Mexico's inland fisheries was turned over to the Ministry of the Navy.

93. Ibid., 5.

94. "Discurso pronunciado por el C. Ing. Alfonso González Gallardo, Subsecretaría de Agricultura y Fomento, en la sesión inaugural de la Primera Convención Forestal," *Boletín de la Dirección General Forestal y de Caza* 2 (October 1941): 10–13. The recent debate over the effects of forests on rainfall and climate has focused on the possible role of trees in increasing precipitation by producing chemicals around which rain drops coalesce and in reducing global warming by removing carbon dioxide from the atmosphere. Al Gore, *Earth in the Balance: Ecology and the Human Spirit*, 106, 115–116.

95. Quevedo, *Relato de mi vida*, 62–63.

96. Ibid., 92.

97. This speech was printed as Quevedo's autobiography.

98. Quevedo, *Relato de mi vida*, 91.

99. Regis Cárdenas, a nephew of Lázaro Cárdenas, proudly pointed out to me the trees that had been planted on the hills above Zacatecas during his uncle's presidency.

6. The Waning of Conservation: 1940–1970

1. Ortiz Monasterio et al., *Tierra profanada,* 232, 305.

2. Daniel Levy and Gabriel Székely, *Mexico: Paradoxes of Stability and Change,* 127.

3. Mauricio Athié Lambari, "El desarrollo de la política ecología en México," in Subdirección de Transformación Industrial, Gerencia de Protección Ecológica, Industrial Petroleros Mexicanos, *Memoria de ExpoEcología*, 10.

4. Luis Macías Arellano, "The Future of Mexico Lies in Education," in *Transactions of the Fifteenth North American Wildlife Conference*, 9–10.

5. Manuel Avila Camacho, *Address to the Mexican Agronomists*, 8.

6. Secretaría de Agricultura y Fomento, "Acuerdo que crea el Departamento de Conservación del Suelo," *Diario Oficial*, 27 April 1942, 2.

7. Ibid., 2–3.

8. Gill, *Land Hunger in Mexico*, 30; Annette L. Flugger and Rosa Dora S. Keatley, comps., *Report on Conservation of Renewable Natural Resources in Latin America*, 31.

9. Secretaría de Agricultura y Fomento, "Ley de Conservacion del Suelo y Agua," *Diario Oficial*, 19 June 1946, 7–9.

10. Ibid., 8.

11. José Navarro Samano, "La conservación de suelos en México hasta 1952," *Suelo y Agua* 2 (1 November 1954): 9.

12. Blanco Macías, "Realizaciones y perspectivas," 94; Gonzalo Blanco Macías and Guillermo Ramírez Cervantes, *La conservación del suelo y agua en México*, 37–38.

13. "'Amigos de la Tierra' Form Central Organization," *Conservation in the Americas* 9 (1950): 24.

14. Flugger and Keatley, *Report on Conservation*, 31.

15. Lorenzo Patiño, *La organización del Servicio del Suelo y Agua Mexicano*, 1–9.

16. Secretaria de Agricultura y Ganaderia, *Informe de labores de la Secretaria de Agricultura y Ganaderia del 1º de septiembre de 1946 al 31 de agosto de 1947*, 131–132.

17. Philip Wagner, "Parras: A Case Study in the Depletion of Natural Resources," *Landscape* 5 (Summer 1955): 22.

18. Ibid., 26.

19. Ibid., 24.

20. Ibid., 28.

21. Gonzalo Blanco Macías, *Agriculture in Mexico*, 16.

22. "Importante llamado del Sr. Presidente [Adolfo Ruiz Cortines] en pro de la conservación de suelos: Afirma que 'El gran enemigo de nuestro progreso económico es la erosión,' " *Suelo y Agua* 3 (2 May 1955): 1, 8.

23. Blanco Macías and Ramírez Cervantes, *La conservación del suelo*, 64, 66.

24. Felipe Salgado Pérez, Director General de Conservación del Suelo y Agua de la Secretaría de Agricultura y Ganadería, *La política actual de trabajo en materia de conservación del suelo y agua*, 3.

25. Blanco Macías, "Realizaciones y perspectivas," 96, 128, 132.

26. Comisión Preparatoria de la Participación de México en la Conferencia de las Naciones Unidas sobre el Medio Ambiente, *Informe nacional*, 48.

27. Levy and Székely, *Mexico*, 137, 139–140; Arturo Warman, *"We Come to Object": The Peasants of Morelos and the National State*, trans. Stephen K. Ault, 195–196, 206–213, 305.

28. Letter from Marte R. Gómez to Raymond Fosdick, 2 April 1943, R.G. 1.1, Series 323, Mexico Agriculture, Box 1, Rockefeller Foundation Archives, Pocantico Hills, New York.

29. Background report by Warren Weaver, 30 September 1950, R.G. 1.1, Series 323, Mexico Agriculture, Box 3, Rockefeller Foundation Archives, Pocantico Hills, New York; "Proposiciones para un memorándum de entendimiento entre la Secretaría de Agricultura y Fomento de México y la Fundación Rockefeller," 1943, R.G. 1.2, Series 323, Agriculture-Agreements 1936, 1941–1943, Box 11, Rockefeller Foundation Archives, Pocantico Hills, New York.

30. For an excellent treatment of one of the legacies of the Green Revolution, pesticide poisoning, see Angus Wright, *The Death of Ramón González: The Modern Agricultural Dilemma*. For a more extensive history of the Green Revolution itself, see Bruce H. Jennings, *Foundations of International Agricultural Research: Science and Politics in Mexican Agriculture*.

31. Enrique Beltrán, *El agua como recurso natural renovable en la vida de México*, 23.

32. Miguel Wionczek, "The Roots of the Mexican Agricultural Crisis: Water Resources Development Policies (1920–1970)," *Development and Change* 13 (1982): 372, 393.

33. Gonzalo Andrade Alcocer, Scientific Investigator of the Soil and Water Conservation Service, Ministry of Agriculture, Embassy of Mexico, Washington, D.C., "Conservation of Mexico's Renewable Resources as Fundamental Base of Its Agricultural Development," in *Proceedings of the Inter-American Conference on Conservation of Renewable Natural Resources*, Denver, Colorado, 7–20 September 1948, 624.

34. Gonzalo Blanco Macías, "Industria y agricultura en una senda de lógica unidad," *El Universal*, 23 and 25 April 1949, reprinted in Secretaría de Agricultura y Ganadería, Dirección General de Conservación del Suelo y Agua, *La filosofía de la conservación del suelo*, 52–53.

35. Dr. William Vogt, "Los recursos naturales de México: Su pasado, presente y futuro," trans. Dr. Bibliano Osorio Tafall, in *Memoria del Segundo Congreso Mexicano de Ciencias Sociales*, 2: 81–82; Guillermo Vogt, *El hombre y la tierra*, foreword by Manuel Alcala, vii, 51.

36. *Memoria del Segundo Congreso Mexicano de Ciencias Sociales,* 2:113.

37. Adolfo Orive Alba, Minister of Hydraulic Resources, Mexico City, "Conservation and the Multiple Use of Water in Mexico," in *Proceedings of the Inter-American Conference on Conservation of Renewable Natural Resources,* 116.

38. Mexico, Comisión de Papaloapan, *General Plan for the Rectification of the Papaloapan River,* 3–4; Flugger and Keatley, *Report on Conservation,* 32. Most of the dams built in Mexico since 1947 were multipurpose dams. In addition to irrigation (the primary purpose of Mexico's first dams), these purposes included the generation of electrical energy, the control of runoff, the storage of potable water, and the promotion of freshwater fisheries. Comisión Preparatoria, *Informe nacional,* 47.

39. Flugger and Keatley, *Report on Conservation,* 32.

40. Ing. José Hernández Terán, Secretario de Recursos Hidráulicos, *México y su política hidráulica,* 38–39.

41. Ibid., 30–31, 37–39; Orive Alba, "Conservation," 116; Patiño, *La organización del Servicio,* 1. The United States was responsible for salinity problems in the Mexicali Valley (along the border with California), as it drained salty waters from an Arizona irrigation district into the Colorado River. For the unfolding of this conflict and its apparent resolution, see Norris Hundley, Jr., "The West against Itself: The Colorado River—An Institutional History," in Gary D. Weatherford and F. Lee Brown, eds., *New Courses for the Colorado River,* 38–39; "Mexican-U.S. Dispute over Colorado River Salt Content," *Hispanic American Report* 15 (May 1962): 207–208; Jennifer Warren, "Troubled Desalting Plant Opens 14 Years Late," *San Francisco Chronicle,* 9 March 1992, A3. For a history of U.S.-Mexican relations over the Colorado, see Norris Hundley, Jr., *Dividing the Waters: A Century of Controversy between the United States and Mexico.*

42. Avila Camacho, *Address to the Mexican Agronomists,* 15.

43. "Discurso pronunciado por el Ing. Fernando Quintana, Director General Forestal y de Caza, con motivo de la Fiesta Principal del Arbol, en la Ciudad de México, Distrito Federal," *Boletín Bimestral de la Dirección General Forestal y de Caza* 2 (March–April 1942): 4.

44. Ibid., 3–4.

45. Secretaría de Agricultura y Fomento, "Ley Forestal de los Estados Unidos Mexicanos," *Diario Oficial,* 17 March 1943, 1–2.

46. Marvin D. Crocker, "Industrial Forest Exploitation Units: A Modern Mexican Forest Management System," *Journal of Forestry* 72 (October 1974): 650–653.

47. "Decreto por el cual se declara veda total e indefinida de recuperación y de servicios para todos los bosques del Estado de México y del Distrito Federal," *Diario Oficial,* 29 March 1947, 2–3; "Decreto que declara veda total e indefinida, de recuperación y de servicios, en los bosques ubicados dentro de los límites del Estado de Querétaro," *Diario Oficial,* 20 July 1950, 4–5; "Decreto que declara zonas protectoras forestales y de repoblación las cuencas de alimentación de las obras de irrigación de los distritos nacionales de riego, y se establece una veda total e indefinida en los montes ubicados dentro de dichas cuencas," *Diario Oficial,* 3 August 1949, 2–4; Instituto Mexicano de Recursos Naturales Renovables, *Mesas redondas sobre utilización y conservación del suelo,* 122.

48. Secretaría de Agricultura y Ganadería, "Ley Forestal," *Diario Oficial,* 10 January 1948, 3–4, 7.

49. Miguel Alemán, *Los árboles, patrimonio de la nación,* 1.

50. Ibid., 1–2.

51. Ing. Reinhart Ruge, "Las presas de almacenamiento y la conservación de los bosques," *Boletín de la Sociedad Mexicana de Geografía y Estadística* 68 (July–October 1949): 152–161.

52. Gill, *Land Hunger in Mexico*, 41.

53. Ibid., 50.

54. B. F. Osorio Tafall, "Soil and Water Problems in Mexico," *Journal of Soil and Water Conservation* 4 (1949): 65.

55. Enrique Beltrán, *Seis lustros de política forestal*, 19.

56. Only a few wealthy Mexicans had adopted this foreign tradition. By contrast, four-fifths of the forests cut in Mexico were cut for charcoal. Gonzalo Blanco Macías, "El hacha de Santa Claus," *El Universal* (Mexico City), 23 December 1949, reprinted in Secretaría de Agricultura y Ganadería, Dirección General de Conservación del Suelo y Agua, *La filosofía de la conservación del suelo*, 169–172; Micallef, "Forest Policy of Mexico," 31; Samuel Solís S., *La industria de los árboles de navidad y su importancia económica*, 10.

57. Macías Arellano, "Future of Mexico," 8.

58. Beltrán, *Seis lustros de política forestal*, 22–23.

59. *Campesino: ¡Defiende tus bosques!*, Cartillas Agrarias 12.

60. Alfredo Barrera and Enrique Beltrán, *El conservacionismo mexicano*, 37.

61. Beltrán, *Seis lustros de política forestal*, 21.

62. Ibid., 24, 26.

63. Secretaría de Agricultura y Ganadería, Subsecretaría Forestal y de Fauna, *Seis años actividades forestales y de fauna, 1959–1964*, 5.

64. Ibid., 170–176; Beltrán, *Seis lustros de política forestal*, 24; Crocker, "Industrial Forest Exploitation Units," 650; *Ley Forestal y su reglamento*, 15.

65. Academia Nacional de Ciencias Forestales, *Homenaje al Dr. Enrique Beltrán*, 29–30.

66. Subsecretaría Forestal y de Caza, *Memoria de la III Convención Nacional Forestal*, 181.

67. The First National Forestry Convention in 1941 had focused on both the biological and economic value of forests. The Second National Forestry Convention in 1962 emphasized the economic value of forests, but did not completely neglect their biological value.

68. Subsecretaría Forestal y de la Fauna, Noé Palomares, *Examen objetivo de la situación forestal de México*, 6. In arguing that mature trees should be cultivated rather than "wasted," Palomares was echoing the management philosophy of foresters in the United States during the twentieth century. Unlike the United States, though, Mexico had not developed a large forest industry. As Palomares regretfully noted, the production of wood had only increased from 3.6 to 5.5 million cubic feet between 1949 and 1968 (Palomares, 4).

69. Ibid.

70. The federal executive signed a draft of the document in November 1940. The Mexican Congress ratified the convention on 27 March 1942. Blanco Macías, "El Parque Internacional," 2; Ruge, "Las presas de almacenamiento," 151.

71. American Committee for International Wild Life Protection, *Brief History and Text of the Convention on Nature Protection and Wild Life Preservation in the Western Hemisphere*, 1.

72. Alemán and López Mateos created three national parks; Avila Camacho created one national park; and Ruiz Cortines and Díaz Ordaz did not create any national parks. Fernando Vargas Márquez, *Parques nacionales de México y reservas equívalentes: Pasado, presente y futuro*, 48–49.

73. Ruge, "La presa de almacenamiento," 151; William Vogt, "Unsolved Problems Concerning Wildlife in Mexican National Parks," in *Transactions of the Tenth American Wildlife Conference*, 357.

74. Carlos Alcérreca Aguirre et al., *Fauna silvestre y areas naturales protegidas*, 90.

75. Vogt, *El hombre y la tierra*, 87. Vargas Márquez, *Parques nacionales*, 133.

76. Vargas Márquez, *Parques nacionales*, 133.

77. Secretaría de Agricultura y Ganadería, *Seis años de actividades forestales*, 27.

78. Beltrán and Vásquez de la Parra, *En defensa del Parque Nacional*, 39.

79. Secretaría de Agricultura y Ganadería, "Ley Federal de Caza," *Diario Oficial*, 5 January 1952, 8–9.

80. A. Starker Leopold, *Wildlife of Mexico: The Game Birds and Mammals*, 81–82.

81. Bernardo Villa R., Institute of Biology, "Fight against Coyotes and Wolves in the North of Mexico (Their Hazards to the Health [and] the Economy, and the Conservation of Wildlife), Instructions for the Use of 1080," ca. 1954, 1, 9, 12, Records of the Fish and Wildlife Service, Predator Control Series, Record Group 22, National Archives, Washington, D.C.

82. U.S. Fish and Wildlife Service, *Mexican Wolf Recovery Plan*, 8, 10.

83. Ben Tinker, *Mexican Wilderness and Wildlife*, with a foreword by A. Starker Leopold, 10.

84. Luis Macías Arellano, "Wildlife Problems in Mexico," in *Transactions of the Fourteenth North American Wildlife Conference*, 14.

85. Ibid.

86. Beltrán also created wildlife refuges, strengthened ties with U.S. game officials, and stepped up policing of transportation centers in an effort to crack down on the illegal trade in wildlife. Secretaría de Agricultura y Ganadería, *Seis años de actividades forestales*, 140–162.

87. Rodolfo Hernández Corzo, "El valor del agua en relación con la fauna y recreación," in Instituto Mexicano de Recursos Naturales Renovables, *Mesas redondas sobre problemas de agua en México*, 226–229.

88. Ibid., 208–209, 221, 224–225, 242.

89. Ibid., 234–237.

90. Ibid., 217.

91. Ibid., 244.

92. Hernández Corzo emphasized the importance of a national inventory of wildlife for ensuring the rational use of this resource. He could not achieve many of his goals (including the survey) because of inadequate funding and the scarcity of wildlife specialists. Subsecretaría Forestal y de Fauna, Dirección General de la Fauna Silvestre, *Fauna silvestre: Expresiones y planteamientos de un recurso, 1964–1970*, 15, 27.

93. Ibid., 2.

94. Ibid., 28.

95. Many Mexican conservationists would argue that the government's interest in the protection of natural resources was minimal for the entire period between 1940 and 1993.

7. Against the Tide: The Conservationists' Crusade

1. Aldo Leopold, *A Sand County Almanac*.
2. Rachel Carson, *Silent Spring*.
3. Enrique Beltrán, "Alfonso L. Herrera (1868–1968): Primera figura de la biología mexicana," *Revista de la Sociedad Mexicana de Historia Natural* 29 (December 1968): 44 and Figure 16; Dr. Leopold Flores, *La dirección de estudios biológicos: Su organización, fines, y resultados que ha alcanzado*, 3, 6, 21; Octavio Solís and Rigoberta Vásquez, "Reseña histórica de los jardines botánicos de México desde antes de la conquista hasta la época actual," *Jardín Botánico* 1 (November 1923): 4.
4. Barrera and Beltrán, *El conservacionismo mexicano*, 24–25.
5. Enrique Beltrán, "La pesca en los litorales del Golfo de México y la necesidad de los estudios de biología marina para desarrollo esa fuente de riqueza," *Memorias y Revista de la Sociedad Científica "Antonio Alzate"* 49 (1929): 421–445.
6. Barrera and Beltrán, *El conservacionismo mexicano*, 25; Academia Nacional de Ciencias Forestales, *Homenaje al Dr. Enrique Beltrán*, 8.
7. Barrera and Beltrán, *El conservacionismo mexicano*, 27–28.
8. Interview with Enrique Beltrán, Mexico City, 7 September 1989.
9. Barrera and Beltrán, *El conservacionismo mexicano*, 29.
10. Interview with Beltrán.
11. Barrera and Beltrán, *El conservacionismo mexicano*, 30.
12. Enrique Beltrán, "Los recursos naturales de México: Lineamientos para una política de conservación," *Revista de la Sociedad Mexicana de Historia Natural* 1 (November 1939): 34.
13. Ibid., 39.
14. Barrera and Beltrán, *El conservacionismo mexicano*, 31; Enrique Beltrán, *Etica, estética y conservación*, 30; Interview with Beltrán.
15. Ambrosio González Cortés, "Evaluación de programas en materia de conservación de recursos naturales en la enseñanza superior en México," in Comité de Recursos Naturales de la Comisión de Geografía, *Segundo mesa redonda sobre recursos naturales*, 162–164.
16. Enrique Beltrán, Gonzalo Blanco Macías, and Roberto Villaseñor, *Homenaje al Dr. Tom Gill, 1891–1972*, 13; Letter from Charles Lathrop Pack Forestry Foundation, 25 January 1952, in Instituto Mexicano de Recursos Naturales Renovables, *En defensa del bienestar y el futuro de nuestra patria*, iii, 16; "Secretary's Report, 1960," 3–4, Charles Lathrop Pack Collection, Environmental Science and Forestry College Archives, Syracuse, New York. Charles Lathrop Pack, who had made his fortune in the timber industry, and his son Arthur Newton Pack established the foundation in 1929. In part, perhaps, Pack supported the cause of forest conservation because he rued his own participation in the destruction of U.S. forests. Interview with Enrique Beltrán; "Jersey Pioneers [Charles Lathrop Pack]," *Asbury (N.J.) Park Sunday Press*, 16 May 1971, F2; Pack Forestry Foundation, *Ten Years of Fact-Finding: A Review of the Accomplishments of the Charles Lathrop Pack Forestry Foundation*, 1.
17. Instituto Mexicano de Recursos Naturales Renovables, *En defensa del bienestar*, 17.
18. *Instituto Mexicano de Recursos Naturales Renovables, 1952–1990: Semblanza*, 6–79.
19. Barrera and Beltrán, *El conservacionismo mexicano*, 17.

20. Interview with Arturo Gómez-Pompa, professor of botany at the University of California, Riverside, and former director of the Instituto Nacional de Investigaciones sobre Recursos Bióticos (National Institute for Research on Biotic Resources), Riverside, California, 5 March 1990.

21. Beltrán, *Etica*, 11.

22. Ibid., 9–10.

23. Enrique Beltrán, "La conservación como instrumento de desarrollo," in Instituto Mexicano de Recursos Naturales Renovables, *Mesas redondas sobre desarrollo y ecología*, 181.

24. Barrera and Beltrán, *El conservacionismo mexicano*, 37; Enrique Beltrán, *La batalla forestal: Lo hecho, lo no hecho, lo por hacer*, 55.

25. Enrique Beltrán, "Use and Conservation: Two Conflicting Principles," in Alexander B. Adams, ed., *First World Conference on National Parks*, 36.

26. Ibid., 38.

27. Ibid.

28. Enrique Beltrán, *La protección de la naturaleza: Principios y problemas*, 9–14.

29. Beltrán, "La conservación," 185.

30. Enrique Beltrán, "Medios de comunicación en conservación," in Comité de Recursos Naturales de la Comisión de Geografía, *Segundo mesa redonda de recursos naturales*, 174–175.

31. Instituto Mexicano de Recursos Naturales Renovables, *En defensa del bienestar*, 18.

32. Beltrán has almost single-handedly directed the institute. The lack of a successor raises definite concerns about how well IMERNAR can function in his absence. Interview with Gómez-Pompa.

33. The U.S. environmental organization Friends of the Earth was established in 1969. The two groups shared a common name and a concern for the conservation of nature, but formed no links.

34. "Los Amigos de la Tierra y su compaña de conservación," *Suelo y Agua* 1 (1 October 1953): 5.

35. Ibid.; "'Amigos de la Tierra' Form a Central Organization," 24.

36. Secretaría de Desarrollo Urbano y Ecología, Subsecretaría de Ecología, Dirección General de Normatividad y Regulación Ecológica, and Cetamex, Centro de Estudios de Tecnologías Apropiadas para México, *Ciudad y medio ambiente: Calidad de vida y percepción ambiental*, 26.

37. Blanco Macías, "El Parque Internacional," 6.

38. Gonzalo Blanco Macías, "Asalto a la naturaleza," *Mensajero Forestal* 29 (November 1970): 10.

39. FUNDAMAT [Foundation Miguel Alvarez del Toro], *Chiapas: A Race against Time*.

40. For a history of forest exploitation in Chiapas, see Cuauhtémoc González Pacheco, *Capital extranjero en la selva de Chiapas, 1863–1982*, and Jan de Vos, *Oro verde: La conquista de la Selva Lacandona por los maderos tabasqueños, 1822–1949*.

41. James D. Nations, "The Lacandones, Gertrude Blom, and the Selva Lacandona," in Alex Harris and Margaret Sator, eds., *Gertrude Blom—Bearing Witness*, 31.

42. Ibid.

43. Evangelina Hernández, "Destruido, el 76% de la Selva Lacandona," *La Jornada* (Mexico City), 21 July 1990, 13.

44. Miguel Alvarez del Toro, "Panorama ecológico de Chiapas," in Instituto Mexicano de Recursos Naturales Renovables, *Mesas redondas sobre Chiapas y sus recursos naturales renovables,* 6–7.

45. Dedication of Miguel Alvarez del Toro to his parents in *Los reptiles de Chiapas,* 2d ed.

46. Miguel Alvarez del Toro, *¡Así era Chiapas!: 42 años de andanzas por montañas, selvas, y caminos en el Estado,* 15–16.

47. Ibid., 12–13, 16–22, 151.

48. Ibid., 23–50.

49. Ibid., 53–55.

50. Ibid., 53–62.

51. Ibid., 66, 70.

52. Ibid., 86–92, 151–152.

53. Ibid., 509–510, 533–539.

54. Cindy Anders, "Building a Better Zoo: Interview with Miguel Alvarez del Toro," *Mexico Journal* 1 (2 May 1988): 3; Instituto de Historia Natural, *Información básica sobre el Instituto de Historia Natural,* 1–3.

55. Some of the signs are: Love the *zenzontle,* bird of 400 voices, love your sisters—the plants and flowers (Aztec poem); Don't sell your memory to sad customs and to the years. Never forget the forest, the wind, and the birds; That the land is a community is the basic concept of ecology, that the land is something to love and respect is an extension of that ethic (Aldo Leopold); Each time that a bird dies, each time that a forest burns, each time that a plant or animal becomes extinct the possibility of the survival of humanity is reduced; Always there is music in the trees of the countryside, but our hearts should be more still to hear it.

56. Instituto de Historia Natural, *Información básica,* 3.

57. Miguel Alvarez del Toro's other daughter, Hebe, illustrates the zoo's literature and his son, Federico, writes music about nature.

58. Wallace Kaufman, "The Zoo in the Forest," *Orion* 9 (Autumn 1990): 30.

59. Anders, "Building a Better Zoo," 3.

60. Ibid., 4.

61. Instituto de Historia Natural, *Información básica,* 6.

62. Kaufman, "Zoo in the Forest," 33.

63. Instituto de Historia Natural, *Información básica,* 4; "El Triunfo: Reserva de la Biosfera," *Ihnforma: Boletín Informativo Trimestral del Instituto de Historia Natural* 3 (April 1990): 1.

64. Wilbur E. Garrett, "La Ruta Maya," *National Geographic* 176 (October 1989): 436.

65. Alvarez del Toro, "Panorama ecológica," 17.

66. Anders, "Building a Better Zoo," 4.

67. Ibid.

68. Ibid.

69. Miguel Alvarez del Toro, "Chiapas, gigante saqueado," *Numero Uno* (Tuxtla Gutiérrez, Chiapas), 24 June 1982, 9.

70. Miguel Alvarez del Toro, "Importancia de las marismas y el error de secarlas," *Informa: Boletín Informativo del Instituto de Historia Natural* 1 (December 1988): 5.

71. Alvarez del Toro, "Chiapas," 9.

72. Ibid.

73. Her name at birth was Gertrude Elizabeth Loertcher. She was briefly married to Kurt Duby in 1924. The biographical material on Gertrude Duby Blom up to her marriage to Frans Blom comes from Gertrude Duby Blom, "Páginas de mi vida, San Cristóbal y Na-Bolom, dos razones fundamentales," 1978, pp. 1–3, Manuscript, Fray Bartolomé de las Casas Library, Na-Bolom House, San Cristóbal de las Casas, Chiapas; Gertrude Duby Blom, *The Story of Na-Bolom*, 9; Alex Harris, "Introduction," in Harris and Sator, eds., *Gertrude Blom—Bearing Witness*, 7–11.

74. Blom, *Story of Na-Bolom*, 2–4.

75. Harris, "Introduction," 13; Nations, "Lacandones," 39.

76. Harris, "Introduction," 6.

77. Gertrude Duby Blom, "Saving the Land of the Lacandón," 1973, p. 5, Manuscript, Fray Bartolomé de las Casas Library, Na-Bolom House, San Cristóbal de las Casas, Chiapas.

78. Gertrude Duby Blom, "La Selva Lacandona Reserva de la Biosfera," *Mujeres* 343 (1979): 24.

79. Gertrude Duby Blom, "Problemas ecológicos de los altos de Chiapas," 1978, p. 5, Manuscript, Fray Bartolomé de las Casas Library, Na-Bolom House, San Cristóbal de las Casas, Chiapas; Interview with Gertrude Duby Blom, San Cristóbal de las Casas, 22 August 1990.

80. Ibid., 6–7.

81. Blom, "Páginas de mi vida," 12; Interview with Blom.

82. Blom, "Problemas ecológicos," 5–6.

83. Blom, "La Selva Lacandona Reserva," 25.

84. Gertrude Duby Blom, "México se olvida de sus tesoros," 1977, p. 4, Manuscript, Fray Bartolomé de las Casas Library, Na-Bolom House, San Cristóbal de las Casas, Chiapas.

85. Gertrude Duby Blom, *La familia de Na-Bolom*, 1:17–18.

86. "The Death of the Lacandón Culture and Rain Forest: An Interview with Gertrude Duby Blom," *Mexico City News*, 18 March 1983, 17; Blom, "Saving the Land," 6.

87. Blom, "Saving the Land," 4.

88. Nations, "Lacandones," 27.

89. Gertrude Duby Blom, "La Selva Lacandona," Paper presented at the Primer Simposio de Ecología, November 1974, 17, Fray Bartolomé de las Casas Library, Na-Bolom House, San Cristóbal de las Casas, Chiapas.

90. "Death of the Lacandón Culture," 16.

91. Blom, "La Selva Lacandona," 8.

92. "Death of the Lacandón Culture," 16.

93. Harris, "Introduction," 15.

8. For Humankind and Nature: The Pursuit of Sustainable Development

1. For an overview of the Biosphere Reserve Program, see Instituto de Ecología, *El futuro del hombre en la naturaleza: Ensayos sobre reservas de la biosfera.*

2. Peter Stone, *Did We Save the Earth at Stockholm?* Appendix: United Nations Conference on the Human Environment, 147–148.

3. United Nations, *Yearbook of the United Nations, 1974*, 28:436.

4. Ul Haq, *The Poverty Curtain*, 82.

5. Comisión Preparatoria, *Informe nacional*, 5.

6. Gonzalo Halffter, "Biosphere Reserves: The Conservation of Nature for Man," in *Conservation, Science, and Society*, 452.

7. Gonzalo Halffter, "Biosphere Reserves: A New Method of Nature Protection," in *Social and Environmental Consequences of Natural Resources Policies with Special Emphasis on Biosphere Reserves*, 4.

8. "Endemism" means found only in a certain region or ecosystem. Conservation International in collaboration with the Instituto Nacional de Investigaciones Sobre Recursos Bióticos, INIREB, *Mexico's Living Endowment: An Overview of Biological Diversity*, an executive summary of Oscar Flores-Villela and Patricia Gerez Fernández, *Conservación en México: Síntesis sobre vertebrados terrestres, vegetación y uso del suelo*, April 1989, 27.

9. Alcérreca Aguirre et al., *Fauna silvestre*, 91.

10. Halffter, "Biosphere Reserves: A New Method," 4.

11. Ibid.

12. Ibid., 3.

13. Ibid., 4.

14. Halffter, "Biosphere Reserves: The Conservation of Nature," 451.

15. With assistance from the National Council of Science and Technology, Gonzalo Halffter in 1974 created the Institute of Ecology to promote ecological research. In that same year, he also became the executive secretary for the Man and Biosphere Program in Mexico.

16. Gonzalo Halffter, ed., *Reservas de la biosfera en el Estado de Durango: Trabajos varios*, 20–21; Instituto de Ecologia, *Homenaje a Gonzalo Halffter*, 30, 48, 61.

17. Halffter, *Reservas de la biosfera*, 34.

18. Gonzalo Halffter, "Local Participation in Conservation and Development," *Ambio* 10 (1981): 95.

19. Not all of the ecological research at La Michilía was applied research. One of the most important nonapplied projects was the transportation of La Michilía's few remaining bears and wolves from the reserve's outer zones to its core area. Halffter, *Reservas de la biosfera*, 22–27.

20. Instituto de Ecología, *Homenaje a Gonzalo Halffter*, 30.

21. Gonzalo Halffter and Exequiel Ezcurra, "Evolution of the Biosphere Reserve Concept," in William P. Gregg, Jr., Stanley L. Krugman, and James D. Wood, Jr., eds., *Proceedings of the Symposium on Biosphere Reserves*, 194; Instituto de Ecología, *El futuro del hombre*, 16.

22. National parks compose approximately 10 percent of the protected natural areas in Mexico. In total, less than 3 percent of Mexico's territory is under some protective land management system. Subsecretaría de Ecología, Dirección General de Conservación Ecología de los Recursos Naturales, *Información básica sobre las areas naturales protegidas de México*.

23. Instituto de Ecología, *El futuro del hombre*, 125.

24. Enrique Carrillo-Barrios-Gómez and Hans Hermann-Martínez, "Sian Ka'an: A New Biosphere Reserve Model in Mexico," in Gregg, Krugman, and Wood, eds., *Proceedings of the Symposium on Biosphere Reserves*, 229, 231.

25. Jerry Emory, "Where the Sky Was Born," *Wilderness* 52 (Summer 1989): 56.

26. Ibid.; Ellen Jones and Glen Wersch, "Developing a Natural Balance," *Americas* 42.3 (1990): 31–32.

27. Emory, "Where the Sky Was Born," 56; Jones and Wersch, "Developing a Natural Balance," 33, 35.

28. In addition to SEDUE's action, salt workers' jobs were being threatened by mechanization. Betty Faust and John Sinton, "Let's Dynamite the Salt Factory! Communication, Coalitions, and Sustainable Use among Users of a Biosphere Reserve," Paper, presented by John Sinton at the American Society for Environmental History Conference, Houston, 28 February–3 March 1991, 1–3, 6–10.

29. A number of these projects require midcourse corrections. For example, irrigation and plastic covers are necessary to provide sufficient water and protection against the salt-laden air for plants grown on the seaweed compost piles. Likewise, fishers prefer another species of crab for catching octopus than the one selected by CINVESTAV. Residents have expressed interest in selling shells as curios, but they want to know how they will market them. Ibid., 1–2, 5, 9–12.

30. Ibid., 4, 13–19.

31. Edward Cody, "Monarchs Rule Mexican Mountains," *Washington Post*, 27 December 1990, A19, A25; Brook Larmer, "Monarch's Wonderland under Siege in Mexico," *Christian Science Monitor*, 29 December 1988, 1, 24; John Ross, "Dangers in Paradise," *Sierra* 77 (July–August 1992): 87–88; Sharon Sullivan, "Guarding the Monarch's Kingdom," *International Wildlife* 17 (November–December 1987): 4–11.

32. The Audubon Society, Ducks Unlimited, and the Nature Conservancy also have conservation programs in Mexico. Jean Kishler, "San Miguel Audubon Society," *Audubon Leader*, Southwest Region (February–March 1989); *Amigos: Friends by Nature*, Dumac annual report for 1988; *Dumac* 11 (September–October 1989); Noel Grove, "Quietly Conserving Nature," *National Geographic* 174 (December 1988): 824; Phone interview with Joe Quiroz of the Nature Conservancy, Phoenix, Arizona, 8 June 1989; Richard Roberts, "South for the Winter," *Los Angeles Times*, 16 January 1990, C10.

33. Interview with Mario Ramos, Head of the Mexican Program for the World Wildlife Fund, Washington, D.C., 7 June 1989.

34. Interview with Martin Goebel, Director of Conservation International's Mexican Program, Washington, D.C., 20 June 1989.

35. Conservation International, "The Sea of Cortez: Understanding and Conserving Its Productivity," *Tropicus* 4 (Fall 1988): 4–5.

36. Conservation International, "In Chiapas: Building Partnerships for Conservation," *Tropicus* 4 (Fall 1988): 6.

37. Juanita Darling, "Mexico to Ease Debt, Help the Environment," *Los Angeles Times*, 20 February 1991, D5; "Mexico Swaps Debt for Nature Conservation," *Orion* 10 (Spring 1991): 62; Rosa Rojas, "Se admitirán 'swaps' en ecología, anuncia Chirinos," *La Jornada* (Mexico City), 25 July 1990, 1; Mark A. Uhlig, "Mexican Debt Deal May Save Jungle," *New York Times*, 26 February 1991, A3.

38. Carlos Alcérreca Aguirre, "El instrumento que nos permite armonizar con la naturaleza es el manejo," *Pronatura* 5 (May–June 1988): 5.

39. Quoted in Césarman, *Crónicas ecológicas*, 42.

40. Víctor Manuel Toledo et al., *Ecología y autosuficiente alimentaría: Hacia una opción basada en la diversidad biológica y cultural de México*, 23.

41. In 1990, the population growth rate in Mexico was 2.5 percent.

42. Juanita Darling, "Mexico's Agricultural Woes: Water Supplies and Thus Abundant Crops Are Drying Up," *San Francisco Chronicle* (Marin/Sonoma edition), 5 December 1990, World news, 4–5.

43. Ibid.

44. In overirrigated fields, groundwater is raised close to the surface (through capillary attraction), suffocating plant roots. This phenomena is known as water-logging.

45. Toledo, *Ecología y autosuficiente*, 38.

46. Rembrandt Reyes Najera and Edmundo Sánchez de la Fuente, "Intoxicación por plaguicidas en la Comarca Lagunera durante el ciclo agrícola de 1974," *Salud Pública de México*, 5ª época, 17 (September–October 1975): 687–698.

47. Lane Simonian, "Pesticide Use in Mexico: Decades of Abuse," *Ecologist* 18.2–3 (1988): 82–87.

48. "U.S. and Mexicans Combating Pests," *New York Times*, 17 September 1972, A15.

49. Angus Wright suggests that these factors are more important than expense in explaining the preference of farmers and bureaucrats for pesticide use over integrated pest management techniques. Wright, *Death of Ramón González*, 36–37, 49, 59–69, 72–76, 206–214. Integrated pest management techniques will become more cost-effective as petroleum prices increase (oil is an important component in pesticides) and as IPM techniques are improved.

50. Toledo, *Ecología y autosuficiente*, 66, 95–98.

51. Ibid., 89–90. The Mexican government has promoted a few small-scale projects with *chinampas* on the lakes and canals of Xochimilco (a southern suburb of Mexico City). Rigoberta López, "El rescate de Xochimilco," *Unomásuno* (Mexico City), 21 October 1989, 10.

52. Toledo, *Ecología y autosuficiente*, 89, 91–92.

53. Gómez-Pompa, "On Maya Silviculture," 1–17.

54. James D. Nations and Ronald B. Nigh, "The Evolutionary Potential of the Sustained-Yield Tropical Forest Agriculture," *Journal of Anthropological Research* 36 (Spring 1980): 26.

55. Toledo, *Ecología y autosuficiente*, 59–66.

56. As of 1980, fish accounted for only 10 percent of the protein consumption by Mexicans.

57. "Política, estrategia y líneas de acción para el desarrollo de la acuacultura, 1989–1994," *Acuavisión*, año IV, 2ª época, 17 (November–December 1989): 10–11.

58. Mexico adopted the polyculture model from China.

59. Some of the waste material is fermented in a biodigestor, a concrete or metal container with holes to put in and to discharge the wastes.

60. Secretaría de Pesca, Fideicomiso Fondo Nacional para el Desarrollo Pesquero, Fondepesca, Biol. Zenaida Martínez Torres and Dr. Jesús Octavio Abrego Ayala, *Modelo mexicano de policultivo: Una alternativa de desarrollo rural*, 11, 13–15, 27–41.

61. Most of the INIREBs sites were in the states of Tabasco and Veracruz. Arturo Gómez-Pompa and J. J. Jiménez-Osornio, "Some Reflections on Intensive Traditional Agriculture," in Christina Gladwin and Kathleen Truman, eds., *Food and Farm: Current Debate and Policies*, 251–253.

62. Ibid., 240.

63. Ibid., 245–248.

64. Some of the polyculture farms were still functioning, but not as a complete system. The Inter-American Foundation provided funding for Chapin's journey.

65. Mac Chapin, "Travels with Eucario: In Search of Ecodevelopment," *Orion* 10 (Spring 1991): 50, 54–59.

9. Reconsidering: Mexican Environmental Policy

1. Stephen P. Mumme, C. Richard Bath, and Valerie J. Assetto, "Political Development and Environmental Policy in Mexico," *Latin American Research Journal Review* 23.1 (1988): 11–12.

2. Secretaría de Salubridad y Asistencia, *Código Sanitario de los Estados Unidos Mexicanos*, 6.

3. Subsecretaría de Mejoramiento del Ambiente, *México: El mejoramiento del ambiente una perspectiva de la nación*, 24.

4. Mexico, Secretaría de la Presidencia, *Medio ambiente humano: Problemas ecológicos nacionales*, 1.

5. Donella Meadows et al., *The Limits to Growth*.

6. Luis Echeverría Alvarez, "Los verdaderos límites del crecimiento," in Joseph Hodara and Iván Restrepo, eds., *¿Tiene límites el crecimiento? Una visión latinoamericana*, 56.

7. Mario R. Redondo, "Contra la contaminación, solo leyes que no se cumplen: Mora M.," *Excelsior* (Mexico City), 24 January 1983, A15.

8. Echeverría Alvarez, "Los verdaderos límites," 56, 59; "Zona económica exclusiva," 1990 Calendar (Mexico City: Fideicomiso Fondo Nacional para el Desarrollo Pesquero).

9. Mexico ratified the Law of the Sea Treaty in 1983.

10. Echeverría Alvarez, "Los verdaderos límites," 56.

11. Secretaría de Salubridad y Asistencia, *Código sanitario*, 6; Subsecretaría de Mejoramiento del Ambiente, *México*, 4.

12. Secretaría de Salubridad y Asistencia, "Reglamento para la prevención y control de la contaminación atmosférica originada por la emisión de humos y polvos," *Diario Oficial*, 17 September 1971, 2.

13. Echeverría Alvarez did not strengthen Mexico's conservation laws. However, by creating scientific institutes, such as the National Council of Science and Technology and the National Institute for Research on Biotic Resources, he did open the floodgates for ecological research and the formation of conservation groups. Interview with Gómez-Pompa.

14. The same was also true for Echeverría Alvarez's successor, José López Portillo.

15. Some people tried to escape constant contact with the pollution in Mexico City by commuting to work from cities outside the valley such as Puebla and Cuernavaca. This partial exodus worsened both Mexico City's air pollution problems and the pollution problems of the surrounding cities.

16. Secretaría de Salubridad y Asistencia, "Ley Federal para Prevenir y Controlar la Contaminación Ambiental," *Diario Oficial*, 23 March 1971, 8–11, and Secretaría de Salubridad y Asistencia, "Reglamento," 2–9.

17. Jesús Galván Moreno, "El papel de los partidos políticos en la solución de los problemas del ambiente," in Subdirección de Transformación Industrial, *Memoria ExpoEcología*, 137.

18. Luis Marco del Pont, *El crimen de la contaminación*, 110.

19. For an overview of the flaws in Mexico's environmental laws, see Rainer Godau Schuking, "La protección ambiental en México: Sobre la conformación de una política pública," *Estudios Sociológicos* 3 (January–April 1985): 47–84.

20. Francisco Vizcaíno Murray, *La contaminación en México*, 20.

21. *La administración ambiental en México: Acciones y resultados de la gestión, 1976–1982*, 1–2.

22. Ibid., 4, 51, 58, 62–64, 73, 84, 100–103.

23. Secretaría de Salubridad y Asistencia, "Ley Federal de Protección del Ambiente," *Diario Oficial*, 11 January 1982, 25–26, 28, 31.

24. Partido Revolucionario Institucional, *Medio ambiente*, 12.

25. Alicia Bárcena Ibarra, "La política ecológica en México: Un instrumento para el cambio," *Logos* 13 (1988): 46.

26. Miguel de la Madrid, *Cien tesis sobre México*, 61.

27. Partido Revolucionario Institucional, *Medio ambiente*, 6.

28. Alejandra Lajous, comp., *Las razones y las obras: Gobierno de Miguel de la Madrid: Crónica del sexenio, 1982–1988*, año 3, p. 312.

29. Ibid., año 6, 598.

30. "El cinturón verde," *Revista de las Revistas* 4100 (26 August 1988): 17; Silvia Arzate, "Representa la Refinería de Azcapotzalco una bomba de tiempo; urgente sacarla: G, Torres," *El Sol de México* (Mexico City), 6 June 1990, Ciudad page.

31. Hernández, "Destruido, el 76% de la Selva Lacandona," 13.

32. Schuking, "La protección ambiental," 72; Ing. Samuel Meléndez Vargas, "Protección de la ecología marina," in Subdirección de Transformación Industrial, *Memoria ExpoEcología*, 133.

33. Lajous, comp., *Las razones*, año 1, pp. 101, 252–253. The peasants' actions might be compared to the ecological sabotage perpetrated by groups such as Earth First! in the United States, although in the case of the peasants the main issue was one of livelihood rather than the protection of wilderness per se.

34. Richard J. Meislin, "In Devastated Mexican Area, the Anger Persists," *New York Times*, 6 December 1984, A6.

35. "Pemex Blamed for Blasts That Took 452 Lives," *Los Angeles Times*, 23 December 1984, I5.

36. Interview with Gómez-Pompa.

37. "La larga marcha de los ecólogos mexicanos: Entrevista con Arturo Gómez-Pompa," *Nexos* 6 (September 1983): 27–28.

38. Interview with Goebel.

39. Wright, *Death of Ramón González*, 77–80.

40. Bárcena Ibarra, "La política ecológica," 47–49. Alicia Bárcena Ibarra was undersecretary of ecology from 1983 until 1986.

41. Ibid., 47–52.

42. "Sizable Portion of SEDUE's Budget Brings Progress on Water Pollution," *International Environment Reporter* 10 (14 October 1987): 513–514. Ironically, the fuel that Pemex developed in 1986 to reduce lead emissions increased ozone. Dawn Gar-

cia, "Smog Stalks Mexico City: Limit on Using Cars Only Hope in Toxic Air Crisis," *San Francisco Chronicle*, 6 December 1989, Briefing section, 2.

43. Comisión Nacional de Ecología, *100 acciones necesarias*. In danger of extinction in Mexico are 379 animal species, 56 species of which are found only in Mexico; 580 plant species are threatened or endangered. Poder Ejecutivo Federal, *Plan Nacional de Desarrollo, 1989–1994*, 122.

44. Malissa McKeith, "Environmental Provisions Affecting Businesses on the U.S.-Mexico Border," *International Environment Reporter* 15 (22 April 1992): 246.

45. Secretaría de Desarrollo Urbano y Ecología, *Acuerdo de cooperación entre los Estados Unidos Mexicanos y los Estados Unidos de América sobre movimiento transfronterizas de desechos y sustancias peligrosas*.

46. "SO Treatment Plant at Copper Smelter Opened to Control U.S.-Mexico Air Pollution," *International Environment Reporter* 11 (14 September 1988): 491.

47. "Sizable Portion of SEDUE's Budget," 514.

48. Ibid.; Lajous, comp., *Las razones*, año 4, p. 584.

49. The depletion of groundwater along the borderlands is one of the critical topics that has not yet been addressed by Mexican and U.S. authorities.

50. Roberto Suro, "Border Boom's Dirty Residue Imperils U.S.-Mexico Trade," *New York Times*, 31 March 1991, I16. The secretary of SEDUE, Patricio Chirinos, estimated in 1991 that it would take at least ten years to resolve border pollution problems. "Border Plants' Growth Brings Jobs, Problems," *Reno Gazette-Journal*, 3 June 1991, A8.

51. William Branigin, "Mexico's Other Contraband—Wildlife," *Washington Post*, 24 June 1989, A18, A24; Movimiento Ecologista Mexicano, "Mexico ante la Convención sobre el Comercio Internacional de Especies Amenazadas de Fauna y Flora Silvestre (CITES)," Press release, 1–3.

52. "Major Legislation Expected to Delegate Regulatory Powers to States, Localities," *International Environment Reporter* 10 (9 December 1987): 655.

53. Secretaría de Desarrollo Urbano y Ecología, "Ley General del Equilibrio Ecológico y la Protección al Ambiente," *Gaceta Ecológica* 1 (June 1989): 8.

54. Ibid., 3–12.

55. Ibid., 21, 26.

56. Ibid., 19–20.

57. Ibid., 12–13.

58. "Major Legislation," 654.

59. Partido Revolucionario Institucional, *Medio ambiente*, 7, 16. Salinas directed de la Madrid's campaign and became his secretary of budget and planning.

60. "Salinas de Gortari Warns of Ecological Disaster," *Mexico City News*, 12 January 1989, 1.

61. Angel Escalante Baranda, "Problemas ecológicos de nuestra capital," *Revista de las Revistas* 4097 (5 August 1988): 11.

62. Rigoberta López, "El rescate de Xochimilco," *Unomásuno* (Mexico City), 21 October 1989, 10.

63. Glenda Hersh, "CSG Unveils Xochimilco Ecological Program," *The News* (Mexico City), 27 September 1989, 5.

64. Partido Verde Mexicano, "Opinión del Partido Verde Mexicano sobre el proyecto de rescate de Xochimilco y el programa de un día sin automóvil. Anuncio de la

integración a la campaña contra la crueldad hacia los animales," Press release, ca. 1990, 1.

65. David Clark Scott, "Slew of Government Programs Target Dirty Air, Scarce Water," *Christian Science Monitor*, 23 October 1991, 11.

66. Víctor Ballinas, "Campaña para cuidar el uso del agua en el D.F., en 1989," *La Jornada* (Mexico City), 9 October 1989, 35.

67. "Frentes políticos," *Excelsior* (Mexico City), 4 June 1990, A30.

68. Juan Manuel Juárez C., "Un árbol a cada niño que nazca aquí," *La Prensa* (Mexico City), 6 June 1990, 3.

69. Garcia, "Smog Stalks Mexico City," 2; Brook Larmer, "New Program Thins Smog, Streets," *Christian Science Monitor*, 31 January 1990, 3; Stephen P. Mumme, "Clearing the Air: Environmental Reform in Mexico," *Environment* 33 (December 1991): 11–12; "Study Shows Car-less Program Effective; Two-Month Extension Announced," *International Environment Reporter* 13 (14 March 1990): 106–107; "World's Most Polluted City Slowly Begins to Clean Up Its Act," *Reno Gazette-Journal*, 16 September 1990, A2.

70. Mumme, "Clearing the Air," 26; Mark A. Uhlig, "Gasping, Mexicans Act to Clear the Capital's Air," *New York Times*, 31 January 1991, A4; Rodrigo Vera, "Manuel Camacho enfrente la contaminación como un asunto de imagen," *Proceso* 738 (24 December 1990): 8.

71. "Fuel Oil Limited in Mexico City to Reduce Smog," *San Francisco Chronicle*, 24 January 1991, A15.

72. "Mexico Finances New Vehicles," *Reno Gazette-Journal*, 20 March 1991, A4; Uhlig, "Gasping," A4. Mumme, "Clearing the Air," 26. Work continues on the expansion of Mexico City's subway system to the settlements in the eastern portion of the Valley.

73. Uhlig, "Gasping," A4.

74. Mark A. Uhlig, "Mexico Closes Giant Oil Refinery to Ease Pollution in the Capital," *New York Times*, 19 March 1991, A1; "Mexico Finances New Vehicles," A4.

75. "Mexico Finances New Vehicles," A4.

76. Mumme, "Clearing the Air," 26.

77. "Pollution," *The News* (Mexico City), 29 July 1990, 4.

78. Mumme, "Clearing the Air," 26; David Clark Scott, "New Smog Plan for Mexico," *Christian Science Monitor*, 27 March 1992, 7.

79. Tim Golden, "Mexico City Emits More Heat over Pollution," *New York Times*, 25 November 1991, A5.

80. Juanita Darling, "Mexico City's Trucks, Buses Must Convert to Clean Fuel," *Los Angeles Times*, 12 February 1992, A1.

81. David Cano and Javier Mejía, "Reducen actividades hasta 75% las 192 industrias contaminantes," *Unomásuno* (Mexico City), 17 March 1992, 1; "Mexico City Smog Hits Danger Levels: Industries Forced to Cut Activity," *International Environment Reporter* 15 (25 March 1992): 163.

82. Juanita Darling, "Mexico's Anti-Smog Plan Meets Industry Resistance," *Los Angeles Times*, 25 March 1992, A4; Scott, "New Smog Plan," 7.

83. Scott, "Slew of Government Programs," 11.

84. Cecilia Rodríguez, "The World's Most Polluted City," *Los Angeles Times*, 21 April 1991, M1.

85. Civil engineer Humberto Castillo of the Democratic Revolutionary Party suggested one of the most quixotic technological "solutions" to Mexico City's air pollution problems: the use of giant wind fans to blow smog out of the Valley of Mexico. The PRI has expressed interest in Castillo's plan despite its impracticality. Paul Iredale, "Critics Deride Mexico City Pollution Plan," *San Francisco Chronicle*, 13 March 1992, A22; "Mexico Considers Wind Machines to Fight Smog," *Reno Gazette-Journal*, 23 February 1992, A14.

86. Leticia Hernández, "Decretó CSG veda forestal de 3 meses en la Lacandona," *Excelsior* (Mexico City), 14 January 1989, Estados section, 1.

87. William Branigin, "Mexico Adopts Campaign to Save the Environment," *Washington Post*, 6 June 1990, A18.

88. Mumme, "Clearing the Air," 26–27.

89. Juanita Darling, "From Lerma River Flows a Tale of Politics and Pollution," *Los Angeles Times*, 22 October 1991, H8.

90. William Branigin, "Imperiled Turtles Slaughtered in Mexico," *Washington Post*, 18 February 1990, A44; Mumme, "Clearing the Air," 27.

91. "Mexico Signs CITES Treaty," *International Environment Reporter* 14 (31 July 1991): 431.

92. David Clark Scott, "US Tuna Ban May Snag Trade Talks with Mexico," *Christian Science Monitor*, 7 November 1990, 6.

93. Homero Aridjis, "Defending Dolphins," *New York Times*, 7 October 1991, A17.

94. Juanita Darling, "Tuna Turnabout: Mexico Announces a Dolphin Protection Plan," *Los Angeles Times*, 25 September 1991, D6; Ignacio Herrera A., "Anuncia SEPESCA un programa para la protección del delfín y el aprovechamiento del atún," *Excelsior* (Mexico City), 2 April 1991, A11, A30.

95. "Pro-Dolphin Accord Made," *New York Times*, 16 July 1992, D9.

96. Barbara Belejack, "The Mexican Wasteland: Interview with Homero Aridjis," *Newsweek*, Latin American edition, 114 (30 October 1989): 50.

97. "Mexican President Salinas Well-Deserving of Environment Awards, Conservationists Say," *International Environment Reporter* 14 (5 June 1991): 308.

98. For the views of Mexican environmentalists regarding the free trade agreement, see "Canadian, Mexican, and American Greens Oppose Free Trade Agreement," *Earth Island Journal* 7 (Winter 1992): 20; Juanita Darling, "Cynics See Political Motivation for Mexico's Move on Pollution," *Los Angeles Times*, 15 April 1991, A6; and David Clark Scott, "US, Mexico Launch Border Cleanup," *Christian Science Monitor*, 28 February 1992, 6.

99. Robert Reinhold, "Mexico Proclaims an End to Sanctuary for Polluters," *New York Times*, 18 April 1991, A20.

100. Secretaría de Desarrollo Urbano y Ecologia, "Ley General del Equilibrio Ecológico," 26–27; idem, "Reglamento de la Ley General del Equilibrio Ecológico y la Protección al Ambiente en Materia de Residuos Peligrosas," *Gaceta Ecológica* 1 (June 1989): 51–59.

101. Suro, "Border Boom's Dirty Residue," 1, 16.

102. Reinhold, "Mexico," A20.

103. Douglas Jehl and Rudy Abramson, "Bush to Seek $100 Million Extra for Border Cleanup," *Los Angeles Times*, 23 January 1992, A1.

104. Seth Mydans, "U.S. and Mexico Take on a Joint Burden: Sewage," *New York Times*, 22 August 1990, A18; "The Texas Border: Whose Dirt?" *Economist* 316 (18 Au-

gust 1990): 20. The United States and Mexico also agreed to equally fund the construction of a thirty-five-million-dollar sewage treatment plant at Nuevo Laredo, Mexico. "Mexico, United States Agree on Cleanup of Pollution along Border, Sharing Costs," *International Environment Reporter* 12 (13 September 1989): 457.

105. Edward Cody, "Expanding Waste Line along Mexico's Border," *Washington Post*, 17 February 1992, A34.

106. Scott, "US, Mexico Launch Border Cleanup," A6

107. "U.S.-Mexico Border Cleanup Plan Set," *Washington Post*, 26 February 1992, A2.

108. John Audley, *A Critique of the February 21, 1992, Draft of the "North American Free Trade Agreement"*; "Environmental Community Cites Flaws in Border Plan, Environmental Review," *International Environment Reporter* 15 (11 March 1992): 136–137.

109. "EPA Unveils Plan to Clean Up Borderlands," *Reno Gazette-Journal*, 4 August 1991, A13.

110. At the insistence of U.S. President Bill Clinton, Mexico and Canada signed an environmental side agreement to the North American Free Trade Agreement in 1993. The compact created a multistep resolution process designed to reverse the course of any North American country that persistently failed to enforce its environmental laws against companies or sectors involved in or affected by trade, if necessary through fines and trade sanctions. However, since the agreement does not provide for citizen participation in the resolution process, most disputes will probably be "settled" behind closed doors by government appointees eager to avoid a trade conflict over environmental matters. If this is the case, then the environmental side agreement will not contribute to the enforcement of environmental laws in Mexico. Mary E. Kelly, *NAFTA's Environmental Side Agreement: A Review and Analysis*.

111. "Fallout from Guadalajara Explosions Expected to Impact Industry, Politics," *International Environment Reporter* 15 (6 May 1992): 255–256; David Clark Scott, "Mexicans Scrutinize Safety Following Guadalajara Blast," *Christian Science Monitor*, 27 April 1992, 6; Jeff Silverstein, "Blasts in Mexico Feed Fear over Growth," *San Francisco Chronicle*, 28 April 1992, A10; Emilio Vázquez and Hilario Monray, "9 Presos en Guadalajara; acusan de negligente al Gobernador Cosío," *Unomásuno* (Mexico City), 28 April 1992, 1, 14, 15.

112. David Clark Scott, "Mexico Shake-Up Rattles Environmentalists," *Christian Science Monitor*, 4 May 1992, 6.

10. The Green Revolution: The Mexican Environmental Movement

1. In Mexico, aesthetic concerns played a less important role in the development of the environmental movement than in the United States, in part because many Mexicans were not affluent enough to take part in outdoor recreation and therefore did not have the opportunity to enjoy nature. In Mexico, there are mountaineering clubs and groups similar to the Boy Scouts and the Girl Scouts, but there is no environmental organization like the Sierra Club to promote outings and the preservation of scenic beauty. For an account of the rise of the environmental movement in the United States, see Samuel P. Hays, *Beauty, Health, and Permanence: Environmental Politics in the United States, 1955–1985*, 21–39.

2. "Ecology Leaders See Their Influence on Official Environmental Policy as Limited," *International Environment Reporter* 11 (13 January 1988): 24.

3. Thirty percent of Mexico City's residents lack toilets. Mark A. Uhlig, "Mexico City's Toxic Residue Worsens Already Filthy Air," *New York Times*, 12 May 1991, I14.

4. Comisión Nacional de Ecología, *Informe General de Ecología*, 119.

5. Uhlig, "Mexico City's Toxic Residue," 14.

6. Garcia, "Smog Stalks Mexico City," 2.

7. Tom Dydek, Ph.D., environmental toxicologist, "Evaluation of Air Quality Monitoring Data for Mexico City," 2–4, enclosed in letter to Jorge González of the Ecologist Alliance, 16 April 1987, in packet of information provided by the Mexican Green Party.

8. Richard J. Meislin, "Smog-bound Mexico City: Has It Seen the Light?," *New York Times*, 25 June 1985, A2; Cecilia Rodríguez, "The World's Most Polluted City," *Los Angeles Times*, 21 April 1991, M1.

9. "Cien intelectuales y artistas mexicanos contra la contaminación de la ciudad," *Unomásuno* (Mexico City), 1 March 1985, 17.

10. Comisión Nacional de Ecología, *Informe General de Ecología*, 31.

11. Arzate, "Representa la Refinería de Azcapotzalco."

12. Ibid.

13. From José Sarukhan's introduction to an issue devoted to Conservation International's programs in Mexico, *Tropicus* 1 (Fall 1988): 1.

14. For a book-length treatment of this latter subject, see Alejandro Toledo with the collaboration of Arturo Nuñez and Héctor Ferreira, *Como destruir el paraíso: El desastre ecológico del sureste.*

15. Centro de Documentación, Comisión Coordinadora para el Desarrollo Agropecuario del Departamento del Distrito Federal, *Recopilación periodística sobre temas ecológicos, resumen semanal*, 1 March 1980–13 August 1982.

16. *Unomásuno* is one of Mexico City's top dailies. *Mexico City News,* which became simply *The News* in 1989, is the English-language daily in Mexico City.

17. For a recompilation of Césarman's articles, see Césarman, *Crónicas ecológicas.*

18. See, for example, "Salvar el medio ambiente mediante la educación ecológica," *Unomásuno* (Mexico City), 17 October 1989, Dosmiluno section, 7.

19. *Mexico City News*, 10 February 1989, 1.

20. Ibid., 4 April 1989, 1.

21. Ibid., 17 April 1989, 1.

22. Ibid., 12 January 1989, 1.

23. "Letter from the Editor," ibid., 11 December 1988, 2.

24. Arturo Sotomayor, *La metropolí mexicana y su agonía.*

25. Fernando Césarman, *Ecocido: Estudio psicoanalítico de la destrucción del medio ambiente.*

26. Ibid., 38–40.

27. A fellow environmentalist, Fernando Ortiz Monasterio, recounts overhearing a couple talking about pollution in their neighborhood while climbing up to the metro station Xola. The woman was worried about the spread of industry and contamination in the *colonia*. The man responded, "That is called ecocide." Fernando Césarman, *Paisaje roto: La ruta del ecocido*, introd. Fernando Ortiz Monasterio, 11.

28. Césarman and Salinas had participated in a PRI-sponsored forum on the environment in 1982, the proceedings of which were published as *Medio ambiente y calidad de la vida*. This may have been the first time the two gentlemen had met, al-

though it is likely that Salinas was already well familiar with Césarman's ideas, if not through his books then at least through his editorials in *Unomásuno*.

29. Shooki Shemirani, "President Cites Environmental Considerations in Development," *Mexico City News*, 20 January 1989, 1.

30. Ortiz Monasterio et al., *Tierra profanada*, 324–325.

31. Interview with Carmen Elizalde Aguilar, head of the Turtle Program for Pronatura, Mexico City, 12 October 1989. Fernando Ortiz Monasterio and Valentina Ortiz Monasterio Garza, *Mariposa Monarca: Vuelo del papel*.

32. Enrique Beltrán, "La conservación como instumento de desarrollo," in Instituto Mexicano de Recursos Naturales Renovables, *Mesas redondas sobre desarrollo y ecología*, 186.

33. "La larga marcha de los ecólogos mexicanos," 26.

34. Secretaría de Desarrollo Urbano y Ecología, *Ciudad y medio ambiente*, 30–46.

35. Ibid., 87–88.

36. Ibid., 89.

37. Ibid.

38. Laura Ríos and Carlos Alonso, "Consejo de visiones guardianes de la tierra," *Unomásuno* (Mexico City), 30 April 1991, Dosmiluno section, 4.

39. Interview with Nigh.

40. Secretaría de Desarrollo Urbano y Ecología, *Ciudad y medio ambiente*, 89–91.

41. "Mexican Fishermen Win Fight over Bay," *San Francisco Chronicle*, 1 August 1992, A20.

42. Huehuecóyotl is both a multiethnic and multinational commune. Alberto Ruiz Buenfil, "Huehuecóyotl: El lugar del viejo, viejo coyote," *México Desconocido* 152 (July 1989): 37–41.

43. Secretaría de Desarrollo Urbano y Ecología, *Ciudad y medio ambiente*, 28. Some appropriate technologies, such as the use of dry latrines and biogas digestors, seem suitable only for small populations in rural areas. Other environmentally benign technologies, such as the use of solar collectors and water flow control devices, potentially have a much wider application.

44. Partido Revolucionario Institucional, *Medio ambiente*, 12.

45. Alfonso Ciprés Villarreal, "Porque el Movimiento Ecologista Mexicano nunca será partido," Press bulletin no. 08/87, 14 April 1987.

46. "Ecology Leaders," 24.

47. During the 1988 presidential election, the Green Party endorsed the Democratic Revolutionary Party candidate, Cuauhtémoc Cárdenas, on the basis of his pledge to confront such environmental issues as deforestation, water and air pollution, soil erosion, and animal trafficking. Like his father Lázaro Cárdenas, Cuauhtémoc vowed to create new jobs through reforestation projects and fisheries development, among other resource management programs. Ibid.; Wright, *Death of Ramón González*, 242.

48. The Audubon Society is also working to preserve the Santa Rosa Forest between Guanajuato and San Miguel de Allende and is running a trees-for-school program in which children are planting and taking care of trees near San Miguel de Allende. Jean Kishler, "San Miguel Audubon Society," *Audubon Leader*, Southwest Region (February–March 1989).

49. Both Mexican and U.S. nationals are members of Tierra Madre (San Miguel

de Allende has a sizable U.S. community). Tierra Madre, *San Miguel de Allende 2000,* and Tierra Madre, *San Miguel de Allende 2000 Summary Projects for 1989.*

50. Alfonso Ciprés Villarreal, *Movimiento Ecologista Mexicano,* 1–2.

51. Secretaría de Desarrollo Urbano y Ecología, *Ciudad y medio ambiente,* 24–25.

52. Among the signatories were the novelist Homero Aridjis (who drafted the declaration), Fernando Benítez, Fernando Césarman, Alfonso Ciprés Villarreal, the anthropologist Miguel León-Portilla, the novelist Octavio Paz, and the painter Rufino Tamayo.

53. "Cien intelectuales," 17.

54. Shooka Shemirani, "Conference Cites Increased Air Pollution Dangers," *Mexico City News,* 17 January 1989, 1–2; Vera, "Manuel Camacho," 6–9.

55. Mark A. Uhlig, "Refinery Closing Outrages Mexican Workers," *New York Times,* 27 March 1991, A11.

56. Belejack, "Mexican Wasteland," 50.

57. Homero Aridjis, "The Death of a Masterpiece," *New Perspective Quarterly* 6 (Spring 1989): 40.

58. Ibid.

59. Ibid., 41, 43. Aridjis, "Defending Dolphins," A17; "A Plea for Mexico [Open Letter from the Group of 100 to President Carlos Salinas de Gortari on the Lacandón Jungle]," *World Press Review* 45 (October 1989): 45, 47; Vera, "Manuel Camacho," 9.

60. Julia Carabias and Víctor Manuel Toledo, coordinators, *Ecología y recursos naturales: Hacia una política del PSUM.*

61. Víctor Manuel Toledo, "La otra guerra florida," *Nexos* 6 (September 1983): 23.

62. Ibid., 21–23.

63. Ibid., 17–18, 20.

64. "La larga marcha," 28.

65. Víctor Ronquillo, "Los verdes a la contienda electoral," *Unomásuno* (Mexico City) 28 April 1991, Páginauno section, 3.

66. Interview with Grieger.

67. Ibid.

68. Partido Verde Mexicano, "Opinión del Partido Verde Mexicano," 2–3.

69. Interview with Grieger; Partido Verde Mexicano, "Los integrantes del Partido Verde Mexicano nos pronunciamos," Press release, 1.

70. Tim Golden, "For Mexico's Green Party, It's a Very Gray World," *New York Times,* 14 August 1991, A3.

71. Ronquillo, "Los verdes," 3.

72. Mumme, "Clearing the Air," 28.

73. "Ecology Leaders," 24; Stephen P. Mumme, "System Maintenance and Environmental Reform in Mexico: Salinas's Preemptive Strategy," *Latin American Perspectives* 19 (Winter 1992): 127–129.

74. Fernando Ortega Pizarro, "Ya obsoleta y con todo y fallas se puso en operación Laguna Verde," *Proceso* 720 (20 August 1990): 8–10. Since Laguna Verde's opening, there have been several more radioactive leaks. John Ross, "Mexico's Reactor Still Plagued by Troubles," *Earth Island Journal* 7 (Spring 1992): 14.

75. Lajous, comp., *Las razones,* año 5, pp. 175–185.

76. Sara Figueroa de Tfeiffer, Elia Arroyo, and Jorge González Torres, "Boletín de Prensa," ca. 1990, 1.

77. Lajous, comp., *Las razones*, año 4, p. 582.

78. Tfeiffer, Arroyo, and González Torres, "Boletín de Prensa," 1; Rosa Rojas, "Otra emergencia real en Laguna Verde: Ecologistas," *La Jornada* (Mexico City), 26 July 1990, 15.

79. Rodrigo Vera, "Solo un simulacro de revisión, hecho por un amigo, se hizo para abrir la planta," *Proceso* 720 (20 August 1990): 7.

80. Allegedly, the PRI attempted to silence the Mothers of Veracruz, in part by threatening to dismiss relatives who worked within the state government of Veracruz. Another allegation was that Carlos Salinas de Gortari closed the National Institute for Research on Biotic Resources (INIREB) because of the involvement of INIREB personnel in the fight against Laguna Verde. Vera, "Solo un simulacro de revisión," 7; Wright, *Death of Ramón González*, 68.

81. Vera, "Solo un simulacro de revisión," 7. As subdirector of the Federal Electricity Commission, Eibenshutz helped develop the first plans for Laguna Verde in 1966. Ortega Pizarro, "Ya obsoleta," 8.

82. Tfeiffer, Arroyo, and González Torres, "Boletín de Prensa." Attached to the bulletin is the Christmas message from the bishops of Veracruz. Seven bishops, including the archbishop of Xalapa collaborated on this message.

83. Ortega Pizarro, "Ya obsoleta," 6.

Conclusion

1. Partido Revolucionario Institucional, *Medio ambiente*, 7, 16.

2. Shooki Shemirani, "Conference Cites Increased Air Pollution Dangers," *Mexico City News*, 17 January 1989, 1–2.

3. Steinbeck, *Log from the Sea of Cortez*, 4.

Bibliography

Abrams, Elliot M., and David J. Rue. "The Causes and Consequences of Deforestation among the Prehistoric Maya." *Human Ecology* 16 (1988): 377–395.

"Abril 18 de 1861.—Reglamento expedido por el Ministerio de Fomento á que deben sujetarse los cortadores de árboles en terrenos nacionales." In *Legislación mexicana o colección completa de las disposiciones legislativas expedidas de independencia de la República*. 160–163. Comp. Manuel Dublán and José María Lozano. Vol. 9 of 13 vols. Mexico City: Imprenta del Comercio Dublán, a cargo de M. Lara, 1878.

Academia Nacional de Ciencias Forestales. *Homenaje al Dr. Enrique Beltrán*. Mexico City: Academia Nacional de Ciencias Forestales, 1980.

Acosta, Joseph de. *Historia natural y moral de las Indias*. Ed. Edmundo O'Gorman. Mexico City: Fondo de Cultura Económica, 1940.

La administración ambiental en México: Acciones y resultados de la gestión, 1976–1982. Mexico City, 1982.

Aguilera, Carmen. *Flora y fauna mexicana: Mitología y tradiciones*. Mexico City: Editorial Everest Mexicana, 1985.

Alcérreca Aguirre, Carlos. "El instrumento que nos permite armonizar con la naturaleza es el manejo." *Pronatura* 5 (May–June 1988): 4–5.

Alcérreca Aguirre, Carlos, Juan José Consejo Dueñas, Oscar Flores Villela, David Gutiérrez Carbonell, Edna Hentschel Ariza, Mónica Herzig Zuercher, Ramón Pérez-Gil Salcido, José María Reyes Gómez, and Víctor Sánchez-Cordero Dávila. *Fauna silvestre y areas naturales protegidas*. Colección Medio Ambiente 7. Fundación Universo Veintiuno. Mexico City: Tonatiuh Gutiérrez, 1988.

Alemán, Miguel. *Los árboles, patrimonio de la nación*. Colección Popular 15. Mexico City: Editorial Ruta, 1951.

Alfaro, Jesús. *Algunas palabras acerca de la influencia higiénica de las arboledas y necesidad de reglamentar su uso entre nosotros*. Mexico City: Terrazas, 1892.

Almaraz, Ramón. *Memoria de los trabajos ejecutados por la comisión científica de Pachuca en el año de 1864.* Mexico City: Imprenta de J. M. Andrade y F. Escalante, 1865.

Alvarado Tezozómoc, Hernando. *Crónica mexicana.* 3d. ed. Ed. Manuel Orozco y Berra. Mexico City: Editorial Porrúa, 1980.

Alvarez del Toro, Miguel. *Los animales silvestres de Chiapas.* Tuxtla Gutiérrez, Chiapas: Gob. del Estado, Departamento de Prensa y Turismo, 1952.

———. *¡Así era Chiapas!: 42 años de andanzas por montañas, selvas y caminos en el Estado.* Colección Chiapas 1. Tuxtla Gutiérrez, Chiapas: Universidad Autónoma de Chiapas, 1985.

———. *Las aves de Chiapas.* Tuxtla Gutiérrez, Chiapas: Instituto de Historia Natural, 1971.

———. "Chiapas, gigante saqueado." *Numero Uno* (Tuxtla Gutiérrez, Chiapas), 24 June 1982, 9.

———. "Importancia de las marismas y el error de secarles." *Informa: Boletín informativo del Instituto de Historia Natural* 1 (December 1988): 5.

———. *Los mamíferos de Chiapas.* Tuxtla Gutiérrez, Chiapas: Universidad Autónoma de Chiapas, 1977.

———. "Panorama ecológico de Chiapas." In Instituto Mexicano de Recursos Naturales Renovables, *Mesas redondas sobre Chiapas y sus recursos naturales renovables.* 6-7.

———. *Los reptiles de Chiapas.* 2d ed. Tuxtla Gutiérrez, Chiapas: Publicaciones del Instituto de Historia Natural, 1972.

Alzate y Ramirez, José Antonio. *Gacetas de literatura de México.* 4 vols. Puebla: N.p., 1831.

American Committee for International Wild Life Protection. *Brief History and Text of the Convention on Nature Protection and Wild Life Preservation in the Western Hemisphere.* N.p.: N.d., 1946.

Amigos: Friends by Nature. Dumac annual report for 1988. "'Amigos de la Tierra' Form Central Organization." *Conservation in the Americas* 9 (April 1951): 24–25.

"Los Amigos de la Tierra y su campaña de conservación." *Suelo y Agua* 1 (1 October 1953): 5, 7.

Anders, Cindy. "Building a Better Zoo: Interview with Miguel Alvarez del Toro." *Mexico Journal* 1 (2 May 1988): 3–4.

Andrade, Antonio. *La erosión.* Mexico City: Fondo de Cultura Económica, 1975.

Andrews, Anthony. *Maya Salt Trade and Production.* Tucson: University of Arizona Press, 1983.

Anonymous Conqueror. *Narrative of Some Things of New Spain and of the Great City of Temestitan, Mexico.* Trans. into English and annotated by Marshall H. Saville. Boston: Milford House, 1917.

Applegate, Howard. *Environmental Problems of the Borderlands.* El Paso: Texas Western Press, 1979.

"El aprovechamiento de las aguas y la agricultura." *El Tiempo* (Mexico City), 23 October 1905.

Aridjis, Homero. "The Death of a Masterpiece." *New Perspectives Quarterly* 6 (Spring 1989): 40–43.

———. "Defending Dolphins." *New York Times,* 7 October 1991, A17.

"El árbol: Fuente de vida y de equilibrio ecológico," *Vuelta* 15 (October 1991): 82.

Arzate, Silvia. "Representa la Refinería de Azcapotzalco una bomba de tiempo; urgente sacarla: G, Torres." *El Sol de México* (Mexico City), 6 June 1990, Ciudad page.

Atwood, Wallace W. *The Protection of Nature in the Americas.* Instituto Panamericano de Geografía e Historia 50. Mexico City: Antigua Imprenta de E. Murguía, 1940.

Audley, John. *A Critique of the February 21, 1992, Draft of the "North American Free Trade Agreement".* Washington, D.C.: Sierra Club Center for Environmental Innovation, 1992.

Audubon, John Woodhouse. *Illustrated Notes of an Expedition through Mexico and California.* New York: Published by J. W. Audubon, 1852.

Avila Camacho, Manuel. *Address to the Mexican Agronomists.* Department of State for Foreign Affairs. International Press Service Bureau. National and International Problem Series. Mexico City: Agencia Editorial Mexicana, 1941.

Baker, Rollin H. "The Future of Wildlife in Northern Mexico." In *Transactions of the Twenty-third North American Wildlife Conference.* 567–575. Washington, D.C.: Wildlife Management Institute, 1958.

Ballinas, Víctor. "Campaña para cuidar el uso del agua en el D.F., en 1989." *La Jornada* (Mexico City), 9 October 1989, 35.

Bancroft, Hubert Howe. *California Pastoral, 1796–1848.* San Francisco: History Company, 1888.

———. *History of California.* 7 vols. San Francisco: A. L. Bancroft and Company and History Company, 1884–1890.

———. *History of Mexico.* 6 vols. San Francisco: A. L. Bancroft and Company and History Company, 1883–1888.

Bárcena, Mariano. Director del Observatorio Meteorológico Central. *Ensayo práctico de repoblación de bosques.* Mexico City: Oficina tip. de la Secretaría de Fomento, 1897.

Bárcena Ibarra, Alicia. "La política ecológica en México: Un instrumento para el cambio." *Logos* 13 (1988): 45–52.

Barco, Miguel del. *Historia natural y crónica de la antigua California.* Ed. Miguel León-Portilla. Mexico City: Universidad Nacional Autónoma de México, Instituto de Investigaciones Históricas, 1973.

Baroja, Julio Caro. *Ritos y mitos equivocos,* Biblioteca de Estudios Criticos, Sección de Antropología 1. Madrid: Ediciones Istmo, 1974.

Barrera, Alfredo, and Enrique Beltrán. *El conservacionismo mexicano.* Folleto 27. Mexico City: Ediciones del Instituto Mexicano de Recursos Naturales Renovables, 1966.

Bartlett, John Russell. *Personal Narrative of Explorations and Incidents in Texas, New Mexico, California, Sonora, and Chihuahua, Connected with the United States and Mexican Boundary Commission during the Years 1850, 1851, 1852, and 1853.* 2 vols. New York: D. Appleton and Company, 1854.

Bath, C. Richard. "Environmental Issues in the United States–Mexican Borderlands." *Journal of Borderland Studies* 1 (Spring 1986): 49–72.

Beals, Ralph L. *The Comparative Ethnology of Northern Mexico before 1750.* Ibero-Americana 2. Berkeley and Los Angeles: University of California Press, 1932.

Belejack, Barbara. "The Mexican Wasteland: Interview with Homero Aridjis." *Newsweek,* Latin American edition, 114 (20 October 1989): 50.

Beltrán, Enrique. Mexico City. Interview, 7 September 1989.

———. *El agua como recurso natural renovable en la vida de México.* Folleto 17. Mexico City: Ediciones del Instituto Mexicano de Recursos Naturales Renovables, 1957.

———. "Alfonso L. Herrera (1868–1968): Primera figura de la biología mexicana." *Revista de la Sociedad Mexicana de Historia Natural* 29 (December 1968): 37–91.

———. "La aplicación de insecticidas en gran escala y los equilibrios naturales." *Revista de la Sociedad Mexicana de Historia Natural* 17 (December 1956): 53–62.

———. *La batalla forestal: Lo hecho, lo no hecho, lo por hacer.* Mexico City: N.p., 1964.

———. "La educación en la conservación de los recursos naturales." *Boletín de la Sociedad Mexicana de Geografía y Estadística* 68 (July–October 1948): 269–279.

———. *Etica, estética y conservación.* Folleto 38. Mexico City: Ediciones del Instituto Mexicano de Recursos Naturales Renovables, 1972.

———. "Forestry and the Public Domain: A Mexican Viewpoint." *American Forests* 75 (December 1969): 36, 57–59; 76 (January 1970): 36–37, 46–47.

———. *El hombre y su ambiente: Ensayo sobre el Valle de México.* Mexico City: Fondo de Cultura Económica, 1958.

———. "El Instituto Mexicano de Recursos Naturales Renovables." *Ciencia Interamericana* 8 (January–February 1967): 15–21.

———. "Man versus Land." *Americas* 2 (April 1950): 24–27, 46.

———. "La pesca en los litorales del Golfo de México y la necesidad de los estudios de biología marina para desarrollo esa fuente de riqueza," *Memorias y Revista de la Sociedad Científica "Antonio Alzate"* 49 (1929): 421–445.

———. *La pesca en Mexico City: Su estado actual y un proyecto para impulsarla.* Mexico City: Editorial E.C.L.A.L., 1952.

———. *Problemas latinoamericanos en la conservación de los recursos naturales.* Folleto 22. Mexico City: Ediciones del Instituto Mexicano de Recursos Naturales Renovables, 1965.

———. *La protección de la naturaleza: Principios y problemas.* Mexico City: Secretaría de Educación Pública, 1949.

———. "Los recursos naturales de México: Lineamientos para una política de conservación." *Revista de la Sociedad Mexicana de Historia Natural* 1 (November 1939): 33–43.

———. "Los recursos naturales de México y nuestra economía." *Revista Mexicana del Trabajo* 1 (September–October 1954): 13–26.

———. *Seis lustros de política forestal.* Folleto 26. Mexico City: Ediciones del Instituto Mexicano de Recursos Naturales Renovables, 1966.

———. *Temas forestales, 1946–1960.* Prologue by Julián Rodríguez Adame. Mexico City: N.p., 1961.

———. *Tres temas forestales.* Folleto 12. Mexico City: Ediciones del Instituto Mexicano de Recursos Naturales Renovables, 1955.

———. "Use and Conservation: Two Conflicting Principles." In Alexander B. Adams, ed., *First World Conference on National Parks.* 35–43. Proceedings of a Conference Organized by the International Union for the Conservation of Nature and Natural Resources. Seattle, Washington, 30 June–1 July 1962. Washington, D.C.: National Park Service, U.S. Department of the Interior, 1964.

———. "El Virrey Revillagigedo y los bosques de San Luis Potosí." *Revista de la Sociedad Mexicana de Historia Natural* 17 (1956): 121–131.

———. Subsecretaría de Recursos Forestales y de Caza. *El problema y la política forestales.* Mexico City: Secretaría de Agricultura y Ganadería, 1959.

Beltrán, Enrique, Gonzalo Blanco Macías, and Roberto Villaseñor. *Homenaje al Dr. Tom Gill, 1891–1972.* Mexico City: Ediciones del Instituto Mexicano de Recursos Naturales Renovables, 1972.

Beltrán, Enrique, and Rigoberta Vázquez de la Parra. *En defensa del Parque Nacional Desierto de los Leones.* Folleto 36. Mexico City: Ediciones del Instituto Mexicano de Recursos Naturales Renovables, 1971.

Beltrán Gutiérrez, Héctor. *Legislación forestal mexicana.* Mexico City: Ciudad Universitaria, 1962.

Benavente [Motolinía], Toribio de. *Historia de los indios de la Nueva España.* Ed. Claudio Esteva Fabregat. Colección Crónicas de América 16. Madrid: Historia 16, 1985.

Berkeley, California. Bancroft Library. Manuscript Collections. Archives of California. 63 vols.

———. *Departmental Records* 49. 9:136–137 "Victoria al Ministerio de Relaciones," 1831.

———. *Legislative Records* 60. 2:68–69. "1834—mayo 13—Diputacional sesión del día de la fecha," 1834–1835.

———. 2:207 "1834—noviembre 3—Diputacional territorial sobre estracción de maderas, California," 1834–1835.

———. *Legislative Records* 61. 4:152. "1845—mayo 16—Angeles (sesión de esta día)," 1841–1846.

———. *Superior Government State Papers. Decrees and Dispatches* 57. 15:128. "1839, México.—Romero a Gobierno de Californias—Villa de Los Angeles, junio 12," 1839.

———. John Daniel Coffman. Mexico, 1936.

———. Will Dakin. "Journals of Mexico." 8 vols. 1935–1937.

Blanco Macías, Gonzalo. *Agriculture in Mexico.* American Agricultural Series 5. Washington, D.C.: Pan American Union, 1950.

———. "Asalto a la Naturaleza." *Mensajero Forestal* 29 (November 1970): 9–11.

———. "El Parque Internacional de las Naciones Amigas y la Presa Falcón." *Suelo y Agua* 1 (16 November 1953): 2, 6.

———. "Realizaciones y perspectivas en la conservación del suelo en México." In Instituto Mexicano de Recursos Naturales Renovables, *Mesas redondas sobre utilización y conservación del suelo en México.* 87–104. Mexico City: Ediciones del Instituto Mexicano de Recursos Naturales Renovables, 1969.

Blanco Macías, Gonzalo, and Guillermo Ramírez Cervantes. *La conservación del suelo y agua en México.* Mexico City: Ediciones del Instituto Mexicano de Recursos Naturales Renovables, 1966.

Blazquez, Pedro. *El cazador mexicano o el arte de la caza en México y en sus relaciones con la historia natural.* Puebla, México: Tipografía de Pedro Alarcón, 1868.

Blom, Frans. "Apuntes sobre los ingenieros mayas." *Irrigación en México* 27 (July–September 1946): 5–16.

Blom, Gertrude Duby. San Cristóbal de las Casas. Interview, 22 August 1990.

———. *La familia de Na-Bolom.* 2 vols. Monterrey: Fondo Nacional para Actividades Sociales, 1979.

———. "La Selva Lacandona." Paper presented at the Primer Simposio de Ecología, November 1974, Fray Bartolomé de las Casas Library, Na-Bolom House, San Cristóbal de las Casas, Chiapas.

———. "La Selva Lacandona, Reserva de la Biosfera." *Mujeres* 343 (1979): 20–29.

————. "La Selva Lacandona, su territorio, su gente y sus problemas." *El Nacional* (Mexico City), 4 December 1968, 4; 5 December 1968, 4.

————. *The Story of Na-Bolom.* San Cristóbal de las Casas, Chiapas: N.p., n.d.

Boletín Bimestral de la Dirección Forestal y de Caza. 9 vols. Mexico City: Secretaría de Agricultura y Fomento, 1940–1949.

Boletín del Departamento Forestal y de Caza y Pesca. 4 vols. Mexico City: D.A.P.P, 1935–1939.

Borah, Woodrow, and Sherburne F. Cook. *The Aboriginal Population of Central Mexico on the Eve of the Spanish Conquest.* Ibero-Americana 45. Berkeley and Los Angeles: University of California Press, 1963.

"Border Plants' Growth Brings Jobs, Problems." *Reno Gazette-Journal,* 3 June 1991, A8.

"Bosques y arbolados." *Boletín de la Sociedad de Geografía y Estadística de la República Mexicana,* 2ª época, 2 (1870): 14–24.

Bradsher, Keith. "U.S. and Mexico Draft Plan to Fight Pollution." *New York Times,* 2 August 1991, D2.

Brambila Paz, Rosa, et al. *El animal en la vida prehispánica.* Mexico City: Instituto Nacional de Antropología e Historia and Secretaría de Educación Publica, 1980.

Brañes Ballesteros, Raúl. *Derecho ambiental mexicano.* Colección Medio Ambiente 1. Fundación Universo Veintiuno. Mexico City: Tonatiuh Gutiérrez, 1987.

Branigin, William. "Imperiled Turtles Slaughtered in Mexico." *Washington Post,* 18 February 1990, A44.

————. "Mexico Adopts Campaign to Save the Environment." *Washington Post,* 6 June 1990, A18.

————. "Mexico's Other Contraband—Wildlife." *Washington Post,* 24 June 1989, A18, A24.

————. "North America's Largest Rain Forest Faces Destruction." *Washington Post,* 17 July 1989, A17, A22.

Brundage, Burr Cartwright. *The Phoenix of the Western World: Quetzalcóatl and the Sky Religion.* Norman: University of Oklahoma Press, 1982.

Burgoa, Francisco de. *Geográfica descripción.* Publicaciones del Archivo General de la Nación 25–26. 2 vols. Mexico City: Talleres Gráficos de la Nación, 1934.

Burland, C. A. *The Gods of Mexico.* New York: G. P. Putnam's Sons, 1967.

Burrus, Ernest J., S.J. "Rivera y Moncada, Explorer and Military Commander of Both Californias, in the Light of His Diary and Other Contemporary Documents." *Hispanic American Historical Review* 50 (November 1970): 684.

Call, Tom Clark. *The Mexican Venture: From Political to Industrial Revolution in Mexico.* New York: Oxford University Press, 1953.

Callicott, J. Baird. "American Indian Land Wisdom." *Journal of Forest History* 39 (January 1989): 35–42.

Campesino: ¡Defiende tus bosques!. Cartillas Agrarias 12. Mexico City: Ediciones del Departamento Agrario, 1957.

"Canadian, Mexican, and American Greens Oppose Free Trade Agreement." *Earth Island Journal* 7 (Winter 1992): 20.

Cano, David, and Javier Mejía. "Reducen actividades hasta 75% las 192 industrias contaminantes." *Unomásuno* (Mexico City), 17 March 1992, 1, 11.

Carabias, Julia, and Víctor Manuel Toledo, coordinators. *Ecología y recursos naturales: Hacia una política del PSUM.* Mexico City: Ediciones del Comité Central, 1983.

Cárdenas, Lázaro. *El problema indígena de México.* Mexico City: Departamento de Asuntos Indígenas, 1940.

Carrillo-Barrios-Gómez, Enrique, and Hans Hermann-Martín. "Sian Ka'an: A New Biosphere Reserve Model in Mexico." In *Proceedings of the Symposium on Biosphere Reserves,* ed. William P. Gregg, Jr., Stanley L. Krugman, and James D. Wood, Jr. Atlanta: U.S. Department of the Interior, National Park Service, 1989.

Carroll, Peter N. *Puritanism and the Wilderness: The Intellectual Significance of the New England Frontier, 1629–1670.* New York: Columbia University Press, 1969.

Carson, Rachel. *Silent Spring.* Boston: Houghton Mifflin, 1962.

Cavallero Carranco, Juan. *The Pearl Hunters in the Gulf of California, 1668.* Summary report of the voyage made to the Californias by Captain Francisco de Lucenilla. Transcribed, translated, and annotated by W. Michael Mathes. Los Angeles: Dawson Book Shop, 1966.

Cave, Marion S. *Forest Legislation in Mexico.* Washington, D.C.: Office of the Coordinator of Inter-American Affairs, 1945.

Centro de Documentación. Comisión Coordinadora para el Desarrollo Agropecuario del Departamento del Distrito Federal. *Recopilación periodística sobre temas ecológicos, resumen semanal,* 1 March 1980–13 August 1982. Mexico City: N.p., 1982.

Cervantes Saavedra, Miguel de. *Don Quijote de La Mancha.* 5th ed. Ed. Francisco Rodríquez Marín of the Real Academia de España. 8 vols. Madrid: Espasa-Calpe, 1948.

Césarman, Fernando. *Crónicas ecológicas.* Mexico City: Fondo de Cultura Económica, 1986.

———. *Ecocido: Estudio psicoanalítico de la destrucción del medio ambiente.* Mexico City: Cuadernos de Joaquín Mortiz, 1972.

———. *Paisaje roto: La ruta del ecocido.* Introd. Fernando Ortiz Monasterio. Mexico City: Ediciones Oceano, 1984.

———. *Yo, naturaleza.* Mexico City: Consejo Nacional de Ciencia y Tecnología, 1981.

Chapin, Mac. "Travels with Eucario: In Search of Ecodevelopment." *Orion* 10 (Spring 1991): 49–59.

Chase, Stuart, in collaboration with Marian Tyler. *Mexico City: A Study of Two Americas.* New York: Macmillan Company, 1937.

Cházari, Esteban. *Piscicultura en agua dulce.* Mexico City: Oficina tip. de Secretaría de Fomento, 1884.

Chilam Balam de Chumayel. Ed. Miguel Rivera Dorado. Colección Crónicas de América 20. Madrid: Historia 16, 1986.

The Chronicles of Michoacán. Trans. and ed. Eugene R. R. Craine and Reginald C. Reindorp. Norman: University of Oklahoma Press, 1970.

"Cien intelectuales y artistas mexicanos contra la contaminación de la ciudad," *Unomásuno* (Mexico City), 1 March 1985, 17.

"El cinturón verde." *Revista de las Revistas* 4100 (26 August 1988): 17.

Ciprés Villarreal, Alfonso. "Movimiento Ecologista Mexicano." Press release, n.d.

———. "Porque el Movimiento Ecologista Mexicano nunca será un partido." Press release, no. 8/87, 14 April 1987.

"Circular de 15 de abril de 1857.—Para que los gobernadores de los estados eviten la destrucción de los bosques y cuiden de su conservación." *Código de colonización y terrenos baldíos de la República Mexicana años de 1451 a 1892.* 662–663. Comp. Francisco F. de la Maza. Mexico City: Oficina de la Secretaría de Fomento, 1893.

"Circular de 15 de febrero de 1880.—Exitando á los gobernadores de los estados á que dicten las medidas á evitar la destrucción de montes y arbolados." *Código de colonización y terrenos baldíos de la República Mexicana años de 1451 a 1892.* 857–858. Comp. Francisco F. de la Maza. Mexico City: Oficina de la Secretaría de Fomento, 1893.

Clar, Raymond C. *Forest Use in Spanish-Mexican California.* Sacramento: Division of Forestry, 1957.

Clavigero, Francisco Javier. *The History of [Lower] California.* Trans. from the Italian by Sara E. Lake. Ed. A. A. Gray. Riverside, Cal.: Manessier Publishing Company, 1971.

Cline, S. L. *Colonial Culhuacan, 1580–1600: A Social History of an Aztec Town.* Albuquerque: University of New Mexico Press, 1988.

Coatsworth, John H. *Growth against Development: The Economic Impact of Railroads in Porfirian Mexico.* Dekalb: Northern Illinois University Press, 1981.

Códice Mendocino o Colección de Mendoza. Mexican manuscript from the sixteenth century, preserved in the Bodleian Library, Oxford University. Ed. José Ignacio Echeagary of the Academia Mexicana Correspondiente del Real de Madrid. Mexico City: San Angel Ediciones, 1979.

Cody, Edward. "Expanding Waste Line along Mexico's Border." *Washington Post,* 17 February 1992, A1, A34.

———. "Monarchs Rule Mexican Mountains." *Washington Post,* 27 December 1990, A19, A25.

Coe, Michael D. *The Maya.* New York: Praeger Publishers, 1973.

Colección de documentos inéditos para la historia de España. Ed. Marquis de Pidal and Miguel Salvá. 113 vols. Madrid: Imprenta de la Viuda de Calero, 1855.

Collier, George A. *Fields of Tzotzil: The Ecological Bases of Tradition in Highland Chiapas.* Austin: University of Texas Press, 1975.

Comisión Nacional de Ecología. *100 acciones necesarias.* Mexico City: Comisión Nacional de Ecología. 1987.

———. *Informe General de Ecología.* Mexico City: Comisión Nacional de Ecología, 1988.

Comisión Preparatoria de la Participación de México en la Conferencia de las Naciones Unidas sobre el Medio Ambiente. *Informe nacional.* Mexico City: N.p., 1971.

Comité de Asesoría Técnica Forestal. *La situación forestal de México es grave.* Mexico City: Camara Nacional de las Industrias del Papel, 1958.

Comité de Recursos Naturales de la Comisión de Geografía. *Segunda mesa redonda sobre recursos naturales.* Mexico City: Comisión de Geografía, 1969.

Comte, Auguste. *A General View of Positivism.* Trans. J. H. Bridges. 1851; rpt. Stanford: Academic Reprints, n.d.

Conservation International. "In Chiapas: Building Partnerships for Conservation." *Tropicus* 4 (Fall 1988): 6.

———. "The Sea of Cortez: Understanding and Conserving Its Productivity." *Tropicus* 4 (Fall 1988): 4–5.

Conservation International, in collaboration with the Instituto Nacional de Investigaciones Sobre Recursos Bióticos (INIREB). *Mexico's Living Endowment: An Overview of Biological Diversity.* N.p.: N.d., 1989. Executive summary of Oscar Flores-Villela and Patricia Gerez Fernández, *Conservación en México: Síntesis sobre vertebrados terrestres, vegetación y uso del suelo.* N.p.: N.p., 1989.

"La contaminación del aire." *Suelo y Agua* 8 (15 May 1960): 3.

Contreras Sánchez, Alicia del C. "El palo de tinte: Motivo de un conflicto entre dos naciones, 1670–1802." *Historia Mexicana* 37 (July–September 1987): 49–74.

"Convenio entre los Estados Unidos Mexicanos y los Estados Unidos de Norteamérica para la protección de aves migratorias y de mamíferos cinegeticos." *Boletín del Departamento Forestal y de Caza y Pesca* 1 (February–March 1936): 153–157.

Cook, Sherburne F. *The Historical Demography and Ecology of the Teotlalpan.* Ibero-Americana 33. Berkeley and Los Angeles: University of California Press, 1948.

———. *Soil Erosion and Population in Central Mexico.* Ibero-Americana 34. Berkeley and Los Angeles: University of California, 1949.

Corominas, Joan. *Diccionario crítico etimológico de la lengua castellana.* 5 vols. Madrid: Editorial Gredos, 1980.

Crocker, Marvin D. "The Evolution of Mexican Forestry Policy and Its Influence upon Forest Reserves." Ph.D. dissertation, Oregon State University, 1973.

———. "Industrial Forest Exploitation Units: A Modern Mexican Forest Management System." *Journal of Forestry* 72 (October 1974): 650–653.

Crosby, Alfred W., Jr. *The Columbian Exchange: Biological and Cultural Consequences of 1492.* Foreword by Otto von Mering. Contribution in American Studies 2. Westport, Conn.: Greenwood Press, 1972.

"Cuestionario relativo á los bosques y montes existentes en la República propuesta por la Junta Central de Bosques á las juntas locales de los estados." *Revista Forestal Mexicana* 1 (December 1909): 119–124.

Culbert, T. Patrick, ed. *The Classic Maya Collapse.* Albuquerque: University of New Mexico Press, 1973.

Dakin, Will. Berkeley, California. Interview, 5 November 1987.

Darling, Juanita. "Cynics See Political Motivation for Mexico's Move on Pollution." *Los Angeles Times,* 15 April 1991, A6.

———. "Firms Cash in on Mexican Bid to Halt Pollution." *Los Angeles Times,* 13 May 1990, D1, D10.

———. "From Lerma River Flows a Tale of Politics and Pollution." *Los Angeles Times,* 22 October 1991, H8.

———. "Mexico City's Trucks, Buses Must Convert to Clean Fuel." *Los Angeles Times,* 12 February 1992, A1, A3.

———. Mexico to Ease Debt, Help the Environment." *Los Angeles Times,* 20 February 1991, D5, D13.

———. "Mexico's Agricultural Woes: Water Supplies and Thus Abundant Crops Are Drying Up." *San Francisco Chronicle* (Marin/Sonoma edition), 5 December 1990, World news, 4–5.

———. "Mexico's Anti-Smog Plan Meets Industrial Resistance." *Los Angeles Times,* 25 March 1992, A4.

———. "Tuna Turnabout: Mexico Announces a Dolphin Protection Plan." *Los Angeles Times,* 25 September 1991, D6.

Darling, Juanita, Larry B. Stammer, and Judith Pasternak. "Can Mexico Clean up Its Act?" *Los Angeles Times,* 17 November 1991, A1, A18, A19.

"The Death of the Lacandón Culture and Rain Forest: An Interview with Gertrude Duby Blom." *Mexico City News,* 18 March 1983, 16–17.

"Decreto de 4 de enero de 1813.—Sobre reducir los terrenos baldíos y otros terrenos comunes á dominio particular: Suertes concedidas á los defensores de la patria y á los ciudadanos no propietarios." In *Código de colonización y terrenos baldíos de la República Mexicana años de 1451 a 1892*. 148–152. Comp. Francisco F. de la Maza. Mexico City: Secretaría de Fomento, 1893.

"Decreto por el cual se declara veda total e indefinida de recuperación y de servicios para todos los bosques del Estado de México y del Distrito Federal." *Diario Oficial*, 29 March 1947, 2–3.

"Decreto que declara veda total e indefinida, de recuperación y de servicios, en los bosques ubicados dentro de los limites del estado del Querétaro."*Diaro Oficial*, 20 July 1950, 4–5.

"Decreto que declara zonas protectoras forestales y de repoblación las cuencas de alimentación de las obras de irrigación de los distritos nacionales de riego, y se establece una veda total e indefinida en los montes ubicados dentro de dichas cuencas." *Diario Oficial*, 3 August 1949, 2–4.

Deevey, Edward S., Jr. "Limnological Studies in Middle America with a Chapter on Aztec Limnology." *Transactions of the Connecticut Academy of Arts and Sciences* 39 (February 1957): 213–328.

Department of Urban Development and Ecology. *General Law on Ecological Balance and Environmental Protection*. Issued on 23 December 1987. Trans. U.S. Environmental Protection Agency, Office of International Activities. Washington, D.C.: N.p., 1988.

Departamento del Distrito Federal. "Reglamento de la Ley General del Equilibrio Ecológica para la prevención y control de la contaminación generada por los vehículos automotores que circulan por el Distrito Federal y los municipios de su zona conurbana." *Gaceta Ecológica* 1 (June 1989): 61–69.

Departamento Forestal y de Caza y Pesca. *Código de pesca de los Estados Unidos Mexicanos*. Mexico City: D.A.P.P., 1939.

———. *Código forestal de los Estados Unidos Mexicanos*. Mexico City: D.A.P.P., 1938.

———. "Decreto que reforma el Artículo 87 de la Ley Forestal." *Diario Oficial*, 21 January 1938, 10.

———. *Disposiciones vigentes en materia de caza*. Mexico City: D.A.P.P., 1938

Díaz del Castillo, Bernal. *Historia verdadera de la conquista de la Nueva España*. Ed. Miguel León-Portillo. 2 vols. Madrid: Raycar, 1984.

"Discurso pronunciado por el C. Ing. Alfonso González Gallardo, Subsecretaría de Agricultura y Fomento, en la sesión inaugural de la Primera Convención Forestal." *Boletín de la Dirección General Forestal y de Caza* 2 (October 1941): 11–19.

"Discurso pronunciado por el Ing. Fernando Quintana, Director General Forestal y de Caza, con motivo de la Fiesta Principal del Arbol, en la Ciudad de México, Distrito Federal." *Boletín Bimestral de la Dirección General Forestal y de Caza* 2 (March–April 1942): 3–6.

Doolittle, William E. *Canal Irrigation in Prehistoric Mexico City: The Sequence of Technological Change*. Austin: University of Texas Press, 1990.

Duby, Gertrude. *Los Lacandones: Su pasado y su presente*. Mexico City: Secretaría de Educación Pública, 1944.

Dumac 11 (September–October 1989).

Durán, Diego. *Ritos y festivos de los antiguos mexicanos*. Introd. and glossary by César Macazaga Ordoño. Mexico City: Editorial Innovación, 1980.

Dydek, Tom. Ph.D., environmental toxicologist. "Evaluation of Air Quality Monitoring Data for Mexico City." Enclosed in letter to Jorge González of the Ecologist Alliance, 16 April 1987; both in packet of information provided by the Mexican Green Party.

"Earth Day Celebrated across the Globe." *The News* (Mexico City), 23 April 1990, 1, 5.

Echeverría Alvarez, Luis. "Los verdaderos límites del crecimiento." In *¿Tiene límites el crecimiento? Una visión latinoamericana*. 551–560. Ed. Joseph Hodara and Iván Restrepo. Mexico City: Editorial El Manual Modern, 1977.

"Ecologists Reject Government Claims That Mexico City's Air Quality Has Improved." *International Environment Reporter* 11 (10 February 1988): 142.

"Ecology Leaders See Their Influence on Official Policy as Limited." *International Environment Reporter* 11 (13 January 1988): 23–24.

Elizalde Aguilar, Carmen. Head of the Turtle Program for Pronatura, Mexico City. Interview, 12 October 1989.

Emory, Jerry. "Where the Sky Was Born." *Wilderness* 52 (Summer 1989): 55–57.

"Environmental Community Cites Flaws in Border Plan, Environmental Review," *International Environmental Reporter* 15 (11 March 1992): 136–137.

"EPA Unveils Plan to Clean Up Borderlands." *Reno Gazette-Journal*, 4 August 1991, A13.

Escalante Baranda, Angel. "Problemas ecológicos de nuestra capital." *Revista de las Revistas* 4097 (5 August 1988): 11.

———. "Problemas y soluciones ecológicas." *Revista de las Revistas* 4098 (12 August 1988): 11.

Escobar, Rómulo. *Economía rural y administración*. Ciudad Juárez: "El Agricultor Mexicano," 1928.

———. *Tratado elemental de agricultura*. Mexico City: Sociedad de Educación y Libertad Franco Americana, 1927.

"Fallout from Guadalajara Explosions Expected to Impact Industry, Politics." *International Environment Reporter* 15 (6 May 1992): 225–226.

Faust, Betty, and John Sinton. "Let's Dynamite the Salt Factory! Communication, Coalitions, and Sustainable Use among Users of a Biosphere Reserve." Paper presented by John Sinton at the American Society for Environmental History Conference, Houston, 28 February–3 March 1991.

Flores, Leopoldo. *La dirección de estudios biológicos: Su organización, fines y resultados que ha alcanzado*. Mexico City: Herrero Hermanos Sucesores, 1924.

Flugger, Annette L., and Rosa Dora S. Keatley, comps. *Report on Conservation of Renewable Natural Resources in Latin America*. Washington, D.C.: Pan American Union, 1950.

"Free Trade and a Cleaner Environment: President Salinas Still Has Something to Prove." *Los Angeles Times*, 21 July 1991, M4.

"Frentes políticos." *Excelsior* (Mexico City), 4 June 1990, A1, A30.

"Fuel Oil Limited in Mexico City to Reduce Smog." *San Francisco Chronicle*, 24 January 1991, A15.

Fuentes, Carlos. "Asphyxiation by Progress." *New Perspectives Quarterly* 6 (Spring 1989): 43–47.

FUNDAMAT. *Chiapas: A Race against Time*. Tuxtla Gutiérrez, Chiapas: Foundation Miguel Alvarez del Toro, n.d.

Galicia, Daniel F. "Mexico's National Parks." *Ecology* 22 (January 1941): 107–110.

Gallegos, Carlos Melo, Coordinator. *Parques nacionales.* Mexico City: Instituto de Geografía, UNAM, 1975.

Garcia, Dawn. "Smog Stalks Mexico City: Limit on Using Cars Only Hope in Toxic Air Crisis." *San Francisco Chronicle,* 6 December 1989, Briefing section, 2.

García Martínez, "La legislación forestal." 233–242.

Garrett, Wilbur E. "La Ruta Maya." *National Geographic* 176 (October 1989): 424–478.

Gibson, Charles. *The Aztecs under Spanish Rule: A History of the Indians of the Valley of Mexico, 1519–1810* Stanford: Stanford University Press, 1964.

Gill, Tom. *Land Hunger in Mexico.* Washington, D.C.: Charles Lathrop Pack Forestry Foundation, 1951.

———. *Tropical Forests of the Caribbean.* Published by the Tropical Plant Research Foundation in cooperation with the Charles Lathrop Pack Forestry Trust. Baltimore: Read-Taylor, 1931.

"GM to Move Truck Plant in Response to Stricter Environmental Enforcement." *International Environment Reporter* 15 (8 April 1992): 190–191.

Goebel, Martin. Director of Conservation International's Mexico Program, Washington, D.C. Interview, 20 June 1989.

Golden, Tim. "For Mexico's Green Party, It's a Very Gray World." *New York Times,* 14 August 1991, A3.

———. "Mexico City Emits More Heat over Pollution." *New York Times,* 25 November 1991, A5.

Gómez-Pompa, Arturo. Professor of botany at the University of California, Riverside, and former director of the Instituto Nacional de Investigaciones sobre Recursos Bióticos (National Institute for Research on Biotic Resources), Riverside, Cal. Interview, 5 March 1990.

———. "On Maya Silviculture." *Mexican Studies/Estudios Mexicanos* 3 (Winter 1987): 1–17.

———. *Los recursos bióticos de México (reflexiones).* Xalapa, Veracruz: Instituto Nacional de Investigaciones sobre Recursos Bióticos, 1985.

———. "Tropical Deforestation and Maya Silviculture: An Ecological Paradox." *Tulane Studies in Zoology and Botany* 26 (1987): 19–37.

Gómez-Pompa, Arturo, José Salvador Flores, and Victoria Sosa. "The 'Pet Kot': A Manmade Tropical Forest of the Maya." Interciencia 12 (January–February 1987): 10–15.

Gómez-Pompa, Arturo, and J. J. Jiménez-Osornio. "Some Reflections on Intensive Traditional Agriculture." In Christina Gladwin and Kathleen Truman, eds. *Food and Farm: Current Debate and Policies.* 231–253. Monographs in Economic Anthropology 7. Lanham, Md.: University Press of America, 1989.

González, Ambrosio, and Víctor Manuel Sánchez L. *Los parques nacionales de México.* Mexico City: Ediciones del Instituto Mexicano de Recursos Naturales Renovables, 1961.

González Pacheco, Cuauhtémoc. *Capital extranjero en la selva de Chiapas, 1863–1982.* Mexico City: Instituto de Investigaciones Económicas, 1983.

González Peña, Carlos. "El amigo de los árboles." *México Forestal* 24 (July–September 1946): 45–47.

———. "El retorno a la barbarie." *El Universal* (Mexico City), 4 January 1940, 3, 5.

Gore, Al. *Earth in the Balance: Ecology and the Human Spirit.* Boston: Houghton Mifflin Company, 1992.

Gossen, Gary H. *Chamulas in the World of the Sun: Time and Space in a Maya Oral Tradition.* Cambridge: Harvard University Press, 1974.

"Government Agrees to Inform Citizens of Daily Pollution Levels in Mexico City." *International Environment Reporter* 9 (2 February 1986): 42–43.

Graham, Wade. "MexEco?: Mexican Attitudes toward the Environment." *Environmental History Review* 15 (Winter 1991): 1–17.

Gregg, William P., Jr., Stanley L. Krugman, and James D. Wood, Jr., eds. *Proceedings of the Symposium on Biosphere Reserves.* Fourth World Wilderness Congress, YMCA at the Rockies, Estes Park, Colorado, USA, 14–17 September 1987. Atlanta: U.S. Department of the Interior, National Park Service, 1989.

Grieger, Natalia. Member of the Mexican Green Party, Mexico City. Interview, 25 October 1989.

"Group of 100 Reaffirms Stand." *The News* (Mexico City), 11 September 1989, 1, 25.

Grove, Noel. "Quietly Conserving Nature." *National Geographic* 174 (December 1988): 818–844.

Guzmán Peredo, Miguel. *Las montañas de México (Testimonio de los cronistas).* Mexico City: B. Costa-Amic, 1968.

Halffter, Gonzalo. "Biosphere Reserves: The Conservation of Nature for Man." In *Conservation, Science, and Society.* 450–457. Contribution to the First International Biosphere Reserve Congress, Minsk, Byelorussia, USSR, 26 September–2 October 1983. Organized by UNESCO and UNEP in cooperation with the FAO and even at the invitation of the USSR. Paris: United Nations, 1983.

———. *Colonización y conservación de recursos bióticos en el trópico.* Mexico City: Instituto de Ecología and Instituto Nacional de Investigaciones sobre Recursos Bióticos, 1976.

———. "Desarrollo industrial y equilibrio ecológico." *Acta Politécnica Mexicana* 14 (July–September 1973): 141–145.

———. "Local Participation in Conservation and Development." *Ambio* 10 (1981): 93–96.

———, ed. *Reservas de la biosfera en el Estado de Durango: Trabajos varios.* Mexico City: Instituto de Ecología, 1978.

Halffter, Gonzalo. Pedro Reyes-Castillo, María Eugenia Maury, Sonia Gallina, and Exequiel Ezcurra. "La conservación del germoplasma: Soluciones en México." *Folia Entomología Mexicana* 46 (1980): 29–64.

Hamblin, Nancy L. *Animal Use by the Cozumel Maya.* Tucson: University of Arizona Press, 1984.

Hardin, Garrett. "The Tragedy of the Commons." *Science* 162 (1968): 1243–1248.

Harner, Michael. "The Ecological Basis for Aztec Sacrifice." *American Ethnologist* 4 (February 1977): 117–135.

Harris, Alex, and Margaret Sartor, eds. *Gertrude Blom—Bearing Witness.* Chapel Hill: University of North Carolina Press, 1984.

Harris, Charles H., III. *A Mexican Family Empire: The Latifundio of the Sánchez-Navarros, 1766–1867.* Austin: University of Texas Press, 1976.

Harrison, Peter D., and B. L. Turner II, eds. *Pre-Hispanic Maya Agriculture.* Albuquerque: University of New Mexico, 1978.

Hassig, Ross. "The Famine of One Rabbit: Ecological Causes and Social Consequences of a Pre-Columbian Calamity." *Journal of Anthropological Research* 37 (Summer 1981): 172–182.

Hays, Samuel P. *Beauty, Health, and Permanence: Environmental Politics in the United States, 1955–1985.* Cambridge: Cambridge University Press, 1987.

Helm, McKinley. *Modern Mexican Painters.* New York: Harper and Brothers, 1941.

Hernández, Evangelina. "Destruido, el 76% de la Selva Lacandona." *La Jornada* (Mexico City), 21 July 1990, 1, 3.

Hernández, Francisco. *Antigüedades de la Nueva España.* Ed. Ascensión H. de León-Portilla. Colección Crónicas de América 28. Madrid: Historia 16, 1986.

Hernández, Letitia. "Decretó CSG veda forestal de 3 meses en la Lacandona." *Excelsior* (Mexico City), 14 January 1989, Estados section, 1, 3.

Hernández Corzo, Rodolfo. *La administración de la fauna silvestre en México.* Folleto 21. Mexico City: Instituto Mexicano de Recursos Naturales Renovables, 1964.

Hernández Téllez, Josefina. "Las Madres Veracruzanas en la lucha nuclear." *Fem* 13 (February 1989): 35–37.

Hernández Terán, José. Secretario de Recursos Hidráulicos. *México y su política hidráulica.* Mexico City: N.p., 1967.

Herrera, Ignacio A. "Anuncia SEPESCA un programa para la protección del delfín y el aprovechamiento del atún." *Excelsior* (Mexico City), 2 April 1991, A11, A30.

Hersh, Glenda. "CSG Unveils Xochimilco Ecological Program." *The News* (Mexico City), 27 September 1989, 1, 5.

Hickel, R. "La idea forestal en México." *Revista Forestal* 3 (May 1911): 7–10.

Hittell, Theodore H. *History of California.* 4 vols. San Francisco: Pacific Publishing House and Occidental Publishing Company, 1885.

Hoberman, Louisa Schell. "Technological Change in a Traditional Society: The Case of the *Desagüe* in Colonial Mexico." *Technology and Culture* 21 (July 1980): 386–407.

Hodara, Joseph, and Iván Restrepo, eds. *¿Tiene límites el crecimiento? Una visión latino-americana.* Mexico City: Editorial El Manuel Moderno, 1977.

Hu-Dehart, Evelyn. *Missionaries, Miners, and Indians: Spanish Contact with the Yaqui Nation of Northwestern New Spain, 1533–1820.* Tucson: University of Arizona Press, 1981.

———. *Yaqui Resistance and Survival: The Struggle for Land and Autonomy, 1821–1910.* Madison: University of Wisconsin Press, 1984.

Huehue Tlatolli. Trans. of the ancient conversations or discourses by Juan de Torquemada and Alonzo de Zurita. Mexico City: Oficina tipográfica de la Secretaría de Fomento, 1901.

Humboldt, Alexander von. *Tablas geográficas políticas del reino de Nueva España y correspondencia mexicana.* Mexico City: Dirección General de Estadística, 1970.

———. *Political Essay on the Kingdom of New Spain.* Trans. from the original French by John Black. 4 vols. London: Longham, Hurst, Rees, Orme, and Brown, 1811.

Hundley, Norris, Jr. *Dividing the Waters: A Century of Controversy between the United States and Mexico.* Berkeley: University of California Press, 1966.

Hutto, Richard L. "Migratory Landbirds in Western Mexico City: A Vanishing Habitat." *Western Wildlands* 11 (Winter 1986): 12–16.

Idolatría y superstición entre los indios de Oaxaca. 2d ed. Mexico City: Ediciones Toledo, 1988.

Imamuddin, S. M. *Muslim Spain, 711–1492 A.D.: A Sociological Study.* Leiden: E. J. Brill, 1981.

"Importante llamado del Sr. Presidente [Adolfo Ruiz Cortines] en pro de la conservación de suelos: Afirma que 'El gran enemigo de nuestro progreso económico es la erosión.' " *Suelo y Agua* 3 (2 May 1955): 1, 8.

Instituto de Ecología. *El futuro del hombre en la naturaleza: Ensayos sobre reservas de la biosfera.* Mexico City: Instituto de Ecología, 1988.

————. *Homenaje a Gonzalo Halffter.* Mexico City: Instituto de Ecología, 1985.

————. *Informe de actividades del Instituto de Ecología, 1981–1982.* Mexico City: Instituto de Ecología, 1982.

Instituto de Historia Natural. *Información básica sobre el Instituto de Historia Natural.* Tuxtla Gutiérrez, Chiapas: N.p., n.d.

Instituto Mexicano de Recursos Naturales Renovables. *Aspectos internacionales de los recursos renovables de Mexico.* Mexico City: Ediciones del Instituto Mexicano de Recursos Naturales Renovables, 1972.

————. *La conservación de la naturaleza y la prensa en la América Latina.* Mexico City: Ediciones del Instituto Mexicano de Recursos Naturales Renovables, 1967.

————. *En defensa del bienestar y el futuro de nuestra patria.* Tacubaya, D.F.: Talleres de la Editorial E.C.L.A.L., 1953.

————. *Mesas redondas sobre Chiapas y sus recursos naturales renovables.* Mexico City: Ediciones del Instituto Mexicano de Recursos Naturales Renovables, 1975.

————. *Mesas redondas sobre contribución de diversos profesiones en la conservación de los recursos naturales renovables.* Mexico City: Ediciones del Instituto Mexicano de Recursos Naturales Renovables, 1966.

————. *Mesas redondas sobre desarrollo y ecología.* Mexico City: Ediciones del Instituto Mexicano de Recursos Naturales Renovables, 1974.

————. *Mesas redondas sobre problemas de agua en México.* Mexico City: Ediciones del Instituto Mexicano de Recursos Naturales Renovables, 1965.

————. *Mesas redondas sobre utilización y conservación del suelo en México.* Mexico City: Ediciones del Instituto Mexicano de Recursos Naturales Renovables, 1969.

Instituto Mexicano de Recursos Naturales Renovables, 1952–1990: Semblanza. Mexico City: Tonatiuh Gutiérrez, 1990.

Instituto Mexicano de Tecnologías Apropiadas and the Instituto de Ecología. *Ecotecnología para el desarrollo de México.* Mexico City: N.p., 1982.

Iredale, Paul. "Critics Deride Mexico City Pollution Plan." *San Francisco Chronicle,* 13 March 1992, A22.

Ixtlilxóchitl, Fernando de Alva. *Historia de la nación chichimeca.* Ed. Germán Vázquez Chamorro. Colección Crónicas de América 11. Madrid: Historia 16, 1985.

Jardel P., E.J., coordinator. *Estrategia para la conservación de la Biosfera Sierra de Manantlán,.* El Grullo, Jalisco: Laboratorio Natural Las Joyas, Universidad de Guadalajara, 1990.

Jehl, Douglas, and Rudy Abramson, "Bush to Seek $100 Million Extra for Border Cleanup." *Los Angeles Times,* 23 January 1992, A1, A22.

Jennings, Bruce H. *Foundations of International Agricultural Research: Science and Politics in Mexican Agriculture.* Boulder, Col.: Westview Press, 1988.

"Jersey Pioneers [Charles Lathrop Pack]," *Asbury (N.J.) Park Sunday Press,* 16 May 1971, F2.

Jones, Ellen, and Glen Wersch. "Developing a Natural Balance." *Americas* 42.3 (1990): 27–35.

Jornada sobre ecología en los asentamientos humanos. Mexico City: N.p., 1977.

Jose María Velasco, 1840–1912. Exhibition organized by the Philadelphia Museum of Art and the Brooklyn Museum with the collaboration of the Dirección General de Educación Extra-Escolar y Estética, Mexico City. Philadelphia—11 November–10 December 1944, Brooklyn—10 January–25 February 1945. Note on Velasco's paintings by Henry Clifford.

Juárez C., Juan Manuel. "Un árbol a cada niño que nazca aquí." *La Prensa* (Mexico City), 6 June 1990, 3.

Juffer, Jane. "Clouds of Concern Near Toxic Plants," *San Francisco Chronicle*, 16 November 1988, Briefing section, 2.

———. "Mexican Border a Chemical Nightmare." *San Francisco Chronicle*, 16 November 1988, Briefing section, 2.

Kaufman, Wallace. "The Zoo in the Forest." *Orion* 9 (Autumn 1990): 26–35.

Kelly, Mary E. *Nafta's Environmental Side Agreement: A Review and Analysis.* Austin: Texas Center for Policy Studies, 1993.

Ker, Annita Melville. *A Survey of Mexican Scientific Periodicals.* Baltimore: Waverly Press, 1931.

Kishler, Jean. "San Miguel Audubon Society." *Audubon Leader.* Southwest Region. February–March 1989.

Klein, Cecelia F. *The Face of the Earth: Frontality in Two-Dimensional Mesoamerican Art.* New York: Garland Publishing Company, 1976.

Klein, Julius. *The Mesta: A Study in Spanish Economic History, 1273–1836.* Cambridge: Harvard University Press, 1920; rpt. Port Washington, N.Y.: Kennikat Press, 1964.

Kroeber, Clifton B. *Man, Land, and Water: Mexico's Farmlands Irrigation Policies, 1885–1911.* Berkeley: University of California Press, 1983.

Lajous, Alejandra, comp. *Las razones y las obras: Gobierno de Miguel de la Madrid Crónica del sexenio, 1982–1988.* 6 vols. Mexico City: Fondo de Cultura Económica, 1982–1988.

Lambari, Mauricio Athié. "El desarrollo de la politica ecología en México." In Subdirección de Transformación Industrial. Gerencia de Protección Ecológica. Industrial Petroleros Mexicanos. *Memoria de ExpoEcología.* Ciclo de Conferencias, 21 noviembre–7 diciembre, Refinería 18 de marzo.

Landa, Diego de. *Relación de las cosas de Yucatán.* Ed. Miguel Rivera Dorado. Colección Crónicas de América 7. Madrid: Historia 16, 1985.

"La larga marcha de los ecólogos mexicanos: Entrevista con Arturo Gómez-Pompa." *Nexos* 6 (September 1983): 25–29.

Larmer, Brook. "Monarch's Wonderland under Siege in Mexico." *Christian Science Monitor,* 29 December 1988, 1, 24.

———. "New Program Thins Smog, Streets." *Christian Science Monitor,* 31 January 1990, 3.

Las Casas, Bartolomé de. *Historia de las Indias.* Ed. Agustín Millares Carlo. Foreword by Lewis Hanke. 3 vols. Mexico City: Fondo de Cultura Económica, 1951.

———. *Los indios de México y Nueva España.* 2d. ed. Ed. Edmundo O'Gorman of the Academia de la Historia with the collaboration of Jorge Alberto Manrique. Mexico City: Editorial Porrúa, 1971.

Lee, Julian C. "Creatures of the Maya." *Natural History* 99 (January 1990): 45–51.

Lees, Susan H. "Oaxaca's Spiraling Race for Water." *Natural History* 84 (April 1975): 30–39.

Leopold, A. Starker. "Status of Mexican Big Game Herds." In *Transactions of the Twelfth North American Wildlife Conference.* 437–448. Washington, D.C.: Wildlife Management Institute, 1947.

———. *Wildlife of Mexico City: The Game Birds and Mammals.* Berkeley: University of California Press, 1959.

Leopold, Aldo. "Conservationist in Mexico." *American Forests* 43 (March 1937): 118–120, 146.

———. *A Sand County Almanac.* New York: Oxford University Press, 1949.

"Letter from the Editor." *Mexico City News,* 11 December 1988, 2.

Levy, Daniel, and Gabriel Székely. *Mexico: Paradoxes of Stability and Change.* Boulder, Col.: Westview Press, 1983.

Ley Forestal, su reglamento y reformas. Durango, Mexico: Ediciones de el Mensajero Forestal, 1952.

Ley Forestal y su reglamento. Mexico City: Ediciones del Departamento de Divulgación Forestal y de Fauna, 1961.

Ley sobre aprovechamiento de aguas de jurisdicción federal de 13 de diciembre de 1910 y reglamento de la misma de 31 de enero de 1911. Hermosillo, Sonora: Imprenta del Gobierno del Estado, 1912.

Lobato González, Rodolfo. "Terrazas prehispánicas en la Selva Lacandona y su importancia en sistemas de producción agrícola." Publicación 28, 3:11–34. In *Alternativas para el uso del suelo en areas forestales del trópico húmedo.* Publicación Especial 26–29, 38. 5 vols. Mexico City: Instituto Mexicano de Investigaciones Forestales, 1981–1982.

Locke, John. *The Second Treatise of Government.* Ed. Thomas P. Peardon. New York: Macmillan Publishing Company, 1962.

López, Rigoberta. "El rescate de Xochimilco." *Unomásuno* (Mexico City), 21 October 1989, 10.

López Portillo y Ramos, Manuel, comp. *El medio ambiente en México: Temas, problemas, alternativas.* Mexico City: Fondo de Cultura Económica, 1982.

Losado, Teresa, and Victor Manuel Juárez. "Chiapas es actualmente una de las últimas grandes de extensiones de bosques de niebla: Alvarez del Toro." *Unomásuno* (Mexico City), 24 November 1987, 14.

Lumholtz, Karl. *Unknown Mexico City: A Record of Five Years' Exploration among the Tribes of the Western Sierra Madre; in the Tierra Caliente of Tepic and Jalisco; and among the Tarascos of Michoacán.* Introd. Evon Z. Vogt. 2 vols. New York: AMS Press, 1973. Reprint of 1902 edition.

Lyons, Richard D. "Gertrude Blom, 92; Long a Chronicler of Mayan Cultures." *New York Times,* 29 December 1993, D19.

McClung de Tapia, Emily. *Ecología y cultura en Mesoamérica.* Mexico City: Universidad Nacional Autónoma de México, 1979.

McDonnell, Patrick J. "Foreign-owned Companies add to Mexico's Pollution." *Los Angeles Times,* 18 November 1991, A1, A16, A17.

Macías Arellano, Luis. "The Future of Mexico Lies in Education." In *Transactions of the Fifteenth North American Wildlife Conference.* 7–10. Washington, D.C.: Wildlife Management Institute, 1950.

———. "Wildlife Problems in Mexico." In *Transactions of the Fourteenth North American Wildlife Conference.* 9–16. Washington, D.C.: Wildlife Management Institute, 1949.

McKeith, Malissa. "Environmental Provisions Affecting Businesses on the U.S.–
Mexico Border." *International Environment Reporter* 15 (22 April 1922): 245–258.

Madrid, Miguel de la. *Cien tesis sobre México.* Mexico City: Partido Revolucionario Institucional, 1982.

———. *Defensa ambiental.* Mexico City: Editorial Porrúa, 1982.

———. *Los grandes problemas nacionales de hoy: El reto del futuro.* Mexico City: Editorial
Diana, 1982.

———. *Prioridades nacionales: Bosques y selvas.* Cuadernos de Pensamiento Político 19.
Mexico City: Partido Revolucionario Institucional, 1982.

"Major Legislation Expected to Delegate Regulatory Powers to States, Localities." *International Environment Reporter* 10 (9 December 1987): 654–655.

Marco del Pont, Luis. *El crimen de la contaminación.* Mexico City: UNAM, 1984.

Martin, Calvin Luther, *In the Spirit of the Earth: Rethinking History and Time.* Baltimore:
Johns Hopkins University Press, 1992.

Martínez, Henrico. *Reportorio de los tiempos e historia natural de Nueva España.* Introd.
Francisco de la Maza. Bibliographic appendix by Francisco González de Cossío.
Mexico City: Secretaría de Educación Pública, 1948.

Meadows, Donella, et al. *The Limits of Growth.* New York: Universe Books, 1972.

Mediz Bolio, Antonio. *La tierra del faisán y del venado.* Lecturas Mexicanas 97. Segunda
serie. Mexico City: Secretaría de Educación Pública, Dirección General de Publicaciones y Medios, 1987.

Meislin, Richard J. "In Devastated Mexican Area, the Anger Persists." *New York Times*,
6 December 1984, A6.

———. "Smog Bound Mexico: Has It Seen the Light?" *New York Times*, 25 June 1985,
A2.

Melville, Elinor G. K. "Environmental and Social Change in the Valle del Mezquital,
Mexico, 1521–1600." *Comparative Studies in Society and History* 32 (January 1990):
24–53.

———. *A Plague of Sheep: Environmental Consequences of the Conquest of Mexico.* Studies
in Environment and History. New York: Cambridge University Press, 1994.

Memoria del Segundo Congreso Mexicano de Ciencias Sociales. Organizado por la Sociedad
Mexicana de Geografía y Estadística y que se reunió en octubre de 1945. 5 vols.
Mexico City: N.p., 1946.

"Mensaje del C. Presidente de la República, General Lázaro Cárdenas, radiado al
pueblo mexicano el 1º de enero de 1935, en lo concerniente a la creación del Departamento Autónomo Forestal y de Caza y Pesca." *Boletín del Departamento Forestal y de Caza y Pesca* 1 (September–October 1935): 36–38.

"Mexican Fishermen Win Fight over Bay." *San Francisco Chronicle*, 1 August 1992, A20.

"Mexican President Salinas Well-Deserving of Environment Award, Conservationists
Say." *International Environment Reporter* 14 (5 June 1991): 308.

"Mexican-U.S. Dispute over Colorado River Salt Content." *Hispanic American Reports*
15 (May 1962): 207–208.

Mexico. Comisión de Papaloapan. *General Plan for the Rectification of the Papaloapan
River.* Mexico City: N.p., 1949.

Mexico. Comisión Nacional de Irrigación. *Apuntes para la historia de los aprovechamien-
tos hidráulicos en México.* Colaboración al Primer Congreso Mexicano de Ciencias
Sociales organizado por la B. Sociedad Mexicana de Geografía y Estadística. Mexico
City: N.p., 1941.

———. *La obra de la Comisión Nacional de Irrigación durante el régimen del Sr. Gral. de División Lázaro Cárdenas*. 2 vols. Mexico City: Estados Unidos Mexicanos, 1940.

Mexico. Dirección General de Conservación del Suelo y Agua. *Principales acciones del programa de conservación del suelo y agua realizado durante el sexenio, 1977–1982.* Mexico City: Secretaría de Agricultura y Recursos Hidráulicos, 1982.

———. Secretaría de Fomento. *El corte de maderas en bosques y terrenos nacionales.* Mexico City: Secretaría de Fomento, 1885.

———. Secretaría de la Presidencia. *Medio ambiente humano: Problemas ecológicos nacionales.* Mexico City: Secretaría de la Presidencia, 1972.

Mexico City. Archivo Histórico de la Ciudad de México. *Arboledas.* Inventario 368, expediente 6. "Orden suprema para se planten árboles en todas las calzadas públicas," 1866.

———. Archivo General de la Nación. Fondo: Fomento y Obras Públicas. Serie: Decretos, Circulares, y Leyes. "Circular en la que se establece que a partir del 1° de octubre se pondrá en practica el nuevo reglamento sobre el corte de madera en terrenos nacionales," 19 September 1881.

———. "Disposición para que los extranjeros residentes en la República pueden adquirir propiedades de todos tipos incluso de minas," 1856.

———. "Disposición para que todos los buques nacionales o extranjeros deban tener permiso para exportar maderas de construcción de ebanistería," 1854.

———. "Prohibición de tirar con armas de fuegos a los pájaros que se encuentran en las islas y costas de parte de los buques nacionales o extranjeros que se acercan a ellos para cargo guano," 1854.

———. Fondo: Presidentes. Serie: Miguel Alemán. Secretaría de Agricultura y Ganadería. Dirección General de Conservación del Suelo y Agua. "Programa de trabajo para los distritos de conservación del suelo y agua," 1948.

———. Serie: Lázaro Cárdenas. "Cargos contra Jefe Miguel Angel de Quevedo."

———. Letter from Ing. Salvador Guerrero to Luis I. Rodríguez, 14 February 1936.

———. "Pide el cese de Efraín Chaparro, como Jefe de la Sección-Forestal y de Caza y Pesca, en virtud de que hostiliza a los tablajeros, leñadores, etc., imponiendoles fuertas y continuas multas."

———. Letter from Miguel Angel de Quevedo to Lázaro Cárdenas, 9 November 1939.

———. Letter from Miguel Angel de Quevedo to Lázaro Cárdenas, 3 April 1936. "Informe sobre la exploración de los lagos de Pátzcuaro y Zirauén, Michoacán."

———. Letter from Miguel Angel de Quevedo to Lázaro Cárdenas, 30 April 1935. "Sobre la destrucción de los bosques en Chiapas."

———. Miguel Angel de Quevedo, "Informe que rinde el Ciudadano Jefe del Departamento Forestal y de Caza y Pesca al Ciudadano Presidente de la República, sobre la exploración forestal y de caza y pesca, a la región sureste," 1937.

———. Miguel Angel de Quevedo, "Informe sobre la exploración forestal llevado a cabo por el jefe del ramo en la región del camino México-Morelia-Guadalajara y en la región norte de Jalisco," 1939.

———. Letter from Miguel Angel de Quevedo to Luis I. Rodríguez, 27 November 1935. "Se informe sobre gira en el asunto de pesca y el asunto forestal en la ciudad de Monterrey y otras poblaciones fronterizas: Dandose a conocer proyectos para los lugares de visitar."

———. "Se informe sobre el estado actual de la organización de la pesca y sus beneficios a la nación," 8 February 1939.

————. Serie: Obregón y Calles. Secretaria de Agricultura y Fomento. Dirección Forestal y de Caza y Pesca. Circular 17 de mayo de 1922 [on the need to prevent deforestation].

————. "Se pide dictar disposiciones para evitar el uso de explosivos en la explotación de pescas," 17 May 1922.

————. Ramo de Cedulas Reales Duplicados, volumen 5, expediente 740. "Licensia para cazar con arcabuz."

————. Ramo de Desagüe, volumen 17, expediente 12. Joseph Antonio Alzate y Ramírez, "Proyecto para desaguar la Laguna de Tescuco y por consiguente las de Chalco y San Cristóval, según las circunstancias, assequible y por el poco costo, apreciable, fundado sobre varias obserbaciones phisicas que comprueban so no difícil execución," 1767.

————. Ramo de Ordenanzas I. "Ordenanza sobre el pastos de ovejas," 19 November 1603, 109v–110.

————. Ordenanzas de Mesta para ganados mayores y menores 81. "No se pegue fuegos en los montes, campos ni caunas," 28.

————. "Para que se observe la ordenanza inserte tocante a la caza," 9 November 1580, 61–61v.

————. "Para que se observe la ordenanza sobre la caza que hizo el Virrey Martín Enríquez (31 octubre 1569)," 31 October 1589, 94–94v.

————. "Se confirme el mandamiento expedido por el corregidor de Veracruz, para que sin su licencia no se pueda salir a cazar en dos leguas de contorno de la ciudad," 12 August 1611, 138.

————. Ramo de Ordenanzas II. "Ordenanza para que se disponga la madera que no tenga marca," 1 October 1579, 229.

————. "Que se guarda la ordenanza hecho por el conde de Monterrey, tocante a cacería con arcabuz," 23 December 1603, 145.

————. "Sobre la orden del cortar en los montes de Yaleo (Chalco)," 21 March 1579, 225v–226.

————. Serie: Bosques. Caja 3, expediente 29. Secretaría de Fomento. Dirección de Bosques. Departamento de Administración. "Comisión de Parasitología Agrícola, denuncia caza inmoderada de garzas en Tehuantepec, Estado de Oaxaca," 22 February 1906.

————. Serie: Bosques. Caja 3, expediente 31. Secretaría de Fomento. Dirección de Bosques. Departamento de Administración. "Se pide a la Dirección General de Obras Públicas autorice a la Junta Central de Bosques para intervenir en todos aquellos montes que están al cuidado de dicha dirección," 9 May 1906.

————. Serie: Bosques. Caja 52, expediente 3. Secretaría de Fomento. Dirección de Bosques. Departamento de Administración. "Informe de los trabajos llevados a cabo por la Sección 3a del Departamento de Bosques, desde el 1º de julio de 1913 al 16 de febrero del año de 1914."

Mexico City Makes Little Progress in Combating Large-Scale Air Pollution." *International Environment Reporter* 10 (14 October 1987): 501–502.

"Mexico City Says L.A.'s Smog Is Worse." *San Francisco Chronicle*, 29 March 1991, World news, A22.

"Mexico City Smog Hits Danger Levels; Industries Forced to Cut Activity." *International Environment Reporter* 15 (25 March 1992): 163.

"Mexico Considers Wind Machines to Fight Smog." *Reno Gazette-Journal,* 23 February 1992, A14.

México Desconocido/Parques Nacionales. Special edition. 2 (July 1992), 2d ed.

"Mexico Finances New Vehicles." *Reno Gazette-Journal* 20 March 1991, A4.

"México Forestal." *México Forestal* 1 (January 1923): 1–2.

Mexico National Railway Company. *Mexico National Railway: Confidential [Report].* Philadelphia: Edward Stern, 1872.

"Mexico Signs CITES Treaty." *International Environment Reporter* 14 (31 July): 431.

"Mexico Swaps Debt for Nature Conservation." *Orion* 10 (Spring 1991): 62.

"Mexico, United States Agree on Cleanup of Pollution along Border, Sharing Costs." *International Environment Reporter* 12 (13 September 1989): 457–458.

Meyer, H. Arthur. "Forestry in Mexico." *Chronica Botanica* 6 (November 1941): 395–399.

Meyer, Michael C. *Water in the Hispanic Southwest: A Social and Legal History, 1550–1850.* Tucson: University of Arizona Press, 1984.

Micallef, Benjamin Anthony. "The Forest Policy of Mexico." Master's thesis, University of California, Berkeley, 1955.

Miguel Alvarez del Toro: Bibliografía. Comp. Rosa Marchetta Alonso. Centro de Información para la Conservación. Tuxtla Gutiérrez, Chiapas: Instituto de Historial Natural and FUNDAMAT, 1989.

Monje, Raúl. "Ni siquiera planes contra la contaminación existe reconoce SEDUE." *Proceso* 482 (27 January 1986): 6–9.

Moral, Camilo del. "Los recursos forestales." *Boletín de la Sociedad Mexicana de Geografía y Estadística* 68 (July–October 1949): 169–.

Morales, Héctor Luis. *¿La revolución azul? Acuacultura y ecodesarrollo.* Centro de Ecodesarrollo. Programa de Naciones Unidas para el Medio Ambiente. Mexico City: Editorial Nueva Imagen, 1978.

Morfi, Juan Agustín de. *Viaje de indios y diario de Nuevo México.* Bibliographic introd. and annotations by Vito Alessio Robles. Mexico City: Antigua Librería Robredo de José Porrúa y Hijos, 1935.

Mota y Escobar, Alonso de la. *Descripción geográfica de los reinos de Nueva Galacia, Nueva Vizcaya, y Nuevo León.* Introd. Joaquín Ramírez Cabañas. Mexico City: Editorial Pedro Robredo, 1940.

Movimiento Ecologista Mexicano. "México ante la Convención sobre el Comercio Internacional de Especies Amenazadas de Fauna y Flora Silvestre (CITES)," Press release, 30 July 1987.

Mulvey, Ruth Watt. "Mexico Unlocks Its Timber Resources." *American Forests* 57 (October 1951): 20–22, 62–64.

Mumme, Stephen P. "Clearing the Air: Environmental Reform in Mexico." *Environment* 33 (December 1991): 7–11, 26–30.

———. "System Maintenance and Environmental Reform in Mexico City: Salinas's Preemptive Strategy." *Latin American Perspectives* 19 (Winter 1992): 123–143.

———. "U.S.-Mexican Groundwater Problems: Bilateral Prospects and Implications." *Journal of Interamerican Studies and World Affairs* 22 (February 1980): 31–55.

Mumme, Stephen P., C. Richard Bath, and Valerie J. Assetto. "Political Development and Environmental Policy in Mexico." *Latin American Research Review* 23.1 (1988): 7–34.

Musgrave, M. E. "The Apostle of the Tree." *American Forests* 46 (May 1940): 203–205, 224–225.

Mydans, Seth. "U.S. and Mexico Take on a Joint Burden: Sewage." *New York Times*, 22 August 1990, A18.

Nabhan, Gary Paul, and Thomas Edward Sheridan. "Living Fencerows on the Río San Miguel, Sonora, Mexico: Traditional Technology of Floodplain Management." *Human Ecology* 5 (June 1977): 97–111.

Nannetti, Guilermo, and Emma Reyes. *Cartilla del Suelo: "Historia de Antonio Arango."* Mexico City: Editorial Ruta, 1950.

Nash, Roderick. *Wilderness and the American Mind.* 3d ed. New Haven: Yale University Press, 1982.

Nations, James D. "The Lacandones, Gertrude Blom, and the Selva Lacandona." In *Gertrude Blom—Bearing Witness,* ed. Alex Harris and Margaret Sator. Chapel Hill: University of North Carolina Press, 1984.

Nations, James D., and Ronald B. Nigh. "The Evolutionary Potential of Sustained-Yield Tropical Forest Agriculture." *Journal of Anthropological Research* 36 (Spring 1980): 1–30.

Nava Vázquez, Telésforo. "Once aspirinas contra la contaminación." *Unomásuno* (Mexico City), 11 April 1991, 11.

Navarro, Samano José. "La conservación de suelos en México hasta 1952." *Suelo y Agua* 2 (1 November 1954): 9.

"New Law Takes Effect, Enveloping 1982 Law; Penalties Based on Norms Not Yet Developed," *International Environment Reporter* 11 (13 April 1988): 249–250.

"New Omnibus Pollution Control Law Requires Environmental Impact Statements." *International Environment Reporter* 5 (13 January 1982): 4–5.

Nigh, Ronald. Asociación de Dana, Mexico City. Interview, 16 October 1989.

"Noviembre 25 de 1854.—Se piden a las diputaciones de minería noticias de los bosques y su extensión." In *Código de colonización y terrenos baldíos de la República Mexicana años de 1451 a 1892.* 582. Comp. Francisco F. de la Maza. Mexico City: Secretaría de Fomento.

Novísima recopilación de las leyes de España. 6 vols. Madrid, 1829.

"Nuestra Revista Forestal." *Revista Forestal Mexicana* 1 (July 1909): 1–2.

"Nuevos prejucios a la agricultura." *El Tiempo* (Mexico City), 9 June 1905.

Ogden, Adele. *The California Sea Otter Trade, 1784–1848.* California Library Reprint Series. University of California Publications in History 26. Berkeley: University of California Press, 1975.

Ordenanzas de tierras y aguas. 5th ed. Abridged by Mariano Galván Rivera. Paris: Librería de Rosa y Bouret, 1868.

"Ordenanzas de 27 de agosto de 1803.—Para el gobierno de los montes y arbolados." In *Código de colonización y terrenos baldíos de la República Mexicana años de 1451 a 1892.* 50–145. Comp. Francisco F. de la Maza. Mexico City: Secretaría de Fomento, 1893.

Ordenes y circulares espedidas por el supremo gobierno desde el año de 1825 hasta la fecha para arreglo y legitimidad del comercio marítimo nacional. Mexico City: Imprenta del Aguila, 1830.

Organization of American States. *Ninth International Conference on the Conservation of Renewable Natural Resources.* 6 vols. Final Act. Inter-American Conference of Renewable Natural Resources. Bogota: Ministerio de Relaciones Exteriores de Colombia, 1953.

Oropesa, Gabriel M. "Las lluvias en Necaxa no han disminuido." *Memorias y Revista de la Sociedad Científica "Antonio Alzate"* 43 (April 1921): 401–407.

Orozco, Enrique. "Utilidad de los pájaros en agricultura." *Memorias y Revista de la Sociedad Científica "Antonio Alzate"* 37 (April 1921): 401–407.

Orozco Jiménez, Francisco. "El apóstol del árbol." *México Forestal* 25 (April–June 1947): 32–34.

Ortega Pizarro, Fernando. "Ya obsoleta y con todo y fallas se puso en operación Laguna Verde." *Proceso* 720 (20 August 1990): 6, 8–11.

Ortiz Monasterio, Fernando, Isabel Fernández Tijero, Alicia Castillo, José Ortiz Monasterio, and Alfonso Bulle. *Tierra profanada: Historia ambiental de México.* Mexico City: Instituto Nacional de Antropología e Historia and Secretaría de Desarrollo Urbano y Ecología, 1987.

Ortiz Monasterio, Fernando, and Valentina Ortiz Monasterio Garza. *Mariposa Monarca: Vuelo del papel.* Coyoacán, D.F.: Centro de Información y Desarrollo de la Comunicación de la Literatura Infantiles, 1987.

Osorio Tafall, B. F. "La planficación del aprovechamiento de los recursos naturales renovables en relación con la industrialización de México." *Boletín de la Sociedad Mexicana de Geografía y Estadística* 65 (March–June 1948): 223–258.

———. "Soil and Water Problems in Mexico." *Journal of Soil and Water Conservation* 4 (1949): 59–66.

Pack Forestry Foundation. *Ten Years of Fact-Finding: A Review of the Accomplishments of the Charles Lathrop Pack Forestry Foundation.* Washington, D.C.: Charles Lathrop Pack Forestry Foundation.

Palavicini, Felix Fulgencio. *Grandes de México.* Mexico City: Bolivariana Departamento Editorial, 1948.

Palerm, Angel. *Obras hidráulicas prehispánicas: En el sistema lacustre del Valle de México.* Mexico City: Instituto Nacional de Antropología e Historia, 1973.

Partido Revolucionario Institucional and Instituto de Estudios Politicos, Económicos y Sociales. *Medio ambiente y la calidad de la vida.* Reuniones de Consulta Popular para la Planeación Democrática, January–April 1982. Mexico City: Imprenta Madero, 1982.

Partido Verde Mexicano. "Los integrantes del Partido Verde Mexicano nos pronunciamos," Press release, n.d.

———. "Opinión del Partido Verde Mexicano, sobre el proyecto de rescate de Xochimilco y el programa de un día sin automóvil. Anuncio de la integración a la campaña contra la crueldad hacia los animales," Press release, 1990.

Patiño, Lorenzo R. *Conservación de los suelos en México.* Mexico City: Comisión Nacional de Irrigación, 1942.

———. Delegate of the National Irrigation Commission of Mexico to the VI Scientific Congress of the Pacific. *A Few Observations on Soil Erosion Control in the Central Plateau of Mexico.* Mexico City: N.p., 1939.

———. *México y su programa de conservación del suelo.* Presentada a la Tercera Conferencia Interamericana de Agricultura. Mexico City: N.p., 1945.

———. *La organización del Servicio de Conservación del Suelo y Agua Mexicano.* Mexico City: N.p., 1949.

————. "Los problemas del agua y del suelo." *Boletín de la Sociedad Mexicana de Geografía y Estadística* 68 (July–October 1949): 131–141.

Payno, Manuel. "Bosques y arbolados." *Boletín de la Sociedad de Geografía y Estadística de la República Mexicana*, 2ª época, 2 (1870): 77–94.

"Pemex Blamed for Blasts That Took 452 Lives." *Los Angeles Times*, 23 December 1984, 5.

Peniche B., Roldán. *Bestiario mexicano*. Mexico City: Panorama Editorial, 1987.

Pepito y el árbol. Mexico City: Ediciones del Departamento de Divulgación Forestal y de Fauna. Mexico, ca. 1960.

Peralta, Carlos M. *Estudio sobre los bosques de Uruapan*. Morelia, Michoacán: Tip. Arte y Trabajo, 1931.

Perera, Víctor, and Robert D. Bruce. *The Last Lords of Palenque: The Lacandón Mayas of the Mexican Rain Forests*. Boston: Little, Brown, and Company, 1982.

Pérez Castro, Lorenzo. "Palabras sobre la vida y obra del Sr. Ing. Miguel A. de Quevedo." *México Forestal* 23 (October–December 1946): 64–70.

Perlin, John. *A Forest Journey: The Role of Wood in the Development of Civilization*. New York: W. W. Norton, 1989.

"A Plea for Mexico." *World Press Review* 45 (October 1989): 45, 47.

Pocantico Hills, New York. Rockefeller Foundation Archives. R.G. 1.1. Series 323: Mexico Agriculture. Box 1. Letter from Marte R. Gómez to Raymond Fosdick, 2 April 1943.

————. Box 2. Letter from J. G. Harrar to Dr. Warren Weaver, 24 February 1947.

————. Box 3. Background Report by Warren Weaver, 30 September 1950.

————. R.G. 1.2. Series 323: Agriculture-Agreements 1936, 1941–1943. Box 11. "Proposiciones para un memorándum de entendimiento entre la Secretaría de Agricultura y Fomento de México y la Fundación Rockefeller," 1943.

————. Agriculture-Agreements 1948–1954. Box 11. Letter from J. G. Harrar to Warren Weaver, 15 January 1954.

————. Series 323D: Mexico Natural Science and Agriculture. Folder 318. Instituto Mexicano de Recursos Naturales Renovables. Grant in Aid to Mexican Institute of Natural Resources, 3 June 1957.

Poder Ejecutivo Federal. *Plan Nacional de Desarrollo, 1989–1994*. Mexico City: Secretaría de Programación y Presupuesto, 1989.

————. *Programa Nacional de Ecología, 1984–1988*. Mexico City: N.p., 1984.

————. Secretaría de Gobernación. "Ley Federal del Mar." *Diario Oficial*, 8 January 1986, 3–9.

Pohl, Mary, ed. *Prehistoric Lowland Maya Environment and Subsistence Economy*. Papers of the Peabody Museum of Archeology and Ethnology 77. Cambridge: Harvard University Press, 1985.

"Política, estrategia, y líneas de acción para el desarrollo de acuacultura, 1989–1994." *Acuavisión*, año IV, 2ª época, 17 (November–December 1989): 10–12.

Pollard, Helen Perlstein, and Shirley Gornstein. "Agrarian Potential, Population, and the Tarascan State." *Science* 209 (11 July 1980): 274–277.

"Polution." *The News* (Mexico City), 29 July 1990, 4.

Pomar, Juan Bautista. *Relación de Tezcoco*. Ed. Joaquín García Icazbalceta. Facsimile of the 1891 edition. Mexico City: Biblioteca Enciclopedia del Estado de México, 1975.

Popul Vuh. Trans. Dennis Tedlock. New York: Simon and Schuster, 1985.

Powell, Frank William. *The Railroads of Mexico.* Boston: Stratford Publishers, 1921.

Prado, Julio. *El apóstol del árbol: Biografía del Señor Ingeniero don Miguel Angel de Quevedo.* Mexico City: Emilio Pardo e Hijos, 1936.

Proceedings of the Inter-American Conference on Conservation of Renewable Natural Resources. Denver, Colorado, 7-20 September 1948. Washington, D.C.: U.S. Department of State, l948.

"Pro-Dolphin Accord Made." *New York Times,* 16 July 1992, D9.

Protección a la Naturaleza. 4 vols. Mexico City: D.A.P.P., 1935–1939.

"La protección a las aves útiles a la agricultura." *Boletín de la Secretaría de Fomento,* 3ª época, 5 (July 1906): 1–22.

"Proyecto de Ley Forestal y de Arboledas." *México Forestal* 1 (February 1923): 1–8.

Quevedo, Miguel Angel de. *Algunas consideraciones sobre nuestro problema agrario.* Mexico City: Victoria, 1916.

———. "Anteproyecto del plan sexenal para el período 1941–1946 en los ramos forestales." *Boletín del Departamento Forestal y de Caza y Pesca* 4 (March–May 1939): 1–18.

———. "Breve reseña de los fundamentos y métodos que han servido para la formación del catálogo forestal de la República." *Revista Forestal Mexicana* 2 (October 1911): 124–131.

———. "La ciudad de Mexico no se hunde por la falta lagos en sus alrededores." *Memorias y Revista de la Sociedad Científica "Antonio Alzate"* 41 (July 1922): 49–61.

———. "Conferencia Internacional Norteamericana sobre Conservación de Recursos Naturales celebradas en Washington durante los días del 18 al 24 de febrero de 1909." *Revista Forestal Mexicana* 1 (October 1909): 78–85.

———. *Conveniencia de estudiar todas las circunstancias en que se distribuye el agua pluvial que cae en las varias cuencas del territorio, de coordinar las observaciones pluviométricas con las de hidrometría en las mismas cuencas, así como también de que se expidan las leyes conducentes á la conservación y repoblación de los bosques.* Trabajo presentado al Congreso Meteorológico Nacional reunido en México del 17 al 20 de diciembre 1901 por el Señor Miguel A. de Quevedo delegado de la Camara de Comercio de Guadalajara a dicho Congreso. Guadalajara: Ancira y Hno. Imp., 1902.

———. "La creación de los parques nacionales y sus ventajas." *Boletín del Departamento Forestal y de Caza y Pesca* 4 (December–February 1939): 61–64.

———. *La cuestión forestal en México y medidas conviene adoptar para su resolución.* Mexico City: Secretaría de Fomento, 1909.

———. "Los desastres de la deforestación en el Valle y Ciudad de México." *México Forestal* 4 (May–June 1926): 67–82.

———. "La desolación forestal de las regiones circunvencias al camino nacional de México a Acapulco." *Memorias y Revista de la Sociedad Científica "Antonio Alzate"* 49 (1929): 375–378.

———. *Espacios libres y reservas forestales de las ciudades: Su adaptación a jardines, parques, y lugares de juego.* Conferencia dada en la Exposición de Higiene por el Ingeniero Miguel Quevedo, Vocal del Consejo Superior de Salubridad, Jefe del Departamento de Bosques. Mexico City: Gomar y Busson, 1911.

———. "La influencia de los bosques en la precipitación pluvial: Su aplicación al territorio mexicano." *Memorias y Revista de la Sociedad Científica "Antonio Alzate"* 43 (January–February 1924): 47–63.

―――. "Informe de los principales trabajos desarrollados por el Departamento Forestal y de Caza y Pesca, en cumplimiento del plan sexenal desde mayo de 1937." *México Forestal* 16 (July–September 1938): 39–47.

―――. "Informe sobre la exploración forestal y de caza y pesca llevado a cabo en la región del sureste del territorio mexicano." *Boletín del Departamento Forestal y de Caza y Pesca* 4 (June–August 1939): 1–19.

―――. "Informe sobre los principales trabajos desarrollados por el Departamento Forestal y de Caza y Pesca durante el año de 1936." *México Forestal* 15 (January–February 1937): 3–9.

―――. "Informe sobre los principales trabajos emprendidos por la Junta Central de Bosques y Arbolados durante el año fiscal 1909–1910, rendido al C. Secretario de Fomento por el Presidente de la Junta, el 30 de junio de 1910." *Revista Forestal Mexicana* 1 (June 1910): 255–266.

―――. *La iniciación de la campaña de protección forestal del territorio nacional y sus desarrollos sucesivos y tropiezos.* Mexico City: N.p., 1941.

―――. "La Junta Central de Bosques." *Revista Forestal Mexicana* 1 (July 1909): 3–12.

―――. *Memoria del Departamento Forestal y de Caza y Pesca.* Mexico City: D.A.P.P., 1938, 1939.

―――. *Memoria sobre el Valle de México, su desagüe y saneamiento.* Presentada a la H. Junta Directiva del Desagüe y mandada por la Secretaría de Fomento para la Exposición Internacional de Paris. Mexico City: Oficina tip. de la Secretaría de Fomento, 1889.

―――. "La necesaria expedición de leyes adecuadas." *Memorias y Revista de la Sociedad Científica "Antonio Alzate"* 37 (January 1917): 107–126.

―――. "Nota sobre la precipitación pluvial en la región de Necaxa." *Memorias y Revista de la Sociedad Científica "Antonio Alzate"* 43 (January–February 1924): 71–77, 91–93.

―――. "La organización del Servicio Forestal por el Departamento Autónomo Forestal y de Caza y Pesca y su programa de labores." *México Forestal* 13 (January–February 1935): 3–5.

―――. "Las polvaderas de los terrenos tequezquitosos del antiguo lago de Texcoco y los procedimientos de enyerbe para remediarlas." *Memorias y Revista de la Sociedad Científica "Antonio Alzate"* 40 (October–December 1922): 533–548.

―――. "El problema de la deforestación en Mexico.—Solución práctica del mismo." *México Forestal* 2 (July–August 1924): 64–69.

―――. *Relato de mi vida.* Mexico City: N.p., 1943.

Quezada, Angelica. "La naturaleza se rebela." *Unomásuno* (Mexico City), 28 April 1991, Páginauno section, 7.

Quiroz, Joe. Natural Conservancy, Phoenix, Arizona. Phone interview, 8 June 1989.

Ramírez, Román. *Zoología agrícola mexicana.* Mexico City: Oficina tip. de la Secretaría de Fomento, 1898.

Ramos, Mario. Head of the Mexican Program for the World Wildlife Fund, Washington, D.C. Interview, 7 June 1989.

Rauber, Paul. "Borderline Crazy." *Sierra* 78 (July–August 1993): 48, 50–51.

Read, Jan. *The Moors in Spain and Portugal.* Totowa, N.J.: Rowman and Littlefield, 1974.

Real ordenanzas para la dirección, régimen y gobierno del importante cuerpo de la minería de Nueva España y de su real tribunal general de orden de su magestad. Madrid, 1783.

Recopilación de las leyes destos reynos. 3 vols. Madrid: Catalina de Barrio y Angulo y Diego Díaz de la Carrera, 1640.

Recopilación de leyes de los reynos de las Indias. Facsimile of the 4th ed. printed in Madrid in 1791. 3 vols. Madrid: Consejo de la Hispanidad, 1943.

Redclift, Michael. "Mexico's Green Movement." *Ecologist* 17 (January–February 1987): 44–46.

Redondo, Mario R. "Contra la contaminación, solo leyes que no cumplen: Mora M." *Excelsior* (Mexico City), 24 January 1983, A1, A15.

Reglamento de huertas y sembrados para el territorio de la Baja California, 18 de agosto de 1862. La Paz, Mexico: Manuel Moreno y López, 1862.

Reglamento para la explotación de los bosques y terrenos baldíos y nacionales. Mexico City: Oficina tip. de la Secretaría de Fomento, 1894.

Reinhold, Robert. "Mexico Proclaims an End to Sanctuary for Polluters." *New York Times,* 18 April 1991, A20.

Relación de las ceremonias y ritos y población y gobierno de los indios de la provincia de Michoacán (1541). Facsimile reproduction of a manuscript in El Escorial with transcription, prologue, introduction, and notes by José Tudela. Revision of the Tarascan voices by José Coruña Nuñez. Foreword by Paul Kirchoff. Madrid: Aguilar, 1954.

"Relación de los parques nacionales que han sido declarados desde la creación del Departamento Forestal y de Caza y Pesca hasta el 24 de noviembre de 1939." *México Forestal* 17 (July–December 1939): 67–74.

Reyes, Tereso e hijos. *México está en peligro de perecer, por la perdida de su agricultura, a causa de la destrucción de los bosques.* Mexico City: N.p., 1932.

Reyes-Castillo, Pedro. *La fauna silvestre en el plan Balancán-Tenosique.* Mexico City: Instituto de Ecología and Instituto Nacional de Investigaciones sobre Recursos Bióticos, 1981.

Reyes Najera, Rembrandt, and Edmundo Sánchez La Fuente. "Intoxicación por plagucidas en la Comarca Lagunera durante el ciclo agrícola de 1974." *Salud Pública de México,* 5ª época, 17 (September–October 1975): 687–698.

Rickards, Constantino J. "Zoolatría entre los Zapotecas." *Memorias y Revista de la Sociedad Científica "Antonio Alzate"* 35 (September 1921): 327–337.

Río de la Loza, Leopoldo. *Escritos de Leopoldo Río de la Loza.* Comp. Juan Manuel Noriega. Published by the Ministry of Public Instruction and Fine Arts in commemoration of the first centennial of the birth of Río de la Loza. Mexico City: Imprenta de Ignacio Escalante, 1911.

Ríos, Laura, and Carlos Alonso. "Consejo de visiones guardianes de la tierra." *Unomásuno* (Mexico City), 30 April 1991, Dosmiluno section, 4–5.

Riquelme Inda, Julio. "Tres años de campaña forestal." *Boletín del Departamento Forestal y de Caza y Pesca* 4 (September–November 1938): 119–127.

Roberts, Richard. "South for the Winter." *Los Angeles Times*, 16 January 1990, C1, C9.

Rodríguez, Cecilia, "The World's Most Polluted City." *Los Angeles Times*, 21 April 1991, M1, M6.

Rojas, Rosa. "Otra emergencia real en Laguna Verde: Ecologistas." *La Jornada* (Mexico City), 25 July 1990, 15.

———. "Se admitirán 'swaps' en ecología anuncia Chirinos." *La Jornada*, 25 July 1990, 1, 8.

Roldán, Angel. "Industria ruinosa para los bosques de Chiapas." *Memorias y Revista de la Sociedad Científica "Antonio Alzate"* 44 (January–February 1925): 23–32.

———. "Movimiento forestal mexicano." *Memorias y Revista de la Sociedad Científica "Antonio Alzate"* 51 (1929): 423–429.

Romanini, Claudio, with the collaboration of Anne Berget and Solange Passari. *Ecotécnicas para el trópico húmedo con especial referencia a México y América Latina.* Centro de Ecodesarrollo del Conacyt and Programa de las Naciones Unidas para el Medio Ambiente. Mexico City: Cired-Cecodes, 1976.

Romero, Matías. "Railways in Mexico." *International Review* 13 (1892): 477–506.

Romero Gil, H. "Selvicultura." *Boletín de la Sociedad de Geografía y Estadística de la República Mexicana,* 2ª época, 1 (1869): 9–14.

Ronquillo, Víctor. "Los verdes a la contienda electoral." *Unomásuno* (Mexico City), 28 April 1991, Páginauno section, 3.

Ross, John. "Dangers in Paradise." *Sierra* 77 (July–August 1992): 44–51, 83–84, 86–88.

———. "Mexico's Reactor Still Plagued by Troubles." *Earth Island Journal* 7 (Spring 1992): 14.

Rotella, Sebastian. "Mexico Creates Fish Sanctuary." *Los Angeles Times,* 11 June 1993, A3, A6.

Ruge, Reinhart. "Las presas de almacenamiento y la conservación de los bosques." *Boletín de la Sociedad Mexicana de Geografía y Estadística* 68 (July–October 1949): 143–168.

Ruiz Benefil, Alberto. "Huehuecóyotl: El lugar del viejo, viejo coyote." *México Desconocido* 152 (July 1989): 37–41.

Runte, Alfred. *National Parks: The American Experience.* 2d ed. Lincoln: University of Nebraska Press, 1987.

Ruxton, Frederick Augustus. *Adventures in Mexico and the Rocky Mountains.* Glorieta, N.M.: Rio Grande Press, 1973.

Sachs, Ignacy. *Ecodesarrollo: Desarrollo sin destrucción.* Mexico City: Colegio de México, 1983.

Sahagún, Bernardino de. *Florentine Codex: General History of the Things of New Spain.* Trans. from Aztec into English with notes and illustrations by Charles E. Dibble and Arthur J. O. Anderson. 12 vols. Santa Fe: School of American Research and the University of Utah, 1963.

Salgado Pérez, Felipe. Director General de Conservación del Suelo y Agua de la Secretaría de Agricultura y Ganadería. *La política actual de trabajo en materia de conservación del suelo y agua.* Mexico City: N.p., 1959.

———. Secretaría de Agricultura y Ganadería. Dirección General de Conservación del Suelo y Agua. *Dinámica de la conservación del suelo y agua en México central de Amigos de la Tierra 4.* 2d ed. Mexico City: N.p., 1961.

"Salinas de Gortari Warns of Ecological Disaster." *Mexico City News,* 12 January 1989, 1.

Salonio, Antonio María. "Reglamento para la conservación y aumento de bosques." *Boletín de la Sociedad de Geografía y Estadística de la República Mexicana,* 2ª época, 1(1869): 14–20.

"Salvar el medio ambiente mediante la educación ecológica." *Unomásuno* (Mexico City), 17 October 1989, Dosmiluno section, 7.

San Cristóbal de las Casas, Chiapas. Na-Bolom House. Fray Bartolomé de Las Casas Library. Gertrude Duby Blom. "Mexico se olvida de sus tesoros." 1977. Manuscript.

———. Gertrude Duby Blom. "Páginas de mi vida, San Cristóbal y Na-Bolom, dos razones fundamentales." 1978. Manuscript.

———. Gertrude Duby Blom. "Problemas ecólogicos de los altos de Chiapas." 1978. Manuscript.

———. Gertrude Duby Blom. "Saving the Land of the Lacandón." 1973. Manuscript.

———. Gertrude Duby Blom. "La Selva Lacandona." Paper presented at the Primer Simposio de Ecología, November 1974, 1–35.

Sánchez Flores, Ramón. *Historia de la tecnología y la invención en México.* Mexico City: Fomento Cultural Banamex, 1980.

Santos Coy, José M. *Hay bosques porque llueve o. ¿Llueve porque hay bosques . . . ? (El interés individual).* San Luis Potosí: Tipografía de M. Esquivel y Compañía, 1901.

Sarukhan, José. Introduction. *Tropicus* l (Fall 1988): 1.

Schaefer, Phillip P., and Sharyn Maria Ehlers, eds. *Proceedings of the National Audubon Society's Symposium on the Birds of Mexico, Their Ecology and Conservation.* Tiburon, Cal.: Western Education Center, 1980.

Schuking, Rainer Godau. "La protección ambiental en México: Sobre la confirmación de una política pública." *Estudios Sociológicos* 3 (January–April 1985): 47–84.

Schumacher, E. F. *Small Is Beautiful: A Study of Economics as if People Mattered.* London: Blond and Briggs, 1973.

Scott, David Clark. "Mexicans Scrutinize Safety Following Guadalajara Blast." *Christian Science Monitor* 27 April 1992, 6.

———. "Mexico Shake-up Rattles Environmentalists." *Christian Science Monitor* 4 May 1992, 6.

———. "New Smog Plan for Mexico." *Christian Science Monitor* 27 March 1992, 7.

———. "Slew of Government Programs Target Dirty Air, Scarce Water." *Christian Science Monitor,* 23 October 1991, 11.

———. "US, Mexico Launch Border Cleanup." *Christian Science Monitor,* 28 February 1992, 6.

———. "US Tuna Ban May Snag Trade Talks with Mexico." *Christian Science Monitor,* 7 November 1990, 6.

Secretaría de Agricultura y Fomento. "Acuerdo que crea el Departamento de Conservación del Suelo." *Diario Oficial,* 27 April 1942, 2–3.

———. *Colección de leyes sobre tierras y demas disposiciones con las mismas.* Mexico City: Talleres Gráficos de la Nación, 1944.

———. "Ley de Caza." *Diario Oficial,* 13 September 1940, 4–5.

———. "Ley de Conservación del Suelo y Agua." *Diario Oficial,* 19 June 1946, 7–9.

———. "Ley Forestal de los Estados Unidos Mexicanos." *Diario Oficial,* 17 March 1943, 1–9.

———. "Reglamento de la Ley Forestal." *Diario Oficial,* 27 October 1927, 1–24.

———. Dirección Forestal y de Caza y Pesca. *Ley Forestal y su reglamento.* Mexico City: Talleres Gráficos de la Nación, 1932.

———. Dirección General Forestal y de Caza. *Memoria de la Primera Convención Nacional Forestal.* August 1941. Mexico City: N.p., 1942.

———. Instituto Biotécnico. *El Instituto Biotécnico al servicio del campesino.* 2d ed. Mexico City: D.A.P.P., 1939.

Secretaría de Agricultura y Ganadería. *Conservación del suelo y agua*. Mexico City: N.p., 1962.

————. *Informe de labores de la Secretaría de Agricultura y Ganadería del 1° de septiembre de 1946 al 31 de agosto de 1947*. Mexico City: Talleres Gráficos de la Nación, 1947.

————. "Ley Federal de Caza." *Diario Oficial*, 5 January 1952, 8–10.

————. "Ley Forestal." *Diario Oficial*, 10 January 1948, 3–10.

————. Dirección General de Conservación del Suelo y Agua. *La filosofía de la conservación del suelo*. Mexico City: N.p., 1962.

————. Subsecretaría Forestal y de Fauna. *Seis años de actividades forestal y de fauna, 1959–1964*. Mexico City: Secretaría de Agricultura y Ganadería, 1964.

Secretaría de Agricultura y Recursos Hidráulicos. "Ley Forestal." *Diario Oficial*, 30 May 1986, 13–28.

————. "Reglamento de la Ley Forestal." *Diario Oficial*, 13 July 1988, 7–45.

————. Subsecretaría de Infraestructura Hidráulica. *Agua y sociedad: Una historia de las obras hidráulicas en México*. Mexico City: N.p., 1980.

Secretaría de Desarrollo Urbano y Ecología. *Acuerdo de cooperación entre los Estados Unidos Mexicanos y los Estados Unidos de América sobre movimiento transfronterizos de desechos y sustancias peligrosas*. Washington, D.C.: N.p., 1986.

————. *La contaminación atmosférica en el Valle de Mexico*. Mexico City: Secretaría de Desarrollo Urbano y Ecología, 1987–1988.

————. *Ecología: Concentración de voluntades*. Mexico City: Talleres Gráficos de la Nación, 1987.

————. *Informe de los labores*. Mexico City: Secretaría de Desarrollo Urbano y Ecología, 1982–1987.

————. "Ley General del Equilibrio Ecológico y la Protección al Ambiente." *Gaceta Ecológica* 1 (June 1989): 2–32.

————. "Reglamento de la Ley General del Equilibrio Ecológico y la Protección al Ambiente en Materia de Impacto Ambiental." *Gaceta Ecológica* 1 (June 1989): 32–42.

————. "Reglamento de la Ley General del Equilibrio Ecológico y la Protección al Ambiente en Materia de Prevención y Control de la Contaminación a la Atmósfera." *Gaceta Ecológica* 1 (June 1989): 42–50.

————. "Reglamento de la Ley General del Equilibrio Ecológico y la Protección al Ambiente en Materia de Residuos Peligrosas." *Gaceta Ecológica* 1 (June 1989): 51–59.

————. Subsecretaría de Ecología. Dirección General de Normatividad y Regulación Ecológica. Cetamex, Centro de Estudios de Tecnologías Apropiadas para México. *Ciudad y medio ambiente: Calidad de vida y percepción ambiental*. Mexico City: N.p., 1986.

Secretaría de Fomento, Colonización é Industria. "Monte vedado del Mineral de Chico." *Diario Oficial*, 22 June 1988, 3–4.

Secretaría de Hacienda y Crédito Público. "Ley de Impuestos sobre la explotación forestal." *Diario Oficial*, 31 December 1935, 1558–1560.

Secretaría de Marina. "Reglamento para prevenir la contaminación del mar por vertimiento de desechos y otras materias." *Diario Oficial*, 23 March 1979, 3–8.

Secretaría de Pesca. Fideicomiso Fondo Nacional para el Desarrollo Pesquero, Fondepesca. Zenaida Martínez Torres and Jesús Octavio Abrego Ayala. *Modelo mexicano de policultivo: Una alternativa de desarrollo rural*. Mexico City: N.p., 1988.

"Una secretaría de protección a la naturaleza." *México Forestal* 36 (September–October 1962): 1–4.

Secretaría de Recursos Naturales. "Reglamento para la prevención y control de la contaminación de aguas." *Diario Oficial*, 29 March 1973, 5–12.

Secretaría de Salubridad y Asistencia. *Código Sanitario de los Estados Unidos Mexicanos*.
Mexico City: Secretaría de Salubridad y Asistencia, 1973.

——. "Ley Federal de Protección al Ambiente." *Diario Oficial*, 11 January 1982,
23–32.

——. "Ley Federal para Prevenir y Controlar la Contaminación Ambiental." *Diario
Oficial*, 23 March 1971, 8–11.

——. "Reglamento para la prevención y control de contaminación atmosférica originada por la emisión de humos y polvos." *Diario Oficial*, 17 September 1971, 2–9.

SEDUE. *Informe sobre el estado del medio ambiente en México*. Mexico City: Editores e im-
presores foc, 1986.

Segunda informe anual del Instituto Mexicano de Recursos Naturales Renovables, A.C.. Mexico City: N.p., 1954.

"Semblanzas: Ing. Agr. Gonzalo Blanco Macías." *Suelo y Agua* 1 (1 November 1953): 3.

"Setiembre 24 de 1856.—Resolución de Ministerio de Hacienda—Sobre adjudicación
de Desierto de Carmelitas." In *Legislación mexicana o colección completa de las disposiciones legislativas expedidas desde la independencia de la República*. 251–252. Comp.
Manuel Dublán and José María Lozano. Vol. 8 of 14 vols. Mexico City: Imprenta del
Comercio Dublán, a cargo de M. Lara, 1878.

Sheldon, Charles. *The Wilderness of Desert Bighorns and Seri Indians*. Phoenix: Arizona
Bighorn Sheep Society, 1979.

Shemirani, Shooka. "Conference Cites Increased Air Pollution Dangers." *Mexico City
News*, 17 January 1989, 1–2.

——. "President Cites Environmental Considerations in Development." *Mexico City
News*, 20 January 1989, 1, 3.

Las siete partidas del Rey don Alfonso el Sabio. Reproduction of the Madrid 1807 edition.
Madrid: Edición Atlas, 1972.

Silverstein, Jeff. "Blasts in Mexico Feed Fear over Growth." *San Francisco Chronicle*,
28 April 1992, A10.

Simonian, Lane. "Pesticide Use in Mexico: Decades of Abuse." *Ecologist*, 18.2–3 (1988):
82–87.

Simpson, Lesley Byrd. *Many Mexicos*. 3d ed. Berkeley: University of California Press,
1960.

Sinclair, M. A. "The Environmental Cooperation Agreement between Mexico and U.S.:
A Response to the Pollution Problem." *Cornell International Law Journal* 19 (Winter
1986): 87–142.

"Sizable Portion of SEDUE's Budget Brings Progress on Water Pollution." *International
Environment Reporter* 10 (14 October 1987): 513–514.

Snow, Anita. "Mexico State Follows D.F.'s Lead, Extends School Vacations to February
1." *Mexico City News*, 15 December 1988, 1, 30.

"SO Treatment Plant at Copper Smelter Opened to Control U.S.-Mexico Air Pollution."
International Environment Reporter 11 (14 September 1988): 491.

*Social and Environmental Consequences of Natural Resource Policies with Special Emphasis
on Biosphere Reserves*. Proceedings of the International Seminar 8–13 April 1980. Durango, Mexico. Technical Coordinators: Peter F. Ffolliott and Gonzalo Halffter.
United States Department of Agriculture. Forest Service. General Technical Report.
Rocky Mountain Region RM-88.

Sociedad de Historia Natural. *Primer concurso científico mexicano.* Mexico City: Oficina tip. de la Secretaría de Fomento, 1895.

Solis, Octavio, and Rigoberta Vásquez. "Reseña histórica de los jardines botánicos de México desde antes de las conquista hasta la época actual." *Jardín Botánico* 1 (November 1923): 4.

Solis S., Samuel. *La industria de los árboles de navidad y su importancia económica.* Mexico City: Ediciones del Instituto Mexicano de Recursos Naturales Renovables, 1962.

———. "La labor del Ingeniero Miguel A. de Quevedo en Veracruz." *México Forestal* 24 (July–September 1946): 59–62.

Sonnenfeld, David A. "Mexico's 'Green Revolution,' 1940–1980: Towards an Environmental History." *Environmental History Review* 16 (Winter 1992): 29–52.

Sosa, Antonio H. "Parque Nacional Cumbres de Ajusco." *México Forestal* 42 (April–June 1938): 31–35.

———. "Los parques nacionales de México." *México Forestal* 42 (November–December 1968): 17–30.

Sotomayor, Arturo. *La metropolí mexicana y su agonía.* Mexico City: Ciudad Universitaria, 1973.

Spores, Ronald. *The Mixtec in Ancient and Colonial Times.* Norman: University of Oklahoma Press, 1984.

Steinbeck, John. *The Log from the Sea of Cortez.* New York: Viking Penguin, 1977.

Stone, Peter. *Did We Save the Earth at Stockholm?* London: Earth Island Institute, 1972.

"Study Shows Car-less Program Effective; Two-Month Extension Announced." *International Environment Reporter* 13 (14 March 1990): 106–107.

Subdirección de Transformación Industrial. Gerencia de Protección Ecológica. Industrial Petroleros Mexicanos. *Memoria ExpoEcología.* Ciclo de Conferencias, 21 noviembre–7 diciembre, Refinería 18 de marzo. Mexico City: N.p., 1984.

Subsecretaría de Ecología. Dirección General de Conservación Ecológica de los Recursos Naturales. *La conservación de los recursos naturales en México.* Mexico City: N.p., 1987.

———. *Información básica sobre las areas naturales protegidas de México.* Mexico City: N.p., 1989.

Subsecretaría de Mejoramiento del Ambiente. *Legislación ambiental de México.* Mexico City: N.p., 1977.

———. *México: El mejoramiento del ambiente una perspectiva de la nación.* Presentación hecha por la Subsecretaría de Mejoramiento del Ambiente a la Primera Conferencia de Salud Nacional. Mexico City, July 1973.

Subsecretaría de Recursos Forestales y de Caza. *Memoria de la Segunda Convención Nacional Forestal.* Mexico City: N.p., 1959.

Subsecretaría Forestal y de Caza. *Memoria de la III Convención National Forestal.* Mexico City: N.p., 1966.

Subsecretaría Forestal y de la Fauna. Dirección General de la Fauna Silvestre. *Fauna silvestre: Expresiones y planteamientos de un recurso, 1964–1970.* Mexico City: Comercial Nadrosa, 1970.

———. Noé Palomares. *Examen objetivo de la situación forestal de México.* Mexico City: N.p., 1970.

Sullivan, Sharon. "Guarding the Monarch's Kingdom." *International Wildlife* 17 (November–December 1987): 4–11.

Suro, Roberto. "Border Boom's Dirty Residue Imperils U.S.-Mexico Trade." *New York Times*, 31 March 1991, I1, I16.

Székely, Francisco, comp. *El medio ambiente en México y América Latina*. Mexico City: Editorial Nueva Imagen, 1978.

Tamayo, Jorge L. Comisión Nacional de Irrigación. *Influencia de la deforestación en las obras hidráulicas*. Mexico City: N.p., 1941.

Taylor, William. *Landlord and Peasant in Colonial Oaxaca*. Stanford: Stanford University Press, 1972.

"The Texas Border: Whose Dirt?" *Economist* 316 (18 August 1990): 20–21.

Tfeiffer, Sara Figueroa de, Elia Arroyo, and Jorge González Torres. "Boletín de Prensa." Ca. 1990.

Tierra Madre, *San Miguel de Allende 2000*. San Miguel de Allende: N.p., n.d.

———. *San Miguel de Allende 2000 Summary Projects for 1989*. San Miguel de Allende: N.p., n.d.

Tinker, Ben. *Mexican Wilderness and Wildlife*. Foreword by A. Starker Leopold. Austin: University of Texas Press, 1978.

Toledo, Alejandro, with the collaboration of Arturo Nuñez and Héctor Ferreira. *Como destruir el paraíso: El desastre ecológico del sureste*. Mexico City: Centro de Ecodesarrollo, 1983.

Toledo, Víctor Manuel. "La otra guerra florida." *Nexos* 6 (September 1983): 15–24.

———. "La naturaleza: Un rostro que se borda." *Nexos* 8 (February 1985): 47–48.

Toledo, Victor Manuel, Julia Carabias, Cristina Mapes, and Carlos Toledo. *Ecología y autosuficiente alimentaría: Hacia una opción basada en la diversidad biológica y cultura de México*. Mexico City: Siglo Veintiuno Editores, 1985.

Torquemada, Juan de. *Los veyente y un libros rituales y monarchia yndiana con el origen y guerras de los Yndos Occidentales de sus poblaçones, descubrimiento, conquista, conuersión y otras cosas marauillosas de la mesma tierra*. 3 vols. Seville: Matthias Clavijo, 1615.

Torres, Luis G. *La reforestación de los médanos en la zona litoral del estado de Veracruz*. Mexico City: Dirección de Estudios Biológicos, 1922.

Torres Quintero, Gregorio. *Mitos aztecas: Relación de los dioses del antiguo México*. Mexico City: Manuel Porrúa, 1978.

Transactions of the Thirty-seventh North American Wildlife and Natural Resources Conference. Washington, D.C.: Wildlife Management Institute, 1972.

Tratado de las idolatrías, supersticiones, dioses, ritos, hechicerías y otras costumbres gentílicas de las razas aborígenes de México. Notes, commentaries, and a study by Francisco del Paso y Troncoso. 2 vols. Mexico City: Ediciones Fuente Cultura, 1892.

"Treatment Plant at Copper Smelter Opened to Control U.S.-Mexico Air Pollution." *International Environment Reporter* 11 (14 September 1988): 491.

"El Triunfo: Reserva de la biosfera." *Informa Boletín Informativo Trimestral del Instituto de Historia Natural* 3 (April 1990): 1–2.

Tumulty, Karen, and Rudy Abramson. "Mexico Trade Pact Shuns Environmental Issues." *Los Angeles Times*, 16 April 1991, D2.

Turner, John Kenneth. *Barbarous Mexico*. Chicago: Charles H. Kerr and Company, 1911.

Uhlig, Mark A. "Gasping, Mexicans Act to Clean the Capital's Air." *New York Times*, 31 January 1991, A4.

———. "Mexican Debt Deal May Save Jungle." *New York Times*, 26 February 1991, A3.

———. "Mexico City's Toxic Residue Worsens Already Filthy Air." *New York Times*, 12 May 1991, I1, I14.

———. "Mexico Closes Giant Oil Refinery to Ease Pollution in the Capital." *New York Times*, 19 March 1991, A1, A6.

———. "Refinery Closing Outrages Mexican Workers." *New York Times*, 27 March 1991, A11.

Ul Haq, Mahbub. *The Poverty Curtain*. New York: Columbia University Press, 1976.

Underhill, Ruth M. *Papago Indian Religion*. Columbia University Contributions to Anthropology 33. New York: Columbia University Press, 1946.

UNESCO. *Ecology in Practice: Insights from the Programme on Man and the Biosphere*. Paris: Beugnet, 1981.

United Nations. *Yearbook of the United Nations, 1974*. Office of Public Information, United Nations, 1975.

"U.S. Assigns Environmental Attaché to Mexico." *The News* (Mexico City), 26 August 1990, 3.

U.S. Fish and Wildlife Service. *Mexican Wolf Recovery Plan*. Albuquerque, N.M.: U.S. Fish and Wildlife Service, 1982.

———. John S. Phelps et al. *Sonoran Pronghorn Recovery Plan*. N.p.: U.S. Fish and Wildlife Service, 1982.

"U.S. and Mexicans Combating Pests." *New York Times*, 17 September 1972, 15.

"U.S.-Mexico Border Cleanup Plan Set." *Washington Post*, 26 February 1992, A2.

Urteaga, Luis. *La tierra esquilmada: Las ideas sobre la conservación de la naturaleza en la cultura española del siglo XVIII*. Madrid: Ediciones del Serbal, 1987.

Vargas Márquez, Fernando. *Parques nacionales de México y reservas equivalentes: Pasado, presente y futuro*. Mexico City: Instituto de Investigaciones Económicas-UNAM, 1984.

Vassberg, David E. *Land and Society in Golden Age Castile*. Cambridge Iberian and Latin American Studies. Cambridge: Cambridge University Press, 1984.

Vásquez, Juan M. "Mexico City Is Strangling on Its Growth." *Los Angeles Times*, 8 December 1983, A1, A16.

Vázquez, Emilio, and Hilario Monray. "9 Presos en Guadalajara; acusan de negligente al Gobernador Cosío." *Unomásuno* (Mexico City), 28 April 1992, 1, 14, 15.

Vázquez, Francisco. Comisión Nacional de Irrigación. *The Social Work of the Mexican Commission on Irrigation*. Mexico City: Departamento de Publicidad, 1936.

Vera, Rodrigo. "Manuel Camacho enfrenta la contaminación como un asunto de imagen." *Proceso* 738 (24 December 1990): 6–9.

———. "Solo un simulacro de revisión, hecha por un amigo, se hizo para abrir la planta." *Proceso* 720 (20 August 1990): 7.

Los virreyes españoles en América durante el gobierno de la Casa de Austria: México. Ed. Lewis Hanke with the collaboration of Celso Rodríguez. Biblioteca de los Autores Españoles 273–277. 5 vols. Madrid: Ediciones Atlas, 1976.

Vitale, Luis. *Hacia una historia del ambiente en América Latina*. Mexico City: Editorial Nueva Imagen, 1983.

Vizcaíno Murray, Francisco. *La contaminación en México*. Mexico City: Fondo de Cultura Económica, 1975.

Vogt, William. *El hombre y la tierra*. Foreword by Manuel Alcala. Biblioteca Enciclopédica 32. Mexico City: Secretaría de Educación Pública, 1944.

———. *Los recursos naturales de México: Su pasado, presente y futuro*. Mexico City: Sociedad Mexicana de Geografía y Estadística, 1965.

———. *Road to Survival*. Introd. Bernard M. Baruch. New York: William Sloane Associates, 1948.

———. "Unsolved Problems Concerning Wildlife in Mexican National Parks." In *Transactions of the Tenth American Wildlife Conference*. 355–358. Washington, D.C.: American Wildlife Institute, 1945.

Voorhies, Barbara, ed. *Ancient Trade and Tribute: Economies of the Soconusco Region of Mesoamerica*. Salt Lake City: University of Utah Press, 1989.

Vos, Jan de. *Oro verde: La conquista de la Selva Lacandona por los madereros tabasqueños, 1822–1949*. Mexico City: Fondo de Cultura Económica, 1988.

Wagner, Helmuth O., and Hans Lenz. *El bosque y la conservación del suelo: Su importancia cultura y económica*. Mexico City: Editorial Cultura, 1948.

Wagner, Philip. "Parras: A Case Study in the Depletion of Natural Resources." *Landscape* 5 (Summer 1955): 19–28.

Warman, Arturo. *"We Come to Object": The Peasants of Morelos and the National State*. Trans. Stephen K. Ault. Baltimore: Johns Hopkins University Press, 1980.

Warren, Jennifer. "Troubled Desalting Plant Opens 14 Years Late." *San Francisco Chronicle*, 9 March 1992, A3.

Washington, D.C. Library of Congress Manuscript Division. Alfred Mordecai Papers.

———. National Archives. Records of the Fish and Wildlife Service. Record Group 22. "Mexico Also Owns the Ducks," ca. 1949.

———. Letter from Jesse F. Thompson and Gustav A. Swanson to Chief Office of Foreign Activities, Fish and Wildlife Service. "Proposed Trip of the Director to Discuss Waterfowl Conditions with Mexico," 4 August 1948.

———. Predator Control Series. Record Group 22. Bernardo Villa R., Institute of Biology. "Fight against Coyotes and Wolves in the North of Mexico (their hazards to the health [and] the economy, and the conservation of wildlife); Instructions for the Use of 1080," ca. 1954.

———. Records of the U.S.-Mexican International Fisheries Commission, 1925–1937. Record Group 22. "Convention between the United States of America and the United States of Mexico for the Preservation of Marine and Aquatic Resources," December 1931.

———. "Draft Convention Regarding Game and Fishing," 21 May 1925.

———. Records of the Foreign Agricultural Service. Narrative Reports. Record Group 166. American Consulate General, Mexico City. Consul Dudley G. Dwyre, Excerpt from "Quarterly Review of Commerce and Industries, December Quarter, 1930," 20 January 1931.

———. Consul Dudley G. Dwyre, "Quarterly Review of Commerce and Industries, September Quarter, 1930," 18 October 1930.

———. American Embassy, Mexico, D.F., 16 February 1951 [on International Parks Commission].

————. American Vice Consuls, John D. Jernegan and S. Roger Tyler, Jr., "Mexico's Conservation Program." Prepared on behalf of the National Park Service of the Department of the Interior, 23 May 1938.

————. Secretaría de Fomento. Poder Ejecutivo. 15 de noviembre de 1917 [creation of Desierto de los Leones National Park].

————. Washington, D.C. Smithsonian Institution Archives. Field reports of Edward A. Goldman.

Weatherford, Gary D., and F. Lee Brown, eds. *New Courses for the Colorado River*. Albuquerque: University of New Mexico Press, 1986.

Weber, David J. *The Mexican Frontier, 1821–1846: The American Southwest under Mexico.* Histories of the American Frontier Series. Albuquerque: University of New Mexico Press, 1982.

West, Robert C. *The Mining Community in Northern New Spain: The Parral Mining District.* Ibero-Americana 30. Berkeley and Los Angeles: University of California Press, 1949.

West, Robert C., and John P. Augeli. *Middle America: Its Lands and People*. Englewood Cliffs, N.J.: Prentice-Hall, 1966.

Wionczek, Miguel. "The Roots of the Mexican Agricultural Crisis: Water Resources Development Policies (1920–1970)." *Development and Change* 13 (1982): 365–399.

Woodward, Laura L., and Ralph L. Woodward, Jr. "Trudi Blom and the Lacandón Rain Forest." *Environmental Review* 9 (Fall 1985): 226–236.

"World's Most Polluted City Slowly Begins to Clean up Its Act." *Reno Gazette-Journal*, 16 September 1990, A2.

"Worst Pollution Alert Ever in Mexico City." *San Francisco Chronicle*, 18 March 1992, A8.

Worster, Donald. *Dust Bowl: The Southern Plains in the 1930s*. Oxford: Oxford University Press, 1979.

Worthington, Richard, and Mauricio Schouet. "The Silence of the Labs." *Los Angeles Times*, 1 July 1993, B7.

Wright, Angus. *The Death of Ramón González: The Modern Agricultural Dilemma*. Austin: University of Texas Press, 1990.

Ximénez, Francisco. *Cuatro libros de la naturaleza y virtudes de las plantas y animales de uso medicinal en la Nueva España*. Mexico City: Oficina tip. de la Secretaría de Fomento, 1888.

Zamora, Michoacán. Biblioteca del Colegio de Michoacán. Archivo Fernández y Fernández. Tema Pesca. "Es incalculable la riqueza de México dentro de los mares: Comisión especial exploradora de la fauna y flora acaba de regresar a la capital, trás recorrer el sureste de la República y opina de industrializada en forma debida la pesquería, sería un renglón de ingresos," 10 June 1938 [from *El Nacional* (Mexico City)].

————. Tema Selvicultura. "Comité Nacional para la Protección de las Aves Silvestre."

————. Ramón Fernández y Fernández. "El retorno a la Secretaría de Agricultura." Manuscript.

————. Miguel Angel de Quevedo. "La creación del Departamento Forestal y de Caza y Pesca." 15 January 1936 [from *El Nacional* (Mexico City)].

Zea, Leopoldo. *El positivismo en México: Nacimiento, apogeo y decadencia*. Mexico City: Fondo de Cultura Económica, 1968.

Zinzer, Juan. "Greetings from Mexico." In *Transactions of the Sixth North American Wildlife Conference*. 11–12. Washington, D.C.: American Wildlife Institute, 1941.

————. "Informe de los principales trabajos desarrollados por la Jefatura del Servicio de

Caza de acuerdo con lo establecido por el plan sexenal." *Boletín del Departamento Forestal y de Caza y Pesca* 4 (December 1938–February 1939): 93–97.

———. "A Message from Mexico." In *Transactions of the Third North American Wildlife Conference*, 8–13. Washington, D.C.: American Wildlife Conference, 1938.

———. "The Mexican Wildlife Situation." In *Proceedings of the First North American Wildlife Conference*. 10–15. Washington, D.C.: American Wildlife Conference, 1938.

Index